Franchise Times®
Guide to Selecting, Buying & Owning a Franchise

Julie Bennett

with Cheryl Babcock, CFE

Foreword by John Hamburger

STERLING

New York / London
www.sterlingpublishing.com

STERLING and the distinctive Sterling logo are registered trademarks of
Sterling Publishing Co., Inc.

Library of Congress Cataloging-in-Publication Data
Bennett, Julie, 1942-
  Franchise times guide to selecting, buying & owning a franchise / Julie Bennett, with Cheryl Babcock ;
foreword by John Hamburger.
      p. cm.
  Includes index.
  ISBN-13: 978-1-4027-4393-1
  ISBN-10: 1-4027-4393-9
  1. Franchises (Retail trade) I. Babcock, Cheryl R. II. Franchise times (Roseville, Minn.) III. Title. IV. Title:
Franchise times guide to selecting, buying & owning a franchise.

  HF5429.23.B46 2008
  658.8'708--dc22

                                                                                    2007045256

  10 9 8 7 6 5 4 3 2 1

Published by Sterling Publishing Co., Inc.
387 Park Avenue South, New York, NY 10016
© 2008 by Franchise Times Corporation
Distributed in Canada by Sterling Publishing
c/o Canadian Manda Group, 165 Dufferin Street
Toronto, Ontario, Canada M6K 3H6
Distributed in the United Kingdom by GMC Distribution Services
Castle Place, 166 High Street, Lewes, East Sussex, England BN7 1XU
Distributed in Australia by Capricorn Link (Australia) Pty. Ltd.
P.O. Box 704, Windsor, NSW 2756, Australia

Book Design and Layout: Alexis Siroc

Manufactured in the United States of America
All rights reserved

Sterling ISBN-13: 978-1-4027-4393-1
        ISBN-10: 1-4027-4393-9

For information about custom editions, special sales, premium and
corporate purchases, please contact Sterling Special Sales
Department at 800-805-5489 or specialsales@sterlingpublishing.com.

To my husband, Michael Lefkow,
my in-house attorney, spell-checker,
and personal chef

Contents

Foreword

Welcome to the *Franchise Times Guide to Selecting, Buying & Owning a Franchise*.

When I started my career in the restaurant industry 30 years ago, the big restaurant chains dotted the franchise landscape—McDonald's, Burger King, and other household names. Franchising back then meant big, recognizable companies selling franchises to individuals, often "mom and pop" operators.

But through the years I've watched franchising grow, and grow exponentially. Today, there are more franchisors and the array of business ideas and opportunities have grown. I've been a restaurant owner; a franchisee; an industry watcher through my first publication, the *Restaurant Finance Monitor*; and now, owner of *Franchise Times* magazine. In addition to publishing *Franchise Times* and the *Monitor*, a monthly newsletter that covers franchised restaurant companies, we run franchise conferences where executives come together to network and discuss their business issues. It's through these vehicles that I have watched franchising move into the big time.

Watching this growth—and the growing pains accompanying it—convinced me that now more than ever prospective franchisees need a compass to help them sort through the opportunities and find the right franchise for them.

Franchising has responded to changing consumer dynamics by offering business opportunities that assist today's time-strapped consumers. Franchising's growth no longer stems just from the restaurant industry; it's everywhere. It's now just as important for your dog to attend a branded doggy daycare center as it is for you to stay at a hotel with a recognized name. Brands dominate. There are franchised spas, house cleaners, driveway sealers, closet designers, coffee houses, tutoring services, battery retailers, muffler shops—need I go on?

Franchise Times has observed and documented with journalistic objectivity the successes and failures of those businesses trying to make their mark with consumers. And after a decade covering franchises, we know that whether their star is rising or falling, they take their franchisees with them.

It's the reason this book is important: Franchising is vast—new players come on the scene monthly and, for that reason alone, finding the right franchise is a daunting task for any individual. Other books and magazines tout this franchise or that one. Web sites proliferate the Internet, advertising various franchised concepts, often misleading franchise buyers.

All of these franchises want one thing: your money. As such, you need to choose if and where to spend your money with care. This book offers a comprehensive plan, outlining the steps necessary to make your decision work for you— *before* you sign on the dotted line. Signing on that line is a life-altering decision.

We won't sugar coat it. We won't tell you that franchising is great for everyone, because it's not. We'll give you the facts to help you decide if it's right for you.

We also differ from other franchise books because we talk to the people on the front lines: franchisees. These are the people you need to hear from. How did they decide to buy a franchise? What do they do each day to run their business? What are their challenges? What advice would they offer a new franchisee? And the big question: Are they making money? Their stories are eye-opening, and you can learn a lot by reading them.

If you've read this far, I'm guessing you're still interested in franchising. We've tried to make this the definitive book on how to buy a franchise. We've put our years of franchise coverage on the line and tackled the biggest issues, from deciding which franchise to buy to how to fund it and where to open it. We've tried to take the legalese out of the legal process, summarizing what you need to examine closely in that mountain of paperwork sent by your "dream" franchise—and reviewing the most common complaints franchisees have against their franchisors. We've shared tips from those already in the trenches, existing franchisees, on marketing, training, and hiring and managing employees. We've tried to anticipate your questions and provide the answers.

We want you to go in to this with your eyes wide open.

My 30 years of franchise experience can tell you this: Read this book. Do your homework. Think carefully before you commit to buying a franchise. No one can tell you what is right for you. Only you can decide. We're just here to help.

John Hamburger, President, Franchise Times Corp.

Acknowledgments

The franchisees who shared their stories are the framework upon which this book is built. I will always be grateful for the time you spent with me, talking about what really happens when you buy a franchise. Thank you for your honesty, your attention to detail, and your willingness to advise our readers about franchising's rough patches, as well as its finer points.

I am also grateful to the many franchisors who were candid about what they look for in franchisees and what happens when a qualified candidate contacts one of them. I'd especially like to thank those at Luxury Bath Systems, Cousins Subs, and Dinner by Design, who bravely allowed me to participate in their franchisee Discovery Day and training sessions.

My colleagues at *Franchise Times* magazine in Minneapolis have been supportive and helpful ever since our president, John Hamburger, first approached me with the idea for this book. Publisher Mary Jo Larson and Editor Nancy Weingartner boosted me up when the research bogged down; and Administrative Manager Gayle Strawn arranged for vital in-person meetings. While I was busy interviewing lively franchisees, Research Director Paul Olson was quietly and efficiently assembling all the information you'll find in the directory at the back of this book. When Mary Jo and I started this project, we assumed our editor, Meredith Hale, of Sterling Publishing, would be a superior wordsmith. Meredith does have a flair for words and organization, but her greater gift is with people. She has been a master motivator and graceful negotiator throughout our collaboration. We at *Franchise Times* express our gratitude for offering us this opportunity and for being the glue holding all the pieces together and keeping us all focused.

The staff at FRANdata—Christine Harris, Edith Wiseman, and Paul Wilbur—were always ready with statistics and answers to our many questions, while FRANdata President Darrell Johnson provided both research and reasoned comments.

Terry Hill, communications director for the International Franchise Association, graciously answered my questions by e-mail or arranged interviews with IFA president Matthew Shay or John Reynolds of Educational Foundation.

The future of franchising must be secure, because the professors teaching our next generation of franchisees are of such high quality. Udo Schlentrich, of the University of New Hampshire, was generous with his time and insights. Cheryl Babcock, of Nova Southeastern University in Florida, drew on her 25 years of experience, as a franchisee, a teacher, and a leader in the international franchise community, to provide wise answers to the questions we posed at the end of most chapters.

Mark and John Siebert, Dave Hood, and Dan Levy of the iFranchise Group were willing to enrich my understanding of franchising, even if that meant answering my questions during weekends or while driving through Chicago traffic.

I owe my new understanding of UFOCs, franchise agreements, and other legal issues to a group of very patient franchise attorneys: Justin Klein and Gerald Marks, of Marks & Klein; Michael Liss; Brett Lowell, of DLA Piper US LLP; Michael Dady, of Dady and Garner, P.A.; and Rupert Barkoff, of Kilpatrick Stockton LLP, who also helped by reading through the chapters that touched on legal matters.

Many other experts also assisted in this project, and I'd like to extend special thanks to Eric Stites, who pulled back the curtain on franchisee lead generation; Cheri Carroll, who has been a franchisee, a franchise executive, a franchise broker, and a franchise developer, and just may be the most versatile person in the industry; and Robert Stidham, who provided a peek at the underside of the franchise sales process.

Dinner by Design's Laurie Hobbs and Duke Marketing's Linda Duke may already regret sharing so many of their marketing tips, and Fred Berni may soon be sorry he offered a free personality profile to our readers. We truly appreciate their help.

Finally, I'd like to thank the adult children of our blended family for their encouragement and for understanding when Mom was too busy to talk—Linda Bennett Davis, Lesley Bennett DeMartini, Steven Bennett, Dave and Mark Lefkow, and Susan Lefkow Tucker.

PART ONE

Getting Started: Finding the Right Franchise for You

Franchises are everywhere. Drive down any highway and you'll pass franchises selling fast food, carpeting, furniture, or even batteries. Open your local Yellow Pages and you'll find dozens of franchises that provide services to your home—from cleaning and landscaping to organizing your closets and replacing your gutters. Other franchises provide staffing, accounting, or printing services to other businesses, while still others offer care to seniors in their homes, or toddlers in day care centers.

Each franchise you see is operated by a franchisee who once held a regular job, just as you do now, but dreamed of doing something on his or her own. As you'll soon see, some of these franchisees are earning less money than they did before, but say they're more content. Many others, however, tell us they're earning more than they ever could as an employee and are enjoying life more, too.

Should you join them? This book is dedicated to helping you answer that question.

The first section of this book tells you what franchising is and what advantages it offers over opening a business on your own. You'll meet four people whose lives were changed by franchising, and you'll be given an opportunity to examine your own life, to help you decide whether this business model is right for you. Finally, you'll be introduced to the amazing variety of franchised businesses you can choose from.

CHAPTER ONE

Who Are Today's Franchisees?

For over a decade, we at *Franchise Times* magazine have explored hundreds of franchise systems and talked to thousands of franchisees. We've met people who've told us that finding a franchise was the best thing they've ever done, and others who said, "Buying this franchise was the biggest mistake of my life." According to the International Franchise Association (IFA), a trade group in Washington, D.C., the United States has about 800,000 franchised businesses, and most of their operators fall into the first category, people who enjoy running their own franchised businesses.

We've met dissatisfied operators, too, people who say they're working hard every day and still not making the money they expected. Some of these franchisees failed to prosper because of outside causes: a competitor came into the marketplace with a better, or cheaper, offering; the public lost interest in the category; a highway closed or something else impacted their local marketplace. But others are failing because the franchisee never should have opened that particular franchise in that location, or because the franchise system's business model never really worked in the first place.

Obviously, you'd like to be part of the first category, and the purpose of this book is to help you do just that. We'll guide you through the maze of franchise choices available today. We'll help you determine which types of franchises you are suited to operate, figure out whether the franchise brokers and franchise salespeople you'll meet along your journey are really on your side, and recognize red flags that indicate that you should drop one franchise system and start looking at another. We'll take you inside a Discovery Day (a day when prospective franchisees are invited to franchise headquarters; see Chapter Ten) and a franchise Training Session. All along the way, we'll provide tips and warnings from real franchisees who are inside this industry now, painting your house, mowing your lawn, cooking your burgers, scooping your ice cream, and scrubbing your dog.

We've also enlisted former Subway franchisee Cheryl Babcock, Certified Franchise Executive (CFE), who is now the director of the International Institute for Franchise Education (IIFE) at the H. Wayne Huizenga School of Business and Entrepreneurship at Nova Southeastern University in Fort Lauderdale, Florida, to give you a more in-depth view of each issue. Cheryl has studied franchising since 1983 and teaches undergraduate and MBA classes in franchising and entrepreneurship. She is also the executive director of the International Society of Franchising and serves on the boards of the IFA's Educational Foundation and Women's Franchise & Distribution Forum. In 2003, the IFA honored her with the prestigious Free Enterprise Award. At the end of each chapter, we include an Ask the Professor section, where we pose the questions we think you'd like to ask her yourself.

Before we get started, we'd like to introduce you to four franchisees whose lives, and livelihoods, changed for the better, once they discovered franchising.

Unlocking Surprises

In 1999, Kelly Waddell, of Grafton, Ohio, was in his early thirties and unhappy with his career, repairing home health care equipment. A friend who operated a Mr. Hero submarine sandwich franchise had just returned from a franchise seminar, so Waddell asked him about franchising.

"He said one system caught his attention, because the franchisees were saying such good things," Waddell says. That system was Pop-A-Lock, a business started in 1991 by Lafayette, Louisiana, law enforcement officers who recognized a need for a car door unlocking service. "I called the franchisor," says Waddell, "who sent me a list of their franchisees. I questioned about 20 of them before my wife, Sandy, and I agreed to go to Louisiana to meet the franchise owners. But we couldn't imagine you could earn a living unlocking cars."

The Waddells paid about $9,000 for the Cleveland territory (current franchise fees begin at $29,000), took the Pop-A-Lock training class, bought two trucks to hold all the equipment their franchisor provided, and set up an office in their basement. Since Pop-A-Lock has contracts with major motor clubs, "we had customers right away," Waddell says. "I answered the phones and sent my friends out to open locks and change tires. Sandy planned to keep working—she was a computer programmer at a bank—but three months in we were paying our bills and she quit her job."

"The biggest shock was the 24-hour demand," Waddell says. "You'd be surprised how many people lose their keys at 3:00 A.M. I worked the midnight shift and my wife answered calls during the day."

Today the Waddells operate Pop-A-Lock territories in three large Ohio cities and have 24 trucks with as many drivers making service calls. Together they're earning about $160,000 a year. They're no longer answering the phone at 3:00 A.M., because all 4,000 calls for roadside assistance that come in each month are routed to a call center.

"We just bought a new motor home and are doing some traveling," says Waddell. "Because everything is Internet-based, I can do business from my laptop while we're parked near Niagara Falls. I can't imagine anything else we could do and make this much money."

Executive Office to Print Shop

Former executive Karen Brinker was in her early forties when the women's apparel company she worked for was purchased in a leveraged buyout. "I thought I'd use my one-and-a-half years' severance to buy a small manufacturing company," she says, "and when my business broker took me to a small printing company, lightbulbs went off. Printing is custom manufacturing in which you make, price, and sell a product."

But, Brinker says, "I didn't want to open Karen's Printing because I realized that technology would play a huge role in this industry and I wanted someone else to do the R&D [research and development]. I contacted AlphaGraphics [in Salt Lake City, Utah] and they had it all figured out."

Brinker opened her franchise in Greenwich, Connecticut, in 1990, on the day she turned forty-five. "The people who worked for me before were Harvard MBAs; the first three people I hired for my franchise were $8 to $10 hourly wage earners, and none of us knew anything about printing," she says.

She did know about marketing, and says she spent three to four hours a day, five days a week in her community, making sales calls. That effort paid off: Brinker was earning as much as her corporate salary within two years. "Every day is still different from the day before," she says, "and I'm still constantly learning. I don't sit in meetings; I don't write memos; I don't give speeches.

I don't do much of anything I don't want to do. I work hard (still probably 50 to 60 hours a week) but play hard (ten-plus weeks a year out of the office), and I have a financial freedom that I would not have achieved working for someone else. My only regret is that I wish I'd had the courage to do this sooner."

Tropical Isles and an Indiana Farm

Carleen Peaper, who's in her mid-forties, was a stay-at-home mom until 2001, when she became a Cruise Planners (Coral Gables, Florida) franchisee. Now she's earning about $90,000 a year booking cruises to the Caribbean and Scandinavia from her home office, on a 40-acre vegetable farm in Indianapolis.

Peaper says, "My first cruise was on our honeymoon, and I've always loved traveling. When our son was in high school and I wanted to start working, I was torn between becoming an independent travel agent or a franchisee. I'd once booked a cruise through a Cruise Planners agent, so I contacted them and several other travel-related franchise companies."

Peaper admits she was apprehensive about investing in a franchise, so she e-mailed a set of questions to 50 Cruise Planners franchisees, asking them how long they'd been in business, how long it took for them to start booking cruises, and if they were happy. "Everyone responded," she says. "That was a big thing, and it made me determined to join them."

She used family savings to pay the franchise fee, which at that time was about $8,000, and she also bought a new computer and phone system. "I sent out an introductory letter to let our friends and family know I'd started a business, and I offered to write a column, 'Cruising by Carleen,' for the local newspaper."

Peaper says it took a few years to build her business, and she still spends hours on the phone each day, talking to her customers. "I'm always educating myself by reading travel publications, so I can tell them about flights to Denali, or alternative places to stay while visiting Rome," she says. "Customers say they come back to me because of the service."

"Now that our son's in college, other mothers are wondering 'What do I do now?' I'm prepared for the empty-nester stage because I created this business," she says. "One of the best benefits is traveling more with our family and friends, because I'm always finding great deals with great itineraries."

An Alternative to Travel

John Dini, who's in his fifties, turned to franchising in 1997 because of too much travel. "I was a consultant in the health care industry and the travel was killing me," he says. One day, while stuck on a runway at LaGuardia, Dini read the classified ads in the *Wall Street Journal*, tore out one for a health care executive in Dallas, and put it in his pocket.

"I forgot about it until I... put on the suit again and felt something crinkle. I looked at the ad, remembered I didn't like the company, and was tossing it... when I saw a tiny ad on the back, promoting an 'executive dream franchise.' I called the 800-number and found the Alternative Board in Denver."

The Alternative Board, or TAB, is a peer advisory group for executives and business owners, who pay dues to meet monthly with a facilitator to share their problems and offer each other solutions. Dini says he'd considered forming peer groups on his own, "but I'm hyperactive and enthusiastic, not organized. I knew I could never get off the ground without someone's system."

Dini worked with an attorney to check out the franchise, took a buyout from his employer, and "plunked down $40,000" to open a TAB franchise in San Antonio. In the first few days, he put together three groups; today, he and a partner manage 12 groups for their 100 dues-paying members.

"I don't make the money I made while flying all over the country," Dini says. "But I make a good living, and now I can make it to my kids' baseball games and recitals. And I've sat in on almost 600 board meetings where I've heard people smarter than me solve incredible problems."

Franchising's Appeal

The people profiled here are not franchise superstars. They are simply four of the more than 600,000 people who operate franchised businesses in the United States today.

"Now I can make it to my kids' baseball games and recitals."

FRANdata, an independent research firm in Arlington, Virginia, and the International Franchise Association, a Washington, D.C. trade group, report that the country has at least 2,500 franchise systems. Their 800,000 franchised units generate $1.5 trillion in sales each year, or about 10 percent of our private-sector economy.

The Franchise Times
Top Ten Franchises

We all know the top ten franchise companies. Here's a more detailed look at their sales and number of units (as of 2005).

Rank	Name	Sales in Millions	Number of Units
1	McDonald's	$52,950	30,771
2	7-Eleven	37,999	29,465
3	Carlson Wagonlit Travel	25,600	2,872
4	KFC	13,200	13,893
5	Ace Hardware	13,000	4,868
6	Burger King	12,004	11,104
7	Pizza Hut	9,100	12,548
8	Coldwell Banker Real Estate Corp.	9,055	3,835
9	Subway Restaurants	9,050	24,810
10	Wendy's	8,684	6,746

But franchising consists of thousands of smaller companies, like Pop-A-Lock (130 units), AlphaGraphics (300), Cruise Planners (640), and The Alternative Board (200), that also provide viable business models. According to the IFA's 2006 Profile of Franchising, only one-third of all franchise companies have more than 100 units and a quarter of all franchised concepts have ten units or fewer.

Franchising is growing dramatically. The IFA reports that 900 new companies started franchising between 2003 and 2006; and, in 2006, 300 more registered to start selling franchises. Most of these are newcomers to well-established franchise categories, like pizza delivery, coffee cafes, and tutoring centers. But others, like Dig It! The Fossil Workshop, in Sandy, Utah—a sand-filled storefront where children can dig up real dinosaur fossils—are entirely new business ideas whose creators feel are worth duplicating. In Chapter Five, we'll talk about the risks, and the opportunities, of joining a brand new franchise system. In the meantime, you must have a more basic question. . . .

Just What Is Franchising, Anyway?

Cheryl Babcock, director of the International Institute for Franchise Education at Nova Southeastern University in Fort Lauderdale, provides this definition:

> Franchise is from the French word *franche*, meaning "to be free from servitude." Franchising is a business strategy, a way of doing business, and a method of distribution of goods and services designed to satisfy customer needs.
>
> Franchising entails a strategic alliance between two different entities, the franchisor and the franchisee. The franchisor lends his/her trademark or trade name and business system to the franchisee. The franchisee, in turn, pays the franchisor a royalty fee and, often, an initial fee, for the right to utilize the franchisor's brand name, operating system, and ongoing support, and agrees to conform to quality standards. The franchise system must provide ongoing value to the franchisee.
>
> The contract or agreement between the franchisor and the franchisee is technically the franchise. However, the term generally refers to the actual business that the franchisee operates.

According to Professor Babcock, franchising can be divided into two types:

- *Product and trade name franchising.* In product and trade name franchising, the franchisee typically sells products that are manufactured by the franchisor, such as automobiles and trucks, automotive accessories, gasoline, and soft drinks. In product and trade name franchising, the franchisor licenses its trademark and logo to the franchisee but does not provide the system for running the business, as in a business format franchise. Examples of product and trade name franchises are Coca-Cola, General Motors, and Goodyear Tire & Rubber.

- *Business format franchising.* In business format franchising, the franchisee uses the parent company's trade name and logo and is provided with the complete system for delivering the product or service and conducting the business. This provides consistency from one franchise to another, no matter where it is located. The franchisee receives a detailed plan of how to set up his or her location and training on how to operate it, including information on how to market and advertise the business; recruit, hire, and train the employees; and how to greet the customers. Examples of business format franchises are Subway, RE/MAX, Home Instead Senior Care, and Two Men and a Truck International.

In this book, we will be discussing the second type of franchising, business format franchising.

Early History of Franchising

As Professor Babcock tells us, today, franchising is the fastest-growing method of doing business in the marketplace, but it is really nothing new. Some believe that franchising dates back to the Middle Ages (476 A.D.–1453 A.D.). During that time period, a feudal lord could grant the rights to others to hold markets or fairs, to operate ferries, and to perform some of the activities traditionally carried out by professional and craft guilds. Regulations governing franchises became embedded in the common law of various countries.

The earliest recorded business franchise was in Germany, in 1845, between brewers and tavern owners for exclusive distribution rights of specific brands of ale.

History of Franchising in the United States

Martha Matilda Harper, an international business visionary, launched one of the earliest business format franchises, in 1891, and helped many poor women become business owners. Using images of her floor-length hair as an advertising tool and the mark of Harper distinctiveness, this resulted in a worldwide empire of more than 500 Harper Method health-conscious hair and skin salons.

Other early examples of franchising in the United States include the McCormick Harvesting Machine Company, which, around 1850, commissioned exclusive local agents to sell and service its machinery, and the Singer Sewing Machine Company, which, in 1863, offered protected territories to individuals, with the exclusive right to sell and service its machines. William E. Metzger of

Detroit became General Motors Corporation's first franchisee in 1898; Coca-Cola sold its first franchise in 1899; and Rexall Drugs began franchising in 1902.

The first franchising boom occurred in the 1920s and 1930s, when the Ben Franklin stores, Western Auto Supply Company, Rexall, Walgreens, Hertz Corporation, and Howard Johnson restaurants and motels began operating business format franchises.

The second boom came in the mid-1950s, when Ray Kroc, a salesman for a milkshake machine called the Multimixer, discovered a chain of fast-food hamburger restaurants in California. He bought the concept from its founders, the McDonald brothers, and used franchising to expand throughout the nation. Kroc imposed standards for food quality and service, developed new products, and utilized creative advertising to create the giant of the franchise field.

During that same time period, Harland Sanders founded Kentucky Fried Chicken (KFC), and the International House of Pancakes (IHOP) and Dairy Queen opened their doors. Nonfood franchises that started up in the 1950s include Manpower and One Hour Martinizing. In the 1960s, these were followed by hotels, convenience stores, business services, and printing operations.

During the 1970s, shady operators used the franchising concept for illegal gains. While solid companies like McDonald's, KFC, and Hertz were building legitimate business opportunities, unscrupulous businesspeople were taking advantage of the lack of regulation to ensnare unsuspecting individuals under the guise of franchising. Celebrities were used to promote unproven concepts, and false and unsubstantiated claims were made for various businesses.

In 1979, the Federal Trade Commission (FTC) passed Rule 436.1, the Franchise Disclosure Act, to protect unsuspecting franchise shoppers. The franchise rule requires, throughout the United States, the franchisor provide minimum disclosure of specific franchise information to a prospective franchisee prior to the establishment of a franchise agreement. You'll read more about this document, called a Uniform Franchise Offering Circular, or UFOC, in Chapter Nine.

How Does Franchising Work?

A well-run franchise system is unique among all business formats, because it balances the interests of two parties: a franchisor who wants to grow a business without spending his or her own money, and franchisees who are willing to spend their money to operate similar businesses.

The typical franchisor is an entrepreneur who planned to start only a single business—whether it's selling ice cream, cleaning carpets, or grooming dogs—but became so successful that others wanted to start similar businesses.

Julie Duffy, for example, was a Grayslake, Illinois, mother who had given up a corporate career to raise her children. "That worked for about six months," she says. "I had an itch to do something, and one night I read an article about a group of women who got together in a church basement to assemble meals they could take home and freeze to feed to their families later. I did some research and found that a few women on the West Coast had made the concept into a business."

Duffy had no prior retail or foodservice experience, but she did have the capital to open a meal preparation store she called Dinner by Design. "The phone started ringing quickly," she says, and soon her storefront kitchen was filled with women who had no time to cook but still wanted to give their families a balanced meal that was at least warmed up in their own ovens or Crock-Pots. "I thought I'd be a one-store wonder," says Duffy, "but many customers told me I had to franchise, because they wanted to open a Dinner by Design in their hometowns."

Becoming a franchisor is not cheap. Duffy says she spent about $35,000 for an attorney to draw up and file the necessary documents. Franchising a complicated business can cost $200,000 or more, says Mark Siebert, founder and CEO of the iFranchise Group in Homewood, Illinois, a consulting firm that helps develop new franchise companies.

Franchisors recoup that investment by charging up-front fees, called franchise fees, to people who want to duplicate their businesses. According to FRANdata, franchise fees vary according to industry. The average fee for restaurants is $35,000; for service companies, it ranges from $22,500 to $25,000; and for retail stores, it ranges from $17,000 to $20,000. Duffy decided to charge new franchisees $35,000.

In most franchise systems, the franchise fee pays for the knowledge you need to become a franchisee—training classes that teach you how to operate the business; manuals that spell out how to accomplish each task, from mixing up special sauces to which chemicals to spray on customers' lawns; detailed plans of how to build out and equip your place of business; lists of how many employees you need for each hour you're open, and more. It's often said that buying a franchise is like buying a "business in a box." That description is more than apt, because, in addition to what they carry home from training classes, new franchisees usually do receive a box filled with instruction manuals, software, and other materials from their franchisor.

> *"It's often said that buying a franchise is like buying a 'business in a box.'"*

However, you don't really "buy" a franchise. The success of a franchise system lies in its consistency—every McDonald's Big Mac, Curves workout, and Red Roof Inn hotel room should be like every other. Franchisors learned early on that they couldn't enforce consistency if they sold their duplicate businesses outright. The best way to keep you from removing the lettuce from a Big Mac, or adding aerobics lessons to your Curves center, is by only leasing you the right to operate your franchise. When you pay a franchise fee and sign a contract, you are agreeing to operate a duplicate business for a specific period of time, usually 10 to 15 years.

If all goes well, at the end of your contract, the franchisor will offer you a renewal contract. But if you haven't operated according to the rules in that big box of manuals, or if your place of business isn't clean enough, or if your revenues are way below the others in your system, the franchisor has every right not to extend your contract. Your contract can even be terminated midterm if you're out of compliance with the franchisor's system.

In addition to paying a franchise fee, you have to share the money you make with your franchisor. Each month, franchisees pay a percentage, called a royalty, of whatever revenues they take in. According to FRANdata, royalties are as low as 4 to 6 percent of sales for low-margin/high-volume businesses like fast-food restaurants, and average as high as 12.5 percent for franchises with high margins, like personnel services. According to FRANdata, the average royalty is 6.7 percent.

The important fact to grasp is that royalties are calculated against gross sales, not profits. Let's say your royalties are 6 percent. If it costs you $20,000 a month to operate your business, and your gross sales are $30,000, you owe

> *"The success of a franchise system lies in its consistency—every McDonald's Big Mac, Curves workout, and Red Roof Inn hotel room should be like every other."*

your franchisor $1,800; you get to keep the remaining $8,200 in profit. But if your gross sales are only $16,000, you still owe your franchisor $960, even if it means paying your employees out of your savings account.

One of the greatest advantages of running a franchise is getting to use the franchisor's brand name and taking advantage of that name's reputation in the marketplace. Every time the brand is promoted, whether through a Super Bowl ad or a flier in the Sunday paper, you may expect more customers. Most franchisees also must pay a share of that promotion budget through an advertising fee, which usually amounts to 1 to 3 percent more of monthly gross sales. If your ad fee is 2 percent, in the above example with $30,000 in monthly sales, you'd be sending your franchisor a royalty of $1,800, plus an ad fee of $600, for a total of $2,400 a month. And if your sales are $16,000, you still have to send off $1,280.

You may be renting the brand, but when you open a franchise, you must actually purchase all the physical items you need to run your business. The total investment for a franchise you run from home, like Carleen Peaper, can be under $10,000, because you don't have to pay for rent, additional utilities, and other expenses. By contrast, according to FRANdata, the average total investment to open a retail store ranges from $129,600 to $248,700 and the average service business franchise costs $64,000 to $136,393 to get started. People who open large franchised restaurants, like Panera Bread or Applebee's, can spend in the millions.

What if something happens during the term of your contract—you get divorced, you want to retire, and so on—and you need to sell your franchise? Franchisors do allow sales, but only to persons they have vetted and approved. And because they don't want that newcomer saddled with excessive debt, they also have the right to pass judgment on your selling price.

And what if you grow to love the business but hate the franchisor? Can you just take down the signs and keep operating as Karen's Printing or Kelly's Lock Shop? Absolutely not, because franchisor attorneys have written noncompete provisions into every franchise agreement. These clauses, which can remain in effect for years, prohibit you from operating a competing business from your old premises, and even from opening a similar business within a specified number of miles from your old location.

So, What's in It for Me?

By now, you must be thinking that the balance tips way too far in the direction of the franchisor. But all the rules that seem to protect franchisors actually protect franchisees as well.

If you open a franchise, you certainly don't want a dirty or badly run unit from the same system operating a few miles away. Nor do you want an unqualified operator taking over a neighboring franchise. And you do not want to compete against a former franchisee whose business looks exactly like yours, except for the signs. Because that renegade operator is no longer paying royalties and ad fees, he or she can simply lower prices and put you out of business.

The advantages of franchising extend beyond such rules, and include:

- *Buying power.* As part of a franchise system, you enjoy efficiencies of scale. Your franchisor negotiates low prices for the products and services you need to run your business and may even arrange to have items delivered to your door.

- *Experience.* Since your franchisor and the system's established franchisees have been operating similar businesses for years, they can guide your progress.

- *Support.* In exchange for your monthly royalty payment, the franchisor provides ongoing help, with a staff to assist you with tasks that range from bookkeeping to hiring tips.

- *R&D.* While you're serving your customers, the franchisor's research and development team is testing time-saving technology, creating new products, and thinking up new services you can offer.

- *Promotion.* Since franchisors make their money from royalties, their main goal is to attract more customers to their franchised units, through advertising, discount coupons, posters, sales campaigns, and other efforts.

- *Internet and 800-number access.* All franchisors have Web sites that provide the addresses and phone numbers of all their franchisees, and many include maps to help potential customers find your local unit. Many, like 1 800-GOT-JUNK, also maintain call centers that route toll-free calls directly to your location.

- *Customer alliances.* Many franchisors provide franchisees with ready-made customer bases; for example, Pop-A-Lock has contracts with motor clubs.

- *Training.* Besides the initial training you receive before opening your business, most franchise companies provide ongoing in-person or computer-based training for you and your employees.

- *Camaraderie.* All the other franchisees in the system provide an instant support group to help you through any problem. Most franchisors provide an intranet connection, where franchisees can ask each other questions and share tips and gripes. Many franchisees tell us that their "new best friends" are the other franchisees they met in training class.

Franchising's Challenges

Operating a franchise also has disadvantages, of course, and many of those correlate closely with franchising's advantages:

- *A proven system.* Agreeing to follow a franchisor's operating system means that you have little or no leeway in the way you run your business. You can't offer additional products, drop services, or even paint your walls the color you want. As we'll see in the next chapter, many people find operating a franchise too stifling.

- *Standardized products.* If your franchisor provides a list of approved products for you to use and/or sell in your unit, you can't make substitutes, even if you find something of better quality or at a lower price.

- *Promotions.* Franchisees often get squeezed financially when their franchisor rolls out a new product or announces a special discount. That two-for-one deal that brings extra customers to your store means you're selling them twice as much product for half the price—and still paying royalties on each sale.

- *Ties to a franchisor.* Franchisors can go public, sell out, or take their companies (and you!) into risky new directions. When you buy into a franchise, you're betting on the continuing integrity of the franchise system. If you own an independent business that falls out of favor with its customers, you can morph it into something else, or simply close down. When you have a ten-year contract with a franchise company, you have no option but to follow your franchisor's lead, even if that direction is downhill.

The biggest problem with franchising comes at the front end. Too many people fall in love with the idea of franchising, or with a single franchised concept, and rush into the field. We at *Franchise Times* talk to them later, when they're not making as much money as they expected, or are working in businesses ill-suited to their personalities and talents.

We don't want you to be among those franchisees, so we're pooling our talents, and our years of research and experience to help guide you through the maze of franchise choices to a business where you, too, can prosper.

People often ask us, "What's the best franchise?" That's the wrong question. We've found sour franchisees in the biggest, most profitable systems and, conversely, happy operators in companies where most of their peers are going bankrupt or filing lawsuits. The right question is, "What's the best franchise, utilizing my special talents and experiences, for me to operate in my community?" This book will help you approach franchising with a market research mind-set, and provide the tools to measure your strengths and assess which franchise companies can best put them to use. We'll also show you how to analyze the strengths and weaknesses of individual franchise companies, so that, like Karen Brinker, your only regret is that you did not do this sooner.

But first we must explore the most important question of all: Are you meant to be a franchisee in the first place?

CHAPTER TWO

Are You Meant to Be a Franchisee?

If someone had asked John Kohler that question a few years ago, his answer would have been a resounding no. But once Kohler explored franchising, he discovered his talents and interests were suited to this unique business model. You, too, might be surprised at how well your personality and drive for success can fit into operating a franchised business.

For 20 years Kohler had been the senior vice president of global operations for telecommunications giant Tellabs, Inc., with 4,700 workers reporting to his division. But in the early 2000s, Tellabs started outsourcing tasks to other countries and laid off 9,800 of its U.S. employees.

"I'd just turned fifty," Kohler says, "and accepted an early retirement package. In the spring of 2004, I decided to find something else to do and signed up for a seminar on franchising arranged by an executive outplacement firm. While driving there, I kept thinking that I was wasting my time." At the seminar, Kohler met a franchise broker, a salesperson who sells franchises on a commission basis, similar to the way a real estate broker sells houses. (See Chapter Seven for more on franchise brokers.)

"I was pretty jaded," says Kohler, "and told the guy I had no intention of making Subway sandwiches. He invited me to his office anyway and suggested six franchises that had nothing to do with food. The one that appealed to me the most was Sport Clips, a Georgetown, Texas, franchisor of sports-themed barbershops. It's a cash business, everyone needs a haircut every few weeks, and it's a service you can't outsource."

Today, Kohler is the Northern Illinois master franchisee (a franchisee who buys a large territory and subfranchises parts of it to other operators—see Chapter Eighteen) for Sport Clips, managing two hair salons himself and overseeing 19 more he's sold to other franchisees. He says that franchising lets him "exercise the sales and marketing muscles I never needed at Tellabs. Franchise sales is fun, because I'm meeting people from varied walks of life, from doctors to mechanics. I realize that only one or two out of each 100 of them will pursue it, and it's interesting to see who will bite."

> *"I tell people I haven't bought a job; I've invested in an adventure."*

Whether you will—or should—bite at an appealing franchise business depends on your goals, your personality, your financial status, whether you have what Kohler calls the "intestinal fortitude" for risk, your stamina level, and your and your family's lifestyle needs and expectations. Plus, of course, you must consider whether you can maintain that tricky balance between operating on your own and operating within the stringent rules and regulations that make up every franchise system.

An Adventure—or a Job Replacement?

The first test of franchisee-fitness is the hardest. Why are you thinking about buying a franchise? If your goal is to replace the steady income and daily routine of your current or last job, trade this book in immediately for one on improving your resume. Even though it may be the hardest work you've ever done, operating a franchise is never a replacement for a job.

"Within the first hour of every interview with prospective franchisees," says Stan Friedman, senior vice president and chief development officer for MaggieMoo's, a premium ice cream franchisor in Columbia, Maryland, "we ask if their purpose is to replace a job. If the answer is yes, we send them home. A franchise is like having another child. In our business, you're not replacing a nine-to-five life. You're creating another life."

As Kohler says, "I tell people I haven't bought a job; I've invested in an adventure."

Business Savvy Required

Part of that adventure is operating a small business. Even though the franchisor creates the business format, designs the facility, and spells out exactly which products are sold or services provided, the franchisee is responsible for all the other aspects of running a business. To be a franchisee, you must be ready to rent and maintain space for your business, hire and manage staff, promote your franchise to your local community, and handle the finances. Although a franchisee is technically not an entrepreneur, because he or she is operating a business created by someone else, a franchisee must have an "entrepreneurial itch," says Kohler, a desire to run things himself or herself, no matter what it takes.

"You have to be prepared to put your time and energy into your business. If you're not motivated to do that, and if you're more concerned about a return on your investment than about the challenge of making your franchise a success, don't buy one. Take your money to a stockbroker," he says.

Here are some ways to measure your own entrepreneurial itch:

- Many of the top franchisees we've met started out as mini-entrepreneurs, setting up their first businesses as teenagers. Did you, too, find ways to make money as a kid?

- Do you have more ideas than you can possibly execute? Are you always inventing things, at least in your head?

- Have you always wished you could be the one in charge?

- Do you take charge of situations outside of work, from running volunteer projects to planning outings?

- When things bog down at work, are you the one who comes up with a solution?

- Are you more willing to take risks than your friends or colleagues?

- Do you prefer to multitask? Can you keep track of several projects at once?

- Are you decisive and, when it's necessary, willing to make a quick decision, even if you could be wrong?

- Are you good at motivating others?

If you answered yes to many of the above questions, you may have the entrepreneurial itch to start a business. The next section will help you determine if you're too entrepreneurial to join a franchise system.

The Independence Seesaw

When Mark Siebert, CEO of the iFranchise Group of Homewood, Illinois, a consortium of franchise consultants, talks to prospective franchisees, he uses the following chart to distinguish true franchisees from those who would flourish in their own businesses. Do you recognize yourself in one of its columns?

Franchisee versus Entrepreneur

Straight-A Student	Bs or Cs in school
Long tenure with job	Moved from job to job
Worked corporate jobs	Owned businesses
Drives family car	Drives sports car
Receives few tickets	Receives lots of tickets
Looking for security	Never saw a rule he or she didn't want to break

Siebert's point is that a true entrepreneur is not a franchisee. If you do have an entrepreneurial itch, and maybe own a sports car and like to take risks, are you prepared to work within the confines of a franchise system? Whenever we at *Franchise Times* ask a franchisee who is not thriving the reasons why, she will list several—the location is bad, competition is fierce, the franchisor charges too much for products, etc. But when we ask any franchisor why a franchisee is not doing well, the answer is always the same: "He didn't follow the system."

People who are too independent to follow a system feel stifled as franchisees. Boyd Harris, for example, spent nine years as a Baskin-Robbins franchisee in Austin, Texas, but when he moved to Laredo, he opened independent ice cream stores instead.

"I found my franchisor to be very inflexible," he says. "Although Baskin-Robbins is headquartered in New England, they insisted that we sell every product they offer. I felt I knew what our Texas customer base wanted better than they did."

Today, he operates three ice cream parlors, including a converted shaved ice stand "that Baskin-Robbins never would have approved," he says. He creates his own sundae concoctions and even sells donuts in one of his

> *"I found my franchisor to be very inflexible. . . . I felt I knew what our Texas customer base wanted better than they did."*

locations. "I'm not making more money than I did as a franchisee," Harris says, "but overall, I'm happier."

Fred Berni, the president of Dynamic Performance Systems, Inc., in Toronto, Canada, a developer of personality tests that are used by about 200 franchisors to screen prospective franchisees, says those who are "too entrepreneurial" will get bored and attempt to find excuses to get out of the system, or they will start changing the system. But people who are "not entrepreneurial enough" also make bad franchisees, Berni says, "because they like to be in constant contact with the head office and seek approval for every little change they are contemplating."

Is there any way of knowing where you fit on the independence/dependence scale? Although no test is perfect, the personality surveys that Berni and his competitors have developed to help franchisors sort through applicants hit surprisingly close to the mark.

While the one-third or so of franchisors who use these tests administer them close to the end of the application process (see Chapter Seven), you can pay

When Testing Gets Personal

When this author took the three main surveys—Berni's FranchiZe Profile; the McQuaig Word Survey, adapted to franchising by Accord Management Systems of Westlake, California; and the Caliper Profile, developed by psychologist Herb Greenberg of Princeton, New Jersey—the results were distressingly similar: I'd make a lousy franchisee. On all three surveys, my independence/entrepreneurial score was too high for comfort, and my tendency to put things off until the last minute meant I'd be a poor boss. I'm too optimistic, as well, meaning I'm likely to have unrealistic expectations; and, according to the FranchiZe Profile, my tendency toward being "over responsive" to customer needs means that I'd be in danger of "giving away the store." Worse, all three surveys found me too sociable, more likely to talk to customers than close sales, and too empathetic. My employees would walk all over me, all three reports said.

a fee to take them on your own right now. You'll find contact information for all three companies in the Resource List at the end of the book.

In the meantime, Berni allowed us to include nine questions, focusing on independence, from his Franchisee Success Forecaster.™ If you submit your answers to his Web site (www.My-Success-Strategies.com/independence), he'll send you back your score.

Fred Berni's Quick Independence Test

Please indicate the extent to which you agree or disagree with the following statements by selecting the appropriate numbers. Each question MUST be answered.

1 - Disagree Strongly   2 - Disagree Somewhat   3 - Neither Agree Nor Disagree
4 - Agree Somewhat   5 - Agree Strongly

1. *I would feel stifled if I had to do every last thing "by the book."*

2. *I am comfortable with other people having power over me at work.*

3. *I don't mind having to answer to a superior.*

4. *I like to make decisions on my own.*

5. *In my ideal job I would be able to do my work any way I want.*

6. *I am very independent.*

7. *Sometimes it bothers me when I am told exactly how to do things.*

Please indicate the extent of your agreement with the following statements by selecting the appropriate response.

1 - Not at all   2 - To a small extent   3 - To a moderate extent
4 - To a large extent   5 - To a great extent

8. *To what extent do you prefer to work independently?*

9. *To what extent do you prefer working with a team of knowledgeable people to working on your own?*

To find your rating, go to Berni's Web site (www.My-Success-Strategies.com/independence).

Other Important Personality Traits

While independence is the most important trait in deciding your franchisee-fitness, other facets of your personality must be considered, too. Let's explore some of the core values listed by Berni as critical to franchisee success.

Your Attitude toward Employees

Labor is usually a franchisee's biggest expense and, often, his or her biggest headache. The turnover rate of workers in U.S. restaurants exceeds 100 percent a year, and employees in other retail establishments also change jobs frequently. If you treat your employees right, Berni says, you can reduce turnover and be more confident that your employees will treat your customers right.

According to the U.S. Bureau of Labor Statistics (BLS), the supply of new workers will begin to tighten in 2010, when the first cohort of Baby Boomers retires. We will not have a serious labor shortage, the BLS says, but the people available to work in your franchise are likely to be immigrants, fifteen to twenty-four years old or over sixty, and may want to work only part-time.

To determine if you would be comfortable managing tomorrow's work-force, ask yourself the following questions:

- Do you believe employees are an asset to a business—or a necessary expense?

- Would you feel comfortable working with people who are less educated than you are?

- Can you communicate with people whose first language is not English?

Can you see yourself:

- Hiring workers who'll do the best job, not those that need a job the most?

- Disciplining an employee who arrives late or who fails to perform required tasks?

- Relating to a workforce that might include both teenagers in their first jobs and people over sixty?

- Showing interest in your employees, but not so much empathy that they'll walk all over you?

If you've been a manager or supervisor at work, or have led a group of volunteers through a major project, you may be well-suited to hiring and managing your own workforce. However, franchisees can be successful without managing people at all. If being a boss seems intimidating, you can find a business, like Carleen Peaper's Cruise Planners franchise, that you can operate all by yourself.

Positive Attitude toward Success

There is no substitute for confidence in your own abilities. As you recall from Chapter One, franchisors have a vested interest in your success. The better you do, the more royalties they'll collect. And if you fail, that failure reflects back on their entire operation.

People with negative attitudes, warns Berni, do not accept responsibility for their own successes or failures and tend to blame their franchisors when something goes wrong. To prevent that, franchisors use personality tests and telephone and in-person interviews to try to ferret out applicants whose attitudes may eventually harm their systems.

Before you begin the application process, here are some questions you can use to assess your own attitude.

- Think back to failures in your own career or relationships. When things went wrong, did you take responsibility, or did you blame your boss or the other people involved?

- Would others describe you as an optimist or a pessimist?

- Do you believe that things generally work out for the best?

- Are you able to ask for and accept help when a task is beyond you?

- Do you get easily discouraged when things don't go your way?

The most successful franchisees we've interviewed are also the most optimistic. They believe their franchise will end up in their concept's top performers; or they make predictions, such as, "By this time next year, I'll have three more employees...two delivery trucks...a sixth team of house cleaners." When we check back, they've usually exceeded their goals. Someone with a positive attitude conveys that spirit to his or her employees, who, in turn, contribute to the unit's success.

Sales Orientation and Marketing

In the next two chapters, you'll meet franchisees from a variety of industries, including people who decorate cookies, tutor kids with learning problems, or sell floor coverings. Despite the differences in their businesses, they share one common denominator: they all spend time in their communities promoting their businesses. Are you willing to do the same? Here are some questions to ask yourself:

- Are you willing to network within your local community to build your business?

- Are you willing to be identified as the owner of your franchise?

- Would you be comfortable hosting a booth and passing out samples at local festivals, or marching in holiday parades?

- Can you see yourself delivering free products or coupons for services to schools or office buildings?

- Are you ready to become an active member of your chamber of commerce and other small business organizations?

- Do you have the drive to do what Karen Brinker did, and spend several hours a day, every day, marketing your franchise?

You may be buying a franchise with a national name, but your customers will be coming from a three- to five-mile radius around your location. Before you can serve them, you have to let them know you're there. By joining the chamber of commerce and other organizations, you're promoting yourself as the local representative of the franchise.

Through the years, I've interviewed hundreds of people who have been proud to introduce themselves as the owner of the local ice cream parlor, packing store, or lawn care franchise. I once interviewed a physician who, for a time, operated a smoothie stand and loved calling himself "Dr. Smoothie."

But I've also talked to former corporate executives who still introduce themselves as a "small business owner," not as the proprietor of such-and-such franchise. And I've met longtime franchisees who admit they still have trouble going out and asking for business.

No matter how badly you want to scratch your entrepreneurial itch, and no matter how well you score on our self-assessment questions, you still must face this fundamental question: Is this something you really want to do?

Level of Drive and Stamina

If you don't care for marketing, you can find a partner or hire an employee to take over some of those chores. But you can't hire someone to take on the initial task of getting your franchise started. As Stan Friedman of MaggieMoo's says, buying a franchise is like creating a new life—a life that seems to demand all of your time and energy. New franchisees often work 80-hour weeks and forgo vacations for years. Are you ambitious enough to work that hard? Are you physically able to work with little sleep and few breaks? And, let's be honest here: Do you want to?

Can You Afford to Buy a Franchise?

As we've seen, initial investments in franchises range from a few thousand dollars for a home-based service business to several million for a sit-down restaurant. But that initial investment, to cover the franchise fee, facility buildout, equipment, initial ingredients or inventory, the Grand Opening, and your first employee salaries, is only the beginning. You also must have enough cash to pay all your business and personal expenses until your franchise starts making a profit. Some franchises start breaking even in the first few months, but many franchisees told us they didn't pay themselves a cent for a year or more.

Even if you have enough savings and a business loan to get your franchise opened, do you have enough working capital to keep it operating? And do you have resources—or a working (and willing) spouse—to pay the mortgage and cover other expenses at home?

The most common reason new franchisees fail is the lack of sufficient capital to stay open until they start to make a profit. Franchisors attempt to prevent such failures by requiring that newcomers meet minimal financial standards. At MaggieMoo's, for example, the total investment for a premium ice cream store is $200,000 to $250,000. To be accepted, new franchisees must have a net worth of $250,000–$75,000 of which must be liquid assets they can access quickly.

Furthermore, in northern climates, ice cream stores make most of their money from May to October. If you open in November, Friedman says, you must have enough working capital to support yourself and your store for several months. "We never want anyone to get down to his last dollar," he says.

"We are always concerned that someone's taking on too much debt," says Jeff Sturgis, regional vice president for FOCUS brands in Atlanta, the corporate parent of Carvel and Cinnabon franchise systems. "The biggest challenge is that people don't understand what assets they have."

Before going any further, sit down with your accountant and figure out just how much money you can allocate to your franchise. We'll go into financing your franchise in Chapter Twelve. The purpose of this analysis is to see what resources you have available before you begin your franchise search. Here are some important questions to ask yourself:

- Do you have equity in your home you could tap into? If you do, Sturgis advises against taking out a home equity loan before you apply for a franchise. "If you've taken $100,000 out of your house so you'll have a bigger bank balance, we see that money as debt and we don't want you to be overleveraged," he says. If you need working capital later, that's the time to consider a home equity loan.

- Do you have a 401(k) or other retirement plan that you could use for at least part of the initial investment? And do you want to put that at risk?

- Do you have a severance package you could use to pay the initial investment for your franchise? Do you possess a stock portfolio that will provide dividend income until you start making money?

- Do you collect Social Security, a pension, or other income to cover your living expenses?

- Will your spouse's or partner's salary cover your personal expenses? What about health insurance?

- If you don't have a working partner, do you have enough available cash to cover your personal expenses for at least a year?

Although there are no hard rules about working capital, most franchise experts suggest that you have at least one and one-half times the highest amount your franchisor says you need for a total investment. In the MaggieMoo's example, for instance, if the total investment is $250,000, you should have a total net worth of $375,000.

See Table 2-1 for a summary of average initial investments by industry.

TABLE 2-1
Total Initial Investment by Industry

INDUSTRY	MINIMUM	MAXIMUM
Automotive	$ 149,000	$ 285,000
Baked Goods	$ 210,250	$ 395,000
Building & Construction	$ 71,255	$ 147,798
Business Services	$ 51,003	$ 84,400
Child-Related	$ 77,550	$ 153,975
Education-Related	$ 36,308	$ 74,911
Fast Food	$ 177,900	$ 2,923,000
Lodging	$ 4,108,700	$ 6,485,250
Maintenance Services	$ 39,400	$ 92,350
Personnel Services	$ 74,117	$ 150,174
Printing	$ 172,500	$ 278,000
Real Estate	$ 31,000	$ 98,300
Restaurants	$ 423,000	$ 920,000
Retail	$ 129,600	$ 248,700
Retail Food	$ 152,100	$ 317,775
Service Businesses	$ 64,900	$ 136,392
Sports & Recreation	$ 4,331	$ 340,186
Travel	$ 67,669	$ 134,950

Source: "The Profile of Franchising 2006" by FRANdata Corp. Reprinted with permission of Franchising World. Note that the total initial investment does not include an estimate of real estate purchasing expenses.

Check Your Expectations at the Door

You've probably read articles about people becoming rich by operating franchises. At *Franchise Times* we often print articles featuring "franchisee millionaires." However, none of the people we've photographed next to the NASCAR racers they sponsor or the private airplanes they fly in earned their riches from a single franchise. These successful franchisees own hundreds of fast-food restaurants, a dozen hotels, or a string of quick oil change establishments.

Someday you, too, may own multiple franchises and be profiled in franchise publications.

But right now you're thinking about buying a single franchise, and it's vital that you understand that the income from one unit will not make you wealthy. The money you get to keep—after paying royalties, ad fees, and all your bills—may be less than your current salary—in some cases, a lot less.

Sturgis says, "Out of every franchise business, you can make a certain amount, and no more. We often see people whose expectations are not achievable. It's completely ridiculous to think you can generate an income of $250,000 a year from a single Carvel ice cream store, for example."

"The money you get to keep—after paying royalties, ad fees, and all your bills—may be less than your current salary—in some cases, a lot less."

In coming chapters we'll tell you how to gauge how much money you can make from different types of franchises. But while you're still measuring your fitness to be a franchisee, it's important to consider how long you and your family can live on the income your first franchise is likely to produce.

Just Who Is Going to Answer the Phone and Mop the Floor?

Since the recession of 2001, the number of corporate refugees looking at franchises has increased dramatically. If you, too, are a current or former executive thinking about using your severance or early retirement package to buy a franchise, you can learn from others who did just that.

It's not the loss of income that bothers most corporate executives who become franchisees; it's the loss of their support staff. "The hardest part about being a franchisee is being willing to suck it up and do things you've never done before," says Kohler. "At Tellabs, we had an IT department to take care of technology, and a human relations department to handle employee problems. Now when the computers go down, I'm the one fixing them, and if an employee needs discipline, I'm HR."

Are you ready for such a change in lifestyle?

Paul Detlefs runs his Alternative Board franchise from a 220-square-foot space he rents in an office building in Glenview, Illinois. Just a few years ago he was working in an office three times its size, as a partner with Accenture Consulting in Chicago. He, too, misses the support services of a large company. He also misses the perks. "I always traveled first class," he says, "and I never thought twice about valet-parking my car. The last time I visited a client in the city, I drove around several blocks, looking for the cheapest parking lot."

When Detlefs wanted to send a copy of a book written by the Alternative Board's founder to his clients and business contacts, he and his teenage son printed out the labels and stuffed the envelopes. "If you're an executive considering a franchise, you must be prepared to roll up your sleeves and do everything yourself," he says.

"If you're an executive considering a franchise, you must be prepared to roll up your sleeves and do everything yourself."

Here are some other things to consider before you ditch the corner office for a delivery van:

- Employees at franchise headquarters are not your new support staff, and "you can't assume they'll do much for you," says Detlefs.

- If you're a big thinker who hates details, don't buy a franchise, warns Detlefs. "You'll frustrate yourself to death."

- Your fellow franchisees will be your new peer group. "You'll be happier," says Keith Gerson, former vice president of global development for AlphaGraphics, "if you join a system that's attractive to others who are leaving the corporate environment."

- Don't assume running a franchise will be easy. "Managing three or four hourly employees while you're trying to get a business off the ground requires more patience, faith, and hard work than managing a department in a big corporation," says executive-turned-AlphaGraphics franchisee Karen Brinker.

- But, also, don't assume you'll have to learn all new skills. Brinker says that having a broad understanding about how a business works is invaluable. "Understanding financial management, profit and loss sheets, cash flow, pricing and margins are all critical to running a franchise," she says.

Finally, expect some skepticism. "My friends and family thought I was nuts when I left my corporate job and opened an AlphaGraphics franchise in 1994," says Dick Moran, a former executive with an MBA from the University of Chicago. "But within a few years I was earning considerably more than my corporate salary, and today I own four AlphaGraphics that my adult children are running for me. Creating my own thing and being successful at it is far more rewarding than being a cog in the wheel of a corporation."

A Final Caveat on Franchisee-Fitness

Are you still not sure whether you'd make a good franchisee? Do you feel as though you're qualified in some areas and weak in others?

You're not alone; even experienced franchisors who use personality profiles and interview hundreds of applicants a year can't always predict who will do well as a franchisee. Sturgis of Carvel says, "During the sales process, a few people we thought would be good franchisees turned out to be really difficult. I felt they had the right attitudes and personalities; but the moment they signed their contracts, their attitudes changed, and they felt we should be beholden to them."

Jim Evanger, CEO of Designs Of The Interior (DOTI) a franchisor of upscale home design stores in Barrington, Illinois, says, "We don't accept anyone we don't think will be successful. But we accepted one person we thought would be a middle-of-the-road owner and in very little time, he became a spectacular owner. Even after testing applicants, and applying our best instincts, people can still surprise us."

You, too, may be surprised when you read about the huge variety of franchise opportunities available today. Like John Kohler, you may not want to make sandwiches all day. But you may find another franchise system that does suit your appetite.

Ask the Professor

At the end of most chapters, we've asked Cheryl Babcock, director of the International Institute for Franchise Education at Nova Southeastern University in Fort Lauderdale to answer questions we think you'd like to ask yourself. Here is what Professor Babcock says about franchisee-fitness:

Can you tell which of your students will succeed as franchisees?

I've taught hundreds of entrepreneurship and franchising students through the years and instinctively know that some of them are cut out to start their own entrepreneurial endeavors, some will be ideal franchisees, and some will be better off in the corporate world.

The students who will do well in the franchising world are risk-averse. Not as big risk takers as some of their fellow classmates, they are willing to take some risks but prefer to control and minimize them. They work diligently in the classroom, and they know there is a strong possibility that they are going to have to work long, hard hours when they enter a franchise system.

We joke that they won't be driving a fancy new sports car or going on an around-the-world trip right after they open a franchise business. These students have realistic expectations and are willing to work hard to achieve them. They really want to be in their own business, are willing to ask for help and be coached, and find comfort in the old franchising motto, "You're in business for yourself, not by yourself." They like the idea of having a proven system to follow.

These students have strong interpersonal skills. Many of them work in the hospitality field while they're at the university in order to help pay their tuition. In our class discussions, they provide examples of how they interact with fellow employees and customers. They discuss how strongly they feel about being empowered to rectify situations to ensure customer satisfaction, and how important it is to inspire loyalty, value, and trust in their business endeavors with fellow employees and customers. These lessons that they've learned early will be beneficial to them when they enter the franchise world.

CHAPTER THREE

Beyond Burgers:
Consumer-Oriented Franchises

Are you having trouble seeing yourself behind a fast-food counter, encouraging your teenage clerks to sell more French fries or extra pizza toppings? Do your savings fall short of the investment required for an upscale franchised children's clothing store or even a budget motel? Please don't give up, because franchising spans 75 different industries, with thousands of opportunities, and almost as many different price tags. One of them may be right for you.

In this chapter, you'll meet a former computer executive who now runs two fondue restaurants, an ex–dolphin trainer who serves up ham sandwiches, and an airline pilot and a former nurse who sell batteries. You'll read advice about how you can "flip" houses for profit and learn how a former professor went from taking golf lessons to giving them.

Let's begin with an overview of how many choices franchising offers.

A Franchise to Fit Every Fancy

FRANdata, the independent research firm in Alexandria, Virginia, that is the keeper of franchise statistics, divides active franchise systems into 18 categories. As you can see in Table 3-1, Fast Food, at 20 percent, is the largest category; and when you add in sit-down Restaurants (8 percent), Retail Food (5 percent), and Baked Goods (2 percent), franchises that serve food in some form make up over one-third of all franchise systems.

Since the early franchise giants—McDonald's, Dunkin' Donuts, Kentucky Fried Chicken (now KFC), and Burger King—were fast-food chains, it's not surprising that food sellers still contain the greatest number of franchisees. What is surprising is the growth of other franchise categories. According to FRANdata, from 2003 to 2005, the Service Businesses category (lawn care, hair cutting, etc.) and Building and Construction category (handyman services, carpet installation, etc.) each grew by about 40 percent. Of the 302 new franchises

TABLE 3-1
Distribution of Franchise Concepts across Categories

CATEGORY	PERCENTAGE OF TOTAL
Fast Food	20
Retail	11
Service Businesses	11
Maintenance Services	8
Restaurants	8
Automotive	6
Building and Construction	5
Business Services	5
Real Estate	5
Retail Food	5
Child-Related	3
Lodging	3
Baked Goods	2
Education-Related	2
Personnel Services	2
Sports and Recreation	2
Printing	1
Travel	1

Source: "The Profile of Franchising 2006" by FRANdata Corp. Reprinted with permission of Franchising World.

introduced in 2006, the largest category was still fast-food restaurants. But 18 new health and fitness concepts also appeared, as did 21 new general services franchises and 27 new business services. If, like John Kohler, you can't see yourself making submarine sandwiches, you still have hundreds of franchises to choose from. In the Franchise Company Directory included in the back of this book, you'll find a list of the country's top 300 franchises.

To give you an idea of what your life might be like inside a particular type of franchise system, we talked to franchisees from each of the 18 categories and asked them the same basic questions. But first, a disclaimer: The franchise systems featured in these vignettes were chosen at random from established systems in each category and many of the franchisees have operated their businesses for years. Please don't think that if you buy a MAACO franchise today, you'll soon be flying in your own airplane, like Fresno, California, franchisee Mike Murphy. Likewise, don't assume that all franchisees of LearningRx are as passionate or successful as Becky McLaughlin, in Greenville, South Carolina.

You will see, however, that success in any franchise system depends on the ability of the operator to market to his or her local community. And you'll learn that franchisees who are successful today endured months, or even years, of lean times before making a profit.

We begin with franchises that provide products to consumers, whether that's batteries, a place to stay, or something to eat. And since fast food is the largest franchise category, we start our tour in a fried chicken restaurant in San Antonio. In Chapter Four, we'll look at franchises that provide services to consumers or other businesses.

Fast Food

Jeffery Davis, president of Sandelman & Associates, a market research firm in Coppell, Texas, reports that 92 percent of the U.S. population eats a fast-food meal every month. What he calls "heavy" users eat fast-food meals 17 times every month, spending about $5.30 during each visit.

So, where are people spending their fast-food dollars? According to the Franchise Finance division of GE Capital Solutions in Scottsdale, Arizona, the United States has about 284,000 fast-food restaurants, the majority of which are franchised. Table 3-2 lists the Top Ten Fast-Food Franchises ranked by sales, from the *Franchise Times* list of the top 300 franchises found in the back of this book.

According to FRANdata, the country has 454 fast-food franchise systems, which the industry calls QSRs, for Quick Serve Restaurants. They range from the top ten, with thousands of units each, to Franktitude, a gourmet hot dog concept in Miami with only a handful of units open. Although U.S. consumers

TABLE 3-2

Franchise Times
Top Ten Fast-Food Franchises
by Systemwide Sales (2005)

Rank	Name	Sales in Millions	Number of Units
1	McDonald's	$52,950	30,771
2	KFC	$13,200	13,89
3	Burger King*	$12,004	11,104
4	Pizza Hut	$ 9,100	12,548
5	Subway	$ 9,050	24,810
6	Wendy's	$ 8,684	6,746
7	Taco Bell	$ 6,400	5,868
8	Domino's Pizza	$ 5,000	8,080
9	Dunkin' Donuts	$ 4,143	7,021
10	Tim Hortons	$ 3,129	2,885

*Data for Burger King reflects fiscal year-end of June 30, 2006.

spend almost $150 billion a year on fast food, it doesn't mean that all QSRs are successful, or that you'd be happy running one.

Church's Chicken

Wayne Baker, age 64, is so happy operating his Church's Chicken franchise in northwest San Antonio that he's there every day, working the counter or the drive-up window.

When Baker graduated from college in 1970, he started working in the corporate office of the fried chicken chain while it was still being run by a person called Church. He rose to the position of vice president, but in 1989, when the company was taken over by someone with another last name, Baker cashed in his stock options and became a franchisee.

Cost Comparison for Selected Fast-Food Chains

Here is a snapshot of average building costs for several top fast-food restaurants. Some concepts require franchisees to buy land and put up their own buildings (if possible). Others expect franchisees to lease space.

CONCEPT	MCDONALD'S
Land cost	$420,000
Building cost	$570,000–$703,000
Leasehold improvements	$499,000–$740,000
Equipment costs	$461,000–$707,000
Average unit sales	$1,985,000
Royalty fees	4%
Franchise fee	$45,000

CONCEPT	DOMINO'S PIZZA
Land cost	—
Building cost	$190,000–$247,000
Leasehold improvements	$25,000–$150,000
Equipment costs	$65,000–$175,000
Average unit sales	$666,000
Royalty fees	5.5%
Franchise fee	$5,000

CONCEPT	SUBWAY
Land cost	—
Building cost	$57,000–$380,000
Leasehold improvements	$45,000–$100,000
Equipment costs	$32,000–$39,000
Average unit sales	$384,000
Royalty fees	8%
Franchise fee	$12,500

CONCEPT	KFC
Land cost	$420,000
Building cost	$475,000–$608,000
Leasehold improvements	$325,000–$500,000
Equipment costs	$250,000–$300,000
Average unit sales	$950,000
Royalty fees	4%
Franchise fee	$25,000

Source: 2006 Chain Restaurant Industry Review, by GE Capital Solutions, Franchise Finance, Scottsdale, Arizona, and the *Franchise Times* Top 200 list.

Wayne Baker,
Church's Chicken Franchisee

What do you do on a daily basis? "I'm the administrator, making sure the employees are trained and operating the right way. I'm fanatical about friendly customer service and cleanliness. When I'm there on a Friday night, I time the drive-through line with a stopwatch. I want to see a car make progress every 30 seconds."

How soon before you started breaking even? "Because my two first franchises were low-volume stores that I took over, I had existing customers and started breaking even fairly quickly."

How do you earn money? Can you make a good living at this? "To make money, we have to control food and labor costs. I know what the numbers should be and control them on a daily basis, by managing the hours people work and by looking at any wasted food items. Today, my one restaurant probably generates as much as all three units did together in the early 2000s."

What's the most difficult part of operating a fast-food franchise? "Time management. It's hard to be both the administrator and the operator, because I want to spend as much time as I can interacting with the folks who come here."

Who should not be a fast-food franchisee? "A great number of people get into quick-serve restaurants and don't make it, because they are not mentally or financially prepared. They don't understand that you're open seven days a week and you'll be working 14 to 16 hours a day, every day. And they don't start out with enough money. When you've borrowed money to get started and need more to stay open, it's a bad time to try to get a loan."

What advice do you have for someone considering a fast-food franchise?

- Get experience by working in a fast-food restaurant before making a decision. Church's now requires prospective franchisees to work for existing franchisees before they're accepted into the system.

- Be aware of the time commitment.

- Make sure you have sufficient operating capital to pay the bills until you start making a profit.

- Get sufficient training and be able to work the business yourself.

> *"I get up every morning and look forward to going in and working a shift. . . . I fill orders and thank every customer who walks in the door."*

At one point, Baker owned three Church's franchises, but he sold two of them "absolutely, at a profit," he says, and hired managers to run the third. Nevertheless, he says, "I get up every morning and look forward to going in and working a shift. I'm not the manager. I fill orders and thank every customer who walks in the door."

You have to have a passion for the business to succeed as a fast-food franchisee, Baker says. "You could certainly do this without the corporate experience I had," he says, "but you have to know about the financial cost and the huge time commitment involved."

Sit-Down Restaurants

The country's 184,000 full-service restaurants take in about $175 billion annually. Unlike QSRs, the majority of sit-down restaurants, including the Greek lunch place around the corner and the expensive steakhouse downtown, are owned by independent operators.

The "2006 Chain Restaurant Overview," issued by the Franchise Finance division of GE Capital Solutions, divides full-service restaurant chains into two subcategories. Franchised family restaurants, like Denny's, Friendly's, Golden Corral, IHOP, and Village Inn, have inexpensive menu items, generally do not serve alcohol, and welcome children. Franchised casual dining restaurants, like Applebee's, Fuddruckers, Chili's Grill & Bar, Red Robin, and T.G.I. Friday's, have higher prices and do serve alcohol.

Family and casual dining franchises are more expensive to build than QSRs, but their annual revenues usually top $1 million; and some, like T.G.I. Friday's, can bring in over $3 million in sales. Full-service restaurants are so costly to build that bankers tend to loan money for them only to experienced operators. If your dream is to greet

---

Franchise Times
TOP FIVE
Casual and Family Dining Franchises*

1. Applebee's
2. Chili's Grill & Bar
3. T.G.I. Friday's
4. Denny's
5. IHOP

*Based on systemwide sales.

Cost Comparison for Selected Casual and Family Dining Concepts

Here are some of the costs incurred by franchisees of various sit-down restaurants:

CONCEPT (FAMILY)	DENNY'S
Land cost	$473,000
Building cost	$823,000
Leasehold improvements	—
Equipment costs	$290,000–$465,000
Average unit sales	$1,493,000
Royalty fees	4%
Franchise fee	$40,000

CONCEPT	GOLDEN CORRAL
Land cost	$1,215,000–$1,485,000
Building cost	$2,013,000
Leasehold improvements	—
Equipment costs	$586,000–$878,000
Average unit sales	$3,100,000
Royalty fees	4%
Franchise fee	$40,000

CONCEPT (CASUAL)	APPLEBEE'S
Land cost	$743,000–$810,000
Building cost	$858,000–$945,000
Leasehold improvements	—
Equipment costs	$370,000–$430,000
Average unit sales	$2,500,000
Royalty fees	4%
Franchise fee	$35,000

CONCEPT	T.G.I. FRIDAY'S
Land cost	—
Building cost	$1,190,000
Leasehold improvements	$615,000–$1,000,000
Equipment costs	$550,000–$800,000
Average unit sales	$3,600,000
Royalty fees	4%
Franchise fee	$75,000

Source: 2006 Chain Restaurant Industry Review, by GE Capital Solutions, Franchise Finance, Scottsdale, Arizona.

Mike Frampton, The Melting Pot Franchisee

What do you do on a daily basis? "Because of my business background, I do the bookkeeping. I set up a computer system so that I can keep a good handle on the finances from anywhere in the world. I'm ultimately responsible for the hiring and firing, and I analyze all the data from our marketing campaigns."

When did you start breaking even? "My Sacramento restaurant is in an amazing location, near a couple of theaters. We opened in the summer and started breaking even within a couple of months. The Rockland location was farther out and it took about a year."

How do you make money? Can you make a good living at this? "As with any restaurant, you make money on the margins between your sales and your expenses. I account for every penny. You can make a living operating one or two Melting Pots. I don't know if you can get rich, but you can be comfortable."

What is the most difficult part of operating a fondue restaurant? "Trying to find the right employees and keeping them motivated is a constant challenge. And occasionally we have some very strange guests. Most people come here to celebrate a special occasion and sometimes they have too much fun."

Who should not be a franchisee of a casual dining restaurant? "Someone who thinks he'll open a restaurant and put his feet up while others do the work should not buy a restaurant franchise. And you need to feel comfortable about your business skills. In my previous career, I signed $30 million contracts. Here, each restaurant is like a $2 million to $3 million corporation. For a lot of people, that's a lot of money."

What advice do you have for someone considering a family or casual dining restaurant?

- Some restaurant franchisors impose a lot of structure, while others leave you on your own. Talk to current franchisees to find out how much leeway they're given, then decide if you'd feel comfortable within that framework.

- If you, too, have no restaurant experience, educate yourself about the industry. I spent a lot of time talking to local restaurant owners here in Sacramento, and communicated online with the California Restaurant Association. I also joined an online foodservice discussion group, called restaurantowners.com, that was very helpful.

(Report from the Trenches continued)

- Compare the menu prices of the restaurant you're thinking about to what they charge at restaurants in your area. I didn't want to be the most expensive.

- Spend time creating a detailed business plan. It took me six months to get a business plan that would work.

- Expect resistance. My family didn't quite understand what I was doing. Now one of my daughters works for me when she's not at college."

customers at the door of your own Red Robin, or to preside over the buffet of a Golden Corral, your first step is to find a partner with restaurant experience.

Or, like the next franchisee interviewed, you can seek out a concept that requires little cooking.

The Melting Pot

Mike Frampton, forty-six, had spent 25 years traveling the world as an executive in the technology industry. In 2002, he says, he was looking for something else to do and started scanning the Internet for franchise opportunities. "I got an e-mail about the Melting Pot, and it said that no experience was necessary," he recalls.

Frampton had never seen The Melting Pot, a casual dining chain based in Tampa, Florida, that specializes in fondue, but asked the company for some information and worked on a preliminary business plan. "When we finally visited one in Phoenix," says Frampton, "some unique things dawned on me. Since customers cook their own meals at the table, you don't need a chef and there's no heat in the kitchen, physically or emotionally. And the meal becomes a social event. I went home and made fondue for my two teenage daughters. We actually talked to each other."

Frampton opened his first The Melting Pot in Sacramento in 2003 and his second in Rockland, California, two years later. "I attend a lot of charity events," he says, "and give out free product."

"Being a franchisee," Frampton says, "was never on the list of things I thought I'd do. I could never see myself operating a regular full-service restaurant, and I'm not interested in fast food. But I'm glad this opportunity came up."

Retail Food

You can also sell food without operating a restaurant at all. The 151 retail food franchise systems encompass everything from grocery and convenience stores to specialty retailers who sell candy, coffee, tea, health foods, liquor, wines, nuts, popcorn, or even gumballs. The retail food category also contains one of the trendiest new franchise concepts—meal preparation kitchens where customers assemble entrees they serve later to their families. You'll read more about easy meal prep franchises in Chapters Ten and Fourteen.

While most retail food franchisees only sell food eaten off premises, some combine retail sales with items eaten on-site, like the Coffee Beanery and It's a Grind coffee houses, and the HoneyBaked Ham Company and Cafe.

HoneyBaked Ham Co. and Café

Nancy and Grady Love met in the 1970s when they were both religious studies majors at Randolph-Macon University in Ashland, Virginia. While waiting for Nancy to graduate, Grady earned his MBA, then both worked for theme parks—Grady in the food and beverage area, while Nancy performed in dolphin, sea lion, and bird shows. "She was the one with the fish in her mouth," Grady quips.

Today, Nancy works the lunch counter and cash register of the couple's HoneyBaked Ham franchise in Rock Hill, South Carolina, while Grady places the product orders, delivers catered meals, and promotes their business. "I know there are times my wife wants to kill me," Grady says, "like the year I ordered too many hams and we had to throw away close to $10,000 worth of product." (For more about their relationship, see "Should You Start a Franchise with Your Spouse or Partner?" in Chapter Five.)

"I know there are times my wife wants to kill me."

The pair became HoneyBaked Ham franchisees by accident. They had purchased a Hickory Hams franchise in 1998, just six weeks before HoneyBaked Ham purchased

Nancy and Grady Love, HoneyBaked Ham Franchisees

What do you do on a daily basis? Nancy: "I take care of the store's daily operations. We serve dine-in or carryout sandwiches at a front counter; and if we paid someone else to manage it, we'd have less money to take home ourselves. Besides, it gives me a chance to talk to our customers and get their feedback." Grady: "I do all the marketing, financial planning, ordering, and reporting to the franchisor. I also do deliveries, because customers like that the owner is bringing them lunch. And once I'm in the door, I can see what else we might sell them."

When did you start breaking even? Nancy: "We planned to lose money the first year, but we made money and had to pay taxes. I started drawing a salary right away, but Grady didn't take one for the first 18 months."

How do you make money? Can you make a good living with a retail food store? Grady: "We make money by closely controlling our inventory and watching our food and labor costs. Out franchisor gives us some discretion on the pricing of items we serve at our lunch counter and I'm always out in the community trying to increase sales. We've finally hit an income we feel good about, because together we're earning in the low six figures, between our salaries, car allowances, and what's left over after paying royalties and all expenses."

What's the most difficult part of operating a retail food franchise? Nancy: "The things you can't control—the weather, road construction, and so on." Grady: "It is difficult dealing with perishable products. Also, customer service is so important, and you never know when an employee will come in after a bad night and tick off one of your best customers."

Who should not be a retail food franchisee? Grady: "Absentee owners, who want to run their stores at arm's length, do not do well."

What advice do you have for people considering retail food franchises?

- Nancy: Have enough money to weather out the slow months.

- Grady: Be certain before you go into a business like this that you're ready to give 100 percent to it. If there's any doubt in your mind, do something else.

- Nancy: If possible, work in an existing franchise first. Because I worked in a HoneyBaked Ham store while ours was being built, I hit the ground running.

- Grady: Choose a system that has a good record of supporting its franchisees.

that company. "We had no idea," says Nancy. Because there were other HoneyBaked Ham stores near their original location in Charlotte, they moved their business to Rock Hill, a nearby suburb. Nancy worked in an existing HoneyBaked Ham store until their unit was ready to open. "The local community embraced us," Grady says.

Baked Goods

FRANdata lists 44 franchise systems that sell baked goods. Category leaders tend to focus on a single product, such as donuts (Dunkin' Donuts and Krispy Kreme), breakfast rolls or bagels (Cinnabon, Einstein Bros., and Big Apple Bagels), or breads (Great Harvest Bread Company and Atlanta Bread Company). Because their menus are so limited, Baked Goods franchises are a good way for someone with no restaurant experience to get involved in a foodservice franchise.

Cookies by Design

A background in art, however, is helpful if you're interested in a Cookies by Design franchise. Franchisees of that Plano, Texas–based company, bake and hand-decorate cookies on sticks that they arrange in gift baskets for customers celebrating birthdays, new babies, holidays, or other occasions.

Charles Arak once designed banks, and his wife, Marilyn, was an art teacher until the early 1990s when they started looking for a business they could run together. "My sister lives in Dallas," says Arak, "and she sent me a catalogue of these wonderful, creative cookie baskets. We drove for two hours from our home in New Jersey through cornfields to the closest franchise, which was in Delaware. When the franchisee told us he was doing sales of over $100,000 a year in the middle of nowhere, we figured a store would do great in our neighborhood."

Arak's sister had sent the catalogue in January of 1993. By March, the couple was in Plano for a Discovery Day, and they opened their first shop in Englewood, New Jersey, that September. "During

Franchise Times
TOP FIVE
Baked Goods Franchises*

1. Dunkin' Donuts
2. Tim Hortons
3. Krispy Kreme
4. Auntie Anne's
5. Cinnabon

*Based on systemwide sales.

Charles and Marilyn Arak, Cookies by Design Franchisees

What do you do on a daily basis? Charles: "We make about 300 cookies a day per store. We've hired bakers, but Marilyn's in charge of production and decorating. I handle the administration of the business, keep the books, pay the bills, order supplies, arrange the advertising, and take care of personnel problems. My workday is 9:00 A.M. to 6:00 P.M. Monday through Friday; Marilyn's is 8:00 A.M. to 3:30 P.M. those days. We don't work Saturdays."

How long before you broke even? "We were making a profit after about two months in our first store; the second one took about 18 months."

How do you make money? Can you make a living at this? "About 20 percent to 25 percent of our orders come in through the Cookies by Design Web site, which is a great benefit. We make money by controlling our materials, labor, rent, and insurance. I've found that larger-volume shops can do things more efficiently and are more profitable. You can make a living, but I don't know if I'd do this again in today's business climate."

What is the most difficult part of running a baked goods franchise? "Dealing with employees. There's always a delicate balance in how far you can go to instruct or criticize someone. Sometimes, you've had it with a person and you want them to walk out."

Who should not be a franchisee of this category? "A person who thinks they can sit back and take cookie orders in a fun business. This is work."

What advice do you have for people considering this type of franchise?

- Understand that your business will go through annual cycles. We have a lot of corporate orders during the holidays; business drops off in the summer.

- To keep good employees, you have to pay medical benefits.

- A lot of couples operate this franchise together. It's important to respect each other's strengths. If Marilyn makes a decision about production, I might think I'd do it differently, but 99 percent of the time I shut my mouth. And I know she's not going to get involved in the books."

the 1990s, we had double-digit growth," Arak says, "and sales are still steady, but the newness is wearing off and now we have more competition." In 2003, the couple opened a second Cookies by Design franchise in East Hanover.

Retail Franchises

FRANdata reports that 11 percent of all franchises are retail stores. Retail franchisors range from mall and Main Street staples like FastFrame, Ace Hardware, Party City, and RadioShack to specialty retailers that sell everything from birdseed (Wild Birds Unlimited) to mattresses (1-800-Mattress).

FRANdata's list of 113 retail concepts also includes storefront operations that provide services to customers, such as barbershops, tanning salons, a printer cartridge refill business, dog care facilities, and sign shops.

According to the International Council of Shopping Centers in New York, the nation has almost 50,000 shopping centers, which attract about 200 million adult shoppers each month. Sales at stores normally found in shopping centers top $2 trillion each year.

But those millions of shoppers are fickle. Because so many new stores are opening so quickly—the Chicagoland area was slated to gain 12 million square feet of new retail development in 2007, for example—shoppers can easily abandon your store for something newer and trendier. Udo Schlentrich, director of the William Rosenberg Center of Franchising at the University of New Hampshire in Durham, warns that people considering a retail franchise should search for a concept that "has legs." In other words, will the business model be around for years, and can it be expanded into other areas? "Will it provide longevity, as opposed to short term trends?" Schlentrich asks.

In 2005 and 2006, hundreds of new franchisees jumped onto a hot trend: franchises that help people sell items on eBay. Several new franchisors, with names like Assist 2 Auction, Auction It Today, iSold It, and Online Outpost, sold franchises to people who believed they were buying into the eBay phenomenon.

The idea sounded great. Customers would drop off their unwanted items for franchisees to research, photograph, and post on the appropriate eBay auction sites. Franchisees would monitor the auctions, collect the proceeds, and ship goods to the winning bidders, all for a commission of about 33 percent of the selling price.

But the concept's legs were weak. Customers balked at paying such high commissions; and franchisees who reduced their rates had trouble paying the rent, and many closed. Today, some of the franchisors who once insisted that franchisees operate their eBay drop-off businesses from separate retail stores now allow franchisees to operate kiosks within other existing businesses, like electronics and hardware stores.

Other retail chains have their legs knocked out from under them. Just a few years ago, several video rental franchise systems flourished. Today, most of the chains have disappeared, and the two remaining leaders—Blockbuster and Hollywood Video—are closing more stores than they are opening. The culprits, of course, are online services like Netflix, DVDs so inexpensive that people can buy instead of rent, and pay-per-view offerings by cable and satellite dish companies. When Blockbuster eliminated late fees to help it compete, franchisees lost so much revenue that many of them were forced into bankruptcy.

Professor Schlentrich says, "Obviously, there are no guarantees in business. If there were, all stock analysts would be millionaires." But in choosing a retail franchise, he says, "look for a system that's been through its trial stages and has at least 40 to 50 units in operation."

> *"Look for a system that's been through its trial stages and has at least 40 to 50 units in operation."*

Batteries Plus

That is exactly the opposite of what Ric and Susan Jensen did in 1993. The couple was living in Fort Wayne, Indiana, when Ric learned that an airline company merger meant he'd soon lose his pilot job. The very first Batteries Plus franchise had just opened there, and Ric says, "I started to think about getting in on the ground level. Susan was a registered nurse and neither of us had any business experience. I figured the franchise was so new the staff would work with us one on one."

Ric and Susan Jensen, Batteries Plus Franchisees

What do you do on a daily basis? Susan: "I still do all the administrative tasks, from hiring and training to advertising. In the past year, I've also taken over commercial sales, which means I'm contacting all local businesses that use some sort of batteries."

How long before you broke even? Ric: "It took us two and a half years to start breaking even on the first store, and the second one was in a less visible location and took even longer."

How do you earn money? Can you make a good living? Ric: "You need to bring in more sales than you have expenses. Ordering inventory is easier now, because a computer program tells you what you should reorder. The amount you can earn depends on the area. A lot of franchisees are earning in the six figures from just one store." Susan: "Corporate has a Web site customers use to order items online that they can pick up at our stores. Even if they handle the entire sale, we get a percentage if it comes from our area."

What is the hardest part? Susan: "You have to wear so many hats. I have to know about accounting, business law, tax codes. I wear an HR hat when I'm hiring or dealing with employee discipline, then I have to do the marketing, advertising, training, quality assurance, and even deal with computer issues. It's hard to find time in the day to get everything done."

Who should not consider a retail franchise? Susan: "Don't do this if you want to make money fast without doing the groundwork. And you must be dedicated to customer service. If you're the type who focuses only on the bottom line, I'm not sure this would work well for you."

What advice do you have for someone considering a retail franchise?

- Try to get some experience first. Ric says he managed a hardware store when he was first laid off from his pilot job and it did help.

- Research your local market for the items you'll be selling. What's your competition today? What competition might you have in the future?

- If you don't have a business background, take some business courses to see what's involved in running a small business. But, adds Ric, "You might be better off studying psychology. You need to understand your employees, so you can keep the good ones and improve those who are not so good."

That staff—there were only five people working in Batteries Plus corporate headquarters in Hartland, Wisconsin—helped Ric and Susan select the Quad Cities of Iowa and Illinois for their store locations and waited for them to move their young family there. When the couple had trouble getting a business loan—"We were opening a business no one had ever heard of in a town where we knew no one," Susan says—the Batteries Plus president and founder drove to Iowa and talked to bankers with them.

"We were opening a business no one had ever heard of in a town where we knew no one."

The couple opened their first store in Davenport, Iowa, in February 1994 and had a very slow start. "In the beginning, we often paid our employees more than we made," Susan says. "One day our accountant called and told us that the minimum wage increase applied to us, and Ric and I had to pay ourselves more."

Ric operated the Davenport store himself for four years, while Susan handled the bookkeeping, advertising, and customer service. They were opening a second Batteries Plus in Moline, Illinois, when Ric was called back to flying. "I trained two managers," Ric says, "and got back into the cockpit when I knew they could handle things." Today, Ric is still flying airplanes and Susan oversees the managers and takes care of administrative tasks, like payroll, marketing, and commercial selling.

"We were pretty naïve when we started this," Ric says. "Our biggest qualm was that our franchisor would go out of business and leave us with no support. The one thing that let us sleep at night was that franchisees bought all batteries directly from the manufacturer. We believed we could at least stay in business, even if the franchisor went away." Instead of going away, Batteries Plus now has almost 300 stores in the United States, and most of the early franchisees, including the operator of the original franchise in Fort Wayne, are still in business."

Lodging

Although only 3 percent of all franchises are hotels or motels, franchising plays an important part in the nation's lodging industry. Of the top 15 U.S. hotel companies listed by the American Hotel & Lodging Association (AH&LA) in Washington, D.C., 11 sell franchises, from budget properties like Days Inn and

Motel 6 to high-end hotels like Doubletrees and Sofitel Hotels & Resorts.

The AH&LA's "2006 Lodging Industry Profile" reports that the United States has 47,509 hotel or motel properties with 4,402,466 guestrooms that, in 2005, took in an average of $57.36 a room.

Smith Travel Research in Hendersonville, Tennessee, reports that the lodging industry generated $122.7 billion in 2005 and grossed $22.6 billion in pretax profits. The greatest number of properties are small, with 75 rooms or fewer. But if you fill most of the beds in any sized property, owning a hotel or motel franchise can be very profitable.

Obtaining a piece of that profit, however, is difficult. Many franchisors, including Carlson Hotels Worldwide in Minneapolis, accept only franchisees with prior hotel operations or development experience. And the cost of opening even a budget hotel is extraordinary. Accor North America, in Carrollton, Texas, for example, will only sell Motel 6 franchises to people with $100,000 to $500,000 start-up cash and the ability to raise the $1.9 to $2.3 million required to build and open a motel. Because of the stiff investment requirements, many lodging franchisees are not individuals, but investor groups.

The exception is the 8,500 members of the Asian American Hotel Owners Association in Atlanta. Most AAHOA members trace their roots to India, and are first- or second-generation Americans who began their careers by buying and renovating independent hotels and motels. As they gained experience and capital, franchise companies offered them branded properties. Today, AAHOA members own more than 20,000 hotels with 1 million rooms, including over half of the country's economy lodging properties and nearly 37 percent of all U.S. hotels and motels. Of these, 12,700 are franchised, while the other 7,300 are independent, including several luxury resorts.

The balance is so clearly tipped in AAHOA's favor that several hotel companies have programs that try to attract Hispanic and African-American franchisees into their systems. (See Chapter Seventeen for more information on minorities and franchising.)

Vijay Dandapani,
Red Roof Inn Franchisee

What do you do on a daily basis? "I go to our properties and manage the managers. As director of operations, I oversee renovations. When you have properties with high occupancies, you do a complete gut job every four or five years, replacing all the decorating, carpeting, furniture, and so on."

How long before you broke even? "The beauty of New York City is that we were at full capacity within three months and well past breakeven by the end of the first year. If you did this in a remote part of the country, it would take longer to ramp up."

How do you earn money? Can you make a good living with a franchised hotel? "The way you make money is managing the system. You have to pick the right franchise for a location and set benchmarks for how much business (via its Web site, 800-numbers, and travel agency affiliations) the franchisor will send you. Smith Travel Research (www.smithtravelresearch.com) can provide you with information on the occupancy and room rates of other hotels in the area. During the good times, hotels can make 30 percent returns on revenue after expenses."

What is the most difficult part? "Adjusting to economic cycles."

Who should not be a hotel franchisee? "Just because someone succeeds running another kind of business does not mean that person can run a hotel. This business is people-intensive."

What advice do you have for someone considering a hotel franchise?

- Start by taking courses in hotel management. When we hire people without experience, we begin by sending them to New York University or Cornell.

- If you lack a lot of investment capital and experience, build up your own sweat equity by buying and cleaning up an independent hotel.

- Once you're qualified, talk to a number of hotel franchise companies to find out what they can do for you.

- When you open your franchised property, do something that sets you apart. We started putting sumptuous fitness centers into our hotels in the mid-1990s, when all our competitors offered were pokey little rooms with single treadmills. We also provide free continental breakfasts. Talk to members of the next generation, to try to see what trend will attract them."

Red Roof Inn

Vijay Dandapani, age fifty, began his hotel career in New Delhi, working in the worldwide management training program of a luxury hotel operator there. He was admitted to the School of Hotel Administration at Cornell University in Ithaca, New York, and accepted a position with Apple Core Hotels in New York City after graduation. Dandapani is now the COO and part owner of Apple Core, a private company that is a franchisee of Accor's Red Roof Inn, La Quinta, Comfort Inn, Super 8, and Ramada.

He says he won his ownership position with "sweat equity" from a project he began in the late 1990s—changing a rundown Manhattan office building into a 171-room Red Roof Inn. "We did an adaptive reuse, by using the building's shell," he says. "I had contractors working night and day for 11 months, adding bathrooms and building new elevator shafts. The construction cost $26 million; today, it would be over $60 million."

The franchise opened in 2000 and did well until 9/11, when the nationwide lodging industry suffered a two-year decline. "We had hard times until business turned around, in 2004," Dandapani says.

Real Estate

Franchisees also provide permanent places for people to stay. Five percent of franchised businesses are real estate companies, including industry giants Century 21, ERA, and RE/MAX, which have thousands of offices. According to the "2006 National Association of Realtors® Profile of Real Estate Firms: An Industry Profile," 23 percent of all firms are affiliated with a franchise, a figure that has remained relatively constant since 1999. However, franchise firms are larger than independent real estate offices, the report says, and account for 55 percent of the total U.S. real estate sales force.

Becoming a real estate franchisee is a two-step process. First, you must start a real estate broker-

Franchise Times
TOP FIVE
Real Estate Franchises*

1. Coldwell Banker Real Estate Corp.
2. Century 21 Real Estate
3. Keller Williams Real Estate
4. GMAC Real Estate
5. ERA Franchise Systems

*Based on systemwide sales.

age, then affiliate it with a franchise system. And you'll have to start small. According to the NAR profile, the typical independent real estate firm has a median of six licensees, usually working as independent contractors, and one staff person. All Realtors must pass extensive tests and be licensed within the states where they work.

Real estate franchises include nontraditional firms, like Sell 4Free Real Estate Systems, of Fishers, Indiana, whose franchisees waive the listing fee for sellers who buy other houses, and Help-U-Sell, a Castle Rock, Colorado, company that provides do-it-yourself assistance to both buyers and sellers. The category also includes property inspection franchises and an unusual company that teaches franchisees how to buy, fix up, and sell ugly houses.

HomeVestors

"We buy ugly houses" is the slogan of HomeVestors of Dallas, the only company whose franchisees trade in rundown houses. The company was started in 1996 by a real estate investor who had made a business out of buying houses at a discount, providing cosmetic or structural improvements, and selling them at a profit. HomeVestors now has about 250 franchisees, who buy and sell a total of about 6,000 houses a year.

One of them is thirty-six-year-old Jennifer Raney, of Rockwall, Texas. "I was an independent investor, buying and selling 10 to 15 houses a year, but I had no name behind me," says Raney. "Once I joined the HomeVestors franchise two years ago, I started buying and selling 100 houses a year."

In what she calls a typical example, three or four siblings inherit a house their parents lived in for 30 years. "It's dated," Raney says, "and might even have structural problems. The executor calls me and I go in and assess what repairs are needed and make an offer based on what the house will retail for once I've fixed it up. I then use independent contractors to paint, replace the carpet and light fixtures and sometimes the countertops, and repair any structural problem, like the roof or foundation. Since I'm a Realtor, I can sell the house myself. I like watching a house go from being almost dilapidated to something light, bright, and fresh."

> *"I like watching a house go from being almost dilapidated to something light, bright, and fresh."*

Jennifer Raney, HomeVestors Franchisee

What do you do on a daily basis? "I now have a team of four buyers, a dig lead generator (who digs up leads on ugly houses), and an office coordinator. I orchestrate their activities and maintain good relationships with investors."

How long before you broke even? "Because I'd been doing this on my own before joining the franchise, I immediately turned a profit." (In a 2006 article on HomeVestors in the *New York Times*, a new franchisee said he expects it will take him two years to recoup his investment and make money.)

How do you make money? Can you make a good living? "It costs me $40,000 a month to operate my franchise. I figure out how many houses I have to buy and what profit margin I must make per property. I set my goals and do it. I'm already earning an executive salary and I'm retaining some of the houses I buy, to rent out. My goal is to own 100 houses free and clear."

What is the most difficult part? "Buying in volume can be overwhelming. To buy and sell 100 houses a year, you have to be a machine that's running constantly. You feel like you can never stop."

Who should not be a franchisee of this category? "Someone who thinks advertising will be enough and just waits for the phone to ring. You have to be constantly proactive in getting leads yourself. Because you're buying houses from people in difficult situations, you must be able to relate to them. Someone without an empathetic personality will not do well. And because you're dealing with market trends and numbers, you won't make it if you don't have that ability."

What advice do you have for someone considering a HomeVestors franchise?

- Understand that this is a business, not a hobby. It is not for fun.

- Be prepared to work very hard the first two to five years.

- Conduct yourself with a level of professionalism, or investors won't work with you.

- If you're going to have a franchise, you need to do what they teach you to do.

- Use the franchise support team to help you hire and motivate the right people.

Raney says she typically owns a house for four months before selling it, but sometimes she "flips" the houses she buys immediately to investors and makes a profit in just a few hours.

Building and Construction

The painters, carpet installers, roofers, foundation repair people, and handymen Raney hires to fix up her ugly houses may also be franchisees. The Building and Construction category surged after 9/11, when the nation's homeowners hunkered down and decided to spend more time in their own homes. But when they looked around, they realized their homes needed organized closets, granite countertops, outdoor lighting, new window treatments, and newly lined bathtubs.

The 80-franchise Building and Construction category makes up 5 percent of all franchises and includes everything from Designs Of The Interior (DOTI), a Barrington, Illinois–based franchisor of upscale interior design stores, to Budget Blinds of Orange, California, and The Crack Team of St. Louis, whose franchisees repair foundation cracks. Franchising has even replaced the neighborhood handyman. Now companies like Handyman Connection of Cincinnati and House Doctors of Milford, Ohio, teach franchisees how to hire independent contractors to make household repairs.

As in many franchise categories, ideal franchisees are not those who can install closet organizers or remodel kitchens themselves, but businesspeople who can market such services. As an extra advantage, you can run many of these businesses from a home office.

Nationwide Floor and Window Coverings

Or in Jeff Stewart's case, a business can be run from a well-stocked van. Stewart, of Hinsdale, Illinois, had been a plant manager for an aluminum manufacturing company until it closed in early 2001. "I left my position in January, and by

Jeff Stewart, Nationwide Floor & Window Coverings Franchisee

What do you do on a daily basis? "I call people to set up appointments and present myself directly to customers or new referral sources. I follow up on initial calls to see if I can warm anything up. I'm also ordering materials, arranging installations, and writing work orders. You have to multitask, and you couldn't do this without cell phones and remote e-mail devices, because you have to be available all the time."

How long before you broke even? "It was a good two years. My wife worked and had benefits, which enabled me to stay with the business long enough to get it viable. I've seen really good people who couldn't make it because they ran out of money."

How do you earn money? Can you make a good living at this? "You have to be very good at fitting products your customers will like to their budgets. And you need to mix big jobs with smaller ones and find client work that's not seasonal. Then you have to figure out the margins on each job and keep track of every line item. I am making a living. It's not as good as I want it to be, but I like my boss."

What's the hardest part? "Making time to continually drive for new business. There are so many things you need to be caught up on, it could occupy all your time."

Who should not be a franchisee of a shop-at-home decorating franchise? "People who don't have the enthusiasm to succeed. You have to get in there and try it. I've seen people come to this from different walks of life—sales managers, personnel directors, computer technicians. And in no case was their previous career a good indicator of success."

What advice do you have for people considering this type of franchise?

- Be realistic. This is a hard row to hoe.

- You have to get a lot of things lined up before you can start selling.

- Find people to network with, because that's essential to your getting customers.

March I decided to seriously consider franchising," Stewart says. "I worked with a franchise broker, and Nationwide (a mobile shop-at-home seller of carpeting, tile, and hardwood floors and draperies and blinds) in Milwaukee was one of the first five he suggested. I rejected it, and looked at about 20 more, before circling back. I liked that I wouldn't have to be tied into a store and that I wouldn't have to process lots of small transactions. And I'm comfortable working with home interiors."

"You have to think that driving a van isn't beneath your dignity. If some people look at me funny, that's their problem."

Stewart carries samples of about 200 floor and window treatments from 20 to 30 manufacturers on his truck and has access to hundreds more. Although he sells directly to homeowners, he says his "real" customers are builders, remodelers, and decorators who recommend him to their clients. To network with such people, he joined the National Association of the Remodeling Industry, and now serves as president of the Chicago chapter.

He has hired a part-time office worker, but subcontracts out all the installation work. "You have to be persistent and detail-oriented to do this," he says. "And you have to think that driving a van isn't beneath your dignity. If some people look at me funny, that's their problem. Of course, I'm older [he's in his late fifties]. If I'd gone from being a plant manager to this when I was forty, it would have killed me."

Sports and Recreation

Sports and Recreation, with 2 percent of all franchise systems, is one of the smallest categories on FRANdata's list, but its 57 franchises pack a huge amount of variety. The category leader is The Athlete's Foot, the Norcross, Georgia-based retailer of sports shoes and accessories, with hundreds of stores. If you dream of hanging out at your own gym all day, and have at least $500,000 to invest, Velocity Sports Performance of Alpharetta, Georgia, will show you how to build and staff a facility to help young athletes improve their skills.

Franchise Times
TOP FIVE
Sports and Recreation Franchises*

1. The Athlete's Foot
2. Play It Again Sports
3. Pro Golf Discount / Pro Golf of America
4. Golf USA
5. The Little Gym

*Based on systemwide sales.

Prefer boats? Franchisees of Sea Tow services of Southold, New York, are the American Automobile Association (AAA) of the high seas, rescuing boaters who have run out of fuel or run into bad weather. Wish you could own a sports team, but lack the millions required for the national leagues? For a total investment of about $50,000, you can become an i9 Sports franchisee, organizing and operating your choice of sports leagues. This Brandon, Florida, company will even help you plan tournaments and select prizes.

Baby boomers love golf, so it's not surprising that franchises that sell golf equipment, arrange tournaments, and give lessons are the largest subcategory. And it's also not surprising that franchisees of these 13 systems tend to be middle-aged golfers themselves.

GolfTEC Enterprises, LLC

Mark Nixon was an adjunct professor at the University of Colorado and trying to change his swing when he decided to change his life as well. "I was taking lessons from a GolfTEC franchise and was happy with the results," Nixon says. "I'm an engineer and I thought if they could teach golf to me, they could teach anyone. I'd been looking for a business that took advantage of the demographics of baby boomers about to retire, so I started researching the company."

GolfTEC was started in the mid-1990s by two young graduates of the University of Mississippi's Golf Management program, who designed a system of biofeedback sensors and video to measure and improve a golfer's swing. Nixon says he was impressed, but the company is based in Centennial, Colorado, and all the Colorado franchise territories were already taken.

In 2005, Nixon sold his Colorado house, moved to Tampa, and opened two GolfTEC franchises there. "It was an eventful year," he says. GolfTEC facilities are about the size of a racquetball court, with 11-foot ceilings, and can be free-standing or located with Golfsmith retail stores. Nixon has one of each, and is building more centers in central Florida malls.

"I'm an engineer and I thought if they could teach golf to me, they could teach anyone."

"We give clients a one-hour evaluation," he says, "and take diagnostics of their swings, where they are today, and where they want to go as golfers. Then we guess

Mark Nixon,
GolfTEC Franchisee

What do you do on a daily basis? "Because I'm still growing, I'm busy with site selection and recruiting, hiring, and training employees for existing stores. I also do marketing, advertising, and promotions to attract new customers."

How long before you broke even? "I started breaking even on the first center after about 15 months."

How do you earn money? Can you make a good living at this? "We're open from 8:00 A.M. to 7:00 P.M. seven days a week, and have three to five teaching bays per store. That's a lot of time to fill, but once we hit capacity, the centers should be profitable. They cost from $200,000 to $350,000 to build, so I'll be a long time out of the gate before I start getting a return on my total investment. I am earning a corporate salary from my first two facilities."

What is the most difficult part? "Finding locations with 11-foot ceilings is the hardest part. Otherwise, I'm just having a ball."

Who should not be a franchisee of this category? "We utilize a lot of technology—sensors, video cameras, and computers all hooked together. If that scares you, look for something else. Also, this is definitely a business where you have to get out in the community, and not for someone who doesn't like meeting people."

What advice do you have for someone considering a sports or recreation franchise?

- Find something you're passionate about.

- Then do twice as much due diligence as you think you need.

- You don't need a sports background to do something like this. But you do need to understand how the system works, so you can provide quality control.

Franchise Times
TOP FIVE
Travel Franchises*

1. Carlson Wagonlit Travel

2. Results Travel

3. UNIGLOBE Travel

4. Cruise Holidays Intl.

5. CruiseOne

*Based on systemwide sales.

how many lessons that will require and sign them up for packages that cost $40 to $73 per lesson." All lessons are provided by PGA professionals that Nixon pays by the hour.

Nixon's new life has just one drawback. He's so busy supervising his centers and building new ones that he has little time for golf himself.

Travel Franchises

The 9/11 terrorist attacks that hurt the lodging industry decimated hundreds of travel agency franchisees and even eliminated entire franchise companies. In the two years when the economy was in a recession and people couldn't afford—or feared—leisure travel, smaller agencies that did survive were acquired by larger players. American Express Travel Services now has 2,200 offices around the world, some of them franchised; and Amsterdam-based Carlson Wagonlit Travel has 1,300 franchised units. UNIGLOBE Travel International, of Vancouver, British Columbia, has 700 franchises, down from a total of 1,200.

FRANdata reports that the travel segment now contains only 1 percent of all franchise systems and lists only seven franchisors that are not owned by the big three.

According to the American Society of Travel Agents (ASTA) in Alexandria, Virginia, the majority of its 20,000 members are independent agents.

The ASTA's 2006 "Agency Profile" outlines a second reason travel franchises' finances are strained. Leisure travelers now book flights themselves on the Internet. The percentage of agency sales coming from airline travel dropped from 56 percent in 2000 to 29 percent in 2005. Hotel and car rental income has also fallen, but two segments remain strong: cruise and tour package bookings.

Cruise Holidays, Carlson Leisure Group

This is exactly the niche Rich Skinner and his partner, Steve Sibley, targeted in 2002 when they opened a Cruise Holidays franchise in Woodinville, Washington. "I'd owned a public relations agency that specialized in travel," says Skinner,

Rich Skinner, Cruise Holidays Franchisee

What do you do on a daily basis? "I work on our marketing plans and on group promotions. We're developing a blog and we're going after specialty travel business, like wine cruises."

How long before you broke even? "We started making money in our third year, because it takes that long to build a referral base. Luckily, we both have working wives. To get started in this type of franchise, you need outside resources."

How do you earn money? Can you make a good living at this? "We're paid on a commission basis, according to the price of each cruise, so we're always trying to sell more upscale products. Since 25 percent of our income is from land travel once our customers get into port, we're always trying to get hotels to give us good rates. We are starting to support ourselves, but we're about two years from making a good living."

What is the most difficult part? "We use an outside sales force and it's difficult to find and develop good travel counselors."

Who should not be a franchisee of this category? "You must be passionate about the business and be people-oriented, empathetic with your customers. If you are not driven to provide good customer service, you shouldn't think of this."

What advice do you have for someone considering a travel franchise?

- Too many people are lured into believing they can make a lot of money working from home as a travel agent. For everyone making $100,000 selling cruises, there are hundreds of people earning $7,000 or $8,000 a year.

- Be very realistic and approach this for the long term.

- Have a focused marketing plan. For example, we do not sell discount $299 cruises. We've targeted a customer base that wants a 65-day Pacific cruise in a suite or a first-class train trip across Europe.

- Sign on with a large franchisor. Carlson provides an online database we could never afford on our own and helps with our supplier negotiations.

> *"We had a Web site, wireless connections, and a state-of-the-art computer system. Our phone didn't ring for six months."*

"and at first we thought we'd buy an independent travel agency, but when we looked around for a better option, we found Cruise Holidays."

Skinner says they opened a storefront office "with a big-screen TV, a couch, and a conference table, because we wanted people who would spend a lot of money with us to feel comfortable. Since Steve's background is technology, we also had a Web site, wireless connections, and a state-of-the-art computer system. Our phone didn't ring for six months."

The long start-up time in attracting customers to a cruise franchise is exacerbated by an even longer payment structure. When you book a cruise, your commission is held in escrow until your customers actually set sail. "I can book a cruise for a group today that doesn't leave for a year, and I'll get no revenue until then," Skinner says. "You must always refill the pipeline and always be selling to the future."

There are, of course, some perks. Skinner says he and his family take one or two cruises a year and he has reserved a huge suite on the stern of a Mediterranean cruise ship to celebrate his next birthday in style.

As we've seen, many of these franchises follow consumer trends. If we become more diet-conscious, will demand ebb for fast food, honey-baked ham, and cookie bouquets? If so, sales at sports-related franchises should soar.

If you prefer not to ride such trends, you may be more comfortable looking at franchises that provide services to other businesses, children, or the elderly. We'll look at those next.

CHAPTER FOUR

Service-Oriented Franchises: Fixing Everything from Cars to Computers

The United States is a service economy, and franchises that provide some kind of service—to other small businesses, to seniors, to car owners, or to time-strapped families and their children—are growing quickly. According to FRANdata, franchises enjoying the largest percentage of unit growth from 2003 to 2005 were computer products and services. And of the more than 300 new franchise systems that registered with state agencies in 2006, 118 fell within the service category.

Professor Udo Schlentrich of the University of New Hampshire predicts we'll see "continuous movement into service sectors, governed by demographics. Baby boomers are moving into retirement age, but they still want creature comforts, which accelerates the demand for housecleaning, window washing, lawn care, and other services. And adult children want their parents looked after, not in a nursing home, but at home, with caregivers to help with their health and personal hygiene needs."

"Another sector that hasn't maxed out yet," Dr. Schlentrich continues, "is child care and childhood education programs for dual-earning couples with kids. These couples need help in the early stages of their kids' lives and then in the development of their minds, with franchises that provide exposure to music, art, and reading through play."

General Service Franchises

Service business franchises now match retail franchises in number, comprising 11 percent of all franchise systems. FRANdata divides general service franchises into 20 subsectors which include: dating services; dry cleaners; limousines and shuttle services; mailing, packing, and shipping stores; movers; diet and fitness centers; general health; and senior care. Category leaders include the UPS Stores, of San Diego, and fitness giant, Curves, of Waco, Texas. But the service category also includes unique franchises, like 1-800-Got-Junk?, of Vancouver, British Columbia, whose franchisees get paid for cleaning out people's basements and attics, then get paid again when they resell that "junk" to used furniture and metal dealers; and Dr. Vinyl and Associates, Ltd., a franchisor in Lee's Summit, Missouri, whose mobile franchisees repair everything from car upholstery to vinyl siding.

FRANdata lists 47 different fitness franchises, from Curves for Women and Cuts Fitness for Men, to specialized franchises catering to baby boomers (Club 50 Fitness Centers) or new mothers (StrollerFit). But in some areas of the country, it may be too late for you to join this trend. While some fitness franchises are still adding units, others are closing. Dr. Schlentrich blames oversaturation in some markets and absentee ownership. In the early 2000s, when Curves was the nation's fastest-growing franchise, copycat franchisors also opened centers where women could get a no-frills workout in 30 minutes or less. Soon franchisees of different fitness concepts were competing for customers, often on price, and franchisees who lost customers, or who never attracted enough to hit a breakeven point, had to close.

Dr. Schlentrich also notes that many fitness center franchisees "who are minding their stores" are still very successful and are earning a nice livelihood. But fitness centers are relationship driven and are dependent on people renewing their contracts. Absentee owners, who during the boom purchased the rights to operate 12, even 14 centers, have no ties to the local communities, and do not generate loyalty among their members, he warns.

Senior in-home care franchises may become the Curves of the later part of this decade. According to the National Alliance for Caregiving, a nonprofit organization in Bethesda, Maryland, nearly one-fourth of all American adults are currently providing daily companionship or assistance to a parent or relative.

The situation will only get more serious, because by 2030, the Alliance reports, the country will have 9.6 million people age eighty-five or over, almost double today's elderly population.

So far, 23 franchises provide assistance to seniors, from Home Instead Senior Care, of Omaha, Nebraska, with more than 700 franchises, to Granny Nannies, of Longwood, Florida, with about 20 franchisees. Many franchisees, like Cathy Murphy of San Francisco, chose this business after taking care of an older relative themselves.

Home Instead Senior Care

Cathy Murphy left her career in sales management and marketing for an office products firm when she was fifty-five and the company was "gobbled up" in an acquisition. She found out about senior care franchising "accidentally, when both my parents became very ill simultaneously. It threw my family into the middle of a lake without a paddle. I began looking for help and discovered Home Instead," she says.

Although Murphy says they hired a Home Instead caregiver for her father, and a family friend was a franchisee in Colorado, she was still "suspicious" of franchising. "A retired CPA who had been a franchisee of another concept helped me see that the business model made sense, especially for someone in my age bracket who didn't have time to develop a business on her own."

Murphy purchased the San Francisco territory from a Home Instead franchisee who had opened his first franchise in Mountain View and was too busy to expand. She says, "He told me to find an office that caregiver candidates could get to easily and to invest in a good staff coordinator. I never would have done those things on my own and I probably wouldn't be as profitable now."

Maintenance Services

Maintenance franchises—those that clean residential or commercial buildings; sanitize the toilets in malls and highway rest stops; and clear cobwebs from ductwork, weeds from lawns, and bugs from just about anywhere—make up 8 percent of franchise systems. The category leader is Jani-King International, of Addison, Texas, the world's largest commercial cleaning company, with about

Cathy Murphy,
Home Instead Franchisee

What do you do on a daily basis? "I'm still involved in marketing activities and I'm always looking for growth opportunities. I attend seminars and meet with key decision makers. I'm involved in the daily management of the operation, approving expenses and dealing with technical issues. And I still do all the service calls to new families, to make assessments of their needs."

How long before you broke even? "I started breaking even after one and a half years, when I had around 50 clients."

How do you earn money? Can you make a good living at this? "The franchisor gives us guidelines for calculating and maintaining a profitable margin, after we pay our workers and cover office expenses. We're constantly monitoring performance factors, like the number of inquiries converted to service. My goal was to start earning my corporate salary again in five years, and I've done that after only three."

What's the most difficult part? "The responsibility for the care that you deliver. If you think it should keep you awake at night, it does. Getting caregivers is also a problem."

Who should not be a franchisee of this category? "Starting a new business is stressful. If your family demands are huge, and you don't have support at home, doing this would be too much."

What advice do you have for people considering a senior care franchise?

- Spend a lot of time talking to current owners before you commit to this type of franchise. And spend time with the franchisor's staff.

- Look carefully at the size of the territory you're offered and its demographics. Some senior care franchisors offer large territories that seem appealing to buyers. But you can't manage a large territory and it may not contain enough seniors.

- It's a big mistake to buy more than one territory at a time. You need to concentrate on just one market.

- If you want to get into this to make money, you probably won't be successful. If the service has an appeal to you, then you can make a good living.

12,000 franchisees around the world. The Dwyer Group, based in Waco, is a holding company for six maintenance concepts: Aire Serve (heating and air conditioning), Glass Doctor (window and windshield replacement), Mr. Appliance, Mr. Electric, Mr. Rooter (plumbing), and Rainbow International (damage restoration, services).

More unique franchises are the Mosquito Squad, of Charlotte, North Carolina, whose franchisees rid areas of those flying pests, and Critter Control, of Traverse City, Michigan, a franchise that teaches franchisees how to get rid of raccoons, moles, bats, rats, and other undesirable creatures.

If you'd rather get rid of dust than bats, then one of the eight franchises that provide cleaning services to residences might hold more appeal. The names of some of them—Maid Brigade, Maid to Perfection, and Merry Maids—are appealing in themselves.

The Maids International

Former Winn-Dixie manager John Ricky Garmon chose a cleaning franchise with the simplest name of all—The Maids International, of Omaha, Nebraska. Garmon, who lives in Jacksonville, Florida, says that after Winn-Dixie's founder died in 2003 "it was time to go," so he started searching for businesses online. "I stumbled into a franchise broker who did an exceptional job of figuring out my requirements—no nights, no weekends, no perishables, no kids working for you. She suggested cleaning franchises, so I looked at six of them and chose The Maids because it charges customers more than the others. I didn't want to be the cheapest."

Garmon says he returned from training and "had one week to hire four people. I trained them, and the next week they started cleaning houses. The very first customer we cleaned, we're still cleaning."

"Good employees will reproduce themselves, by bringing in their friends and relatives to work, too."

John Ricky Garmon, The Maids International Franchisee

What do you do on a daily basis? "Today I talked to ten customers who wanted to change their schedules. I cut weekly checks for my workers after my accountant sent me a summary page of the hours they've worked. And I answered questions from an insurance auditor."

How long before you broke even? "It took about six months before I was bringing in more than was going out."

How do you earn money? Can you make a good living at this? "I charge more for cleaning than my expenses will be. The difference is my profit. As you grow larger, the percentage you're spending on fixed expenses gets smaller and more falls to the bottom line. I could be making a good living, but I keep throwing the profit back into the business."

What is the most difficult part? "Turnover will kill you, because your customers like seeing the same faces. The key to the whole thing is getting good people and keeping them."

Who should not be a franchisee of this category? "Someone who doesn't like dealing with customers. You have to be able to adapt really quickly when someone calls and says she needs to move her cleaning day because of a party. And you have to be good with numbers."

What advice do you have for someone considering a cleaning franchise?

- Do a lot of due diligence on the franchise company.

- The most important thing is to be good to your people. They don't need big bonuses, but they do like the little things, like ice cream after a hard Friday.

- Good employees will reproduce themselves, by bringing in their friends and relatives to work, too.

Garmon now supervises six adult cleaning teams who drive to weekday jobs in bright yellow Honda CRVs with The Maids name and logo displayed along each side. "It's a very easy operation to run," he says.

Automotive Franchises

Franchises devoted to the care and maintenance of motor vehicles make up 6 percent of all U.S. franchised businesses. This category includes gas stations, car washes, rental car companies, tire retailers, and franchises that provide body work, oil changes, muffler replacements, engine tune-ups, and transmission repairs.

According to Plunkett Research, Inc., of Houston, Texas, there were 240 million vehicles in operation in the United States at the end of 2006. Of those, only 16.5 million were brand-new cars and light trucks; the vast majority were older vehicles that will eventually require new parts and maintenance to keep rolling.

A few years ago, the future of franchises that specialize in specific maintenance functions, like muffler replacement and transmission repair, looked dismal. New vehicles, especially those produced by Asian manufacturers, are more efficient and require fewer repairs and replacement parts. But franchisors retooled their business models and expanded their service lines. Franchisees of AAMCO Transmissions, of Bala Cynwyd, Pennsylvania, no longer just fix transmissions. They also service brakes, do tune-ups, and change oil. Meineke, of Charlotte, North Carolina, even changed its name, from Meineke Mufflers to Meineke Car Care Centers.

However, the Automotive category still includes specialized niches. Franchisees of AutoQual USA of Warren, Michigan, shine up the cars on dealer lots after each test drive. Oil Butler, of Union, New Jersey, is a home-based franchise whose operators service individuals or fleets of cars by changing the oil and replacing windshields while the cars are parked where their owners work.

Cars may be more efficient, but drivers aren't, and franchises that repair and repaint cars after accidents will always have customers.

Franchise Times
TOP FIVE
Automotive Franchises*

1. Midas
2. Jiffy Lube
3. Dollar Rent A Car
4. Thrifty Car Rental
5. Big O Tires

*Based on systemwide sales.

Mike Murphy, MAACO Franchisee

What do you do on a daily basis? "As little as I can. I have people who manage my shops, and I manage them. I'm still involved in marketing and maintaining good relationships with our customers."

How long before you broke even? "It took about a year. And after about three years we were making a profit."

How do you make money? Can you make a good living? "MAACO doesn't tell us what to charge customers, so we set rates on our own, depending on prevailing hourly wages. Insurance work comes in prepriced and I try to hit a 30 percent margin on the rest. You can definitely do okay. I live in a nice house and fly my own airplane."

What's the hardest part? "The customers are fine. You fix whatever they want, and they're gone. But it's never easy to get good workers. No one says, 'I want to be a body man,' and our industry doesn't have a respectable image. Most of my workers are guys or girls who made mistakes and learned this trade while incarcerated. At any time, half my workers are on parole, and their values are different. It's hard to figure out ways to motivate them."

Who should not be a franchisee of an automotive shop? "If you're not aggressive, opinionated, and innovative, you've got no business in this. If you're an eight-to-five shop steward, keep going. And if you work best in a structured environment, keep going, too. I'm a neat freak and I'm in here every day mopping the floors. If you can't maintain some sort of organization, you'll lose a lot of money quickly."

What advice do you have for someone considering an automotive franchise?

- Besides checking out other franchisees at work, see where they're living. Then you can tell if they're making decent money.

- Work in the franchise you're considering before you sign on.

- You have to be competitive, but you also have to be compassionate. Your car is the second most valuable thing you own, and you want to feel good about the people taking care of it.

- Follow the system. When you come into my shops, you'll see everything you read about in the MAACO manuals. I didn't reinvent anything, because everything they've done for 30 years is still working.

MAACO Enterprises, Inc.

Mike Murphy, of Fresno, California, was a highway patrolman in the mid-1990s when he started looking at franchises. He says he talked to franchisees from a lot of systems and discovered that MAACO owners were the most satisfied. "I worked in one guy's store for two months, for free. It was probably the best investment I ever made, because when I went to MAACO School for training, I had a reference point to work from. I knew why you answered the phone a certain way and that you measure days in minutes, not hours."

> *"At any time, half my workers are on parole, and their values are different. It's hard to figure out ways to motivate them."*

Buying a MAACO franchise was a hefty investment and, Murphy says, "When we started, I maxed out our credit cards, mortgaged the house, sold the car, and at one point I even mailed the keys back to corporate headquarters, but they were returned to sender. And it was a tough adjustment coming out of a government environment, where you worked just eight hours a day and took long vacations."

Murphy attracted customers using guerilla marketing techniques that you'll read about in Chapter Fifteen. He now has two MAACO franchises, employing 60 people. He's moved from that original mortgaged house into an upscale gated community. "But I still wear jeans to work," he says. "And sometimes a guard at our entrance asks if I'll get those weeds the next time I come through."

Services to Other Businesses

Eight percent of all franchises provide services to other businesses. FRANdata splits these into three categories: Business Services (5 percent), Personnel Services (2 percent), and Printing (1 percent).

Business-Related Services

Business-related services include direct mailers, like Money Mailer, of Garden Grove, California, and Valpak of Largo, Florida, whose franchisees sell and send local merchant advertising; check-cashing services like Ace Cash Express, in Irving, Texas; business brokers (Sunbelt Business Advisors, in Duluth, Georgia, is the largest); and companies that provide packing and shipping, payroll, or tax services.

However, you should be wary of several business consulting and advisory franchises in this category. Many of them have corporate-sounding names and glossy brochures, but have failed to attract many franchisees or customers. Be especially suspicious of an Internet franchisor who promises you can get rich by building Web sites for business owners. One such franchise advertises heavily and claims to have thousands of franchisees, but it's under investigation by the Federal Trade Commission. You'll learn how to spot such scams in Chapter Nine.

There is no dispute over computer usage. We have become so technology-dependent that the Pew Internet and American Life Project in Washington, D.C., estimates that 68 percent of all Americans use the Internet on a regular basis. Our businesses rely on computers for connections to customers and suppliers and for internal processing of information. It's not surprising that computer services is the fastest-growing Business Services sector.

FRANdata lists 20 computer repair franchises, including Geeks on Call (also called 1 800 905 Geek), of Norfolk, Virginia, which started franchising in 2001 and now has hundreds of franchisees—all of whom have graduated from Geek University. Then there's the aptly named Computer Troubleshooters, of Decatur, Georgia. Another franchise, out of North Las Vegas, Nevada, purporting to deliver high-tech service with a smile, is named Friendly Computers.

Friendly Computers

Franchising is central to Robert and Diana Formanek's lives. They met at a corporate training session in Boulder, Colorado, when they both were managers for different Domino's Pizza franchisees in Denver. They married, moved to Omaha, and started a Friendly Computers franchise in 2002, between the births of their second and third children.

Robert and Diana Formanek, Friendly Computers Franchisees

What do you do on a daily basis? "We have six technicians and I schedule their appointments, do some marketing, keep the books, and perform other administrative tasks."

How long did it take you to break even? "We were fortunate, and started doing $6,500 in sales the first month. We were paying our bills quickly; but I wanted to be sure I could support our family, so I worked another job for several months."

How do you earn money? Can you make a good living in computer services? "We charge customers by the hour, around $80 for standard labor and $90 for networking. I pay my technicians around $14 an hour for their skills, less if they're driving to or from an appointment. Our average ticket is $137, and we need 40 appointments a week to make a profit in Omaha. You can make a living, although it was Diana's corporate job that enabled us to buy a bigger house."

What is the most difficult part? "As a small business owner, the hardest thing to do is to think about marketing when you're really busy. You think all is going fine, then a month later, you're dead."

What advice do you have for someone considering a computer services franchise?

- Make sure you have enough money for the slow times.

- Check out your potential market area, to see how many other companies are out there and what they charge for their services. Some competition is good, but if there's too much, you may be disappointed.

- Find good vendors who give you good prices and have liberal return policies.

- Since a lot of the vendors are in California, be sure they have good shipping departments that will send you parts quickly.

> *"Diana picked up and delivered computers while she was pregnant with our third child. I was working 70 to 75 hours a week at this and a regular job I was afraid to leave."*

Robert says, "We'd saved some money and started looking at franchises in 2001. The management part was no problem for us, but we needed a system that would teach us everything else. We had no computer training, but liked the field and chose Friendly Computers because they charged lower royalties than their competitors."

The couple started working together from a home office. (You'll read about their insights into both home offices and working with your spouse in Chapter Five. Here's a preview: Diana left the franchise and now works a corporate job.). "We worked from our 1,600-square-foot upstairs [office] and hired two technicians, who checked in and out all day," Robert says. "Diana picked up and delivered computers while she was pregnant with our third child. I was working 70 to 75 hours a week at this and a regular job I was afraid to leave."

After four years, when they were doing $30,000 in sales each month from home, they moved to an office in Omaha and have since opened two more franchises in Kansas City, Missouri, and Kansas City, Kansas. Robert says their business is 60 percent residential and 40 percent business. "We have some businesses on maintenance plans, and promise them four-hour service," he says. "If we have to repair a computer in our shop, we offer free pickup, and when it's fixed, will deliver it for $35. Most customers don't want to wait, and pick up their computers themselves."

Personnel-Related Services

Personnel services could vie with senior care as the franchise growth area of the future. According to the American Staffing Association (ASA), the industry's trade group, the U.S. temporary staffing industry will grow by 3.8 percent a year through 2014. The U.S. Bureau of Labor Statistics says the industry is poised to add more jobs and grow faster than any other industry it tracks. The ASA reports that staffing companies provide more than three million workers a day to the U.S. companies, and so far, only 15 percent of employers use their services. Larger companies are more likely to use temporary employees than those with fewer than 100 workers, the ASA says.

The Personnel Services category, which makes up 2 percent of all franchised businesses, is poised to take advantage of that projected growth. FRANdata lists 34 personnel franchisors—2 executive recruiting firms (MRI Network of Philadelphia is the larger)—and 32 staffing firms. The category leader is Express Personnel Services of Oklahoma City; others include Labor Finders, of Palm Beach Gardens, Florida, whose franchisees place temporary industrial laborers, and Spherion Corporation of Alpharetta, Georgia.

Express Personnel

Becky Kortjohn, who, with her husband Richard, has run an Express Personnel Services office in Dayton, Ohio, since 1989, is ready for the good times. During the recession that followed 9/11, the income of staffing and recruiting firms plunged, and hundreds of offices closed. "During that period," Becky says, "Dick and I were earning less than the person working our front desk. But we managed to stay open and kept our core staff. The temporary workers we place have usually lost something—a job, a spouse, a home, because they just moved here. After the difficult year we experienced, I feel I can be more sympathetic toward them."

"If the procedures manual said to write all reports with my left hand, in red ink, on Monday through Wednesday and with my right hand, in black ink, on Thursday and Friday, I'd do it."

The Kortjohns had joined the franchise because they did not want to leave their own home. "The corporation Dick worked for," Becky says, "was moving and we didn't want to go. We both have human resources backgrounds and, after a lot of research, we chose Express. Of course, the business has nothing to do with HR. It's all about sales."

The Kortjohns divide the selling. Dick does placements into engineering, finance, and accounting jobs, while Becky handles the rest. Together, they send out about 300 workers a day to their clients' companies.

Becky and Richard Kortjohn, Express Personnel Franchisees

What do you do on a daily basis? "I interview candidates who come in looking for a job and talk to our clients about their employment needs. I work a lot with one manufacturer, and it's more of a problem-solving relationship. I'm a partner, rather than a vendor."

How long before you broke even? "About one and a half years. We had two little boys then, and lived very frugally."

How do you earn money? Can you make a good living with a staffing service? "The money we make is the difference between what we pay our workers and what our clients pay us. For example, we might bill a client $15 an hour and pay our worker $10. Since the recession, we are earning executive salaries again and the firm is making a profit."

What's the most difficult part? "We have seven full-time workers, and finding good internal staff is always a challenge. And it's always a balancing act between recruiting the right types of temporary workers, then finding a place to put them."

Who should not be a franchisee of this category? "Someone with no sense of humor. We'd sent a worker to the Dayton Salvation Army once, and her supervisor there called to complain that the young woman had been painting her toenails at her desk. Instead of getting upset, I asked, 'What color?' If you're afraid to make mistakes, you'll never get anything done. I put myself personally on the line for my clients. If you don't have that attitude, you won't make it."

What advice do you have for someone considering a staffing franchise?

- Follow the system. If the procedures manual said to write all reports with my left hand, in red ink, on Monday through Wednesday and with my right hand, in black ink, on Thursday and Friday, I'd do it. I will follow everything, because it works.

- Don't avoid this type of business because you think you're not a salesperson. If you'd asked me if I could sell before we opened, I'd have said absolutely not. But I am a salesperson, and you can be one, too.

- The secret to success in a staffing company is to have a diverse client base. If you have people sitting around for 10 to 14 days between jobs, they'll go to another firm.

Printing-Related Franchises

A quick printer is a small commercial printer that provides quick turnaround and short-run work for its customers. Quick print shops flourished in the 1980s, but their future may not be as rosy. The 11 printing franchises on FRANdata's list make up 1 percent of all franchise companies, and their unit numbers are dwindling.

In its "2006 Annual Franchise Review," *Quick Printing Magazine*, of Melville, New York, reports that the Quick Printing segment had 2,667 shops in 2005, a loss of 107 locations over 2004. Total systemwide sales for all franchise companies was $1.631 billion, down almost 8 percent from the previous year. Sales at one Texas-based franchisor with three printing concepts fell by 60 percent, and 32 of its units closed. Another franchisor lost 37 of its franchisees; only three systems gained units.

The problem is technology. More software programs and speedier computers and copiers allow businesses to do small printing jobs themselves, instead of sending them out to quick printers. And the high-speed, high-color, digital printing jobs that businesses do send out require expensive new equipment that is beyond the reach of some franchisees.

Average sales per quick printing franchise in 2005 were $611,623, down 4 percent from the previous year.

Despite these numbers, QuickPrinting's report says, "The majority of the franchise segment appears strong." AlphaGraphics, of Salt Lake City, is the revenue leader, with franchisees open more than a year averaging $996,000 in sales in 2005. If you're interested in this franchise segment, research companies carefully and avoid those whose franchisees are closing or not renewing their contracts.

The best route to becoming a printing franchisee may be through the office of an existing franchisee. Quick printer franchisees who opened their shops in the 1970s and 1980s are ready to retire and purchasing one of their existing businesses, with their existing customer bases, could be your best approach. (See Chapter Fourteen for more on purchasing a franchise unit from a current owner.) Some quick printing franchisors, in fact, are actively seeking candidates to take over established locations.

Bill Kaufman,
Allegra Printing Franchisee

What do you do on a daily basis? "I've never run a press or done production. I do outside sales, buy equipment, and handle the administration."

How long did it take you to break even? "I made 10 cents the first day I was open, for selling one copy. My wife was not thrilled. It took us close to a year to break even, but we haven't had a down year since."

How do you earn money? Can you make a good living running a quick print shop? "I have to sit down and figure the pricing on each job. What's the cost to run the equipment? How many hours should it take someone to print the job, and what's that person's hourly rate? Then I punch all those numbers into a computer program, and it gives me a price that provides a good margin. Yes, I'm making a good living, doing $1.6 million a year in sales."

What's the most difficult part? "Hiring and keeping good people. My production manager and pressmen are career people. If one leaves, it can take six months to two years to train a new one."

Who should not be a franchisee of this category? "I've seen people buy a printing franchise, then run a press all day. They just bought themselves a job. If you just want a job, work in a bait shop or a bar. And no one should go into this who's not prepared to work hard."

What advice do you have for someone considering a printing franchise?

- Make sure you have plenty of working capital. I had some savings, or I wouldn't have made it.

- Research how much structure your franchisor will impose and decide if you're comfortable with it. Allegra doesn't tell me what equipment to buy, and if you walk into my shop, it will not look like another unit doing $1.5 million in sales. I like it that way."

- You must be comfortable with technology and change.

- To keep good employees, you must pay them well. I pay good wages and provide health insurance, vacations, sick days, and 401(k) plans.

Allegra Print & Imaging

You can't buy Bill Kaufman's Allegra Printing shop in Portage, Michigan—he's selling it to his son. Kaufman, who'd been a manager at Xerox for 22 years, says he opened his franchise in 1988 "when the business was booming. We had technology that would do print and copy jobs that used to take weeks to complete. People were beating down our doors. One year my sales grew by 50 percent."

> *"If you just want a job, work in a bait shop or a bar."*

Back then, Kaufman says, his shop had one computer. "Now we have more computers than employees." Of course, his customers have computers, too, and are doing small jobs, of 500 to 1,000 pieces, themselves. "Now we're doing employee handbooks and jobs requiring 50,000 copies or more," he says.

Kaufman knows his industry is shrinking. He opened a second store that attracted walk-in customers, and closed it when his business moved to mostly commercial printing. "We used to charge $5 to send a fax, and made $500 to $1,000 a month from that. Now fax requests are so seldom we do them for free."

Child-Related Franchises

Franchises that provide services to children, from day care (Primrose Schools, in Acworth, Georgia) to haircuts (Snip-its, of Natick, Massachusetts) to slightly worn clothing (Once Upon a Child, of Minneapolis) to birthday parties (Pump It Up, of Pleasanton, California) are proliferating. Child-related services make up 3 percent of all franchises today, but they are increasing quickly. As is their target market. According to the U.S. government's "2007 Statistical Abstract," by 2010, the country will have more than 21 million children under five and almost 21 million more aged five to nine.

The U.S. Department of Labor reports that in 2004 (the most recent year for which statistics are

Franchise Times
TOP FIVE
Child-Related Franchises*

1. Sylvan Learning Centers
2. The Goddard School
3. Primrose School Franchising Co.
4. Huntington Learning Centers
5. Once Upon a Child

*Based on systemwide sales.

available) 62.2 percent of mothers with children under six were working. That number jumps to 77.5 percent for mothers with children aged six to seventeen. It's not surprising that The Goddard School of King of Prussia, Pennsylvania, has more than 200 franchised day care centers in operation.

Obviously, running a day care center is a full-time responsibility. But many children's services franchises offer opportunities to people who prefer only a part-time commitment. Franchisees of concepts that provide after-school enrichment, like children's art, music, and drama classes, can often fit their business schedules around their lifestyles.

Abrakadoodle

Linda Schaeffer, of Moorestown, New Jersey, says she knows Abrakadoodle franchisees "who work nonstop." But she is not one of them. "I chose this franchise," she says, "because I have three kids and other things in my life."

Schaeffer says she'd owned a ComputerTots franchise back in the 1990s, which she sold after her children were born. "When I learned that company's founder, Mary Rogers, had started a new franchise, I signed on that day," she says.

Abrakadoodle, in Reston, Virginia, offers after-school art and enrichment classes, introducing art to children whose parents don't have time to take them to museums or supervise projects at home. Since 2004, Schaeffer has held classes in schools, YMCAs, Jewish community centers, and park and recreation facilities, paying the establishments a percentage of the fees she collects. She hires art and certified early childhood education teachers to conduct the classes, and pays them by the hour.

Schaeffer runs the franchise from an old gym in her family's finished basement. "I like the flexibility of working from home and not being locked into a storefront. But I can't interview new teachers here," she says, "so I meet them at Starbucks."

Education-Related Franchises

Do you yearn to make a living by helping others? The 2 percent of franchises that are education-related may offer that opportunity, but they hold traps as well. Many of the 46 franchises in this category provide math and/or reading

Linda Schaeffer, Abrakadoodle Franchisee

What do you do on a daily basis? "I get up in the morning and check my e-mails. If there are no fires to put out, I start doing marketing, by checking in with the sites where I hold classes and dropping off brochures at new schools. I schedule future classes, plan curricula, order supplies, train new teachers, and observe those who are working now."

How long before you broke even? "That's tricky, I do this as a second income. Abrakadoodle is profitable, there's no huge overhead, and the first month I was netting something. But I'm not taking a salary and I'm putting almost everything back, although I do pay all my car expenses through the business."

How do you make money? Can you make a good living? "Each session of classes lasts 4 to 12 weeks, although I have some after-school clubs that run all year. I charge parents around $15 a class. What I keep after paying for the facilities, the teachers, and the materials is my profit margin. Franchisees who do this full time are certainly meeting their needs."

What is the most difficult part? "You have no idea what it takes to plan who is doing what at what school and to put together the right supplies for each class. We never repeat projects, and any day I may have six classes running."

Who should not be a franchisee of this category? "You have to have an outgoing personality to market your services to PTA groups, day care centers, and park and recreation departments. They're all looking for someone they'd feel safe leaving kids with. If you're too slick, you won't get their business."

What advice do you have for people considering a children's enrichment franchise?

- Decide first if you are self-motivated and can work alone a lot. This is my second home-based business and it can get a little lonely.

- Can you also get out there and market? Today, I'll get into my car and pop in at 20 schools. If you hire someone to do your marketing, it's difficult to make money.

- Understand that this is not something glamorous or sophisticated. I'm a CPA (certified public accountant) and I'm cutting paper and sorting Crayola crayons.

- Don't do this as a hobby. It's a lot of work, and you'll get your hands dirty.

> *"Understand that this is not something glamorous or sophisticated. I'm a CPA and I'm cutting paper and sorting Crayola crayons."*

tutoring for young children through high school. Some franchisees whose franchisors require them to rent visible facilities in shopping centers and to buy expensive materials tell us they have a hard time making a profit.

Also be wary of franchise systems that concentrate on a specific skill. Franchise companies designed around teaching computer skills, for example, lost some of their appeal when technology become more user-friendly.

This category also includes old standbys—the Arthur Murray and Fred Astaire dance studios. If your dream is to tango into the sunset, give one of them a whirl.

LearningRx

Betsy McLaughlin, of Greenville, South Carolina, has more serious things on her mind. McLaughlin had taught math for 30 years when her husband took a new job and they moved to South Carolina. "I didn't want to land at the end of the substitute list," she says, "and I always wanted my own learning center. I found LearningRx , in Colorado Springs, Colorado, online. It provides one-on-one help for kids with learning or reading difficulties. Since I'd never worked with such kids, I asked my sister-in-law, who does have that experience, to travel to Colorado with me. She's now a LearningRx franchisee, too."

McLaughlin first visited LearningRx headquarters in September 2003. "I took everything to a lawyer, took a personality test, then pondered this for a month and a half. My husband said to trust my gut, so I signed the franchise agreement in November and went back to Colorado for training."

She enlisted her daughter to help and set up shop in her house. "Our first student was the son of a friend. We needed someone to practice on," she says. By the end of the first year, McLaughlin put an addition on the back of her house to accommodate her students, which can number 80 during the summer months. She's purchased a second territory and set up a satellite office there.

"Our students are between the ages of four and fifty-three," McLaughlin says, "but the biggest group is nine-year-old boys. Many young kids have auditory processing deficiencies, which keeps them from developing reading skills.

Betsy McLaughlin, LearningRx Franchisee

What do you do on a daily basis? "I did train, but now I have four full-time staff people, including my daughter, who is making this her life's work, and 20 part-time teacher-trainers. I consult with parents and oversee our operations. I invite parents in for monthly seminars to see what we do and to watch our one-on-one training. Because I can tell our story best, I meet with principals, headmasters, and administrators of assisted living centers."

How long before you broke even? "My daughter and I figured that we needed four students a month to pay her salary and our bills. We had four within a couple of weeks, then added staff and more students."

How do you earn money? Can you make a good living at this? "We charge parents $1,150 for a directed program, in which we teach them to do what we do to help their children. Fees can reach $8,000 if they send a child here for a long reading program, five days a week for five or six months. You absolutely can make a good living. I am taking a salary now, but I'm reinvesting all my profits back into the business."

What is the most difficult part? "The mundane problem solving. You get a call that this child is not coming in and you have to explain that parents have to cancel 24 hours in advance for a refund. And making sure that parents are willing to wait for results. They're putting a lot of time and money into this. Also, I'm too comfortable in my office. I have to make myself do marketing calls."

Who should not be a franchisee of a learning center? "You need compassion for these kids and their parents, who have struggled for so long. If you can't muster that, you're hurting them both."

What advice do you have for people considering a learning center franchise?

- Consider the franchise part first. I spent time watching other franchises in our community. Sometimes something really popular would open and close a few months later. I learned that if I chose something too trendy, I could be in trouble.

(continued)

(Report from the Trenches continued)

- When I found a solid franchise, I'd ask the franchisee for advice. What did you do before? Can you see a schoolteacher doing this?

- Check out the franchisor carefully. I felt confident because once my sister-in-law saw the LearningRx system, she said, "This is what we should have been doing all along."

- Be careful about choosing a territory. One of our franchisees is struggling because his territory is not as vibrant as mine.

- If you start this while you have a young family, it will be tough. I work long hours and have grown children who can help me.

We measure success by giving them tests when they arrive, and more tests six months later. One thing that improves is their processing speed. Parents tell me that once a child feels he can learn, he does his homework more quickly. An assignment that used to take two hours now takes only 20 minutes."

By now, you should have an idea of the types of franchises that appeal to you. But will that category of franchise fit into you lifestyle? In the next chapter, we'll help you measure yourself for your ideal franchise fit.

CHAPTER FIVE

Finding Your Perfect Franchise Fit

Dr. Udo Schlentrich, who directs the William Rosenberg Research Center of Franchising at the University of New Hampshire says, "When I was a student at Cornell University in 1968, a business professor asked our class of about 150 students how many of us wanted a career in the corporate world. About 98 percent of the hands went up. Now when I ask students that question, there's a complete reversal. Ninety-eight percent want to be their own boss. The entrepreneurial spirit is stronger than at any other time in my career."

Sometimes that spirit is too strong. Finding a franchise is like getting married, he says. You may fall in love with a particular franchise system. But you must do your own self-assessment first. Is it suited to your skills? Are you a people person? Do you have the money and time to commit? Where does your family stand?

"And," Dr. Schlentrich says, "you must see how the franchise fits into the external environment. Does it take advantage of economic and social trends? Does your community have the demographics to support it?"

If you skip any of these steps, he warns, and propose on the first date, you'll have a bad marriage. This chapter will try to keep you from such a fate, by exploring in depth two self-assessment issues we mentioned earlier: Could you operate a home-based business? And should you plan to operate a franchise with your spouse? We'll look at the wisdom of buying a franchise that fits today's trends and the risks of buying one designed to fit tomorrow's. We'll show you how franchisees managed to find their own franchise fits and we'll meet a franchisee who wishes she'd shopped a little longer.

Operating a Franchise Near Your Washer and Dryer

According to FRANdata, at least 164 different franchises can be run from your home. These include low-investment concepts like selling cruises or putting together direct mail packages to maintenance services like lawn care or carpet

> *"It's hard to make yourself work when there's laundry to be folded or a leaking faucet to repair."*

cleaning. You can sell window treatments and floor coverings from a truck, like Jeff Stewart of Nationwide, or start up a business services franchise at home, like Robert and Diana Formanek did with Friendly Computers, then move to an office when you have enough customers to pay the rent.

Or can you? Some municipalities frown on people who try to run businesses in residential neighborhoods. Local ordinances may prohibit you from parking service vehicles within sight of your neighbors' homes. Some communities and homeowners' associations restrict the number of deliveries from Federal Express or other services you can receive each day. And while your local government can't control what you do by yourself within your own home, they can prevent you from having employees or letting customers drop off or pick up merchandise or items to be repaired.

Call your local city hall and ask if they have restrictions on home-based businesses or require you to apply for a Home Occupation Permit. If they do have restrictions, you might ask how often those ordinances are enforced and what the penalties are for violations. Many communities have a "Don't ask, don't tell" approach to such laws and will take action only if neighbors complain.

The Advantages of a Down Home Office

Despite such potential run-ins, home offices offer several advantages, especially when you're trying to start a new business. They include:

- *Low overhead.* If you're operating from home, you don't have to pay the rent, utilities, insurance, and other expenses for a separate location.

- *Physical disability.* If you have some kind of mobility difficulty or other problem, working from home may be a good option.

- *Time.* Commuting from the bedroom takes only a couple of seconds. And you can work at any hour of the day or night.

- *Wardrobe.* Why spend money on business suits when you can wear sweats all day?

- *Taxes.* The IRS allows deductions for home-based businesses.

- *Peace of mind.* If you haven't made a great investment in building out and equipping a separate location, you won't have as much money on the line, and should be less stressed about failing. Some franchises will even let you ramp up part-time from home while you're still working your old job.

- *Child care.* Many home-based franchisees find it's impossible to watch little children and run a business. But if your children are school-aged, like Abrakadoodle franchisee Linda Schaeffer's, you can take care of them and your business at the same time.

Disadvantages of Making Your Home the Home Office

On the flip side, here are some reasons you may prefer to find another space for your business endeavor:

- *Isolation.* Many franchisees, like Schaeffer, say working by yourself can get lonely.

- *Lack of motivation.* Gerry Lev, president and CEO of LeaderBoard Tournament Systems in Vancouver, British Columbia, says two of his franchisees, who arrange charity golfing events from home offices, closed down after a couple of years. "They said they needed 15 other people around them to keep them going," Lev says.

- *Lack of commitment.* If you haven't invested much to get started, you may not have the tenacity to hit breakeven and start making a profit.

- *Work/life balance.* If the business is always there, it's easy to keep working it all the time.

- *Family resentment.* See above. Family members may also grow tired of business calls interrupting dinner and order forms on the kitchen table.

- *Lack of professionalism.* Some people look down on home offices, even if they can't see you in your sweats.

- *Distractions.* It's hard to make yourself work when there's laundry to be folded or a leaking faucet to repair.

- *Pantry proximity.* "You can get fat working from home," warns Schaeffer.

Location, Location—Even If It's Just Down the Hall

Despite the drawbacks, the Department of Labor reports 15 percent of all U.S. workers now work from home at least one day each week. The more education the worker has, the more likely he or she will work at least part-time from home. If you want to join them, franchisees say that the best way to make a home-based business work, and incur the least resentment from housemates, is to locate it in a defined space, with separate phone lines.

Bob and Linda Kaplan have operated their Money Mailer franchise from their Chicago home for over ten years. "It would be tough to do this in a small apartment," says Bob, "because it would take over all our living space."

When the Kaplans started their franchise, which provides regular mailings of coupons and promotional materials for local merchants, they rented an office. But when they moved to a larger house, they decided to bring their business home. "I was really nervous about it," Linda says, "but it's working wonderfully. We have a downstairs bedroom that is separate from the rest of the house, and we even have an office manager who works there during the week."

But sometimes it's hard staying in one place. Abrakadoodle franchisee Schaeffer set up an office and stores materials in her home's basement. "But nobody's home during the day, and it's so much more pleasant working from the kitchen table with my puppy at my feet," Schaeffer says. "Of course, my family hates it when I leave my stuff all over the house."

Sometimes the situation is reversed. We once interviewed a lawn care franchisee who'd outfitted his home office with the newest in computer equipment. Every day after school, his sons moved in there with him, to do their homework and IM (instant message) their friends.

"Clients who don't know we work from home think they're leaving messages, instead of waking us up."

Usually, the boundaries broken are not physical. Cruise Planners franchisee Carleen Peaper says the hardest part is balancing her business with her home life. "The phone can ring at any time," she says, "even when we're entertaining on the weekend. It's hard for me to let a single call go to voicemail."

Linda Kaplan says, "Our phone can ring on Sunday night as much as it does on Monday morning. Clients who don't know we work from home think they're leaving messages, instead of waking us up."

Another cruise agent franchisee we met admits that her home business has taken over her life. She is so afraid of losing sales or disappointing clients with problems that she installed extensions of her business line all over her house, and answers all calls, even if they come in during dinner with her family or at one in the morning.

At the other extreme was an Alabama franchisee of a handyman concept we interviewed, who transformed his basement recreation room into an office, then posted office hours on the door. He and his wife, who did the paperwork, worked exactly those hours, no more, no less. Four years later, by the way, the handyman had gone out of business, and the workaholic cruise franchisee was thriving.

Obviously, there are no rules for home-based franchises, except those that may be imposed by your community. If you have limited funds to invest, you may have to find a franchisor who allows you to at least start your business at home. You can find lists of home-based franchises on several Web sites, including

Are You Home Office Material?

Before you start pacing off your spare bedroom for a desk and a computer, here are some things to consider:

- Are you self-motivated?

- Do you have friends who have offices nearby, or who don't work at all? The best way to beat loneliness is to have people you can telephone and meet on a regular basis.

- Is your family supportive? Self-sufficient? Kelly Waddell of Pop-A-Lock says, "You couldn't start something like this with a baby in the house. We were fortunate our son was able to make his own toast if he had to."

- Do you have the self-discipline to make yourself work while the laundry room mess, the family room TV, and the refrigerator beckon? And can you stop working at appropriate hours?

www.entrepreneur.com or by checking businesses under the low-investment tabs on sites like www.worldfranchising.com. A Google search for home office tips will give you ideas of how to design and equip an office in your home.

Should You Start a Franchise with Your Spouse or Partner?

Many franchise companies, including restaurants, retail stores, and many service businesses, encourage couples to become franchisees together. Couples who can divide the tasks, and share the concerns, often prosper more than individual franchisees.

"We thought we had the kind of relationship that would let us work together. Now we see we have our limits."

But not always. The combination of working at home and working together was too much for Rob and Diana Formanek. "We started our Friendly Computer Services franchise at home, thinking we could work together in comfort and keep a flexible schedule," says Rob. "But after a couple of years, that got old. We were stuck together, and stuck in the house, 24/7. I was always in our upstairs office, doing accounting or ordering parts, and my wife wasn't happy, because she thought I should be downstairs, playing with the kids."

Moving to an outside office didn't solve things. "Diana and I have always been best friends and we thought we had the kind of relationship that would let us work together. Now we see we have our limits. Diana has gone back into the corporate world. I think we just burned ourselves out," Rob says.

Finding Your Limits

Becky Kortjohn, who has run an Express Personnel office with her husband, Dick, since 1989, says that working together can put a strain on the best relationship. "I quit once," she says. "But you can't quit what you own."

When Grady Love suggested that he and Nancy run a HoneyBaked Ham franchise together, Nancy says, "I was afraid to be in the same building with him all day, because it would damage our family relationship." The Loves reached a compromise. Most partnership agreements divide control of a company on a 49–51 percent basis, to prevent decision deadlocks. "We told our lawyer we wanted a 50–50 split," Nancy says, "so we would be in the same position legally."

Before Bob and Linda Kaplan started their franchise, they'd been in truly unequal positions. Bob had been a partner in an ad agency where Linda was the office manager. Now they, too, are equal partners. "Mutuality is the key," says Bob. "Don't do this if one of you obviously dominates the other."

For Better or for Worse?

Other partnerships end at the close of the workday. But you and your spouse have to get along 24/7, and couples who plan to operate franchises together should heed the following advice:

- Decide how tasks and responsibilities will be divided, and stick with those lines of demarcation. "If you see your partner doing something you don't agree with, shut your mouth," says Bob Kaplan. "Walk away and let it happen. More often than not, things will work out for the best." "You can't second-guess each other," says Becky Kortjohn.

- "Make sure the rest of your life is settled first," says Kelly Waddell. "If you don't, cracks will become craters."

- "Take the same salary," Waddell says. "That moves any money issues out of the way."

- "Be careful about hiring relatives," Waddell says. "My mother-in-law does 80 percent of our motor club billing from her own home. At one point, we had more relatives and friends working for us, which was tough when discipline and staff reduction times came."

- Is at least one of you a neat freak? Linda says a home-based franchise generates a lot of paperwork. "If you allowed it to accumulate, it would overwhelm you."

- Don't talk about the business all the time, advises Kortjohn. "It's a bad habit to get into, especially when you have children at home."

- Don't take things personally, says Love. "I know my wife loves me, even when she wants to kill me."

- "Have stress release points, and do things that don't involve your spouse. We've even taken separate vacations," Love says.

From Submarine to Senior Care

Curt Maier, who had spent five years in a nuclear submarine patrolling the coast of Russia during the Cold War, now runs an adult day care center in the Lehigh Valley of Pennsylvania. Before he started his franchise search, Maier says, "I never knew such a business existed."

After leaving the Navy, Maier spent 20 years as a general manager with a Fortune 500 chemical company, working out of several global offices. In 2004, when his company went through a restructuring, Maier took a severance package. "I had a bag of money I could use to buy or start a business or buy a franchise," he says. "Franchising looked perfect for me, because I'm an executor, not an innovator. I can get a plan done."

Maier enlisted a franchise broker he'd met at a networking event to introduce him to concepts. He looked closely at three of them: a child development franchise, a janitorial brokerage service, and a franchise that provides in-home senior care. "I asked the broker about alternatives in the senior market, and he sent me to an adult day care franchise in North Carolina," Maier says. "I liked the concept, but the company had no experience in Pennsylvania. Since such services are licensed by state agencies, I thought that was important."

"One day, while I was reading the *Wall Street Journal*, I saw an ad for SarahCare, an adult day care franchise in Canton, Ohio," he says. "I contacted them directly—they were not on my broker's list—and went to Ohio to meet the principals. My mother-in-law is in her mid-eighties and my wife and I had been thinking about care options. I liked the idea of owning something where seniors could feel safe and respected." Maier opened his first franchise in November 2005. Although he has about 14 clients, who pay $60 to $68 a day for care and activities, he was not breaking even 14 months later. Once he does, he'll open more SarahCare centers, he says.

If you and your partner feel you can work through control issues and run a franchise as equal partners, you can begin to explore franchises that play off each other's skills. If one of you is strong in salesmanship and the other prefers keeping the books and doing back-office work, you might thrive together in a franchise with a retail location, for example.

But if you feel that you and your partner really aren't suited to spending time together 24/7, don't feel too bad. Linda Kaplan says, "Half of Money Mailer's franchisees are couples that work together. The other half say they could never work with their spouses. They'd kill each other."

Franchises That Ride the Trends

When you're browsing franchise Web sites, walking franchise trade shows, and reading print ads for franchises, the word "NEW" pops out incessantly. "Get in on the ground floor of this great concept," the promotional materials say. "This will be the next McDonald's," the salesman whispers from his booth.

As we've seen, almost 500 new companies register to start franchising every year. Starting a franchise is expensive, and newcomers need franchisees quickly, to expand and to defray their start-up expenses. To attract those candidates, new companies are likely to accept franchisees who might otherwise not be qualified, just as Batteries Plus took on Susan and Ric Jensen, a nurse and a pilot, instead of experienced businesspeople. Franchisors desperate for candidates may offer reduced franchise fees or delayed royalty plans. Some might even offer to finance your first unit, just to prove they've "sold" one.

New franchises have some advantages, says Eric Stites, president of the Franchise Business Review in Kittery, Maine, a market research firm. "Often," he says, "they're tapping into some new, unique product, service, or hot trend. If a system isn't fully developed, you can play a major role. And if you get in early, you may be given first dibs on additional territories, before they're sold to someone else."

"Franchising," says Stites, "is all about risk and reward. The earlier you get into a system, the greater the risk and, if it succeeds, the greater the reward."

Some franchise insiders feel the risk is too great. "Franchising is a natural selection process," says Professor Schlentrich. "It's survival of the fittest. Once the kinks are worked out, a franchised unit can survive, whether you open it in

> *"Franchising is all about risk and reward. The earlier you get into a system, the greater the risk and, if it succeeds, the greater the reward."*

Georgia or on the West Coast. It's dangerous to purchase a franchise that doesn't have an established five-year track record. Look only at systems that have "gone through the trial stages, shown success, and have 40 or 50 units operating," he says. In other words, stay away from franchise trends.

Which expert is right? To find out, we contacted all 70 new franchises that had registered in 2001 and that *Entrepreneur Magazine* had featured in an article, "70 Brand-New Opportunities for 2002!" Of the 70, only 32 companies were still in business six years later. The other 28 had either disappeared altogether, had stopped selling franchises, or had been purchased by another company. Of those still franchising, some had only a handful of units. One window-washing franchisor had sold one unit and given up. The president of a medical billing company said she sold a few franchises, then terminated them all. "I thought it would be easier," she says.

If you had purchased a franchise from one of those concepts, your life wouldn't be easy, either. But 15 of the 70 newcomers, including Dippin' Dots Franchising, It's a Grind Coffee Houses, Rubio's Baja Grill, 1-800-Dryclean, and Super Wash, have grown into viable systems. If you'd bypassed all the new franchises, you would have missed an early jump onto the computer services trend, because both Geeks on Call (now 1800 905 GEEK) and Friendly Computers started franchising in 2001. And you would have missed being one of the first operators of Wireless Toyz, a retail store that sells cell phones and satellite TV services and accessories.

Deciding to fit your future into a trendy new franchise is certainly risky. In our simple survey, only 21 percent of the new systems sold 30 or more units in six years. More recently, eBay drop-off stores were the hot trend of 2005. Many of the franchisees who purchased units from a franchise before it had an established track record lost their investments. "If it's a trend, it can go away as quickly as it came," warns Stites.

Other trendy franchises that are struggling are some ink cartridge refillers—office products, electronics, discount, and even drug stores have entered the marketplace and are competing on price—and medspas. Several franchises that provided Botox injections and laser hair removal appeared and went away just as quickly in the mid-2000s. As with eBay drop-off stores, the business model had not been adequately tested.

The hot trend of 2006 was easy meal preparation. By the end of the year, the country had 1,091 kitchens, where time-strapped moms could assemble meals to cook at home later, and 361 meal preparation companies, including about 27 franchises. While some operators are doing well, others are feeling the pinch of increased competition; 84 franchised and independent meal prep stores have already closed. Franchise industry insiders predict that the meal prep sector will go through a consolidation process—some franchisors will be acquired by larger players, while others will be squeezed out of the marketplace.

Taking a chance on a new franchise system depends on your risk tolerance. But please be aware that the phone numbers of almost half of the "NEW" franchises you see today may be disconnected within six years, too. Academic research underscores this point. In the mid-1990s, Scott Shane, now a professor of economics and entrepreneurship at Case Western Reserve University in Cleveland, published

> "If it's a trend, it can go away as quickly as it came."

research on the franchises he'd tracked from 1983 to 1993. Less than 50 percent of the companies that started franchising in 1983 were still franchising four years later. By 1993, only 25 percent of the original cohort were still around, Dr. Shane reports.

If you really want something new, you might be safer looking at one of the two exceptions Dr. Schlentrich makes to his five-year, 50-units rules. You can take a chance on a new concept, he says, if:

1. The franchise is emerging in a sector that is within your professional experience and you can see that it would fly in your area.

2. The franchise system has been started by people with experience in similar franchise companies. For example, if a group with a background at T.G.I. Friday's or Applebee's started a new restaurant company, "there's a higher level of chance that they would understand the real estate markets and food business than someone new to the field," he says.

Trends to Watch

Here are a few trends gathered from news stories, women's magazines, and franchise experts. As you become attuned to searching for new business ideas, you'll spot many more:

- Franchises that provide art, music, dance, and physical activities for children—as a supplement to schools that have cut back on extracurricular programs.
- Children's party places. Dual-earning couples are spending lots of money on their kids' birthday parties.
- Day care centers for children, seniors, or dogs
- Hair, nail, and beauty spas for teens and preteens
- Book clubs are hot and, so far, no one has tapped this trend for franchising.
- Back-office services for small and midsized companies, including debt collection and background checks
- Tutoring centers for kids and adults with learning problems
- Healthy fast food for kids
- Restaurants that serve organic food
- Music stores where you "mix and burn," paying to download music to CDs or iPods
- Scrapbooking and a new variation, online scrapbooks

The Task Ahead

Some people spend months, or even years, looking at franchises and never buy one at all. Others fall in love quickly, and feel ready to sign a franchise agreement within a few weeks. Average franchise shoppers spend three to six months narrowing down their franchise choices, more if they are still working full-time. What's most surprising is that almost all franchisees we've met say they started their search with one type of concept in mind—and ended up buying something very different.

A Father/Daughter Duo

When Toney Anaya and his daughter, Kimberly Segotta, began thinking about franchises they could manage together, "we were looking at storage units and other concepts that require little day-to-day management," he says. In mid-2007, they opened their first unit of Chef Dane's, a gourmet meal preparation concept started by Santa Clara, California, chef Dane Mechlin.

Anaya, who served as governor of New Mexico during the 1980s, is an attorney in Santa Fe, while Segotta and her family, which includes young children, live in Albuquerque. "We found a franchise broker," Anaya says, "and told him we had no preconceived ideas of what we wanted to do. Kimberly, who will ultimately take over the entire business, likes food and furniture, and wanted flexible hours so she could take care of her children after school."

The pair spent almost a year looking at different concepts and attended two Discovery Days before selecting Chef Dane's. They signed regional director rights for the state of New Mexico; and El Paso, Texas, will build three stores themselves and subfranchise others, Anaya says.

"I'd advise prospective franchisees to learn as much as they can about the franchise industry and the companies they're considering through the Internet, newspapers, and magazines," Anaya says. "We felt Chef Dane's was a good fit for a lot of reasons. It's a new company in a new industry, and we're getting in on the ground floor, although we are aware that brings some risks, as well as rewards. The business model of three meal preparation sessions a day fits my daughter's schedule better than the other franchises we'd looked at. And it's something my daughter can get passionate about. There's no need to get into a business you don't want to go to every morning."

The Woman Who Leapt Too Soon

A woman with an MBA in finance, who asked us not to use her name, says she spent over a year looking at franchises. "I decided against food concepts, a packing and shipping business, and hair salons," she says, "because it's hard to get employees, and they're cash businesses and subject to employee theft." She finally settled on tutoring centers because she'd always loved teaching, the business required no cash payments and little inventory, and "all the employees were part-time teachers who'd already been prequalified by the state." But the franchise she liked best had no units available in her area, so she went with her second choice.

After two years, the woman is breaking even some months, but says she wishes she'd never joined the franchise system. The franchise support is weak, she says, and the business model leaves local franchisees competing over students.

"You reach a point when you're read up on everything and it just becomes a leap of faith. I found what seemed to me as my best option, as far as my interests and my finances go," she says. "Now, if someone researching franchises calls and asks if they should join this one, I tell them no."

Ask the Professor

Do certain types of franchises have longer legs?

A few of the businesses that started franchising in recent years have the potential to be around for a long time. There will always be a need for business-to-business services. Franchise systems that assist other businesses with everything from office support, consulting services, advertising, and paralegal support have a niche to fill. I remember when a friend of mine purchased a Shred-It, Inc., franchise. This is a mobile franchise that specializes in paper shredding and recycling and targets companies that need assistance with document security and reducing clutter. Now I see these trucks in many cities outside office buildings.

Another type of franchise that will probably be around for a long time is any that is related to our pets. Americans have a love affair with their pets. In fact, according to the American Pet Association 63 percent of U.S. households own a pet, and in 2005 we spent $36.3 million on them. More than 90.5 million cats and 73.9 million dogs can equate to big sales for franchisees that get into a business providing services to our furry friends. Look at franchise opportunities that specialize in pet grooming centers, including mobile pet grooming franchises like Aussie Pet Mobile; pet day care centers, kennels, and obedience schools; or pet food delivery services.

Of course, Americans' other love affair is with food. Food franchises have been around for a long time. Trends have come and gone. We have preferred casual dining establishments for several years. Perhaps it is because through carryout or delivery, we can have some barbecue or a box of wings at home sitting in front of the big-screen television and be with our pets.

We must also consider the ever-growing population of seniors in America today, and the franchises offering children's services. For the last 15 years I've been telling my students to look at these types of businesses, and I should have taken my own advice and done it myself.

We spend money on our pets and on our kids. Franchise systems that provide services to make our kids smarter, healthier, and happier continue to do well. According to *Entrepreneur Magazine*'s twenty-eighth Annual Franchise 500, children's enrichment learning programs increased by 850-plus units, from 2005 to 2006. Additionally, many diverse new programs and franchise opportunities appeared on the scene in 2006, such as a cooking school and an abacus learning program.

(continued)

Abrakadoodle and Young Rembrandts are examples of franchises that cater to the growing interest in children's well-rounded educational experiences and provide them another outlet besides the computer and video games.

Baby Boomers (those born between 1946 and 1964) will start turning 65 in 2011, and the number of older people will increase dramatically during the 2010 to 2030 period, according to the U.S. Census Bureau. Look at franchise opportunities like Home Instead Senior Care, Comfort Keepers, and so on, that offer home care services for the elderly, or other franchise opportunities catering to this growing segment of the population.

What new, trendy franchisees did very well?

Specialty coffee has been around for about 40 years, and although it had its heyday in the 1990s when the number of coffeehouses doubled every two years, it is still growing. The Specialty Coffee Association of America (SCAA) reports that independent owners (one to three units) maintain about 57 percent of the market share. Larger coffeehouse chains (those with more than ten units) seem to be on every corner today, but they only represent 40 percent of the market. Although there hasn't been a huge explosion in coffeehouse franchising, given the sheer size of the industry, the expanding customer base—with baby boomers continuing to drink coffee into their senior years and young kids starting to drink coffee in junior high—and the skyrocketing appeal and availability of specialty coffee, several savvy franchise systems have helped their franchisees do quite well. It appears this trend will continue because, according to the National Coffee Association USA, 49 percent of Americans age eighteen or older drink some type of coffee beverage daily, and a lot of them are waiting in lines at specialty coffee retailers like The Coffee Beanery, which began franchising in 1985, or It's A Grind, which opened in 1995, to get their java fix. Starbucks has grown considerably, and it is a strong competitor, but there seems to be room for more specialty coffeehouses as people tend to drink coffee every day. Now they can even have iced coffee beverages.

We must reiterate the popularity of senior care franchises. They have been around for ten-plus years, the market they serve is growing, and the franchisees that run the business according to the system appear to be doing quite well. More franchise companies are entering into this sector, providing all types of services to capture a part of this lucrative market.

CHAPTER SIX

Beginning Your Franchise Search

Now that you've read through the franchise categories, you're ready to start looking at individual franchises. Which seems easy, because franchises are everywhere—in local shopping centers, along the highway, and listed in local Yellow Pages. All you have to do is drive around your community and decide which business you want to duplicate.

But it's not that simple. The franchises you shop in, drive by, and call up for services may be all sold out in your area. Some of the franchises you see may not be the category leaders that could offer a better opportunity for you. The closest unit of the best franchise to introduce to your town may be hundreds of miles away, where you'll never see it if you depend on franchise shopping locally.

It's easy to assume that none of this is a problem, that the thousands of franchises available are all listed in some orderly fashion in a book or database you can sort through until you find several that appeal. But there is no single database of franchisee opportunities, no directory that lists every franchise available today, no trade show where every franchise seeking new applicants has a booth. In fact, there is no way to tell just how many franchise companies are operating today.

Franchise experts give lots of reasons for this information gap:

- Franchising is not, technically, an industry, but a form of doing business that encompasses 75 different industries. Therefore, its businesses fail to fit nicely into a single Standard Industrial Classification (SIC) code, or even a handful of codes.

- No single entity keeps a list of all franchises because none is required to. Since the 1970s, franchising has been loosely governed by the Federal Trade Commission, under what is called the Franchise Rule. This rule requires all franchisors to present disclosure documents called Uniform Franchise Offering Circulars to prospective franchisees at least 14 days before they sign a contract. (We'll cover UFOCs in detail in Chapter Eight.) Here's the surprising part: Although the FTC requires that franchisors produce and update UFOCs, it does not require them to file those documents with the Commission.

- Fifteen states—California, Hawaii, Illinois, Indiana, Maryland, Michigan, Minnesota, New York, North Dakota, Oregon, Rhode Island, South Dakota, Virginia, Washington, and Wisconsin—do require that UFOCs be filed with their departments of commerce, attorney generals, or other offices. FRANdata maintains its listings of active franchise systems by researching the UFOC filings in these states. But filing a UFOC in registration states can be cumbersome. State officials insist on reading the lengthy documents, which can take months if scores of new franchises try to register at the same time; and some states require changes, usually to make them more favorable to franchisees. To avoid such scrutiny, an uncounted number of franchise companies restrict their franchise sales to the other 35 states.

- Likewise, there's no repository of franchise companies that have sold out all their territories, simply stopped selling franchises, or gone out of business. Therefore, whatever listings do exist contain information about franchise companies that no longer want your application, or no longer exist. If you try to reach one or more of the latter, you'll find that their phone numbers have been disconnected and their Web site domain names are up for sale.

So, how do you search for franchises? Let's take a look at some of the resources available to you.

Print Directories: All the Information Franchisors Want You to Know

Several companies publish annual, or even quarterly, directories of franchise companies. But none of them are comprehensive, because the companies listed all paid to be there, paid for a membership, or paid someone to fill out complicated forms.

The International Franchise Association, in Washington, D.C., is the industry's trade group, and about 1,200 franchise companies are members. These members, which pay dues of $1,650 to $2,200 a year, are listed in the *Franchise*

Opportunities Guide the IFA publishes twice a year and on its Web site (www.franchise.org). Small franchisors may find the dues too expensive, and some large franchisors choose to join trade associations within their own industries instead, like the American Hotel and Motel Association. The IFA is a lobbying group, and franchisors of any size that do not agree with its stand on issues may not be members.

The Franchise Handbook is a quarterly published by Enterprise Magazines, Inc., of Milwaukee. Listings are free, but only franchises that pay for display ads, at costs of $610 to $3,790, or pay to have their logos included, are guaranteed placement. Franchises listed in *The Franchise Handbook* are also on its Web site (www.franchise1.com).

Bond's *Franchise Guide*, published annually by Rob Bond's Source Book Publications of Oakland, California, contains expanded listings of about a thousand franchise companies. Franchisors pay $500 a year to be included in the directory and on Bond's Web site (www.worldfranchising.com).

No one pays to be in the *Franchise Times* annual directory of the 200 Top Franchises, nor on the list of 100 Up and Comers, which are included in this book. Since companies are ranked by size—number of units and annual revenues—the lists include only franchising's largest players. Franchisors do pay to be listed in the *Franchise Times* annual *Super Book*, in print and on the Web. Listings cost $995 to $1,495, depending on length.

Entrepreneur Magazine's Annual Franchise 500, published each January, also ranks franchise systems. Again, companies do not pay to be listed. But they do have to fill out long questionnaires and send in copies of their UFOCs and financial statements several months in advance. Entrepreneur's staff members read through the documents, checking the systems' size, growth and termination rates, litigation problems, and other factors. An independent CPA analyzes each system's financial data. Then staff members apply what the Irvine, California–based publication says is a "secret formula," to choose the Top 500 franchises. These franchises are also ranked within 114 separate categories, from Automotive Appearance Services to Technology.

Fewer than one-third of franchise systems participate in the Franchise 500 each year. Franchises that have fewer than ten units don't qualify; franchisors having a bad year prefer not to send in their information; and franchises that are thriving, like many fast-food chains, don't bother with all the paperwork.

Franchises that do participate use their rankings for marketing purposes. When you see a franchise that proclaims itself number one in its Entrepreneur category, be aware that the category may be very small and may not include that segment's leading companies.

These shortcomings do not mean you shouldn't head to your local book-store to buy one or more of the directories available. Just understand when reading through them that many more franchises are also out there, waiting to be found.

Finding Franchises Online

Put on your skepticism glasses before you type "franchise" into the Google search box. The leading search engine will take you to at least 25 sites that rank, sell, and promote franchises.

Some of the promotion is downright misleading. One site quotes a U.S. Chamber of Commerce study on the fantastic success of franchising as a business model compared to independent businesses. The only problem is that no rep-utable expert within the franchising community has ever seen the study. Another site quotes annual income figures for franchisees that, if they were true, would replace those Entrepreneur rankings in every system's marketing materials.

Franchisors pay a lot of money for their listings on these Web sites, at rates that can cost thousands of dollars each year. Many sites contain boxes you can click for a list of the "Five Best" or "Ten Hottest" franchise concepts. By now we don't have to mention that places on those listings are for sale. So are listings for "Premium," "Gold," and "Silver" franchise systems. Also for sale are places on lists that promise to take you to "The Ten Best Franchises for Making Money Fast" or "The Best Home-based Businesses for 2008."

If you fill out a questionnaire on some Web sites—to qualify for a free book on franchising or to be matched to franchise companies that fit your finances—you become a franchise lead. The Web site operator may then sell your informa-tion to a franchise broker (more about them in Chapter Seven) or directly to franchisors who are looking for candidates with your qualifications.

But if you can get past the hype, and refrain from typing your name, address, and net worth information into every empty box you encounter, the Internet can be one of the best ways to research franchises, because each of those directories will also link you directly into the Web sites of the franchises they list.

What Should You Look for Online?

You can get a great deal of information about different franchise systems by looking at their Web sites. Vibrant systems have sites that include corporate histories; photos of franchisees serving food, selling merchandise, or dispensing services; recent press releases and news articles about the company; information about, and often photos of, company officers; and, best of all, lists of all their franchisees.

"If you can refrain from typing your name, address, and net worth into every empty box you encounter, the Internet can be one of the best ways to research franchises."

"Tired" systems have Web sites that are less appealing. Press releases and news articles are old—a line at the bottom of the homepage may show that it was last updated years ago. Solid franchisors provide ways for you to contact them by phone and/or e-mail. Financially strapped franchise companies just provide online application forms.

What if you come across a franchise whose concept sounds worth exploring, but its Web site needs a makeover? Here's the beauty of the Internet. Go to one or more of the online directories and do a search for other franchises within that subcategory. You can then check out the Web sites of the franchise's competitors. If you've purchased a print directory, you can do the same thing. Look up the first franchise in the index, then see which other systems are listed in the same category.

Here's a tip that will save you a lot of time: If a franchise and its Web site look really appealing, do not fill out the online application and ask for more information right away. If you do, and you meet the financial criteria the franchises are looking for, you'll be inundated with phone calls and e-mails from franchise salespeople long before you even know if you want to buy a franchise in the first place. Instead, click on the link to franchise locations. Are there fewer than 30? You'll read about the risks of joining new and/or small franchise systems in later chapters. Right now, you'd be wise to put those franchises aside and search for larger systems in the same category.

Are there units of the franchises you like nearby? If you're looking at food-related businesses, retail stores, or other storefront operations—like fitness centers, packing and shipping services, or sign shops—it's time to get into your car.

Shopping for Franchises at the Mall

After you've spent several hours browsing franchise directories and Web sites, you'll realize that many of the stores and businesses you thought were unique to your community are franchises. You really can shop for franchises by going shopping. Drive to area malls and strip centers, and walk into franchised stores, restaurants, hair or nail salons, dry cleaners, automotive shops, or other service providers. Can you see yourself running such an operation? Eating the food? Managing the employees?

How busy are these units? Ask someone there to point out the franchisee. Does that person seem relaxed or stressed? Does he or she look like someone who might spend time with you, talking honestly about his or her operation, should you decide to explore that concept more deeply?

Are there franchises that looked great on paper and on the Internet that aren't in your area? Open the Yellow Pages and see if those systems have franchised or independent competitors nearby. While you're driving around, you can check them out, too, to see if there's a market for the product or service you're considering.

Shopping by Phone

If your preliminary research is making you think about franchises that are run from home, vans, office buildings, or locations within industrial parks, you'll have to begin your explorations by telephone. Does the franchisee answer on the first ring? That may be a sign that business is lagging. But it also can be an opportunity for a longer phone call. You can then ask the franchisee a few questions to get an idea of whether this is a concept with a solid customer base. How long does it take to make an appointment or schedule a service call? When is the franchise the busiest? How many people work there?

Franchise Shopping from Afar

Your perfect franchise may be a concept that's strong in a local region that's just beginning to franchise nationally. Maid-Rite in Des Moines, Iowa, for example, has been franchising its loose meat sandwich shops locally for over 80 years. In 2007, the company announced that it would start expanding across the nation. Here are some tips for finding franchise companies that are not in your area:

- Send e-mails to people you know around the country, telling them about your search. Ask them to send you information when they come across appealing franchised businesses.

- Search for the term "franchises" on the Web sites of newspapers from various U.S. cities. A good source of information is the American City Business Journals Web site (www.bizjournals.com).

- Set up an alert for articles and press releases under the word "franchise" (be sure to exclude sports teams) on sites like Yahoo! Finance and Google.

- Local newspapers often contain features about new franchise openings. Pick up such papers while traveling and ask friends to bring newspapers back to you from their trips, too.

- Many franchise companies are operated by women. Spend an afternoon in your public library, flipping through women's magazines for articles about female business owners.

- Subscribe to the International Franchise Association's newsletter, the "IFA SmartBrief," at www.smartbrief.com.

- *Franchise Times* magazine often features new franchises. Subscription information is available on our Web site (www.franchisetimes.com).

Remember MAACO franchisee Mike Murphy's tip about checking out where the franchisee lives, to see if he or she is making any money? In the case of franchises without storefronts, you can check out the office and industrial buildings where they're located. You can even drive by a franchisee's house and check out the condition of the service van in the driveway.

Franchise Trade Shows

Before the Internet, prospective franchisees shopped for franchises by attending trade shows, where hundreds of franchisors set up booths. During the 1990s, a permanent Franchise Exposition area was even installed in Chicago's Merchandise Mart. Scores of franchisors had booths that were often miniature replicas of their franchises, set out literature, and assigned sales representatives to wait for prospective franchisees. But the expo area never attracted enough traffic to make it viable, and it closed.

After the Internet became popular, franchise companies pulled out of trade shows, too. Why spend the money to set up a booth when thousands of franchise leads were arriving each month from cyberspace?

The trend is reversing, says Tom Portesy, president of MFV Expositions in Paramus, New Jersey. "The Internet was the big buzz for a long time," Portesy says, "but franchisors are realizing that while the Internet provides quantity, it doesn't provide quality leads. For that you need a good face-to-face meeting with a prospect." MFV holds three U.S. franchise shows a year and may expand that number soon.

Franchisors spend at least $3,600 for a booth at MFV's regional shows—held in Miami in January and in Los Angeles in November—and a minimum of $5,000 for the International Franchise Expo, held each spring in Washington,

"Franchisors are realizing that while the Internet provides quantity, it doesn't provide quality leads. For that you need a good face-to-face meeting with a prospect."

D.C. They must also cover the expense of sending franchise staff people to man those booths and the cost of the brochures and freebies they distribute there.

The MFV shows are good places to shop for franchises for two reasons. Because of the cost to exhibit, only franchisors interested in expanding and meeting new franchisee candidates will be there. More important, the shows are co-sponsored by the IFA, and only their members, or franchises whose documents have been approved by the IFA staff, are allowed in, although some new, untested concepts do exhibit.

This is not the case for the dozen or so U.S. shows put on each year by National Event Management of

Project Fal$e Hope$

In December 2006, the FTC announced a federal and state law enforcement action targeting bogus business opportunities and work-at-home schemes. Some of the businesses targeted by Project Fal$e Hope$ include:

- The Results Group of Phoenix charged $99 to $599 for an opportunity to sell items on commission through Web sites affiliated with Fortune 500 retail companies. But, the FTC charges, the targeted companies were unaware of any affiliation.

- Making Money Secret charged consumers between $47 and $129 to enter a members-only Web site that promised "Top 12 Programs to Make Big Money." The programs did not exist, or were simply links to government grant programs.

- Business Card Experts falsely claimed that consumers could earn $150,000 in their first year and recoup their initial investment of $10,000 to $25,000. But all that investment provided was the right to order colored business cards from the company.

Markham, Ontario in Canada. Those events are billed National Franchise and Business Opportunity Shows, and exhibitors are a blend of established and brand-new franchises, plus businesses that try to look like franchises. Business Opportunities are also governed by the FTC, and most of the commission's investigations and court actions focus on them.

When you walk by their booths, Business Opportunities look just like franchises. In exchange for an up-front fee, you get the equipment to operate a business, often a vending machine, coffee kiosk, or T-shirt printing press. But that's all you get. Unlike a franchise, you get no ongoing support, official territory, or recognized brand name. Some Business Opportunities are legitimate, but others could be scams. Give a Business Opportunity salesperson a check and you may never hear from him or her again.

Nor does National Event Management vet the franchises that exhibit in its shows, says company vice president Fred Cox, Sr. "We're not researching companies to see if they're real franchises, or if they're registered in the states where our shows are held," Cox says. "If the authorities have questions, we cooperate with them."

Of the 77 exhibitors at a recent Franchise and Business Opportunities Show in Rosemont, Illinois, near Chicago, 14 were franchisors with more than 30 units, but one of these was the Internet consulting franchise that is under investigation by the FTC. The rest were Business Opportunities, selling machines that construct curbs, whirl fruits and vegetables into smoothies, or press designs onto clothing; franchise systems with only a handful of units operating; or franchise industry suppliers, like consultants and brokers.

This does not mean you should stay away from such events. Once you've started thinking about franchising, it's important to meet franchisors and see what franchise businesses are available. "You don't wake up one day and say, 'I'd love to be in the sign business,'" says Portesy. "But you may go to a franchise show and meet a representative from a sign franchise, who tells you it's a business you can get into for a total investment of under $200,000 that uses your business skill sets and lets you work nine to five on weekdays." The booth for an established sign company at the Chicago-area show was, in fact, very busy.

Portesy says his shows attract 180 to 300 franchise exhibitors and 6,000 to 18,000 attendees, over 80 percent of whom are already in the process of shopping for a franchise. "They've visited stores, talked to franchisors, and are more educated than attendees were a few years ago," he says. Do your homework before attending a franchise show, he advises.

By now, your desk is probably piled high with franchise magazines, printouts from intriguing Web sites, and all the brochures you gathered at that trade show. Does something jump out as looking especially promising? If so, you'll want to focus on that concept or category when you start your in-depth research. If not, try to sort all the information into some kind of order, either using our categories or those you create yourself.

Showtime Tips

The FTC has published a "Consumer Guide to Buying a Franchise" you can download from its Web site, www.ftc.gov. The following advice for getting the most out of a franchise exposition comes from that guide, from Portesy and other franchise insiders, and from franchisees.

Before you go to the show:

- Check the show's Web site to see which franchisors are exhibiting. If they include established franchisors you're interested in, write down some questions to ask them. Common questions are: How much do I have to invest? Do you provide protected territories? What qualifications do you look for in a franchisee? (You'll find many more questions to ask in Chapter Nine, on due diligence.)

- If the list includes franchisors you've never heard of, check out their Web sites and count the number of franchises they have operating now. If they have ten or fewer, make a note to visit their booths only if you have time. But if they have 30 or more units and an appealing Web site, read through their Web site material and, if possible, visit a nearby location. If one or more of them look interesting, make a note to visit them early.

- Have an idea of how much you can invest in a franchise. If you know you can't afford to open a sit-down restaurant, for example, cross those booths off your list.

- Put your checkbook in a drawer. The salespeople for Business Opportunities can be really charming and persuasive.

At the show:

- Go early, on the first morning it's open, when the franchise representatives are fresh.

- Go directly to the booths of the franchises you're interested in. Ask your questions, and then stay for a few minutes to listen to the questions asked by other franchisee candidates and the answers they receive. You may learn something valuable. Take notes.

(continued)

(Showtime Tips continued)

- Collect brochures and business cards from the people you talk to. Ask if you can call them the following week with more questions.

- If you don't have specific franchises to visit, begin touring the show by turning left and starting with the farthest row of booths. Since most people start from the right, you'll have more time to chat with franchise representatives before the crowds arrive.

- If a concept looks interesting, visit the booths of all similar franchisors, so you can comparison shop later.

Beware of:

- Any salesperson who tells you his or her franchise is perfect for you. He or she is telling everyone else the same thing.

- Any franchise salesperson who tells you an offer is limited, that there is only one territory left, or that the franchise fee is reduced for this day only.

- Any representative who tells you how much money you can make. The FTC requires any franchise making earning claims to back them up with written substantiation. Numbers whispered at a trade show are worthless.

- Any franchise that promotes itself by promising wealth or riches.

Trade Show Extras

Franchise expos include free seminars. Most of the speakers are franchise brokers or representatives from companies that help you buy a franchise by tapping into your 401(k) plan or other retirement funds. If you attend, be aware that the speaker is trying to sell you something.

Some exhibitors, the FTC guide says, may offer you prizes, free samples, or free dinners if you attend a promotional meeting to discuss the franchise in greater detail. Go if you're interested in the company, not the giveaway. And walk out if the meeting turns into a high-pressure sales pitch.

Ask the Professor

Why is the franchising count always in flux?

The IFA Educational Foundation and FRANdata, a franchise industry source for objective information and analysis, released the first of a series of reports in August 2006 indicating that franchised businesses are expanding at a fast pace, and new franchise concepts are appearing in greater numbers. Many more industries are choosing franchising as a method of expanding their business. Many of these concepts are designed to meet the changing wants and needs of the American consumer, fueled by their desire for ethnic food tastes, child-related services, and other service businesses. Businesses are being franchised today that didn't exist a few years ago.

Remember those entrepreneurial students of mine who didn't go into franchising? They, and their entrepreneurial counterparts across the country, are creating new franchise concepts with increasing frequency, according to the study that drew from a database of nearly 2,500 franchise concepts. Nearly 900 concepts started franchising over the last three years, and 500 concepts started franchising in 2005.

What do you tell your students about finding franchises?

The students provide weekly reports to the class on issues pertaining to franchising and our course reading. One of the reports focuses on franchise opportunities. I always bring copies of the different franchise directories, that is, Rob Bond's *Franchise Guide* (from Source Book Publications) that lists over 1,000 franchise companies, or the latest *IFA Franchise Opportunities Guide* that lists the franchisors that are members of the International Franchise Association. I find that students today are very Internet savvy. They go directly to the franchise company's Web site or to one of the numerous Internet sites that provide directories of franchise companies. I direct them to the IFA Web site (www.franchise.org), *Franchise Times* site (www.franchisetimes.com), and *Entrepreneur Magazine* (www.entrepreneur.com). This way, they can see which systems they qualify for financially and can begin filling out applications.

CHAPTER SEVEN

You're Interested...Now What?

By now, you've done your preliminary research—on yourself, on the franchise industry in general, and on categories that may be suited to your skills, interest level, and finances. You have lists of the franchises you've visited nearby, as well as those you've learned about from Internet searches, reading consumer and franchise publications, and visiting trade shows. Perhaps your sister in another state alerted you to something that's doing well in her neighborhood. Now it's time to let those franchisors know you're interested.

However, if you contact them all at once, you'll be overwhelmed with material and confused by competing sales pitches. The best way to begin is to sort the concepts by category and subcategory. If you can see yourself fitting into a Business Services category but you're not sure which one, sort the systems you like into subcategories and contact all the packing and shipping concepts, for example, first. You should be able to research three to five systems at the same time. This way, you'll be able to compare your selected companies' management teams, royalty structures, and marketing materials.

This chapter will tell you what really happens when you send in an online application and how to respond when franchise salespeople contact you. You'll learn about the highly controversial field of franchise brokers and receive tips on taking an online personality test.

Contacting Franchisors on Your Own

Although print and online directories all include phone numbers for each franchise's development office, almost all their initial contacts come through the Internet. At Home Instead Senior Care, in Omaha, for example, about 85 percent of new leads arrive online. The other 15 percent, says Tim Connelly, director of franchise development at Home Instead, are referrals from existing franchisees. If you do call a franchise development office, the likelihood is that someone will refer you to the system's online request form anyway.

Franchises get thousands of online leads each month, but you can stand out, just by being qualified. As Tom Portesy, president of MFV Expositions says, franchises are drowning in online requests from people who click on their names by mistake or are just browsing. Many browsers are lured in by advertisements on Web sites that proclaim you can "Be Your Own Boss" in an "Exciting Industry." When they see the industry is making signs, and that they'll have to come up with $200,000 to get started, these prospects move on to something else.

> *"Many browsers are lured in by advertisements on Web sites that proclaim you can 'Be Your Own Boss' in an 'Exciting Industry.'"*

Obviously, you can go directly to a franchisor's Web site and ask for additional information. However, Web sites that let you fill out a single information request, with the promise of sending it to all the franchises you've checked, may work to your advantage. Eric Stites, president of the Franchise Business Review in Kittery, Maine, says, "If you check off several companies of the same concept, like five handyman franchises, all five companies will see that list. Franchise salespeople will see how focused you are, and will try to be the first to contact you." But the opposite is also true. "If you check off 50 companies in as many categories, franchisors will figure your focus is all over the map, and following up won't be a high priority."

The Follow-Up: Waiting by the Phone

Say you want to own a dessert franchise and one appealing one is Carvel, an ice cream and cake concept owned by FOCUS Brands of Atlanta. Carvel's minimum financial requirements—$100,000 liquid cash and $300,000 total net worth—are within your range, so you ask for more information. What happens?

Jeff Sturgis, the regional vice president of franchise development for Carvel and its sister brand, Cinnabon, says the two concepts get a total of 10,000 to 12,000 Internet leads a year. Your request will be sent to Carvel's franchising department and you'll be sent a preliminary online application, asking about your occupation, net worth, and your reasons for choosing Carvel. Only about 20 percent of those who receive the form ever fill it out, Sturgis says.

> *"The reality is, if your application meets the requirements of a franchisor that is expanding aggressively, someone will call you right away."*

Like all franchisors, Carvel requires a minimum amount of liquid capital that you must have available to invest. "We'll eventually verify its presence by asking for bank statements," Sturgis says. "If you took out a $100,000 home equity loan a few months ago and put that money into a savings account, we couldn't deny you had $100,000. But home equity is debt and we don't encourage it, unless you can repay the home equity loan with other income." The biggest problem with financial qualifying forms, he adds, "is that people don't understand what they have."

If your form passes muster, and you live in an area where Carvel wants to sell more units, someone from the Atlanta sales office will telephone you, probably within 24 to 48 hours. Stites says: "When most prospective franchisees complete online forms, they think they'll probably hear back by e-mail. They don't expect their phones to ring. The reality is, if your application meets the requirements of a franchisor that is expanding aggressively, someone will call you right away."

The Carvel salesperson "will try to engage you in conversation about what motivated you to contact us," Sturgis says. "He will verbally validate the financial information you sent us and will talk about the area where you'd like to open an ice cream store." During that 30- to 45-minute conversation, the salesperson will also be evaluating your qualifications.

Often, your investigation will end with that first phone call. The franchise may not be selling units in your area, the business model may be different from what you thought, or your expectations may not mesh with the franchisor's reality. "We tell people they'll be devoting 50 to 60 hours a week to this and still won't make any money in the first year," Connelly says of Home Instead.

Getting Serious

If you've made it through the initial phone call, you're in an elite group. At Carvel, of 100 initial leads, only 10 will qualify, and only 1 of them will buy a franchise. In 2006, Home Instead awarded franchises to less than 1 percent of the 4,500 to 6,000 leads it received.

Surviving the Initial Phone Interview

As you'll soon see, franchise salespeople work on commission and only want to spend their time with committed potential buyers. If a salesperson calls and it's not a convenient time to talk—your baby's upset or your dogs are barking at the landscapers—make an appointment to talk later. Here are some tips to follow when you do converse:

- *Be honest.* When the salesperson asks what other franchises you're looking at, tell the truth. If you're also researching Baskin-Robbins and MaggieMoo's, it will show the Carvel sales department that you're a serious candidate.

- *Be yourself.* Home Instead's Connelly says, "I always see through it if an applicant is telling me what she thinks I want to hear."

- *Be realistic.* The salesperson will ask what you expect to earn from your Carvel franchise. "If you're making $250,000 now and say you want to replace your income, that's ridiculous," says Sturgis. "We don't want to deal with anyone whose expectations are not achievable."

- *Show an understanding of how franchising works.* "We want to deal with people who really understand what this is," Sturgis says. "If you start asking questions like, 'Can I also sell bagels? What about flowers?,' that's not a good sign."

- *Have a timeline.* The sales department wants to know how quickly you can act. Do you have a severance package you want to invest in a franchise within the next few months? Or are you just exploring franchising, in case you get laid off next year?

- *Ask questions.* Appropriate inquiries include: How many Carvel stores are in my market now? How many do you want here? Are franchisees in the process of opening more? Where? Do you have research on the ice cream industry that could help me with my decision? Do I need experience in the food industry to be considered for a franchise? What skills/qualifications do you look for in new franchisees?

(continued)

(Surviving the Initial Phone Interview continued)

Red Flags

Salespeople earn commissions on each franchise lead they turn into a sale. You can expect them to be aggressively promoting their brand. But back off if a franchise salesperson says:

- You have to act quickly, because territories in your area are almost sold out.

- You have only a few days to take part in a "limited time offer"— a reduction in franchise fees, for example.

- You can make a certain amount of money with this franchise. Under the FTC rule, no one in a franchise company can make an earnings claim without also providing written verification. If you are quoted a revenue figure, ask for written back-up.

- You sound perfect for this franchise. Like the salesperson in the franchise trade show booth, he or she is telling everyone the same thing.

"Franchise experts agree that you should never sign a franchise agreement without paying a competent franchise attorney to read through—and possibly change—the UFOC and franchise agreement."

At this point, the franchise company must send you its disclosure documents, the Uniform Franchise Offering Circular (UFOC) you've heard about. We'll go into detail on UFOCs in Chapter Eight, but for now, you should know that UFOCs are hefty documents, often 300 pages or longer, and are written in legalese. They are divided into 23 items that cover everything about the franchise opportunity—from details on the owners and their finances to specifics on what the franchise will cost to start and operate. In most cases, the UFOC will be on your doorstep the next morning. Under a revision to the Franchise Rule, franchisors now have the option of sending UFOCs even faster, by delivering them electronically to your e-mail.

Kurt Landwehr, the former national development director for Great Clips, in Minneapolis, now runs brandONE, a business that acts as an outsourced sales department for smaller franchisors. He says, "Once I feel a candidate is qualified, I want to get him the UFOC as quickly as possible, so I send it by overnight delivery. That gives the lead a sense of urgency. And I'll include a cover letter that says I'll be calling shortly to discuss it."

Franchise experts agree that you should never sign a franchise agreement without paying a competent franchise attorney to read through—and possibly change—the UFOC and franchise agreement. But such professional analysis is expensive and will cost anywhere between $300 and $900 per UFOC. If you're researching several franchises at the same time and are weeks from committing to one, you can save money by reading Chapter Eight and doing the initial analysis yourself.

Read through the UFOC carefully, highlighting areas where you have questions and putting sticky notes on those pages, so you can find them again. Besides being prepared for your second call with the franchisor's sales representative, you'll be ready for that expensive date with an attorney, should this be the franchise you eventually like best.

UFOC Warning Signs

You want to go on to the next franchise on your list if you find one or more of these red flags in the UFOC:

- *Item 3: Litigation.* Is the franchisor involved in lawsuits with some of its franchisees? Toney Anaya says he dropped a franchise when he saw that three lawsuits pending against the franchise showed a pattern of alleged misrepresentation.

- *Item 4: Bankruptcy.* Has the company, its predecessors, or any of its principals filed for bankruptcy recently?

- *Item 20: High number of terminations.* Banks won't lend money for new franchises in systems where 10 percent or more of franchisees closed down in a given year. Some have even stricter guidelines.

The Second Phone Call

The franchise sales representative will call again to go through the UFOC with you, and this conversation may last for hours. The next chapter will give you ideas of questions to ask on items that are generic to all franchise disclosure documents. Items 5 through 12 are exclusive to each franchise, because they spell out what it costs to join and what obligations you and the franchisor have to each other during the term of the franchise contract. This is the time for you to inquire about fees, what it will cost you to open a unit, and who'll help you find a location. If this franchise doesn't provide protected territories and another in its subcategory does, be sure to ask why.

Below are samples of the types of questions you should be asking. Make a list of your own questions, leaving space to write in the answers. When you're comparing two or three different franchise offerings, you'll be glad you did.

- Will you help with financing?
- Do your franchisees qualify for Small Business Administration (SBA)-guaranteed loans?
- When do I have to make a deposit? Pay my entire franchise fee?
- How soon do you start collecting royalties? Do you impose late fees?
- Will someone help me find a location for my unit? Who negotiates the lease? Who signs it?
- Will I need a special license? If so, will you help me get it?
- Do I have to purchase equipment, or can I lease it? Do you have arrangements with equipment vendors?
- What if I want to use a product that's not on your approved list?
- Will someone from corporate be there to help with my opening?
- How do I find my first customers?

Obviously, you want answers to these and scores of other questions. But you also want to see how forthcoming the salesperson is with the answers. If the salesperson sounds uninformed or defensive, it may raise doubts about the viability of this concept. And if the salesperson just seems to want to push you on to the next stage, that, too, is a bad sign.

Again, while you're evaluating the UFOC, the franchise is evaluating you. Landwehr says, "We're looking for people who are excited about this business opportunity. If you act like you're really not interested, by missing phone appointments or by cutting conversations short, we'll lose interest in you, too." Landwehr says some of his clients worry about forming a partnership with someone who is not articulate over the phone, or who doesn't sound like he or she has a professional background.

At any point in the process, says Home Instead's Connelly, "We may say, 'We don't think this is a good match for you.'" If after the second conversation, you feel the franchise is not right for you, tell them so. Remember, only one in ten of the qualified people they talk to will become franchisees. You don't have to worry about hurting anyone's feelings.

A Personality Check

At this point in the sales process, some franchisors will ask you to take a personality test, to see if you have the skills and traits they look for in franchisees. Usually, you'll be asked to take a test online before you attend the system's Discovery Day. The most common tests ask you to choose which words best describe you (for example, strong-willed, full of enthusiasm, dependable, or easily influenced), or have you rate your answers to certain statements, like "I need a lot of time to myself." Each test takes less than half an hour to complete. You send your answers via the Internet to the testing company, which scores them, puts them into a customized report, and sends them off to the franchisor.

Personality profiling is relatively new to franchising, and less than half of all systems use such tests. IFA president Matthew Shay says, "Franchisors are much more sophisticated today than they were a generation ago, and are more ready to embrace analytical tools, including personality evaluations." And since so many people are choosing franchising for a second career after being corporate managers or executives, the tests help franchisors know "whether the candidate who interviews

> *"Franchisors are much more sophisticated today than they were a generation ago, and are more ready to embrace analytical tools, including personality evaluations."*

well really has the mind-set to exchange some of his or her independence and autonomy for a recognized brand and business plan," Shay says.

Robert Bingham, CEO of Little Gym International in Scottsdale, Arizona, says his company has been using personality tests since 2004. "We don't have a tremendous amount of time to spend with people to decide whether they should join us or not. I see the tests as a tool to help us do a better job of screening candidates," he says.

At Little Gym, owners spend their days leading children through gymnastics, dance, and exercise classes. "We need operators who are comfortable interacting with kids and their parents," Bingham says. Since starting the testing program, the franchisor has turned down applicants whose profiles show "they'd rather be in a back room crunching numbers," he says.

To operate an It's a Grind Coffee House, franchisees have to go out in their communities to promote their businesses, says CEO Steve Shoeman in Long Beach, California. If your personality test whispers introvert, "We'll be watching your comfort level during the interview process. If you're really quiet, but score well in other areas, we can teach you how to hire managers or find a partner more suited to the coffeehouse environment."

Cottman Transmissions, an automotive franchisor in Horsham, Pennsylvania, would never accept this author as a franchisee. As you recall from Chapter Two, I flunked all three leading personality tests because I'm too empathetic and would let employees walk all over me. At Cottman, the tests are used to flag applicants who may be too indulgent with their employees. Candidates who are likely to be too lax, letting employees arrive late and leave early, for example, get extra coaching in "boss skills" at franchisee training.

Other franchisors are more scientific. They've studied the personality profiles of their current top performers and try to match new franchisees to that ideal. As you might expect, such an approach is controversial. Bob Kreisberg, president of Opus Marketing, a Laguna Hills, California, company that administers personality profiles in the information-technology industry, wonders whether choosing franchisees for certain traits really builds a stronger company. "Franchise companies that say, 'We have one culture: If you don't fit, we don't want you,' are missing out on the advantages that different people bring to the table," he says.

If you're asked to take a personality test, don't worry about flunking. If your personality doesn't fit into a system's profile of an ideal franchisee, you can easily find a system where it does. One caveat: Don't try to answer the way you think the franchisor wants you to. All the tests have "fail-safe" questions, designed to flag disingenuous answers.

Finally, if you take a test, ask the franchisor to send you the testing company's report. Some of the comments may smart, but ever since I scored low on all three leading tests, I'm more comfortable with my flaws. I didn't make that deadline? Don't blame me. Blame my sociable, procrastinating personality.

"Franchise companies that say, 'We have one culture: If you don't fit, we don't want you,' are missing out on the advantages that different people bring to the table."

If your preferred franchisor doesn't do personality testing, it may have other ways of assessing your suitability. At Home Instead, for example, Connelly says, "We do a telephone personality interview, to determine if you have the leadership skills needed to run an in-home care franchise."

If you pass a personality test or get through a telephone interview, your sales representative will now suggest that you start a due diligence investigation of the franchise by calling other franchisees in the system. As you'll see in Chapter Nine, due diligence is critical and takes a lot of time. Don't let your sales representative rush you by putting a time limit on your investigation. If you're looking at several different franchise systems, you may want to get through the preliminary stages on all of them, so you can start talking to, and visiting, franchisees of all those systems at the same time.

Using a Broker to Help You Find Franchises

Several of the franchisees you've read about found their franchise fits by working with franchise brokers, and you may want to pursue that approach as well. Before you do, you should know that few people within franchising are neutral about brokers. Some see them as professional matchmakers, leading prospective franchisees through the clutter of thousands of options to a franchise that's suited to their interests, expectations, and skills. But other people see them as the used-car salesmen of the industry, intent on force-fitting potential franchisees into the concepts they represent.

Franchise brokers work something like real estate brokers. Their services are (or should be) free. They ask you questions about what you want in a franchise company and show you a variety of options that meet your criteria. When you buy a franchise, they earn a commission from the franchisor.

But here's the rub: Their average commission ranges from one-third to one-half of the franchise fee. Thriving franchisors who are getting a steady stream of new franchisees on their own don't need to pay brokers that much and will not deal with them. And most brokerage firms won't deal with low-investment franchisors, whose franchisee fees are so small that earning 40 percent of one isn't worth the effort. Thus, each franchise broker firm works only with the franchisors who have agreed to pay large commissions on each franchise they help to sell, usually about 60 to 100 companies. If you enlist a broker to help in your franchise search, these are the only companies you'll see.

Positive Broker Experiences

This is just fine with many prospective franchisees, including Toney Anaya. "I was never worried about the limited choices the franchise broker offered us," he says. "My wife's been a real estate broker for over 20 years and I understand how the brokerage community works. There are more honest people in that arena than not."

Mary Doize, of San Antonio, a former executive with a software firm, says she spent six months looking for franchises on her own before enlisting a franchise broker. "There were so many franchises out there and I had so many questions," she says, "I had to get a consultant to help me."

"There were so many franchises out there and I had so many questions, I had to get a consultant to help me."

She says that before she met broker Kathy Hill, of the small Dallas firm Entrepreneur Authority, she'd been looking at business-to-business franchises. "Kathy had me fill out a questionnaire, and based on it, said my skills of running a team and hiring and recruiting employees would work well with DOTI, a home decorating franchise," Doize says. She followed through on the advice and opened her store in 2007.

DOTI (short for Designs Of The Interior) CEO Jim Evanger says, "We were getting 50 or 60 Internet solicitations every month, but they weren't the right people. We want prospects who can handle the investment and are strong managers. So we decided to let broker networks do our filtering, and we've been pleased. Our franchisees must manage teams of decorators, and the candidates they're presenting are generally former executives who are used to getting results through other people."

Unlike some firms that troll for prospective franchisees on the Internet, Entrepreneur Authority CEO David Omholt says he and his 15 consultants find candidates in their local communities, through business networks. "It's our philosophy to work with only two to four concepts in any category, so we only represent about 100 companies. We research companies and their UFOCs before accepting them, and turn down about 90 percent that approach us, often because they're too new."

Cheri Carroll, a former broker with FranNet, of Carlsbad, California, says that firm, which is the oldest in the industry, is even more selective. Every year a committee of brokers, she says, selects one type of franchise from each category for their inventory of about 60 well-established companies. Her biggest problems, she says, had nothing to do with the small selection. "I once had a former chemical engineer who wanted a sign franchise. I told him, 'I'm not going to sell it to you, because you won't like it after two months.' He bought one directly from a franchisor, and closed it three months later."

The Negative Side

Longtime franchise executive Robert Stidham, who is now president of Franchise Dynamics, LLC in Naperville, Illinois, a franchise sales outsourcing company, says he has "mixed emotions" about brokers. "They often present themselves as coaches," he says, "and hold themselves out to be objective, when their function is really sales." He says his concern is not so much with FranNet and its rival, FranChoice of Minneapolis, whose brokers are mostly seasoned franchise salespeople, but with firms whose consultants have minimal franchise experience.

> *"They often present themselves as coaches, and hold themselves out to be objective, when their function is really sales."*

"They're giving the industry a black eye," he says.

Two other brokerage firms are actually franchises. "When you contact them, the first thing their consultants do," says Eric Stites, "is try to sell you a franchise in their own companies."

And because some of a broker's client companies pay higher commissions than others, there's a danger that the franchise a broker says is "just right" for you may be the one who's paying him or her the most, Stites warns.

Other Franchise Salespeople

Outside sales agents, like Landwehr and Stidham, are paid a small retainer by the franchisors who hire them and, like brokers, earn commissions on each franchise sale. They're hired by young franchise companies that don't want to invest in in-house sales departments, by systems in midgrowth that have hit a plateau at between 100 and 250 units and want someone to jump-start the sales process, or by large franchisors testing new concepts who don't want to dilute their existing sales forces, Stidham says.

They should tell you they don't work directly for the franchise company, Stidham says, but if they don't, you probably won't know the difference.

Area developers are people like Toney Anaya, who pay franchisors a fee to sell subfranchises in a given territory. If an area developer controls franchise sales in your area, the franchisor will send your request for information to his or her office and someone from the sales office will contact you.

The area developer collects a percentage of the fee you pay to join the franchise and an ongoing percentage of the royalties you'll pay on your revenues. In exchange, it's his or her job to help you open your franchise and to provide ongoing support. Sometimes area developers are so busy opening their own units that they don't have the resources to support anyone else. Checking out the quality of the area developer's support should be an important part of your due diligence.

Making Your Broker Work for You

If you feel you could use some guidance from a broker, here are some simple tips to follow to ensure a smooth relationship:

- Interview more than one, says SarahCare franchisee Curt Maier, who franchise-shopped with Ford Myers, a broker with a single office in Radnor, Pennsylvania.

- Do your homework first, says Myers, and "don't contact a broker unless you're pretty serious."

- Work with a broker in your area, advises Cheri Carroll. "She'll know what franchises are sold out and whether another One Hour Martinizing dry cleaner is needed in your city." And a local broker, who wants more referrals, is unlikely to put you into any system that will fail.

- If you, like Maier, start with a broker, and then end up buying a franchise that's not on the broker's list, don't feel too bad. Only about 20 percent of brokers' assignments result in commissioned sales.

Drop a broker who:

- Asks for a fee. Their costs are paid by franchisors.

- Tries to steer you away from a concept you like, especially if the franchise fee is lower than others on his or her list.

- Has no experience in franchising.

- Works at it part-time. You can't know enough about the franchise systems you're representing if you're just doing this at night.

- Wants you to sign an exclusivity agreement stating that you won't work with another broker for a certain length of time.

- Is on a retainer with some of his or her clients. Since brokers represent a variety of systems, some franchisors try to stack the odds in their favor by offering brokers extra incentives to bring them candidates. You want to find a franchise that's the best fit for you, not for the broker's pockets.

- Shows you only companies that are less than two years old and have less than ten units. These companies are the most risky, and established brokers will not represent them.

Ask the Professor

Is there any correlation between how quickly a franchise responds to a request and the strength of the system itself?

Numerous studies conclude that immediate and continuous communication is an important factor in keeping a lead's interest. One could surmise that the longer the response time, the more questionable the franchisor's business system. If the franchisor doesn't have the support people in place to follow up on leads, it makes you wonder if there will be a sufficient, energetic team in place to support you once you become a franchisee. You are looking for a franchise system that focuses on continuously evaluating and improving its system standards. This indicates the franchisor's commitment to upholding its concepts. You should be looking for a system where the franchisor's leadership team is comprised of people who are happy and excited, full of energy, and have strong positive feelings toward the brand.

Do you believe a personality test can predict who will make a good franchisee?

An increasing number of franchise systems have started using personality profiles over the last few years to screen potential franchisees, and these profiles are increasingly popular. I've been a bit skeptical that any test could tell if you would make a good franchisee. What was happening in your life the day you took the test? Would the results be the same if you took the same test next week, or next month? I would like to see a little more academic rigor that shows me they work.

I've often been asked, "Is there a profile for the ideal franchisee?" Each individual system has its own expectations of the ideal franchisee. Behavioral surveys could identify some of the common traits to function in a franchise system, that is, the ability to communicate, willingness to collaborate, assertiveness, and so on. Perhaps if the personality tests were based on a franchise company profiling the characteristics of its present franchisees, and then trying to match prospective franchisees' traits to those of their top performers—all the while avoiding the qualities of its underperforming franchisees—then the tests would be providing some valuable information. However, isn't this something you could accomplish by looking the prospective franchisee in the eye during Discovery Day? You might find that this person has other admirable qualities and traits—not included in the personality profile—that would be a benefit to your system.

Who should use a broker and why?

The prospective franchisee who has no clue as to what type of franchise he or she wants to go into—he or she simply knows he or she wants to get into a franchised business—would be a candidate for working with a franchise broker.

A good broker can provide you with a wealth of information about franchising, urge you to ignore any preconceived notions about products or services, and get you to focus on the results you want to achieve. A good broker will try to determine what drives you, where you want to live, what you like to do with your time at work, and what your passions are. Beware of a potential conflict of interest, however, if the broker leads you to believe that he or she is your coach, adviser, or consultant. Remember, brokers are paid and are agents for the franchisor.

The Nuts and Bolts: Investigating and Buying a Franchise

Until now, your franchise search has been straightforward. You learned what franchising is; decided if your personality, attitudes, and experiences make you fit to be a franchisee; and explored franchise opportunities. The next steps are not linear, so read Part Two as a unit, because you'll be going in several directions simultaneously.

At this point, you'll start going through UFOCs in earnest (Chapter Eight) and may want to hire an attorney (Chapter Eleven) to help you interpret them. Due diligence (Chapter Nine)—a thorough investigation of each franchise opportunity—should be an ongoing activity. As you'll see in Chapter Ten, you may be invited to attend a Discovery Day, a face-to-face meeting with a franchisor's staff, at any point in the process. And many prospective franchisees enlist a banker (Chapter Twelve) to help them review franchise opportunities. Budget Blinds franchisee Dell Cannon, of Lubbock, Texas, for example, told a local banker about his franchise search at the very beginning of the process, so the loan officer could research concepts right along with him.

To get you started, the Federal Trade Commission has prepared "A Consumer Guide to Buying a Franchise" that you can download from www.ftc.gov by putting its title in the search box. The 11-page handbook reviews what you've learned about franchising, summarizes important sections of the UFOC, and includes lists of questions for you to ask franchisors and their franchisees throughout your research.

CHAPTER EIGHT

The UFOC: Not Exactly Beach Reading

We'll begin the investigative process with the Uniform Franchise Offering Circular (UFOC) because it's the framework behind every franchise—a huge, clunky framework that you'd prefer to leave in its overnight delivery envelope.

Which is just fine with many franchisors. One serious problem in franchising is that people are signing franchise agreements without studying the UFOCs and, therefore, without really knowing their obligations or the franchisors' restrictions on their new businesses. We've heard franchisees complain, for example, that their franchisor "unfairly cannibalized" their sales by opening another franchised or corporate unit nearby. But when we checked the system's UFOC, that document's Item 12 said very clearly that the franchisor could open additional units wherever it chose to.

The most obvious reason why people don't study UFOCs is that they are long (we've seen some that top 500 pages), boring, repetitive, and written by franchise lawyers. Franchisee attorney Justin Klein, of Marks & Klein, LLP in Red Bank, New Jersey, and New York, says people also don't read them because the first page of every UFOC says it provides information for prospective franchisees "as required by the Federal Trade Commission." "They've been handed a book that says the federal government requires us to give this to you. So they think the federal government has reviewed the document and given it a stamp of approval," Klein says.

This is not true. As you recall from Chapter Six, the FTC doesn't even collect UFOCs, let alone read them. Agencies in the 15 states that do require franchises to register their UFOCs may be too short-staffed to read each one carefully and have little authority to point out problem areas.

Another reason is what Klein calls "the McDonald's myth. People hear the word 'franchise,'" he says, "and they jump at the opportunity. They've convinced themselves that franchising equals McDonald's equals success. I had a client

> *"I said to him, 'You didn't even read these documents. You just smelled the French fries.'"*

who'd owned a chain of independent retail stores and now wanted to buy a fried chicken franchise. I wondered why he was willing to work under the restrictions listed in their UFOC, when I suddenly realized something and said to him, 'You didn't even read these documents. You just smelled the French fries.'"

"He called me the next day and said I was right. He was so caught up in the idea, he just wanted to do it. Once he read the UFOC, he changed his mind," Klein says.

From Minnie Pearl to Ronald Reagan

You might be more inclined to read UFOCs if you knew their origins. Although franchising began during the Civil War, the first food franchise didn't arrive until 1925, when California businessmen Roy Allen and Frank Wright launched A&W Root Beer, a chain of franchised drive-in restaurants. Other franchisors, including McDonald's, Kentucky Fried Chicken, and Dairy Queen, arrived and multiplied quickly. In the 1960s, franchising entered its "Wild West" era. Since there was no regulation of this business model, new franchisors rode into town almost daily, and many of them were operated by opportunists looking to make a quick buck.

Promoters of a fried chicken chain named after country singer Minnie Pearl took their franchise public. An investigation by the Securities and Exchange Commission (SEC) disclosed that what the operators of these and other systems had declared as revenues were really uncollected franchise fees. Several franchise schemes collapsed into a series of bankruptcies and lawsuits.

By 1970, so many complaints about fraudulent franchises were coming in to the office of Anthony Pierno, then California's Commissioner of Corporations, that Pierno turned to his state's governor, Ronald Reagan, for help. Governor Reagan allowed Pierno to call in representatives from the IFA and the country's few franchise law practices to write the first law regulating franchising. The drafters thought of franchising as a form of investment, albeit in pizza parlors instead of stocks, and patterned the California Franchise Investment Law after existing securities laws.

Other states passed similar laws, also based on securities disclosure documents, and in the mid-1970s, an association of Midwest securities administrators developed the first Uniform Franchise Offering Circular. The FTC adopted the UFOC format—detailing 23 items a franchisor must reveal to a prospective franchisee—in 1979.

Like a stock prospectus, a UFOC tells you only what you need to know before you buy a franchise. It does not govern franchise relationships after a franchise is sold. And just like a stock prospectus, a UFOC is designed to prevent future lawsuits. Every UFOC also contains a sample of the Franchise Agreement that you'll sign, if and when you decide to join the system. Since the UFOC puts all the elements of the Franchise Agreement into contract form, it accounts for almost half of the document's heft.

What to Look for When Reading a UFOC

Now that you're convinced that UFOCs are worth reading, here's the best part. You don't have to wait for a franchisor to send you one to get started. Any franchise operating in the state of California must file its current UFOC with the California Department of Corporations, which makes them available free online at http://134.186.208.228/caleasi/Pub/Exsearch.htm.

The California site stores UFOCs in sections, and downloading all of them can take some time. If you're willing to spend $200 or so, you can buy print or downloadable UFOCs from several companies, including FRANdata in Arlington, Virginia, or FranchiseHelp, Inc., in Elmsford, New York. You shouldn't have to pay for UFOCs of franchises you're considering, because the sales office is glad to send them to you. But if you want to compare a franchise you're researching to others in its industry, obtaining additional UFOCs is a good strategy.

Besides being long, UFOCs are complicated, so we've asked two leading franchise attorneys to help you decipher them. They are J. Michael Dady, a partner with Dady & Garner, P.A. in Minneapolis and New York; and Rupert Barkoff, a partner with Kilpatrick Stockton, LLP in Atlanta. Barkoff edited the *Fundamentals of Franchising* for the American Bar Association's Forum on Franchising, along with Andy Selden, of Briggs & Morgan P.A. in Minneapolis. Many of his comments come from that 2004 volume.

Grab that UFOC, a red pen, a pile of sticky notes, and a strong cup of coffee and let's begin.

Item 1: The Franchisor, Its Predecessors, and Affiliates

This item provides a history and description of the franchisor. Note when the company was founded and when it started selling franchises.

Read between the Lines

What type of experience does the franchisor have with this concept? Has it been in business for a number of years? Has it actually, and successfully, operated businesses of the type you are being asked to purchase? —Dady

Watch Out For...

an untested franchisor that has not operated corporate locations for at least two years before selling franchises. Also be wary of a system that's been offering franchises for several years, but has only managed to sell a handful.

Item 2: Business Experience

This section lists the franchisor's executives and summarizes their professional backgrounds and, sometimes, their educations.

Read between the Lines

Do the individuals who will be running the franchise have significant experience—in franchising and in the industry? —Dady

Have any of the individuals been involved in other franchises that have failed? —Barkoff

Watch Out For...

serial franchisors, who start franchises in response to trends, then move on to other concepts. Look out for executives who job-hop from one franchise to the next. They may be unqualified, or they may be window dressing, hired on for a short period to lend the appearance of experience to a new system.

Item 3: Litigation

This section lists pending and past litigation in which the franchisor is or has been involved.

Read between the Lines

Has there been significant litigation with franchisees who allege that the opportunity has been oversold or claim that they are not earning as much as they had been told they would? —Dady

Watch Out For...

most systems that have one or two pending lawsuits from disgruntled franchisees or suppliers. Be concerned if there are several lawsuits that seem to follow a pattern. Ask the franchisor if additional litigation has been filed since the UFOC was printed.

Item 4: Bankruptcy

If the franchisor or any of its key executives have gone bankrupt, it must be disclosed here.

Read between the Lines

Prior bankruptcies by the franchisor or its officers are a bad sign. —Dady

Watch Out For...

recent bankruptcy filings that may impact the future of the franchise. If the franchisor or its executives have lost money on one venture, it makes it less likely that they'll be profitable in this one. Vendors don't like to deal with companies that have gone bankrupt, making it more difficult for franchisees to order supplies.

Items 5 and 6: Initial Franchise Fee and Other Fees

These sections are long charts of fees you'll have to pay to the franchisor.

Read between the Lines

Are the fees so high, particularly the ongoing royalty percentage, that it will be difficult to make money with this concept? How do the royalties and other fees compare to this system's competitors? —Dady

Does the franchisor have the right to impose additional fees unilaterally, subsequent to the execution of the franchise agreement? —Barkoff

Watch Out For...

franchisors that charge royalty and advertising fees that are a percentage of gross sales. Almost all of them do. Additional monthly fees for Internet and 800-number referrals, bookkeeping and other back-office services, software usage, equipment rental, and so on can add up quickly and erode your bottom line. Beware of high late fees and ask when they are imposed.

Item 7: Initial Investment

This chart lists all the money you'll have to spend to become a franchisee, from paying the franchise fee through your Grand Opening, and to stay afloat for the first three months.

Read between the Lines

The initial investments listed in UFOCs never cover all initial expenses. The cost of building out your unit varies according to regions of the country, for example. Construction labor and materials costs may have increased significantly since the UFOC was printed. Your local community may impose additional restrictions, calling for expensive modifications of your plans. —Barkoff

Are the total investments required within the magnitude of what you can afford? Do you have additional funds to live on for three months? A year? Ask the franchisor when you can expect to start breaking even. If the franchisor won't tell you, consider that a negative. —Dady

Watch Out For...

being undercapitalized. Most UFOCs include three months of working capital investment analysis. Many concepts take a year or more to start breaking even. In your calculations, multiply the working capital number by at least 4—more if you don't have a working partner or other means to support your family.

Item 8: Restrictions on Sources of Products and Services

To ensure consistency, franchisors usually limit the products and services you can use. If you're looking at a restaurant or retail store concept, this section will be very long and explicit.

Read between the Lines

Does the franchisor commit to using its best efforts to get you the best possible pricing on the products and services you need as a franchisee? Is the franchisor taking payments or rebates from vendors based on franchisee purchases? If so, what are those payments used for—the advertising fund, to benefit all franchisees, or for whatever purpose the franchisor desires? —Dady

Can you use competitive, independent sources of supply? —Barkoff

Watch Out For...

franchisors that require you to buy certain products, even if less expensive alternatives are available. A major issue in franchising is the commissions, or rebates, some franchisors collect from vendors. If the franchisor does collect such monies, they must disclose that in Item 8 of their UFOC, but you'll need an experienced franchisee attorney to help you ferret out the information. Other issues arise when franchisors become the suppliers and/or distributors of the products they require you to purchase, or when franchisors require minimum purchases.

Item 9: Franchisee's Obligations

Since a franchisee's obligations are implicit throughout the UFOC, franchisors design Item 9 as a chart, listing other UFOC sections and places in their Franchise Agreement where each obligation is described in detail.

Read between the Lines

Are your obligations of the type you are able and willing to accept, including your renewal opportunity, your posttermination obligations, and your noncompetition restrictions? Look out for UFOCs that do not offer realistic renewal opportunities or include obligations to sell your unit back to your franchisor for just the value of its hard assets (excluding the customer base and goodwill you've built up during the term of your contract). Also look out for clauses that require you to resolve your disputes with your franchisor in some place other than your home state. —Dady

Watch Out For...

everything! It is vital that you understand every requirement of Item 9. As you flip back and forth through the document, leave a trail of sticky notes so you can find each section again when you're discussing the UFOC with the franchisor. As you'll see in Chapter Eleven's discussion of why you need a franchisee attorney, lawyers focus on details you're likely to gloss over, including sections that describe what will happen if you aren't making money and want to leave the system.

Item 10: Financing

Over half of all franchisors say they offer some type of financing help to new franchisees, but what they offer ranges from financing part of your investment themselves to giving you the phone numbers of bankers with whom they have relationships. Our attorney panel recommends that you go over this section with your own lawyer and accountant.

Watch Out For...

franchises that are finance companies in disguise.

Item 11: Franchisor's Obligations

You'll be relieved to see that the section listing the Franchisor's Obligations to you—support, training, marketing, and so on—is almost as long as the Franchisee's Obligations section.

Read between the Lines

Make sure the types of franchisor obligations specified are consistent with the types of things the franchisor told you it would do for you. —Dady

Watch for firm commitments of services the franchisee obtains from the franchisor before and after start-up. (One of the most common complaints of

The Lopsided UFOC

In the late 1990s, I investigated roasted chicken concept Boston Market for *Franchise Times*. When I opened its UFOC, which weighed over three pounds, or about the size of one of its products, I discovered hundreds of pages devoted to financing, and only a handful that talked about chicken. The former executives had hatched an elaborate scheme to loan money to area developers who would open restaurants and, when they reached a certain sales volume, sell them back to the franchisor. Because of their heavy financing costs, however, the franchisees never had the resources to build sales. The publicly traded company kept borrowing more money to stay afloat. When the scheme cracked apart, Boston Market's stock price fell quickly and many franchisees filed for bankruptcy. (Boston Market is now owned by Sun Capital, a private equity firm.)

franchisees is that franchisors are unclear with respect to the level and types of services they will provide once a franchisee has opened for business; be wary of promises of support services qualified by phrases such as "in our discretion" or "as needed.") —Barkoff

Watch Out For...

any discrepancy between what the salesperson has told you and what you see written in the UFOC. The training requirements, for example, may be tougher, or more lenient, than what you believed. Or if the salesperson has given you assurances that a person from corporate will be at your side during your Grand Opening, make sure that promise is part of the franchisor's official obligations. Item 11 also provides information on how the system's ad fund is administered. Are franchisees involved in advertising and marketing decisions, or are ad monies spent according to the franchisor's discretion?

> *"Be wary of promises of support services qualified by phrases such as 'in our discretion' or 'as needed.'"*

Item 12: Territory

This section states whether or not you'll operate your franchise within an exclusive territory. If the system provides protected territories, Item 12 describes its parameters.

Read between the Lines

Does the franchisor offer protections against encroachment? ("Encroachment" is the legal term for infringing on your territory—when another franchised or corporate unit opens nearby and steals away some of your customers.) —Barkoff

Make sure you have the type of protection against same-brand competition you realistically need. —Dady

Watch Out For...

UFOCs that provide no protected territory, because you'll be competing against your fellow franchisees. Beware of salespeople who tell you not to worry about not having an exclusive territory because the franchisor will never open another unit within a mile or two of yours. If you're successful, the chances are good that it will.

If a franchisor is selling you a protected territory with "100,000 customers," for example, ask how that number is calculated. After all, "100,000 people" is very different from "100,000 adults earning over $50,000 a year." If you are doing well, can you buy adjacent territories at reduced fees?

Item 13: Trademarks

One of the greatest advantages of a franchise is its brand. This section describes what trademarks the franchisor holds for its name, product names, and slogans.

Read between the Lines

Look for assurances that the franchisor's trademark is valid. What happens if the franchisor loses the rights to that mark? Are there conflicting—and possibly superior—local uses of the same, or similar, trademarks by third parties? —Barkoff

Watch Out For...

trademark conflicts in new systems. A well-known Mexican concept had to change its name—and the franchisees all their signs—twice when it first started.

Item 14: Patents, Copyrights, and Proprietary Information

Franchises that use specialized equipment list their patents here.

Read between the Lines

Every franchise has a proprietary "Confidential Operations Manual," where most day-to-day operations rules are buried. You should review it before you sign a contract, even if you have to sign a confidentiality agreement to do so. Can the franchisor change its operations at will, or are franchisees involved in manual revisions? —Barkoff

Watch Out For...

franchises that do not hold the patents or exclusive rights to products or equipment that are vital to their operations.

> "A well-known Mexican concept had to change its name—and the franchisees all their signs—twice when it first started."

Item 15: Obligation to Participate in the Actual Operation of the Franchise Business

This section tells you whether franchisors require their owners to operate their franchises themselves.

Read between the Lines

If you are planning on operating other businesses, or if you believe you have a right to be able to open additional stores if the first one is successful, see if you can get a written commitment to this effect. —Dady

Watch Out For...

franchise systems that allow absentee owners. Studies show that owner-operated franchises perform best.

Item 16: Restrictions on What the Franchisee May Sell

To provide consistency, franchisees usually must all sell the same items. Since the restrictions listed in this item are unique to each franchise system, the attorneys had no general comments.

Watch Out For...

franchisors that allow franchisees wide latitude in what they sell, because that dilutes the value of the brand.

Item 17: Renewal, Termination, Transfer, and Dispute Resolution

No franchise contract lasts forever. This item describes what happens when your contract expires and you want to renew it, or when you want to sell your franchise. It also cites what will happen if you don't follow the rules laid out in Item 9 and where and how your disagreements with the franchisor will be settled or adjudicated.

Read between the lines

How is dispute resolution really done? Is there a franchisee-franchisor review or advisory council? Does the franchisor "stack the deck" in the contract so it has the upper hand in disputes? In the event you default on your payments to your franchisor, are adequate cure periods provided? Can the franchise term be renewed or extended? On what terms? If the renewal terms are unacceptable, does a posttermination covenant not to complete cripple your future plans? What are the restrictions on transferring ownership of the franchise? What are the impacts of those restrictions on your estate planning? —Barkoff

See if you can perpetually renew so long as you are capable of performing. See if your attorney can get the franchisor to limit future royalties and advertising fund increases so that they don't exceed a particular percentage. See if the franchisor will limit its right to transfer ownership of the company only to successor franchisors who are capable and willing to assume your franchisor's obligations to you. Look out for dispute resolution provisions that require you to resolve a dispute somewhere other than in your home state and before more than one arbitrator (if there is an arbitration clause). —Dady

The Macadamia Test

As part of an investigation of a gourmet ice cream brand, I met with a franchisee who complained that his franchisor was harassing him. The franchisor was sending inspectors into his store to give him bad marks on customer service, cleanliness, and product quality, he said. To check things out for myself, I went to his shop and ordered my favorite treat—cake batter ice cream with macadamia nuts. When I bit into the concoction, I realized that the nuts were stale, almost rancid, and I had to throw it away. It was disappointing, but at least I didn't accuse his franchisor of being unfair. (The store is now closed.)

Watch Out For...

Franchisors may make you sign a much more onerous contract—higher royalties, smaller territories, and so on—when your first one expires. Does Item 17 mention renewal options? Also beware of stringent termination clauses. All UFOCs list behaviors that will prompt the franchisor to remove you from its system, such as failure to pay royalties and keep your premises clean. Compare this Item 17 with others in the industry, to see if its termination restrictions are similar or overly punitive. As you'll learn in Chapter Eleven, franchisee attorneys feel most Item 17 sections are tipped too far in favor of the franchisor. While an attorney will probably not be able to reduce your royalties during contract negotiations, he or she may be able to win some concessions on termination, renewal, and transfer issues.

Item 18: Public Figures

This item goes back to the Minnie Pearl era, when celebrities were used to promote franchises. It has almost no relevance today.

Item 19: Earnings Claims

About 25 percent of all franchisors elect to publish information on how much money their franchisees make. In other UFOCs, this item is limited to a single sentence: "We do not make earnings claims."

Read between the Lines

Favor those franchisors who give you some information about how much their franchisees earn. The Earnings Claim should include the factual basis for the information set forth, based on unit revenues and expenses. Look out for franchises that say one thing about revenues, expenses, and cash flows when they are trying to sell you the opportunity, but say something different, or nothing at all, in their Item 19. —Dady

Watch Out For...

earnings claims that are too general. A claim that the average franchisee's total revenues are $900,000 a year doesn't help you if most units are in the city and you're opening one in a rural area.

Item 20: List of Franchise Outlets

Typically, your UFOC will contain a list of the operators of all existing franchised units and of units that have closed within the last year.

Read between the Lines

Look and see if there have been lots of transfers or closings. Look to see if there are other units in your area that will promote some cost-effective media advertising. —Dady

Analyze the number of franchises sold, open units, terminations, and closures. Does Item 20 break out multiunit data? Does it display a pattern of openings followed by closures or resales, that is, churning? —Barkoff

Watch Out For...

a long list of units sold but not yet open. It can signal that the franchisor is more interested in collecting franchise fees than in helping new franchisees get started. Also be on the lookout for a list that's a year or more old. You need current contact information to perform due diligence, and an old list may not reflect recent closures.

Item 21: Financial Statements

The FTC requires franchisors to include audited financial statements on their companies in Item 21.

Read between the Lines

Does the UFOC contain stale financials? A UFOC can legally be used with financials that are over a year old. What is the franchisor's current financial condition? —Barkoff

Is the franchisor making money? Are company-owned stores, if any, making money? Does the franchisor have staying power? What happens if sales of new franchises slow down? —Dady

Watch Out For...

unusual line items, like loans to officers. How do they calculate unused gift cards? Franchise fees for units not yet open? A young franchisor that's operating at a loss may need additional franchise fees just to stay afloat—a situation you'd best avoid.

Item 22: Contracts

The UFOC also contains the Franchise Agreement and other contracts you'll have to sign to join the system. We'll discuss contract provisions in Chapter Eleven.

Item 23: The Receipt

The franchisor must provide you with a UFOC at least 14 days before you sign a contract, and keep a file of signed receipts to prove it did so. Sign the receipt and send it back.

> "A young franchisor that's operating at a loss may need additional franchise fees just to stay afloat—a situation you'd best avoid."

Is the UFOC Fair?

By now, you must be thinking that the UFOC and Franchise Agreements are the most one-sided documents you've ever encountered. Obviously, they were written by the franchisor's attorneys to take advantage of you.

We'll admit we had the same reaction the first time we read one. But after years of researching franchise systems and talking to franchisees, franchisors, and the attorneys who represent both sides, we've learned to appreciate the documents. A franchise is a duplication of an existing business. In order to ensure consistency across an entire country, a franchisor must set out long lists of obligations and responsibilities for its franchisees to follow. And in order for you to make an informed decision, you must be privy to information on who's running the franchise system, whether it's profitable, and who else has opened, and perhaps closed, franchise outlets.

If you're still skeptical, go to the California Department of Corporations Web site and download the UFOC for McDonald's. You'll see that franchisees of that system must abide by rules set out in a UFOC that closely resembles the one you just looked at. In fact, its UFOC is probably longer.

Ask the Professor

Are there clues within a UFOC that indicate you're dealing with a reputable franchisor?

The UFOC is a remarkable document that provides a wealth of information about the franchisor. It provides prospective franchisees with a decided advantage compared to other types of investments. It actually spells out all the material information you need to know about the franchisor, the franchise system, and the financial dynamics of the investment that you are contemplating.

This is a wise time to secure the services of a franchise attorney who is knowledgeable in reviewing franchise agreements. Don't pinch your pennies now. You're getting ready to make a major investment, and it is important for you to realize and fully understand what you're getting into. You will find some clues that indicate if you're dealing with a reputable franchisor through your review of the 23-item narrative description in the Uniform Franchise Offering Circular (UFOC). Crucially important information includes the background history (business, litigation, and bankruptcy) of the franchisor, its officers, and directors. In addition, you will find information pertaining to the fees you'll pay the franchisor; estimates of your total investment in the franchise; your inventory and other purchasing requirements; financing provided by the franchisor; the contractual service obligations of the franchisor; trademarks, copyrights, and patents; renewal, transfer, and termination provisions; earnings claim information; and statistical summaries of the entire franchise system.

You may also want to secure the services of an independent CPA to review the franchise company's audited financial statements for the previous three years. This will give you insight into the financial health of the franchisor, and you can determine for yourself if you think they are financially solid or not.

Do you have a rule of thumb on what constitutes too much litigation or too many franchisee turnovers?

Unfortunately, lawsuits are prevalent in today's society, and one must be wary of overreacting to them. However, a prospective franchisee should be prudent and evaluate the UFOC for the number and types of complaints filed against the franchisor. Both the number and the type of complaints could be warning flags about the integrity of the franchise system. You are looking for franchisors that exhibit integrity and keep their word. This should result in a smaller percentage of lawsuits filed against the company.

The UFOC should include information on franchisees that have left the system. In doing your due diligence, you are looking for a stable franchise system. You should contact as many of those past franchisees as possible for their input and their reason for leaving the business. Did they leave because they weren't making as much money as they expected in establishing and growing their business? Did the franchisor not live up to their expectations and provide the support they anticipated? Most franchise companies will have some turnover of franchisees. However, a high percentage of turnovers can be an indication that something is amiss with the franchise.

CHAPTER NINE

Checking Out Your Franchise of Choice

Now that you've read through one (or several) UFOC(s) and asked the franchise salesperson questions about sections that concerned you, it's time to start a serious investigation of the franchise system (or systems) you like best. This phase is called due diligence, but we like to think of it as high-stakes detective work.

Once you sign a contract, you and the franchisor are married for the next 10 to 20 years. But this contract comes with stiff divorce provisions. If you want to close your unit and move on to something more attractive, you are still liable for all the obligations you pledged to in the Franchise Agreement, including monthly royalty payments (see Chapter Eleven). And because you've learned the franchisor's proprietary recipes, training methods, and/or operations secrets, you're not allowed to open a competing business for several years.

It's important to know as much as you can about the franchise company and the people running it beforehand. Do they pay their bills? Are they respected in the industry? Have any of the major players been involved in previous business failures? Thanks to the Internet, finding out such basic information is fairly easy.

Checking Out the Franchisor Online

Take a good look at franchisors' Web sites and marketing materials. Do what they promise match with what you've learned about the company through the UFOC and discussions with the salesperson? Do they project an image you're comfortable with?

Go to Google and type in the name of the franchise company. By now, you're aware of the franchisor's good points, because they've been repeated to you many times by the franchise salesperson and are highlighted in the brochures he or she has sent you. Ignore links to all the puff piece news stories about how much the franchisor is contributing to a local charity and announcements that the franchisor has opened yet another unit somewhere. Look for problems—

news stories about units closing, lawsuits from suppliers, information about acquisitions or major expansions that, as far as you know, never happened. Has the franchisor been involved in legal matters since its UFOC was printed? Find and print out press releases about new executive hirings, because they may unearth a pattern of firings as well. Don't stop after the first few Google pages; negative information may not show up until the twenty-fifth or thirtieth page of citings. When you're finished, set up a Google News Alert, so that search engine can send fresh news about the franchisor directly to your e-mail.

"Look for problems— news stories about units closing, lawsuits from suppliers, information about acquisitions or major expansions that, as far as you know, never happened."

Now go to the Web sites of local newspapers in or near the franchisor's corporate headquarters (you can find them at www.newsdirectory.com) and do the same thing. Excellent sources of information are the American Business Journals that are published in many major cities. You can find that Web site at (www.bizjournals.com). National franchisors may be mentioned in articles in the *New York Times* (www.nytimes.com) or the *Wall Street Journal* (www.wsj.com). Is the franchisor under investigation by the FTC? Go to www.ftc.gov and type the franchisor's name into the search engine there to find out.

When I'm doing an investigation of a company for *Franchise Times* or another publication, I do an even more thorough search of news stories on LexisNexis, the online research tool developed for lawyers by Reed Elsevier, Inc., headquartered in the Netherlands. For details, go to www.lexisnexis.com. But be careful. Each article you order costs about $3.

If the franchisor is publicly traded, you can find a wealth of information in its filings with the Securities and Exchange Commission (SEC) via www.edgar-online.com. The William Rosenberg Center for International Franchising at the University of New Hampshire keeps track of publicly traded franchisors in its Franchise 50 analysis and newsletters at http://wsbe.unh.edu/centers_wrcif/home.cfm. If you type the franchisor's stock symbol into Yahoo! Finance, you'll find stock charts, links to current news stories, and places where you can order stock analyst reports.

Depending on the industry the franchisor is in, you can also search trade publications. *Nation's Restaurant News*, for example, has a Web site (www.nrn.com) that you can search for articles about restaurant franchisors. Again, you'll have to pay for full articles.

Is the franchisor a member of the International Franchise Association trade group? Members are listed at www.franchise.org. Young systems sometimes can't afford IFA dues, and are too busy getting started to get involved in anything else. But if an older franchise is not a member, make a note to ask why. While at the site, you can sign up for the IFA's "SmartBrief," a daily newsletter that contains links to news stories about franchisors or issues concerning franchising.

In the past, you had to be a business member to check on the financial status of another company via a Dun & Bradstreet report. Now all you need is a credit card. To see if the franchisor is paying its bills, go to www.dnb.com/us and order a report. Have complaints against the franchisor or its franchisees been filed with the Better Business Bureau? Go to www.bbb.org to find out.

Several franchise blogs allow franchisees and customers to share information on franchise companies online. Read postings with a grain of salt. While many tend to be filed by cranky franchisees, you may learn something about the franchisor by checking them out. Certainly, if a blog or chat board has a lot of negative information about the franchisor you're investigating, you should get in touch with the bloggers for more details. Relevant blog sites include Blue Mau Mau (www.bluemaumau.org), Franchise Pick (www.franchisepick.com), and Franchise Law Blog (www.franchiselawblog.com), posted by the law firm of Wiggin & Dana in New Haven, Connecticut. Franchise blogs are transitory. Search for new ones on Google. Some sites, including Franchise Chat (www.franchise-chat.com), link to franchise-related news stories from around the world.

Checking Out the People Running the Franchise

Item 2 of the UFOC provides miniprofiles of the franchisor's key executives. Do they have previous experience in franchising? In their franchise's industry? Look carefully at where they worked before. Sometimes several executives of one franchise company leave to start a new one. This isn't necessarily bad, but do find out what happened to their original employer.

The Biggest Mistakes People Make When Shopping for a Franchise

- Mistaking a great product for a franchise system where individual franchisees can make a profit.

- Mistaking longevity for success. Just because the same fast-food franchise has been in the same place for several years doesn't mean the franchisee is successful. The franchisor may be replacing failing franchisees with new ones every few years.

- Believing that fast growth means that the current franchisees are making money. The franchisor may be devoting all its resources to selling more units, not supporting current franchisees.

- Overestimating how much money they'll make, often based on whispered promises from franchise salespeople.

- Underestimating how much capital they'll need to get started.

- Not doing enough preliminary research.

- Getting so lost in research minutiae that they never make a decision.

Some UFOCs include enough detailed information that you can look for job gaps, while others simply list other places the executives have worked. Pick up the press releases you printed out about executive hirings. Does the information match up with what's in the profiles?

Turn to Item 4 in the UFOC to see if any of the key players filed for bankruptcy. If someone did, was another franchise company involved? Make a note to ask about the bankruptcy while you're attending Discovery Day or when you're next talking to a franchisor salesperson.

You're now ready to run Internet searches on key executives. Unless something in another profile jumps out, you can limit this search to the chief executive officer (CEO) and/or president, the chief financial officer (CFO), the chief operations officer (COO), and the person in charge of franchise development. Again, start with Google, but this time your search will be faster, because you'll probably find only a handful of links for each one. You can also search newspapers and business journals in the cities where their previous employers are located. If they worked for public companies, the executives may be mentioned in *Wall Street Journal* articles or on the Web sites of business publications like *Fortune* or *BusinessWeek*.

Again, you're only looking for problems that might impair your future relationship with the franchisor. Once, while investigating a sports-related franchise for an article I was writing, I did an Internet search on one of its principals and discovered he'd been fired from a coaching position at a public university because of a sexual harassment allegation concerning a student. This is the type of information I'd like to know before I invested in a franchise whose main customers are children.

Checking Out a New Franchise System

If the franchise you're looking at is brand new, there may be nothing about it on the Internet to research, besides checking into the backgrounds of its principals. Before we give you tips on how to evaluate a new franchise, we want to repeat again: Half of all new franchisors fail. And that statistic is based on research from a few years ago, when fewer than 100 new franchisors arrived annually. In 2006, FRANdata found that 302 new franchisors had registered to start selling franchises. Even if half of this crop also survives, that means that 151 franchises launched in 2006 will be gone by 2011 or sooner. And if you invest in an untested concept, your savings, and possibly your house and retirement funds, will be gone, too.

"Franchisees in new systems are always guinea pigs," says attorney Justin Klein of Marks & Klein in Red Bank, New Jersey. "When people come to me because they want to invest in a new system, I tell them what they're getting into. There's risk in any business and you never know if a new system will even work. All you can do is hope that they have the right people in marketing, operations, and other key positions. Sometimes a young system does do well, if it's trendy—and very lucky."

> *"Franchisees in new systems are always guinea pigs."*

Robert Stidham, president of Franchise Dynamics LLC in Naperville, Illinois, says his company acts as an

A Guinea Pig Success Story

Susan and Dan Manwaring opened the very first Batteries Plus franchise in Fort Wayne, Indiana, in 1992. "We were living in Milwaukee," says Susan, "and Dan played golf with someone who was having problems with his battery-powered golf cart. The next time they played, the cart was working perfectly, and the man said that he'd finally found the right battery for it, at a Batteries Plus store. After Dan lost his corporate job and we'd moved back home to Indiana, he couldn't stop thinking about the store that sold only batteries. He called his old golfing partner for the name and number of the owner. I still have the piece of paper he wrote the phone number on."

The owner, Ron Rezetko, had five corporate Batteries Plus stores in Wisconsin and had just registered to start selling franchises, Susan says. After visiting the company stores and meeting Rezetko and his three corporate employees, the Manwarings signed the company's first franchise contract. "We pledged everything we owned to borrow enough money to build a store," Susan says. "Then Dan took another corporate job—we had four children and felt someone should have a regular paycheck—and left me to run the store. My background was in business and accounting. I knew nothing about batteries."

Susan was a fast learner and opened a second store in 1993. Dan left his job in 1996 and the couple now operates seven Batteries Plus franchises. "All our kids went to college and two of our sons are involved in the business," Susan says.

"We knew it was risky to sign on with a brand-new franchise system," Susan says. "But we'd researched the battery industry and knew it was about to take off. Of course, we never imagined where we'd be today, with cell phones, computers, and iPods. As I think back, we put a lot of trust in Mr. Rezetko, but we felt he had a lot of integrity and would deliver on his promises."

outsourced sales department for franchisors, including emerging concepts with 10 to 15 franchised and corporate units. He evaluates new systems according to the following considerations, and says he turns away 90 percent of them. You can use his questions to measure the new systems you're talking to.

- Does the franchisor offer a unique value proposition? If you can't differentiate it from others in its category, there's no way to attract and keep customers.

- Is there room for development or growth in its category? "I can't see us representing a new burger concept," Stidham says, "because there are so many strong national and regional burger brands."

- What is the depth and capability of the management team? What is their experience in other franchises or in the industry they're entering? Sometimes franchises are started by nice people, Stidham says, who have a good idea, but no management experience.

- Do they have the money to reinvest consistently to build their business and support their franchisees? "I've had people send in balance sheets that show they have no equity and that they funded their start-up with debt. They're looking for your franchise fees to get them out of debt," he says.

- Do they offer to meet you at a hotel or fancy restaurant? "If you can't even go to see their premises, it scares me," he says.

- Do all your phone calls go to voicemail? If you can never get a live person now, what will happen when you're open and need support?

> *"Sometimes franchises are started by nice people who have a good idea, but no management experience."*

- Do they have contracts with equipment vendors and product suppliers? If they haven't established those relationships yet, something is wrong with their credit. Attorney Klein adds another red flag. "I've seen UFOCs with misspelled words that are stapled together. If the franchisor isn't taking the time to create professional recruiting documents, how is he going to generate enough capital to support his franchisees?"

If the young franchise company you're looking at sent you a neatly bound UFOC, has at least ten units operating, and passes all of Stidham's tests, then you can move on to the rest of your due diligence detective work. But if it doesn't, please move on to another concept.

Checking Out the Franchisor's Industry

You're not just marrying a franchisor. You're also joining a family of companies within a certain industry, be it fast food, sign-making, or educational services. Even if the franchisor checks out, how do you know you're getting into an industry with staying power? In 15 years, will you, like the Manwarings, have a business you can turn over to your adult children?

Most major industries have associations, like the National Restaurant Association and the National Association of Realtors, that provide statistics on the industry and predict future trends. There's a National Association of Professional Pet Sitters whose Web site (www.petsitters.org) provides material you can read through as you investigate pet-sitting franchises (yes, there are some!). Several hobby associations keep statistics you can use while deciding whether to open a HobbyTown USA franchise; and the National Association of Resale and Thrift Shops has information you should look over before considering a Children's Orchard, Plato's Closet, or other franchise that deals in slightly used clothing and wares.

If the industry you're considering is a big employer, like lodging, you can go to the Bureau of Labor Statistics (www.bls.gov) and click on the Occupational Outlook Handbook to study future trends. Trade publications like the *Quick Printing* magazine we mentioned in Chapter Four also provide industry overviews. You can also use Google and national newspaper search engines for articles on trendy industries, like Botox spas, easy meal preparation centers, and doggy day care establishments, to see if the segment is still growing.

Checking In with Current Franchisees

No government report or association survey can give you as much information about a franchise as its current franchisees. If the UFOC doesn't include an Earnings Claim, they can tell you how much they make. They can tell you how quickly the franchise support person answers their calls, how often the franchisor provides them with new products or services and fresh marketing ideas, and whether the system has an independent franchisee association. They can also tell you if they're losing money, if franchise support is weak, and if the franchisor makes demands they consider punitive, like insisting they use suppliers that charge high prices.

The experiences of current franchisees are so vital to your decision that the franchise salesperson typically points to Item 20 in the UFOC, the list of franchised outlets, and urges you to talk to them.

But that's not as easy as it sounds. Franchisees are busy people who don't have time to chat. Often, I have less trouble scheduling an interview with a system's CEO than with one of its franchisees.

Or they may talk, but give you information that's in their own best interest. If you're thinking of opening a unit nearby, a franchisee may see you as competition, and tell you he or she is earning less than he or she really is. Or franchisees in an area may want you to open a unit nearby, so that you can join their purchasing co-op or contribute to their marketing fund, and they'll tell you things are rosier than they really are.

This is what happened to the "Woman Who Leapt Too Soon," whom we met in Chapter Six. She says, "I talked to other franchisees in my state, but I don't feel they gave me a clear picture. My research was skewed because the people who were answering my questions wanted my contributions to their regional ad fund. They had a dog in the fight." She says that if the franchisees had been honest about their support issues and other types of problems, she would not have purchased her franchise.

"The people who were answering my questions wanted my contributions to their regional ad fund. They had a dog in the fight."

Michael Liss, a franchise attorney in Oak Brook, Illinois, says you can lessen the impact of misleading information by talking to a great number of franchisees. "I tell my clients to call 60 franchisees," says Liss. "You'll find that 20 won't talk to you, 20 will talk but will be very neutral, and the last third will talk for half an hour to two hours. They'll invite you to their stores and, when you get there, show you their books."

The Dangers in Taking Shortcuts

Jim Railing, of Indianapolis, had been a trial lawyer for 20 years before making a career move into investment banking in the early 2000s. He put together large financial transactions for multiunit franchisees and became intrigued by franchising. "My family owned land that was being developed into a strip center," he says, "and I thought a sub sandwich shop would go well there. My daughter, Shantel Hawkins, had been a district manager for Wendy's for ten years, and was ready to go into business with me."

> "They didn't want to tell me they were losing their shirts, but when I calculated their food costs, I knew you couldn't make any money with this concept."

Railing was approved as a franchisee of a leading sub concept. During his due diligence, he talked to franchisees in Indiana and Illinois. "They were both having good experiences," Railing says. "But then I started reading that other franchisees had filed lawsuits against the company. The further I got into it, the more I knew what to ask other franchisees. They didn't want to tell me they were losing their shirts, but when I calculated their food costs, I knew you couldn't make any money with this concept. I'm so glad I never wrote that check."

So, Are You Making Any Money?

Obviously, you want to know if the franchise is financially feasible. But you can't simply call 60 franchisees and ask how much they're making—first, because it's rude, and second, because they won't tell you until you've established some kind of trust. Sometimes competitors will pose as prospective franchisees to dig up information, and sometimes the franchisor will hire "mystery shoppers" to make such calls, to see what their franchisees say about the company.

Besides, you can't measure a franchise just by its profits. The "Woman Who Leapt Too Soon" is making money, but she still doesn't recommend her franchise to anyone who calls.

Railing, who finally bought area development rights for Cousins Subs, in Menomenee Falls, Wisconsin, developed a strategy for getting franchisees to talk to him about what they're earning. His tips include:

> *"Remind them that at one point they, too, were calling existing franchisees about the concept and asking the same kinds of questions."*

- Select people from the UFOC who won't feel you'll be in competition with them. Find franchisees in towns or cities that are similar in size to your own.

- Avoid busy times. And when you do call, your first question should be, "Is this a good time to talk?"

- Tell them a little about your background, so they'll know you're a legitimate caller. Remind them that at one point they, too, were calling existing franchisees about the concept and asking the same kinds of questions.

- Ask general questions first: How long have you been a franchisee? Are you still pleased with your decision?

- If someone is not forthcoming, back off and call the next person on your list.

- If the person seems willing to talk, ask about his or her cost structure: What do you have to pay for supplies? What do you pay your hourly workers? That way, you can ease him or her into the real question of whether he or she is making any money and, if so, how much.

Other Things to Ask About

Once you start calling franchisees, you'll develop your own list of questions, based on what the first few have told you. If one franchisee says he feels his franchisor backed him into too expensive a location, for example, you'll want to ask others about their site selection process. If you uncover complaints—not enough advertising, new stores opening too close to existing ones, and so on—you'll want to see if this is a real problem, or just the perceptions of one or two cranky individuals.

Here are some questions to get you started:

- How long have you operated your franchise? Why did you choose it?

- What surprised you the most about it after you opened?

- Is it hard finding and hiring employees?

- How did you attract your first customers?

- When did you start breaking even?

- Does the franchisor help you get good prices on products and supplies?

- How do you rate the franchisor's training program? Support? Marketing programs?

- How often are you in touch with other franchisees? Do you have an intranet connection on which you share ideas? Do you have an independent franchisee association?

- What is the hardest thing about running this franchise?

- Would you buy this franchise again?

More Grains of Salt

In the ideal world, every franchisee you reach would answer each question the same way and you'd know at the end of talking to 40 of them (and trying to reach 20 others) whether this system is the one or not. That's not likely to happen. If you call a new franchisee who's still in his or her honeymoon phase, you may get more positive answers than from a franchisee who's been in the system for a long time and wondering why he or she is still paying so much in royalties. Newer franchisees welcome frequent visits from the franchisor's support team; older franchisees find them intrusive.

You can disregard a handful of complaints, unless they fit into a pattern that might signal serious problems. You don't want to toss out a good opportunity because you called a few franchisees on a bad day.

Seeing the Books

Ultimately, you'd like a franchisee within reasonable driving distance to invite you into her store and let you go over the business's financial statements. If you've talked to many franchisees and already know a lot about the system, you've established yourself as a credible candidate. Now is the time to call back a nearby franchisee who was nice to you during your initial phone call and ask about looking over her books.

It may take some persuasion. People are reluctant to share what they're earning, either because they think they should be making more or because they're embarrassed they bought a franchise that's a loser. You can try Railing's strategy: "We're all in the same boat. You looked at a franchisee's financials once yourself, or wish you had. And I'll be showing my books to prospective franchisees in a few years, too." If the franchisee still turns you down, be very gracious—you may be sitting next to her at a regional ad fund meeting soon—and move on to someone else.

When you do get to look at a franchisee's books, take careful notes about all revenues and expenses. If possible, look at several years of financials. You'll need this information to share with your accountant before you make a final decision about joining the franchise. And if you do join, the numbers will help you write the business plan you'll need to get a loan.

Contacting Franchisees Who Have Left the System

You also want to talk to franchisees who are no longer operating their units. Did they lose so much money they closed down? Did they have serious disagreements with the franchisor over other issues? Were there health problems or other personal reasons for the closing? Or did they sell their units at a profit and move to golf course communities in Arizona?

"The people who can have the most bearing on your decision are the hardest to find."

The people who can have the most bearing on your decision are the hardest to find. If the UFOC lists only franchise unit phone numbers, and that unit is closed, all you'll get is a recording that the line has been disconnected. You'll have to play detective, and here are some tips that may help:

- Call 411, or type the person's name into an online phone directory, to see if you can locate the franchisee's home number. If that fails, start calling people in the area with the same last name. You may locate a brother—or an ex-spouse—who's willing to talk and pass on a current phone number.

- Call other franchisees in your target person's area and ask if they know what happened, and how to reach that person.

- Use reverse telephone directories to locate the businesses near the franchisee's old location, and call them. Someone may know what happened.

- Try Google first, and then search local newspapers for clues. You may find an old press release or news story about the franchisee's Grand Opening that includes valuable clues, like spouse's name and occupation, the community organizations he or she belongs to, and more.

Even if you do manage to reach a former franchisee, you may not learn anything. Sometimes a franchisor will let an unhappy franchisee out of its system without penalty, if he or she promises not to talk about it. Or the ex-franchisee may be so disheartened, or embarrassed, he or she won't talk to you. Be persistent, because sometimes there's an unexpected payoff. I once tracked down a former franchisee of a sports training concept who said, "The concept is terrific and I've never met such high-quality people. I simply went into this without enough capital to stay open. It's the biggest regret of my life."

> *"The concept is terrific... I simply went into this without enough capital to stay open. It's the biggest regret of my life."*

Checking Out a Franchise from the Parking Lot

If there's a location of the franchise you like nearby, you can figure out how much business it does by... spying. If it's a concept with a retail location, like a store, restaurant, or business services franchise, park your car where you can see the unit's front door. Make notes about how many people go in and out in an hour or two. Are they carrying anything away? Do they look satisfied, or do some of them seem angry?

Go inside and act like a customer. Ask the manager how business is and when it's the busiest. Check out the attitude of the people behind the counter and running the cash registers. Are they pleasant? Surly employees can be the fault of an individual operator or can reflect the culture of an entire system. Are the shelves well stocked? Is the food served hot?

> *"Check out the attitude of the people behind the counter and running the cash registers. Are they pleasant?"*

If it's a home-based concept or a service business run out of an industrial park, call up and ask how soon you can get its service—your house cleaned or painted, your dog washed, or your basement cracks sealed. If they're not busy, and can get to you tomorrow morning at nine, there may not be enough demand for you to open another unit of this franchise.

Do a competitive analysis. Check out the competitors' locations in the same way, or call competing service businesses. Do they seem busier? Or are they the ones with the surly employees?

If there's no competition in the area, will there be by the time you open? Drive through strip malls and look for "Coming Soon" signs. Go to the Web sites of your chosen franchisor's competitors and see if they flag your area as one to soon be served by its concept.

Ask your potential franchisor for demographic information about the territory you're considering. Who are the potential customers? Are there enough of them in your area, or should you negotiate for a larger territory?

Every community has a finite number of customers. Before you invest in a franchise, even one that current franchisees love to operate, you must feel secure that you'll have enough business to keep it going.

Trying the Franchise On

A few franchisors, including McDonald's, require you to work in existing units before they qualify you to buy a franchise. Even if it's not a requirement, the best way to know if you're suited to run a franchise is to work in one first.

You may recall that Mike Murphy, the MAACO franchisee in Fresno, California, said that working for free in another owner's store "was the best investment I ever made."

Besides getting experience, you'll gain insight into how the business operates and how it makes money. And when you open, you'll be a better franchisee. Nancy Love says that because she worked in another Honey-Baked Ham store for six months before she and her husband opened theirs, she "hit the ground running."

"Working for free in another owner's store was the best investment I ever made."

If you mention taking time out of your search to work in someone else's franchise to your salesperson or broker, he or she will probably try to talk you out of it. Remember, he or she won't get paid until you sign a franchise agreement.

But if you can afford it, call a franchisee in the area and offer to work in his or her unit for at least a week. You'll pick up great information, plus, if you join the franchise, a grateful new colleague.

Other Tips for Investigating a Franchise

You may be able to extend your search by attending franchise-industry events or reading proprietary material. Here are some suggestions for investigating franchises through these channels:

- Ask if you can attend a national convention or regional franchisee meeting, to see if the franchisees are people like you. While there, ask them what they would have done differently if they were looking at the concept today.

- Ask your salesperson to send you copies of company newsletters. Often, they feature profiles of top-performing franchisees. Do you share some of their traits? Their backgrounds?

- The American Association of Franchisees and Dealers in San Diego (www.AAFD.org) is a nonprofit trade association that represents the interests of franchisees. The AAFD has developed what it calls the Standards of Fair Franchising and awards a Fair Franchising Seal to franchisors that comply. Is the franchise you're looking at a member?

- The American Franchisee Association in Chicago (www.franchisee.org) is the industry's watchdog. If you're having doubts about the viability of a franchise system, contact the organization to see if franchisee members have filed complaints or lawsuits.

- Ask your salesperson if the system's franchisees have been surveyed for their satisfaction. Two companies—FranSurvey in Lincoln, Nebraska, and Franchise Business Review in Kittery, Maine—now survey franchisees about their experiences with their franchisors. The surveys are sanctioned by franchisors, which have the choice of making the results public or not. If the franchise system you're looking at scored well on its franchisee satisfaction survey, the salesperson has probably told you so several times. But if it did not score well, there may be problems you'd rather not jump into.

As we've seen, joining a franchise, finally, becomes a leap of faith. But spending a week or two learning as much as you can about a system and its principals gives you the best chance of landing on your feet.

Ask the Professor

What other methods do you suggest to your students to check out the viability of a franchise system?

You're ready to commit, but there are many concepts from which to choose. It's time to begin the elimination process, look beyond what first attracted you to a concept, and dig a little deeper.

An early decision is whether to go with a large, well-known brand, a smaller system that has regional dominance, or a new start-up system. The smaller regional systems often have a strong following, and if you open in the region, you can take advantage of the brand awareness and marketing power and have a chance to grow with the system. You may run into difficulty in importing the smaller regional systems and the new start-up systems to another area where there is no name recognition. You probably won't receive as much marketing support as you would if you were closer to their regional dominance and could take advantage of their media campaigns.

Look for a franchisor that is innovative, committed, and focused on building the brand and the concept's integrity, and one that is dedicated to helping you with your growth plans. You probably aren't going to get rich in the franchise business if you have just one location. You need to be thinking about building your franchise company. Will the franchisor help you beyond same-store sales and assist you in achieving your dreams of moving from a single-unit operator to a multiunit operator?

It all comes back to the numbers. You need to analyze the unit economics. Check out the per-unit sales volume for the last several years. Make projections on where the business is going. Identify the franchisor's expansion plans. How many stores have opened and closed in the last few years? It is essential to visit with the existing franchisees. Pick their brains and get an insider's point of view. I always give my students a list of questions to ask franchisees. The last question I tell them to ask is, "If you had the opportunity to go into this franchise again, would you?" It always produces some interesting responses.

What are the signs that a franchise system is struggling?

Signs of a struggling franchise system include extremely low franchisee confidence in the system, low renewal rates, tension and distrust between the franchisees and the franchisor's staff, franchisee dissatisfaction, and poor franchisee profitability.

CHAPTER TEN

Discovery Day—or the Time I Almost Bought a Sub Shop

In every franchise search process, there comes a time when you want to do more than just talk on the phone. The franchise salesperson of the concept you like best has told you so much about his or her training program in Ice Cream College or Battery University, for example, that you'd like to see that "campus" for yourself. And you've done such thorough background checks on the CEO, CFO, and other executives, you're more than ready to shake their hands.

Luckily, the franchisor is just as interested in seeing you, and every franchise system includes a face-to-face meeting in its sales process. Usually, these sessions are called Discovery Days and are conducted at the franchisor's corporate headquarters. Your salesperson will start talking about your attending a Discovery Day early in the process—probably during your second phone conversation.

While it would be wonderful to visit the corporate headquarters of every system you're researching, that's simply not practical. First, there's the cost of getting there. Franchisors want you and your spouse or partner to attend together, because buying a franchise is a family commitment. If your spouse is opposed to the idea, your chances for success are low. This means your expenses will include plane fare for both of you to fly in the day before, plus one or two nights in a hotel. The second cost is psychic. It's very hard to leave a well-run Discovery Day without wanting to join the franchise on the spot.

> *"It's very hard to leave a well-run Discovery Day without wanting to join the franchise on the spot."*

On with the Show

I discovered this for myself a few summers ago, when an assignment to write about a Discovery Day led me to Cousins Subs in Menomonee Falls, Wisconsin. I chose Cousins randomly—it was within driving distance, it had a Discovery Day scheduled before my deadline, and the franchise development people agreed to let me attend. But by the end of the eight-hour session, I was convinced that Cousins was the best franchise on the planet, and that I should open one myself.

This kind of reaction is not accidental. Cheri Carroll, of FranDevelop Consulting in San Diego, says that all Discovery Days have serious agendas and have been carefully choreographed to convince you to buy their franchise offering immediately.

No matter what the concept, Discovery Day agendas contain most of the same elements, says John Siebert, a consultant with the iFranchise Group in Homewood, Illinois, a firm that helps businesses become franchisors. The day includes a general overview of the franchise and its history, which is usually a PowerPoint presentation by the company's founder, CEO, or the person in charge of franchise development; a series of meetings with the heads of various departments, including support, training, technology, purchasing, real estate, marketing, and so forth; and tours of corporate headquarters and a nearby franchised or corporate location. You'll get to sample the franchise's products or view a demonstration of its services.

Just as important, you'll get a feel for the franchise system's culture. Do people greet each other in the halls as well as in the conference room? Are presenters engaging? When they offer examples of great marketing campaigns, for example, do they mention the franchisees who developed them by name? Do they insert humor in their talks and also mention what didn't work in the past and why? Is the event well organized, and does it stick to a schedule? "If the Discovery Day sales machine is haphazard and doesn't run well, the situation will only get worse when it comes to training and helping you run the business," warns Todd Vieyra, the founder of the Furniture Medic franchise (now a ServiceMaster subsidiary).

The Discovery Day at Cousins Subs ran like clockwork, including the cookie breaks. The real estate manager talked about helping new franchisees find the best location, preferably at the end of a strip mall, where there's room for a drive-through lane, and showed slides of well-situated restaurants. The CFO reported that Cousins has a relationship with a national bank "that will let you borrow 70 percent of your total investment."

The director of purchasing made putting away weekly deliveries of hundreds of pounds of meats, cheeses, and frozen bread dough sound as easy as unloading a few bags from the neighborhood grocer's. The vice president of marketing showed photos of the finalists in a franchisee's contest to find lookalike cousins. And company cofounder Bill Specht stopped by to tell us about starting the chain in 1972 with his real cousin, Jim Sheppard. "I'd moved here from New Jersey," Specht said, "and I missed the submarine sandwiches we could buy there, so Jim and I started making them ourselves."

We also toured two local Cousins Subs shops, one decorated in the old-style red and yellow and another with a new, softer palette of greens and golds. We walked into freezers, peered over counters, checked out restrooms, and, best of all, sampled lots of different kinds of sandwiches. The Cousins executives even handed us bags of subs and cookies to eat on the way home. Who could resist all that?

Since then, Kerry Espich, Cousins' new manager of franchise sales and recruitment, says their Discovery Day program has gotten even better. "Instead of showing you slides of restaurant locations," Espich says, "we now take you on a driving tour, to show you existing stores and sites that may, or may not, be approved by our real estate department. This is more interactive than sitting in a conference room, and it gives you an idea of the characteristics we're looking for in a location." And back at company headquarters, prospective franchisees now spend time in Cousins' test kitchen, watching sub assembly lines—and picking out their own lunches.

When attorney Jim Railing, of Indianapolis, and his wife and daughter attended a Cousins' Discovery Day in August 2006, he says he was so impressed that he signed a franchise agreement three weeks later. "The Discovery Day showed me they had the things I was looking for in a sandwich concept—sound finances, the right resources in place in terms of technology and personnel, and a great product," says Railing.

Behind the Choreography

Discovery Days are designed to have just that impact. Everything is planned, right down to the conference room seating chart. Presentations are well-rehearsed

"Everything is planned, right down to the conference room seating chart."

and presenters are wearing their best suits and attitudes. Lunch is always brought in because "it's easy to lose control of a group in a restaurant," says Vieyra. And prospective franchisees are never left without a staff person present, because that short-circuits negative conversations.

The cookie breaks are timed, not to provide a treat, but to let you walk around so you'll be more alert for the next speaker. And speakers are alert for attendees who ask too many questions, because taking time to answer them all can throw off the well-rehearsed itinerary, Vieyra says. Instead, speakers will offer to answer all questions at the end of the day.

Sometimes the Discovery Day dance will include what Vieyra calls the "singers." These are the system's top franchisees, and the franchisor may pay their expenses to come in and give testimonials either during the day itself or at a dinner the night before. "The franchisor makes it very convenient for you to have a dialogue with people who'll tell you what you want to hear," Vieyra warns.

"At the end of Discovery Day, you'll probably be more excited than at any other time in the search process," says Brian Schnell, co-chair of the franchise team at Faegre & Benson LLP, a Minneapolis law firm. "The franchisor wants to catch you on that emotional high, and wants you to sign the franchise agreement that day, or shortly thereafter."

"The franchisor makes it very convenient for you to have a dialogue with people who'll tell you what you want to hear."

Which may not, of course, be in your best interest. We've asked franchisees, franchisors, consultants, and attorneys for tips to help you get the most out of a Discovery Day and ways to help you resist signing a franchise agreement on the spot.

When Should You Attend a Discovery Day?

Ideally, you'd attend only one Discovery Day at the end of your research process. By then, you would have chosen this franchise above all others, completed a thorough due diligence, lined up a franchisee attorney who's read through the UFOC and is ready to negotiate the franchise agreement, and talked to bankers about a start-up loan. You would have the assurances of existing franchisees that the system is viable and is one you could fit into easily. You may have even worked in one of their locations. In this ideal scenario, Discovery Day would be an in-person affirmation of everything you know about the franchise system and you'd be ready for that emotional high.

But franchise-hunting is rarely ideal. You may have completed due diligence on two, or even three, franchises and are still undecided about which one to choose. You might like one in particular but you, or your attorney, may have some reservations. You may be only partway through due diligence, and far from nailing down a lawyer or banker, when the franchise salesperson announces that an upcoming Discovery Day is the last one the franchise will host for several weeks. If you agree to attend a Discovery Day under such circumstances, are you wasting your time, or betraying the franchisor's hospitality?

"Only about half the people attending any franchise system's Discovery Day end up buying that franchise."

Certainly not, say franchise industry insiders. Only about half the people attending any franchise system's Discovery Day end up buying that franchise. Some are rejected by the franchisor, but most simply move on to another concept, or don't buy a franchise at all. If you're torn between two or three choices, plan to visit all of them and hope that the culture of one appeals to you more than the others. If you have concerns about a system, you can ask your questions in person and watch the reactions of the people who try to answer them. And if you have doubts about a franchisor's finances, you can check out the state of their corporate headquarters.

If you're planning to attend more than one, go to the one offered by the largest, most sophisticated franchisor first, advises Vieyra. "Even if that system's not your first choice," he says, "the event will teach you what a well-organized Discovery Day is like, so you can make comparisons when you visit smaller systems."

Rules for Attending a Discovery Day

Remember that Discovery Day, no matter how informal it may seem, is a high-powered sales event. Here are some tips to get the most out of attending one (and to return home without signing a contract):

1. Vieyra's first rule is, leave your checkbook at home.

2. Ask if the franchisor will pay some of your expenses to attend. Finding qualified leads is expensive, and franchisors spend $2,500 to $6,000 in advertising and Web site fees and salesperson salaries for each candidate they get this far in the sales process. Most will agree to spend another $300 or so to defray your travel costs. Some franchisors refund your Discovery Day expenses if you buy a franchise; others hand every attendee a check of around $200. Sign-A-Rama pays the airfare of everyone who attends a Discovery Day at its West Palm Beach, Florida, headquarters, for example.

3. Ask how many other prospective franchisees will be attending. The ideal number, says Vieyra, is 6 to 15 people. A franchise shopper who attended a Discovery Day with more than 100 others says it was obvious that all the franchisor wanted to do was sell franchises, not build relationships.

4. Be prepared. Make a list of questions that are still unanswered after reading the UFOC and completing due diligence.

5. Dress professionally, so that the franchisor knows you're serious about the concept and have the means to invest in it.

6. Take business cards. You'll want to collect contact information from the other attendees, and you'd like them to be able to reach you, too.

7. Take your spouse or partner. Franchisors doubt the commitment of a prospect who attends alone.

8. Be prepared to talk about your background and the reasons you've chosen this franchise.

9. Show your enthusiasm. If you like what you see, let the franchise staff know it. Some prospects are turned down because they just didn't seem very engaged during Discovery Day. Franchisors also turn down candidates who don't fit the company culture—are not outgoing enough to make the community contacts required, for example.

10. Wander around, suggests The Maids franchisee John Ricky Garmon. "The people making the presentations are supposed to be impressive," Garmon says. "Go into the IT department and supply room and meet the people who'll be helping you when you have a problem."

11. Take notes. Write down the names and direct phone lines of key people from the support, training, marketing, and real estate teams. Make careful note of any promise, so that your lawyer can get it in writing later.

12. Ask questions about anything you don't understand. "There's no better time to get your marketing questions answered than when the vice president of marketing is sitting right across from you," says Schnell.

13. Listen to the questions of other prospective franchisees. You may learn something valuable.

14. Ask what happens next. Do the executives you've met today get together to decide who will be invited into their system? How will you know?

At Cousins, Espich says, "By the end of the day, people are pretty glassed over and we don't ask them to make any decisions. I typically wait five business days before I call prospects we like to see if they're interested in moving forward. If we decide someone's not a fit, we wait until they're back home to tell them we're sorry."

Things the Franchisor May Not Want You to Discover

Discovery Day can also unearth negatives about a company. The most obvious is the condition of its corporate headquarters. If the place is shabby, you may decide you'd rather commit your life savings to a more prosperous entity. But be suspicious, too, of offices that are sleek and extremely well appointed. We've visited scores of franchise offices, and most of them are clean, comfortable, and pretty nondescript. Often, like Cousins, they're in industrial parks, and many have attached warehouses. A franchisor that's trying to impress you with glitz may be in the business of selling franchises, not supporting franchisees.

Other things to watch out for include:

- *Vague answers to your questions.* "If you ask about support," says John Siebert, "and the answer is, 'We have great support,' be wary. The answer should be, 'Our support person is ____, and here's her phone number.'"

- *Generic presentations.* Mr. Railing says he attended a Discovery Day of another sandwich concept where "they tried to pump us up with a 40-minute video of franchisees saying how thrilled they were to be their own boss."

- *Whispered earnings claims.* If the franchise does not include an earnings claim in Item 19, no one should be telling you how much money you can make. If it's not in writing, it's not trustworthy, and probably not true.

- *Solo singers.* If you're invited out to dinner with the system's top performers, and no one from the home office is present, warns Vieyra, don't lose perspective. These success stories can talk about earnings, just like any other franchisee. But be aware that they are the best franchisees in the system, and you may never reach their sales numbers.

- *High-pressure sales tactics.* Even if you're riding an emotional high, you should not sign a franchise agreement that day, and no one should insist that you do.

Variations on the Discovery Day Theme

Some franchisors, however, do expect you to sign on the day you visit, and they let you know that up front. Schnell says he has franchise clients who call their face-to-face sessions Decision Days: "They want prospects to come in at the end of their research process, meet everyone on the team, and feel really excited and good about joining it. Rather than have the prospects leave and lose that momentum, they want them to sign on the dotted line. As an attorney, I still feel that's a bad idea."

Instead of asking all prospects to fly in to visit their headquarters, some franchisors schedule regional Discovery Days in major cities. If you attend one, you'll meet key executives and hear their presentations, but you won't be able to tour and evaluate the corporate offices.

And some franchises, like Home Instead Senior Care, hold no Discovery Day events at all. "We invite a good candidate to Omaha for a day to meet with the executive staff one-on-one. That way, we can ask each other questions and decide if it's a good match," says Tim Connelly, director of franchise development.

Ask the Professor

How many Discovery Days do most prospective franchisees attend?

It depends on how far the franchisor's headquarters are located from the prospective franchisee, how much the travel costs will be, whether the franchisor is willing to share any of the costs for the trip, how much money the franchisee has available and allocated to explore various franchise opportunities, and how serious the franchisee is about opening a unit of the respective franchisor's.

Many prospective franchisees have tunnel vision and only want to pursue one opportunity that they think will do extremely well in their community, and they choose to attend that franchisor's Discovery Day. Other prospective franchisees who are more interested in a concept than a particular brand and have the finances to do it will probably attend a couple of Discovery Days based on their interactions with the franchise salespeople or brokers, and their own investigations.

What's the biggest mistake prospective franchisees make when attending these events?

They bring their checkbooks! By the time prospective franchisees get to Discovery Day, most of them are pretty sold on the idea of going into the business. They are attending Discovery Day because they want to meet a few more of the leaders at the franchisor's headquarters to see if they like and respect them, want to be in business with them for the next 10 to 20 years, and if they have trust in the system and people in which they are willing to invest their money.

In the more sophisticated franchise systems, Discovery Day is a finely tuned, well-orchestrated event with an agenda that is designed to highlight the system and the people who work in it. Many franchisors may utilize hard-sell tactics during the day because their purpose is closing franchise sales.

If you decide to accept an invitation to attend a franchisor's Discovery Day, turn it to your advantage. Get to know the people at the franchise headquarters and start building a relationship. Ask to meet the department heads, and then ask them specific questions. Find out a rough estimate of how long it will take to get your unit open after you have paid the initial franchise fee, and try to spot any red flags that may arise and make you determine that you need to consider moving on to the next opportunity.

CHAPTER ELEVEN

Franchise Attorneys: Pay Now—or Pay More Later

If the complexity of the UFOC and the issues you've come across during your preliminary due diligence haven't convinced you to hire a franchisee attorney, here's something that will send you running to the phone. Almost all the franchisors we've ever talked to want you to engage an attorney to read through their documents. Their success depends on the well-being of their franchisees, and franchisees who sign contracts they don't understand make poor partners.

The people who don't want you to use a lawyer are franchise salespeople and less-than-scrupulous brokers. These people are paid a hefty commission after you sign a contract, and your hiring an attorney can delay their checks, or quash the deal altogether.

One of them says he asks candidates, "Why do you need to see an attorney? Franchise contracts are non-negotiable documents, offered on a take-it-or-leave-it basis. We won't change the language, because it's important to us that all franchisees are on a level playing field. Why pay an attorney to read the same things you are, if he can't change anything? It's money not real well spent."

Home Instead's director of franchise development, Tim Connelly, disagrees. "Candidates will often ask me why they should go to an attorney if we don't change our contract. I tell them, 'I'm not trying to surprise you in any way. If you take your contract to a lawyer, there should be no surprises later, and we'll both sleep better.'"

Beyond a Good Night's Sleep

Despite what every franchisor, broker, and franchise salesperson says, franchise contracts can be negotiated, often in ways that would never occur to you, or to an attorney who doesn't specialize in this field. But the reasons to engage a lawyer go beyond a few changes to your contract. Let's take a look at some of the most important ones.

Reinforcement of Your Decision to Become a Franchisee

Michael Liss, a franchise attorney in Oak Brook, Illinois, says clients arrive at his office after they've spent a year or more thinking about owning their own business. "If they start from scratch, they know there's a high failure rate," he says. "Then they try to buy an existing independent business and find out there are 200 to 500 prospective buyers for every good business that's for sale. They come to me after they realize there's a third option, buying a franchise."

If you find an attorney like Liss, who says that one-third of his practice is devoted to clients getting into franchises, you'll feel more confident about the process. If hundreds of other people he's seen through the years are running franchises, you can, too.

A Dose of Reality

If you've fallen in love with a particular franchise concept and want to get married immediately, visiting an attorney can be just like premarital counseling—only more expensive.

In *Fundamentals of Franchising*, attorneys Rupert Barkoff and Andrew Selden say a big part of a franchisee attorney's job is educating clients about the industry. "Give the client a 'Miranda warning' about franchising," their book advises. "It is a long-term relationship; to become an independent businessperson, the client must give up a significant amount of independence; there are no guarantees of financial results; owning a franchise frequently involves long hours and hard work; the contract probably is enforceable and probably not easy to 'get out of' later; and franchise investments and relationships entail risks that are different from and usually above and beyond the ordinary business risks associated with business ownership."

If that doesn't make you want to hold onto that engagement ring a little longer, perhaps what Liss calls his "eyes wide open" approach will work. "When clients come in, they're 90 percent sure 'this is the franchise for me.' My effort is to really flood with light on who the franchisor is and what they are really selling you. We'll go through important sections of the UFOC paragraph by paragraph, and I'll tell you how to contact franchisees in

"Visiting an attorney can be just like premarital counseling—only more expensive."

the system and what to ask them. If the franchisees are not like you, and they're the ones doing okay in the system, that's a big warning flag. If they are like you, and they're doing well, that's a great predictor."

By the end of this process, Liss says his clients are either "tremendously more certain this is the right thing, or they go the other way and start looking at other concepts."

You may feel the $300-or-so-an-hour franchisee attorneys charge for their premarital counseling isn't that costly after all, compared to a difficult divorce.

Insight into Franchise Operations

Franchisee attorneys who guide their clients through investigations of various franchise systems, and who stay in touch with them after they've opened, can provide you with valuable inside information.

Michael Dady, for example, says, "We've handled matters for clients in over 300 different systems. We can say to a prospective franchisee, 'We hear that there's a problem getting enough people through the lunch line of this particular franchise. If you do business with them, make sure you have enough people to help you during the busy times.'"

Insight into Franchisee-Franchisor Disputes

Disputes between franchisees and their franchisors seldom make headlines. As you'll see in a moment, even the most contentious disagreements are usually settled by arbitration and do not go to public trials. If a California franchisor is involved in a heated dispute with its franchisees in Arizona, for example, you may never hear about it in Vermont.

But the approximately 2,000 attorneys who are members of the American Bar Association's Forum on Franchising get together for formal sessions each fall and share information throughout the year. The forum also publishes a yearly wrap-up of franchise-related legal actions in its Annual Franchise and Distribution Law Developments books.

If the franchisee-franchisor relationship in the system you're looking at is going south, a franchisee attorney can wave you off before you unwittingly jump into a bad situation.

Insight into Mergers and Acquisitions

Private equity has discovered franchising. In the past few years, investment firms have purchased dozens of franchise systems. Some franchises have even had two different private equity owners. Often the new owners, with their business savvy and Wall Street connections, improve the company and, with it, the fortunes of its franchisees. But if you're negotiating with a franchisor, you'd like to know whether the company is in play.

Franchisee attorneys attend finance conferences, read industry publications, and have contacts that can keep them informed about merger and acquisition activity.

Contract Review and Negotiations

You can get the greatest return on your investment from a franchisee attorney if he or she can negotiate better terms to your franchise contract. Although a few items—the franchise fee and royalty and ad fund percentages—are almost always sacrosanct, franchisee attorneys say they have won concessions on many other issues.

Justin Klein says, "Even without changing the terms, there are some great things you can do. Sometimes I'll say something like, 'My client really wants to do this, but can't afford the cost of spending two weeks at your headquarters location for training. Why don't you split that cost with him?' Other times, a franchisor will agree to pick up the cost of some piece of equipment, like a computer."

Liss says that franchisors with 100 units or fewer are more likely to negotiate than larger systems. "About 80 to 90 percent of smaller franchisors will negotiate changes," he says. "When you get over 100 units, it changes radically the other way; but 10 to 20 percent of larger franchisors will also make some changes." Liss says he'll review a UFOC with a client and make a checklist of its good and bad points. "If there are 20 things you want changed, that's far too much to ask for, and you'll get nothing," he warns.

> *"If there are 20 things you want changed, that's far too much to ask for, and you'll get nothing."*

So what can you get? Let's take a look at some concessions a good franchisee attorney can help you win.

Early Out Rights

When you sign a franchise agreement, you're pledging to pay the franchisor monthly royalties for a period of time, from 10 to 20 years. But what if, after a few years, you're losing money and decide to close down?

Under the majority of franchise contracts, you'd still owe that royalty payment, even though you're no longer in business. In September 2006, Lady of America, a fitness center franchisor in Fort Lauderdale, for example, won a lawsuit against a former franchisee who had closed her facility. A court ordered the woman to pay Lady of America almost $60,000, a sum that represented the royalties she would have paid, had she remained open. Liss says such decisions are not uncommon. "The judge assumes you were smart enough to know about that provision when you signed the contract."

Attorneys often negotiate early out rights for their clients, releasing them from future royalty requirements. Dady says, "We've convinced even some of the largest franchisors to change contract clauses and allow franchisees to stop paying royalties when they exit the system."

Better Renewal Terms

When you're signing a franchise agreement, you're thinking about next month, when you start training. But your franchisee attorney is thinking ten years ahead, when this agreement expires and you have to sign a new contract.

"When you're buying a franchise, ten years looks like a lifetime," Dady says. "But renewals are a killer. Royalties are up, ad fees are up, and your territory may be smaller." Dady negotiates future royalties before you sign your present agreement. "You can't say, my client is paying 5 percent now and doesn't want to pay more than 6 percent then," he says. "But you can negotiate a change that says royalties will not exceed x percentage of current rates."

"If they want you to buy a franchise, they'll often negotiate the area you'll operate in."

Territory Size or Shape

"There's no science behind the way franchisors come up with the size of their protected territories," says Liss. "If they want you to buy a franchise, they'll often negotiate the area you'll operate in."

Remodeling Requirements

Brian Schnell is an attorney who represents franchisors in contract negotiations at Faegre & Benson, LLP in Minneapolis. He says his clients, who are mostly large franchise companies, will sometimes negotiate remodeling provisions. Instead of making you liable for unlimited remodeling and updating expenses, they will agree to a maximum amount you should have to spend, and include that figure in their contract.

Option to Purchase

What happens when you want to sell your franchise? Another killer, lawyers say, are contract clauses that give the franchisor first rights to buy back your unit for the value of your hard assets.

"You may have operated a restaurant for ten years and believe its market value is $600,000," says Liss. But to the franchisor, it's a rented building stocked with old equipment and worth only $6,000. "We can often change those clauses so that the franchisor agrees to pay you a fair market value for your unit," Liss says.

Dispute Resolution

Franchisee attorneys tend to take more issue with Item 17—Renewal, Termination, Transfers, and Dispute Resolution—than with any other UFOC section.

"Problems can arise in a franchise system that are not the fault of good operators. Your franchisor can sell to a bad buyer, for instance," says Dady, "who may operate a competing system. You may have conflicts over requirements to buy equipment or supplies from a vendor you don't want to deal with, or you and your fellow franchisees may believe the franchisor is opening too many stores or not dealing with your ad monies correctly."

Under 75 percent of all franchise agreements, he says, you can't file a lawsuit and have your complaints heard by a judge and a jury. Instead, disputes are settled by arbitration, usually in the home state of the franchisor. "Arbitration is more expensive than a trial," Dady says, "because arbitrators cost $400 an hour and the franchisee has to pay for half. Often, franchise agreements insist on a panel of three arbitrators. Judges are free." When you add in the cost of

"Utilize your bargaining power when you have it."

traveling to the franchisor's state for an arbitration hearing, most franchisees can't afford to stand up to their franchisors, Dady says.

During contract negotiations, he tries to get franchisors to agree to limit arbitration proceedings to just one arbitrator and to move the venue to the franchisee's home state. "Utilize your bargaining power when you have it," he says.

If One Franchise Is Good, Why Aren't Three, or Thirty, Better?

A franchisee attorney can also advise you against signing a deal to open more than one franchise or becoming an area developer, in charge of selling franchises yourself throughout a large territory or even an entire state.

We've talked to many new franchisees who had planned to buy just one unit. But in the emotional high of Discovery Day, or after a positive due diligence process, they listened to a salesperson who suggested they buy two or three territories at the same time, at a reduced fee. While this may sound like a good idea—I'm going to do so well, I'll want to lock up adjacent territories right now—it rarely is. Think about the franchisor's motivations. We know it spent at least $6,000 to find and woo you. Wouldn't it get a better return on that investment if you agreed to buy multiple franchise locations, instead of just one?

If you have to pay the additional franchise fees up front, this reduces the money you'll have available to launch your first franchise. Even if the fee payments are postponed, being committed to opening more units can take your focus off that first location, which, as we've seen, requires all your time and energy. The time to think about additional units is after your first franchise is breaking even and you're starting to see a profit.

Established franchisors only offer area development agreements—in which you pay the franchisor for the rights to develop a large territory, by putting up units yourself and finding prospective franchisees to build the others—to seasoned businesspeople or investor groups. But young franchisors that are raring to expand sometimes offer these deals to franchise neophytes.

It's easy to see why. Whenever you sell a new franchise, you receive half the franchise fee. But when an outsourced salesperson or franchise broker sells a

Finding Franchisee Attorneys

Just a few years ago, the country only had a few attorneys who represented franchisees. Now the specialty is becoming common. Here are some ways you can find one:

- Ask other franchisees who they used.

- Contact the offices of franchisee attorneys you read about. Often, they'll work long distance, over the phone. If not, they'll refer you to an attorney in your area.

- Look for franchisee attorney listings under "Suppliers" in print and online franchise directories.

- Purchase the ABA's Forum on Franchising Directory of about 2,000 attorneys who specialize in franchising. It's $35, and available at www.abanet.org/forums/franchising.

franchise, he or she, too, collects half the franchise fee. He or she just hasn't paid for the right to make that sale.

Think about what the franchisor had to do to find you—pay to list the business in print and online directories, maintain a Web site, hire a franchise sales force, conduct credit checks, run Discovery Days, and more. Are you prepared to extend that kind of effort when you're trying to open a franchise yourself?

If your franchisee attorney keeps you from buying additional territories or signing an area development agreement you're not qualified to fulfill, he or she has more than earned his or her fee.

What Will It Cost?

Fees vary, but some franchisee law firms, like Dady & Garner in Minneapolis and New York, do UFOC and Franchise Agreement reviews "as a service to prospective franchisees, for about $950," Dady says. Klein says his fees, which include counseling, begin at $1,500; and Liss charges about $300 an hour for document reviews that usually take three to four hours. No matter what they charge, "It's less expensive seeing me before you sign a contract than afterwards," says Klein.

Ask the Professor

What other value can an experienced attorney bring to the table?

An experienced franchisee attorney will help you make a more informed decision about purchasing the franchise; help you better understand your rights and obligations as a franchisee, and the rights and obligations of the franchisor; and help you discover any misleading disclosures or a failure to disclose when there is a duty to do so by the franchisor that could give rise to common-law actions against the franchisor for fraudulent misrepresentation or concealment. A qualified attorney who is experienced in dealing with franchise relationships can provide you with guidance and assist you in determining the overall desirability of the franchise offering by interpreting the UFOC and protecting your interests as a potential franchisee.

Why can't I use the lawyer who helped me buy my house?

The UFOC is one of the most significant documents that you will receive from the franchisor, and it is important that you secure the services of an attorney familiar with franchising to review it with you. Federal and state laws require that information pertaining to each of the 23 items in the UFOC must be fully and completely disclosed. These disclosures will assist you and an experienced franchisee attorney who is familiar with franchise regulation in analyzing the merits of the potential franchisor, and help you to make a more educated investment decision. Although state and federal law requires that these disclosures be made, neither the FTC nor the individual states review the UFOC for accuracy. While the attorney who helped you buy your house or draw up your will may be a highly qualified person, he or she doesn't have a thorough understanding of franchise law. You're getting ready to make a huge investment, and quite possibly a life change. You will be wise to spend a few hundred dollars having a knowledgeable attorney review the documents with you.

CHAPTER TWELVE

Financing Your Franchise

Unless you have a large severance package or are looking at a low-investment concept, you'll have to find a way to finance your franchise. Luckily, this has gotten easier. A decade or so ago, first-time franchisees could rarely obtain start-up bank loans; today, some franchisees tell us they attract half a dozen or more loan offers from bank and nonbank lenders.

The marketplace is so rich that it has spawned two new industries: franchise loan brokers who help you borrow money on the best terms, like mortgage brokers, and firms that help you turn your IRA or 401(k) funds into a franchise investment.

But you shouldn't wander into the franchise finance marketplace without a guide. If you didn't talk to an accountant when you started analyzing your financial ability to look at franchises in the first place, it's time to hire one now. You don't have to find a specialist, like your franchisee attorney. When it comes to numbers, a franchise is like any small business, except it has the additional expenses of royalties and ad fees.

You might be able to find an accountant skilled in small business, who can help you read through franchisor financials now, work with you through the loan application process, and handle bookkeeping and tax chores after you open. If you don't know one, ask small business owners, including franchisees, in your community for referrals.

So, Can I Make Any Money?

An accountant may not be able to answer that question, but he or she should be able to help you with your due diligence. We've known prospective franchisees—okay, prospective franchisees with MBAs—who arranged all the financial information they gleaned from UFOCs and existing franchisees into spreadsheets. They could then tweak the numbers to determine, for example, how many dogs their mobile grooming van attendants would have to bathe in one day to clear a profit, and how much more they'd earn if they bathed all the collies and poodles themselves. If you have enough information, your account-ant can set up a similar program.

An accountant can also help you analyze the numbers you copied from the books of existing franchisees. Although franchise units look alike, and fran-chisees must buy the same products and pay the same fees, the ways franchisees handle the money left over can vary greatly. Some franchisees pay themselves regular salaries; others never do, but pay their car and other expenses through the business. Some take whatever money is left over each month and reinvest it into the business or pay down their loans faster. Others take vacations. An accountant can help you sort through these variables and get you closer to knowing how profitable the franchise you're looking at might be.

Getting Ready for the Loan Process—at Home

To obtain that profitable franchise, you'll probably have to apply for a loan. Franchise lenders say there's a strong correlation between repayment of a busi-ness loan and an applicant's personal credit history. Kyle Huffman, vice presi-dent of GE Capital Solutions, Franchise Finance, in the Bellevue, Washington, office, says his nonbank lender seeks applicants who pay their bills on time and have no liens or judgments filed against them. "If you've gone through a divorce and your late-payment window is limited to six months or less, we'll still con-sider you if the rest of the past four or five years are okay," he says.

Here are some tips to help you become a good credit risk:

- Get a copy of your credit report from each reporting agency, advises Robin Griggs, vice president and credit specialist with Huntington National Bank in Cleveland. Make sure everything's correct. Sometimes a report will contain a bill you didn't realize you owed. Pay it, she says, and follow through with the reporting agency until that bad mark goes away. The three major credit reporting agencies—Equifax, Experion, and TransUnion—now will provide you with a free report every 12 months. Information is available on a special Web site (www.annualcredit report.com).

- Most lenders want credit scores of 650 or better. If yours is too low, try paying off a couple of smaller credit cards and see if it rises.

- Lenders expect you to "inject skin into the game," says Griggs, by making a 20 to 30 percent down payment on your franchise investment out of your own assets. Be sure you have that capital saved up or available before you apply for a loan.

- Don't make any big financial moves, says Rick Anderson, general manager of Franchise Finance, a nonbank lender and loan packager in Little Rock, Arkansas. "Just freeze where you are now," he says. "Don't get new credit cards, don't pay big bills off, don't pay the house off, and don't buy a car. A lot of people think if they take out a big home equity loan and pay off all their other debt, they'll look more attractive. But borrowing from home equity is still debt. What lenders really want to see is cash in the bank."

- Don't quit your day job, or let your spouse quit his or hers. Most start-up franchise loans require a Small Business Administration (SBA) guarantee, says Anderson, and "the SBA doesn't want people betting the farm on a franchise." Maintain outside sources of income.

"Borrowing from home equity is still debt. What lenders really want to see is cash in the bank."

Choose Your Franchise Carefully

The Franchise Finance division of GE Capital Solutions has more than 6,000 borrowers with more than 20,000 franchise locations, says Huffman, but is choosy about which franchise systems it backs. His company will not loan money to someone buying into a franchise system where same-store sales are falling, he says.

He and other lenders say obtaining a loan is easier if you:

- Avoid franchise systems where 5 percent or more of the existing units closed in the past year.

- Stay away from brand-new franchise systems with no track records of loan repayments.

- Select one of the 600-plus franchises preapproved for SBA guarantees listed at www.franchiseregistry.com. As you'll soon see, a registry listing can streamline the SBA approval process by several weeks.

- Avoid franchises where previous franchisees have defaulted on SBA loans. According to finance industry insiders, the SBA keeps a list of "bad" systems it will no longer deal with. As part of your due diligence, ask the franchisor if it's listed on the SBA Registry and if its franchisees can obtain SBA-guaranteed loans.

Finding a Lender: Start with Your Franchisor

Once you've signed the franchise agreement—or know you will—your first stop on your finance search is in the franchisor's office. Over half of all franchisors help franchisees with financing, although what they provide varies greatly.

Darrell Johnson, president of FRANdata, says his research shows that franchisors have four ways of dealing with financing:

- *Figure it out for yourself.* The franchisee is on his or her own to hunt down and procure financing.

- *The passive approach.* "Here's a list of approved lenders. Go talk to them."

- *The proactive approach.* The franchise is on the SBA Registry, helps franchisees prepare loan documents and business plans, and establishes relationships with banks and other lenders.

- *Franchisor direct lending.*

Let's take a look at the last option now.

Will You Sell Me a Franchise and Pay for It, Too?

A few large franchisors are both business partner and banker to new franchisees. Mike Hawkins, vice president of franchising for the Dwyer Group in Waco, Texas, parent of Mr. Electric, Mr. Rooter, Mr. Appliance, Glass Doctor, Aire Serve, and Rainbow International, says his company finances up to 80 percent of a new franchisee's fee, which can range from $20,000 to over $200,000, depending on the size of his territory. Most of his company's franchisees are independent contractors who convert their businesses to franchises, Hawkins says, and about 60 percent of them opt for direct financing. Dwyer Group collects the loans over five years and charges an interest rate of 9 to 12 percent, depending on the franchisee's credit status.

"I think this helps a lot of people get into franchising who couldn't do it any other way," Hawkins says. Direct financing also leaves new franchisees with more working capital to grow their businesses, and it leaves their lines of credit open so they can buy more vehicles and equipment.

FRANdata lists Express Personnel Services, Michelin Retread Technologies, Jackson Hewitt Tax Service, and Hot Stuff Foods, among other systems, that offer direct loans.

"It got to a point where we didn't know if we were in franchising or financing."

But some franchisors that once offered direct financing have backed off. Lonnie Helgerson, former CEO of computer repair concept Expectec, in Orlando, says that his franchisor discontinued its direct lending program. "We had to keep a big doubtful loans allowance on our books," he says, "and it was knocking the dickens out of our earnings. It got to a point where we didn't know if we were in franchising or financing."

You can ask your franchisor about direct financing, but don't be surprised if no program is available.

Proactive Assistance

Your franchisor may not be able to lend you money, but it can help you borrow some. Lenders want to see business plans, and most franchisors will give you a template that you can fill in with your specific information. If your franchisor does not provide such help, many books, including *How to Write a Business Plan*, published by Nolo Press (www.nolo.com), provide step-by-step guides you can follow. SCORE, the Service Corps of Retired Executives, provides free counseling to small business owners, including assistance with developing business plans. You can find the closest chapter of SCORE at www.score.org. Community colleges frequently hold classes on the subject, and you can ask your accountant for help.

Some franchisors have relationships with national banks that are so familiar with their franchise programs that they may approve you for a loan based solely on your credit history.

But finding money is not always that easy.

Finding a Loan on Main Street

Former insurance salesman Dell Cannon of Lubbock, Texas, used the personal approach to getting a loan. He'd met Bob Cosby, the senior vice president of City Bank in Lubbock, at a social event. During the months Cannon was checking out franchises, he visited Cosby at the bank to give him updates. Once he'd chosen Budget Blinds, of Orange, California, Cannon dropped the franchisor's UFOC on Cosby's desk, so the banker could perform his own due diligence.

"I wanted to see how long the franchise had been in business," says Cosby, "and the total number of franchises they had. I wanted to see how many franchises had closed and how long they were open before they closed. I especially wanted to confirm that Budget Blinds provides excellent training, because this is something Dell had never done before."

By the end of his research process, Cosby was so convinced Cannon would succeed that he approved a conventional (not SBA-guaranteed) loan for the franchise. And became its first customer. "My family and I had recently moved to Lubbock and I knew how hard it was to find someone to help you pick out window coverings. As soon as Dell was open, we used his services," Cosby says.

If you have a longtime relationship with a local bank, you, too, can drop in and ask about its business loan policies. But be forewarned. Some local bankers, especially in rural areas, are not up to speed on franchising and will not handle franchise loans, even if you and the bank vice president play golf together every week.

SBA-Guaranteed Loans

Most small business loans do require an SBA guarantee, a pledge that if you default, the federal government will reimburse your lender for up to 80 percent of the amount you borrowed. The SBA, which has been helping small business owners get started since 1953, guarantees billions of dollars worth of loans each year. The number of SBA-guaranteed loans to franchisees has increased dramatically, and franchising's relationship with the agency received a boost in 2006, when Steven C. Preston, a former executive vice president with franchisor ServiceMaster Co., was confirmed as the SBA's administrator.

Since the SBA's loan programs change frequently, go to www.sba.gov for the latest information. Most franchisees apply for SBA 7(a) guarantees on loans from $75,000 to $2,000,000, although some are eligible for what the agency calls micro-loan guarantees, (loans under $50,000).

SBA loans do, however, have three disadvantages compared to conventional loans:

1. They carry a higher interest rate.
2. They require personal guarantees, which to most applicants means pledging their homes as collateral.
3. Approvals can take several weeks.

Any bank or nonbank lending institution may be eligible for SBA lending status, although some elect not to participate. Institutions dispensing SBA guarantees are divided into Certified and Preferred lender categories. Certified Lenders cannot approve loans on-site; they must pass the documents on to a regional SBA office. Preferred Lenders are institutions with strong track records with the agency (i.e., few defaults) that are deemed capable of making loan approvals themselves. Applying for a loan through a Preferred Lender can take weeks off the approval process. The SBA has given Preferred Lender status to more than 450 institutions, and you'll find them listed on www.sba.gov.

In 2005, when Terry Plemons of Southlake, Texas, needed to borrow $100,000 to open a CertaPro Painters franchise, he went to the SBA site and made a list of the 30 to 40 Preferred Lenders in the Dallas–Forth Worth area. "I started dialing for dollars," he says. "I narrowed the list to banks near where I live or within the territory where I would be operating, and sent personal financial statements, a full business plan, and a lot of documents to half a dozen of them. I had serious offers from four or five, and didn't meet the banker I selected until very near the end of the process."

But "dialing for dollars" only works with established franchise systems like CertaPro, based in Oaks, Pennsylvania, that have hundreds of franchisees with strong repayment histories. When Texan Brian McMullin purchased the second franchise sold by Snip-its, a children's hair salon concept based in Natick, Massachusetts, he assumed he would have no trouble getting financing. After all, his credentials included an MBA, a long corporate career, and volunteer service in his community, the Woodlands.

But when McMullin and his wife applied for an SBA-guaranteed loan at their local bank, the SBA's regional office in Houston ruled that Snip-its did not qualify for its program. The SBA has clear guidelines on what qualifies as a small business. But UFOCs are so complicated it's often difficult to determine whether the local franchisee has enough leeway to operate as an independent business owner and not as an employee of the franchisor.

McMullin researched the SBA's approval process and finally sent the Snip-its UFOC to the SBA general counsel's office in Washington, D.C., where the agency's top attorney overruled the Houston office and approved the loan.

Subsequent Snip-its franchisees escaped similar frustrations, because Snip-its' vice president of franchising, Derek Skaletsky, immediately applied for a listing on the Franchise Registry. For a fee of $2,500, plus a $500 annual renewal fee, franchisors can send their UFOCs to FRANdata in Arlington, Virginia. If the documents meet SBA loan qualification criteria, the franchise is listed on a public Web site (www.franchiseregistry.com), which all banks making SBA loans can access in seconds.

A few weeks later, when another new Snip-its franchisee, Robert Goldstein, applied for a loan to open a salon in the Nashville area, 10 of the 12 banks he visited were interested and 6 made loan offers. "They could check the registry and see that Snip-its is the real deal," Goldstein says.

Persistence Pays

Eric Hamilton's chosen franchise, Signs By Tomorrow, is listed on the registry, but the Maple Heights, Ohio, former executive was still turned down by SBA lenders.

"It's a weeding-out process, and people who give up are not meant to be business owners."

"I took my business plan to several banks, but when the loan officers looked over my anticipated cash flow, they were concerned that I wouldn't be making enough to support our lifestyle and expenses," Hamilton says.

Finally, Hamilton found a banker willing to take a chance and who did approve his loan. The entire process took six months. "Be persistent," Hamilton advises.

"I think it's a weeding-out process, and people who give up are not meant to be business owners."

Paying Someone Else to Do the Legwork

You can bypass the time involved in finding financing by turning the process over to one of the loan brokers suggested by your franchisor or listed in franchise directories. According to Reginald Heard, national accounts manager for CIT Small Business Lending in Livingston, New Jersey, a nonbank lender, "An experienced broker should be able to size up the financing needs of an operator and guide him to the right lending sources." Another advantage, says Skaletsky of Snip-its, is that a broker can work with new franchisees from parts of the country where local bankers may have never heard of your concept.

There are, of course, some caveats. Franchise loan brokers, who operate like mortgage brokers, are a new business concept, and like most new concepts, have no standards or regulations. Some brokerages are established concerns, but others may be run by a single individual who has little more experience than you do. And although franchise brokers, like mortgage brokers, earn a commission for each loan they place, they still charge borrowers fees of $1,000 to over $6,000.

Loan broker Steve Mariani, president of Diamond Financial, in Raleigh, North Carolina, says he helps arrange SBA-guaranteed loans for new franchisees of systems whose UFOCs he's vetted. "We start by looking over the applicant's prequalification letter from the franchisor, his resume, and his personal financial history. Sometimes we see a credit score so low we'll work with the applicant

"It took us eight months to help one guy whose credit was a disaster."

to bring it up first. It took us eight months to help one guy whose credit was a disaster," Mariani says.

Mariani says he works mostly with nonbank lenders like CIT and Banco Popular. He charges borrowers a $1,000 processing fee and refunds $750 of it if they never qualify for a loan. "You won't know who the lender is until you're approved," he says.

Here's some advice for working with franchise loan brokers:

- *Begin by asking the broker how much the service costs.* Since the broker is earning a commission from your lender, charging you a high fee may seem excessive. Try to negotiate, or move on to someone else.

- *Ask what services are included in the fee.* Some brokers quote low processing fees, then charge $3,000 or more to write your business plan.

- *Watch out for brokers who want to charge you a percentage of your total loan.* With an SBA-guaranteed loan, such a fee may be illegal.

- *Get referrals and ask franchisees the broker has worked with if they'd recommend the experience.* Has the broker worked with your franchise system before?

- *Beware of exclusivity agreements.* Several franchisees say they felt agreeing to let a single broker source their loan was too restrictive.

- *Beware of people really selling other services, like IRA and 401(k) conversions, posing as franchise loan brokers.*

Do You Want to Rent That Fryer?

Most franchisors help new franchisees defray start-up expenses by arranging for them to rent the equipment they need to operate their units. A lending company purchases necessary equipment—deep-fat fryers, delivery vans, printing presses, and so on—from franchisor-approved vendors, then leases it to you on a rent-to-own basis. When the lease expires, you pay the lender an extra dollar, and it's yours.

For example, if a new ShapeXpress franchisee had to buy all the exercise equipment and tanning beds he needed to open his first fitness club, it would cost about $50,000. Instead, ShapeXpress arranges with vendors to lease that equipment to franchisees, who pay about $1,500 a month for terms of three to five years before they own it outright.

Again, leasing companies only want to do business with good credit risks. But because the equipment acts as collateral for their loans, just like car loans, their qualifications are less stringent than conventional lenders. If you haven't done so yet, pull your credit report and score and clear up any problems before applying for an equipment lease contract.

Betting Your Nest Egg on a Franchise

Harry Johns' retirement depends on how fast Rutgers University students use up their printer cartridges. Johns, the former IT manager for a chain of drug stores, has invested some of his retirement savings into the Cartridge World franchise he opened near the college in New Brunswick, New Jersey.

Investing your nest egg into your own business has been legal since Congress passed the Employee Retirement Income Security Act of 1974 (ERISA) setting up the IRA and 401(k) plans that make you responsible for your own retirement. But tapping into those monies to purchase franchises didn't become popular until 2001, when the dot-com crash made owning the stock of other companies seem less attractive and corporate downsizings sent hundreds of executives—and their fat 401(k)s—out looking for something else to do.

Since then, three companies—Guidant Financial Group, in Bellevue, Washington; BeneTrends, Inc., of San Diego; and SD Cooper Company in Huntington Beach, California—have helped several thousand people like Johns become franchisees. Basically, representatives of the three main companies charge you about $5,000 to help you cash out all, or part, of your retirement plan without IRS penalties, and reinvest that money into a new C corporation—your franchise—of which you are the trustee and sole stockholder.

Johns says he used BeneTrends to take $70,000 from his 401(k) plan and financed another $70,000 to pay the Cartridge World franchise fee and build out his location. "Since the amount I had to borrow was lower," says Johns, "I qualified for a conventional loan and didn't have to put up my house as collateral. And the smaller loan means smaller payments, which helps my cash flow."

Some franchisees use a portion of their retirement funds to cover the 20 to 30 percent down payment required for SBA-guaranteed loans. Others, like William Mitchell, use their entire retirement packages to buy franchises they could otherwise not afford. Mitchell says he used his IRA monies to help pay the $2.5 million cost of the Primrose School he opened recently in Charlotte, North Carolina. "I expect to get a good return from this investment," says Mitchell, "and I'm also helping children."

> *"The smaller loan means smaller payments, which helps my cash flow."*

There are, of course, restrictions and potential problems:

- You must have stopped working for your employer before you can tap into a 401(k) plan you've accumulated there.
- You must operate the franchise yourself.
- If you have less than $40,000 in your retirement plan, the companies that facilitate these transactions won't work with you.
- When you sell your franchise, your profits must go back into your IRA or 401(k) plan.
- And the biggest danger of all—you may lose all your retirement money.

Dr. Germain Boer, professor of management at Vanderbilt University's Owen Graduate School of Business in Nashville, says, "These plans buy stock in your own company, just as if it were General Motors. And you're buying a franchise with pretax dollars. I think the risk decision depends on your age. If you're a thirty-year-old, it's a smart thing to do. If you're sixty, it's not so smart."

Johns, by the way, was only thirty-seven when he made his transaction, and he did not use his entire retirement savings. "I'm not worried about making a $70,000 investment in myself," Johns says.

Borrowing from Uncle Alfred

If you have no retirement savings and don't qualify for a bank loan, your only recourse may be getting friends or relatives to invest in your franchise or loan you the money you need. But think carefully about asking for help. Many friendships have been destroyed and families torn apart over money matters.

If you are borrowing money, approach your friendly lenders as you would

"You don't want a subpoena server to be chasing Uncle Alfred's cart across the golf course."

a bank, with a business plan and a detailed report on the franchisor and your due diligence. Ask your accountant to draw up official loan documents and to look over the terms. Under federal and state tax laws, putting money into your franchise may make your investors liable for taxes if you're successful and for bankruptcy restitution if you fail. You certainly don't want a subpoena server to be chasing Uncle Alfred's cart across the golf course.

Ask the Professor

How do most people finance their franchises?

Most people first consider their savings, family and friends, and partners or investors. The majority of people finance their franchise through national banks and finance companies. Typically, this requires a guarantee by the U.S. Small Business Administration (SBA). The SBA is the guarantor of most small business loans.

Some people are fortunate enough to have a nest egg they can tap into, and in the last few years many people have started looking at their retirement funds and 401(k)s. Prospective franchisees are using their retirement accounts to meet the hefty down payment that the SBA requires for loans.

Finance companies usually are more flexible than banks because they can take on a wider variety of loans and move faster in response to market changes and customer needs. Additionally, some franchisors provide financial assistance in one form or another, for example, equipment lease packages.

What do I have to know about loan rates and prepayment penalties?

You need to take a close look at the paperwork and read the fine print before signing any loan agreements. Look at the collateral requirements and hidden costs, like prepayment penalties and loan restrictions. You need to consider the impact of down payments. When you are comparing a bank's interest rate of 8 or 9 percent to an equipment-leasing company's interest rate of 10 or 11 percent, it might sound like a terrific deal. However, the bank might require a hefty down payment of 25 to 30 percent, and it will leave you cash-poor. You need all the available cash up front when you are starting your franchise. You might want to try to secure a loan that requires very little or nothing down and low payments for the first six to nine months to help you get through the start-up phase.

If I want to open my franchise quickly, does it pay to shop around for better rates?

Now is a good time to borrow money to buy your franchise. Local bankers have become more savvy about franchise financing. Many banks and finance companies have the capital to lend; waits are getting shorter for SBA loans; and close to 600 franchise systems seeking new franchisees are listed on the SBA's Franchise Registry. Why not shop for the best rate and keep that extra cash?

PART THREE

Getting Ready for Business: How to Hit the Ground Running

You've passed all the initial hurdles, from selecting a franchise to obtaining the financing to purchase it. The next steps—getting trained, finding a site, building out your location, hiring employees, and planning your Grand Opening—are the most exciting in your journey. As you'll learn, most new franchisees adapt quickly to becoming business owners. In fact, most of them wish the process would move along even faster.

In the next few chapters, we'll explore how you can move through the initial steps of setting up your business and arrive at a successful Grand Opening (also called Opening Day). We'll look at typical questions that come up in this part of the process, such as whether you should purchase an existing franchise location or build a new one (Chapter Fourteen) and where to find reliable employees (Chapter Fifteen). We'll also hear from franchisees about how to keep your business running smoothly after the opening-day ribbon has been cut, through effective local marketing and superior customer service.

CHAPTER THIRTEEN

Franchisee Training (Yes, There Are Tests)

The most important thing a franchisor does is train new franchisees to follow its system. "If you thoroughly understand the philosophy and operating systems of the franchise you're joining, you have a great chance of succeeding on a day-to-day basis," says Dave Hood, the president of the iFranchise Group in Homewood, Illinois, a consortium of franchise experts who consult to existing franchisors and help transform businesses into franchises.

If franchisees are well-trained, Hood says, customers in different regions or states will all have the same level of experience. "Some businesses are technical in nature, like the construction industry or computer services," he says, "and their franchisees must be highly trained, because the quality of each franchisee's work has an impact on the entire system."

Getting Somewhat Trained at Installing Bathtub Liners

A few years ago I stood in a real bathtub and, with a partner, attached an acrylic panel to a fake bathroom wall. The scene was the cavernous warehouse classroom of Luxury Bath Systems, a franchisor in Glendale Heights, Illinois, whose franchisees cover old cast-iron or pressed-steel tubs and ceramic tile walls or drywall with shiny new liners.

It was the hands-on segment of a franchisee training class, and my partner, who was more experienced and a whole lot taller, was doing most of the work. We'd spent the morning taking notes while a trainer—a young man who announced he'd lined 1,000 old tubs himself—walked us through the wall installation process. He told horror stories of what can go wrong, like the time a customer's cat had crawled into a wall opening when the installer went to retrieve something from his truck and went missing for days. He reassured us that the job gets easier after 50 or so bathrooms. And he used videos, in which he also starred, to show us how to clean the old wall, measure and cut the new panel,

> *"If I'd been a real franchisee, I would have flunked Luxury Bath Systems training."*

and apply three tubes of caulk to the wall to hold the panel on.

I let my partner do the caulking, because I had trouble getting my caulk gun to work, and because our trainer had just shown us his "Popeye muscles" from squirting all those tubes of caulk himself. But my partner let me guide the panel that fits into the outside corner of the bath enclosure, called a bullnose, through a whirling jigsaw. I cut it too short, so when the trainer inspected the row of fake walls, ours was the only one with a gap at the top.

If I'd been a real franchisee, I would have flunked Luxury Bath Systems training. Luckily, I was just a guest, learning how franchisee training classes are conducted. It was the first day of a five-day session and we'd begun with a tour of the franchisor's headquarters, where the acrylic liners are manufactured to fit into 648 types and shapes of tubs. We couldn't see the area where the liners are made—the process is a secret—but we did view towers of tub molds and walls full of finished white, almond, and gray tub liners.

The five men in the class and I met the women who fill franchisees' orders by figuring out what types of tubs their customers have, and saw the shipping area, where all liners are photographed with a digital camera before they leave, in case they get scratched en route. Company executives dropped by during our breakfast and lunch breaks to answer questions and to ask the real students about their backgrounds. I don't know if they returned at the end of the day to check on our wall installations, because my partner was glaring at me and I cut out a few minutes early.

Except for the glaring, Dan Levy, who writes manuals and designs training classes for franchisor clients of the iFranchise Group, says my experience at Luxury Bath Systems is what you can expect when you attend your franchisor's training classes. Training classes generally last from five days to three weeks, he says, and should contain the following elements:

- A textbook, which is the franchise operations manual that breaks down everything you'll have to do to run your franchise.

- Outside speakers, videos, and PowerPoint presentations, because "it's too boring if you just sit and read through the manual," Levy says.

- Role-playing, during which you and your classmates act out your future roles—closing sales, dealing with difficult customers, disciplining employees, and so on.

- Overnight assignments that must be done with your classmates, so you'll build relationships while learning to solve problems together.

- Meetings with and instruction from the heads of the marketing, operations, human resources, ordering, quality control, and other departments.

- Overviews of the support each department will provide when you return home, and phone numbers to reach them when you have questions or problems. (The Luxury Bath trainer said he keeps his cell phone on 24/7 to answer questions from the field. Whenever it rang during class, he answered it.)

- Lessons in the business requirements of the franchise—pricing, keeping the books, managing payroll, paying taxes, managing inventory, and so forth.

- A hands-on introduction to any technology you'll be using and 24/7 numbers for the franchisor's tech support team.

- Detailed information from the real estate department on finding a site and building out your unit.

- A description of any permits you'll have to get from your local government, and information on how to obtain them.

- Presentations by franchisees about their real-life experiences.

- Opening day budgets, schedules, and promotion suggestions. Announcements of who will be at your side as you prepare to open.

- Information on employee recruiting, training, and scheduling.

- On-the-job training at a corporate-owned training facility or a nearby franchisee's site. (In the past, trainees at Luxury Bath Systems installed wall treatments and tub liners in corporate employees' homes. "But we're dealing with water here," says company founder and president Davis

Glassberg, "and if a trainee does something wrong, it can cause quite a mess." Today, all hands-on training is done in the warehouse class-room. Before they start working for paying customers, Glassberg says, "We recommend installers do their own bathroom or one in a neighbor's house, where they can take their time and there's no pressure.")

Franchisees can also expect daily quizzes and, on the last day, a final exam. Franchisees who flunk the final may be given remedial help and tested again, or they may be told they're not a good fit for the system, after all. When that happens, franchisors refund their franchise fees, but may deduct the cost of the training classes from the payment.

Who Pays for All This?

Your franchise fee should cover the cost of training you (and your spouse or partner if you're doing this together) and, often, training your manager or other key employee. Included in the fee are the operations manual and other materials distributed in class, training videos, software programs, and some of the tools you'll need to get started.

In most systems, you'll have to cover the costs of traveling to franchise headquarters and staying at a nearby hotel yourself.

"The month my manager and I spent at Ice Cream University in Burbank, California, was very costly," says a new Baskin–Robbins franchisee. "I rented apartments for us to stay in there. But if you have to train somewhere, it was a wonderful place to be."

> *"The month my manager and I spent at Ice Cream University in Burbank, California, was very costly."*

Northern Illinois isn't as wonderful, but Joe Serina, the current director of training at Luxury Bath Systems, says that all costs for their training, including airfare and lodging for two installers, are covered in the franchise fee. Franchisees who will not be doing installations themselves attend a one-and-a-half day overview.

You can find details about the training programs of franchisors you're researching in Item 11 of their UFOCs.

Making Italian Meatloaf for the Masses

There are no bullnoses to ruin at Dinner by Design training classes, but you do run the risk of making customers sick if you don't handle and prepare food just right. This was the biggest lesson I learned when attending the first day of a training session for that easy meal preparation franchise in Grayslake, Illinois.

The day began on a less scary note. Four franchisee groups (two couples, a single man, and a couple plus their investor partner) sat in a real classroom in the College of Lake County, a community college located conveniently across the street from the franchisor's corporate training store. Company founder Julie Duffy appeared in person, and in dozens of video news clips projected on a movie screen, talking about how she left a corporate job when her kids were born and discovered how hard it is to feed a family healthy food every night. She opened a store where other moms could meet and assemble a few weeks' worth of meals; soon, her customers wanted to open one, too, so she started franchising.

The in-person Duffy talked about what it takes to be a franchisee—"You have to be a self-starter. However much work you think it's going to be, double that"—and gave an overview of what the trainees could expect during the week. This agenda included sessions on ordering food, maintaining an online

> *"However much work you think it's going to be, double that."*

menu board for customer orders, creating a customer database, scheduling employees, building units, financial record-keeping, and daily operating procedures. Because easy meal prep is so competitive, many of the sessions focus on marketing and promotion, including planning the franchisees' Grand Openings.

Before they can graduate, each Dinner by Design franchisee must spend six days as an apprentice in another franchisee's store, in charge of such tasks as the End of the Month Breakdown, taking down old recipe cards, stashing away unused ingredients, and cleaning all equipment. They must also host a private party and prepare the food for a day's sessions.

When the franchisor's food scientist, Mark Morgan, talked about developing recipes, the director of operations looked queasy and said, "He made me try 13 different variations of his salmon asparagus tart. I'll never touch it again." Morgan told franchisees how bulk buying saves them money. "I negotiate with

> *"He made me try 13 different variations of his salmon asparagus tart. I'll never touch it again."*

Tyson, because we use 300,000 pounds of chicken each year." He also told them how to make money by mixing up entrees from their leftovers and selling them as premade meals from their store's freezer case.

Director of training and development Pat Argoudelis had a long agenda, but mostly talked about washing your hands between putting together the ingredients for separate entrees, and whenever you blow your nose, touch your hair, or touch a customer. A trip to the bathroom requires a full-scale scrubdown. Meal preparation franchises walk an awkward line between restaurants and grocery stores because customers assemble meals in their facilities, but take them home to freeze and cook later. Each freezer pack comes with a label that tells the customer to defrost the meal slowly in his or her refrigerator for a day or two before cooking. But should a careless parent leave a meal to melt on a sunny kitchen counter where it gets warm, and stray germs start to breed, the result could be catastrophic.

The day ended with a course in crisis management and a trek to that corporate kitchen, where we all stood at assembly stations and put together sample meals. I was happily stuffing pork chops with breadcrumbs, dried cherries, and pecans when it happened. I sneezed. I dashed to the sink, but it was too late. The kitchen help and trainees were all glaring at me.

Getting the Most Out of Your Training Experience

Franchisees who did pass their final exams give the following tips:

- Don't go to training too early. Wait until about a month before you're scheduled to open. Franchisees who jumped into training, then had to wait months while their units were built out, say they forgot too much.

- While you're waiting, work in an existing franchise. Then, when you get to training, everything will make more sense, says Fresno, California, MAACO franchisee Mike Murphy.

- If your franchisor doesn't provide them, ask for materials you can go through beforehand—vendor instruction booklets, training videos, even that massive operations manual.

- Call back some of the existing franchisees you talked to during due diligence and ask what they wish they'd paid more attention to during training. Tom Albanito, who was in the training class I visited at Dinner by Design, says that when established franchisees made their presentations, "I wish I'd questioned them more about their labor and food costs. We bought an existing store in Kenosha, Wisconsin, and we're not coming close to their numbers."

- Build a rapport with the other trainees. They'll be going through the same things you are, and you can share tips and bolster each other through rough times.

- Leave with a firm understanding of the help you'll get during your Grand Opening and a schedule of future training sessions for yourself and your employees.

- When you return home, watch for an evaluation form that many franchisors send their training class graduates. It will highlight the strengths you bring to the system and then list the areas where you might need some additional work before you go out on your own.

Training Never Stops

Think of initial training as getting a medical degree. You've learned the basics, but it's only through the specialized training and hands-on experience you get during your internships and residency that you really become a doctor.

Besides sending someone to help you train your employees and open your unit, your franchisor may send support personnel back as frequently as once a quarter in your first year of operation, to check on your progress and to help with any procedures that may be causing you problems. At Dinner by Design, CEO Julie Duffy visits each start-up franchisee every six weeks herself.

The franchisor should also provide training materials for your employees. To get the attention of your young workers, many of these programs are online, interactive, and short. If your workforce will include Hispanics or other immigrants, ask if your franchisor has training programs in Spanish or other languages.

Most franchisors host regional training sessions whenever they introduce new products or add new services. Training is also a component of each franchise system's national convention. If a new piece of equipment is being introduced, the vendor may be there to teach you how to use it. At Luxury Bath Systems' conventions, the top installers are invited to top-gun roundtable discussions, in which they share war stories and best practices.

At Express Personnel Services in Oklahoma City, training is a nine-step process:

1. Two weeks of new franchisee training at Express University in Oklahoma for new owners and their staffs, plus a week of on-the-job training at a certified franchisee's office.
2. "Fast Track" weekly phone calls during franchisees' first 26 weeks in business.
3. On Track Boot Camp, a two-day drill to help newcomers build confidence and refine their skills.
4. Tele-Seminars, one-hour sessions on hot issues that may include visual presentations or online training.
5. Express University Online Learning, a series of e-learning courses for employees.
6. Power Train for inside and outside salespeople. Franchisees use online learning, software training, and learning exercises to get new employees up to speed during their first two weeks on the job.
7. Express University Certification for franchisees and their employees.
8. LearnLink, a training plan for employees that covers one subject a week.
9. Live Learning Events at annual leadership conferences and at two-day regional sales summits.

If all this seems a little excessive, think about McDonald's. To qualify for a McDonald's franchise you must spend 9 to 18 months training in a restaurant near your home, attend seminars and one-on-one training sessions, and take advanced courses at Hamburger University in Oak Brook, Illinois. Do you still wonder why McDonald's equals success?

Ask the Professor

What are the components of a good training program?

One of the real strengths of franchising is the training and support that a good franchisor provides. A solid training program should adequately prepare you to run the business. It should provide information on how to deliver the product or service and be comprehensive enough to teach you the financial, marketing, and day-to-day aspects of operating the business. It should provide management training, and, depending on the product or service you're offering, it could include information pertaining to safe food preparation and handling. Other relevant factors it should include are:

- How to find your location and negotiate a lease
- How to complete the building permits and build-out of the location
- How to find, hire, and manage employees
- How to design your marketing program to obtain customers
- How to order supplies and/or inventory necessary to operate your business
- How to develop and maintain a record-keeping system for the business
- How to secure the equipment you will need to operate the business
- How to protect the brand identity

You won't remember everything you've learned in the training program after you are finished, and it might be some time before you open your doors for business. Therefore, it is important to find out if the franchisor is providing you with how-to manuals that are easy to access, and/or if the franchisor will be providing training support through the intranet. Find out which personnel (and how many) from your business will be able to attend the training program. Once you open your doors for business, you are going to want your questions answered quickly and easily. Leave the training class with a list of the names and contact information for the other franchisees who attended. They will be a strong support network for you.

(continued)

Are there red flags at training that should make you decide not to proceed?

As a franchisee who has paid a great deal of money to become a part of a franchise system, you are expecting a comprehensive initial training program from the franchisor, as well as ongoing training and support. The most valuable source of information will come from the existing franchisees. Most of them will be happy and supportive of the franchisor. However, it is also important for you to visit with those who have recently left the system for one reason or another and are unhappy with their experience. Find out why they left the system. Do the existing franchisees, as well as those who have left the system, feel that the franchisor's training program was adequate for them to start and operate their business successfully? If the franchisees had a lot of issues that the franchisor was unwilling to address, this would be a huge red flag. If the franchisor has a substandard training program and you discover in your conversations with existing franchisees that the franchisor is lax in its ongoing support, this would be another red flag because it would not enable you to successfully run your business. The franchisor would not be fulfilling its responsibility.

CHAPTER FOURTEEN

Finding a Home for Your New Enterprise

If you thought finding a franchise was difficult, just wait until you step into the commercial real estate marketplace. "Commercial real estate is a very odd business," says Cartridge World franchisee Harry Johns. "Negotiating for sites is a slow process, not like buying a house." Johns signed his franchise agreement with Cartridge World of San Francisco in February 2006, spent four months looking for sites, signed a lease in June, and opened his store in New Brunswick, New Jersey, in November.

That seemed like an eternity to Johns, who says he used the time to join a networking group and his local chamber of commerce and to help form an advertising co-operative with other local Cartridge World franchisees. He even developed a few customers, by driving their empty ink cartridges to other Cartridge World stores to be filled.

But national commercial real estate broker Phil Baugh, of the Baum Realty Group in Chicago, says that six to nine months to find a site and get a franchise open is about average. "We understand that you've just committed $40,000 to over $200,000 to a concept and are ready to make a major change in your life. But if you don't take the proper steps and you choose a site too quickly, you'll regret it later," he says.

> *"If you choose a site too quickly, you'll regret it later."*

Sidestepping the Process

Chris and Tina Butler had no such lag time, because they bought an existing Comfort Keepers franchise in Muskegon, Michigan. Chris says he'd sent for information on Comfort Keepers, a franchise based in Dayton, Ohio, that provides nonmedical in-home care for seniors, in 2001, but backed off when he realized that his local territory was already taken.

> *"The day you buy is the day you start making money."*

"Eighteen months later," Chris says, "the owner of that territory contacted me and asked if I'd like to buy it." The franchisee had been promoted to a position in Comfort Keepers' corporate office. "He was not only desperate to sell, but he also didn't want the business to fail," Chris says.

The couple started due diligence immediately, by hiring an accountant to go over the seller's books, talking to other franchisees, and talking to the franchisor's executives in Dayton. "We figured his asking price was probably 50 percent less than what it would cost to start a new franchise, and we were also getting a furnished office, employees, and a customer base," Chris says. Tina hurried off to Dayton for training (Chris kept his day job for the first nine months) and within eight weeks of that initial phone call, the couple was in business.

Franchise attorney Michael Liss of Oak Brook, Illinois, says that buying an existing franchise "is the best of all worlds. You're getting a history of financial statements, the day you buy is the day you start making money, and your employees and marketing plans are in place. You don't even have to worry about choosing the wrong site, because the franchise is operating there now."

Unless you, too, are very lucky, an existing franchise won't fall into your lap. You can, however, look for existing units that may be for sale by:

- Contacting your franchisor. Many franchisors keep lists of franchisees who want to sell their units. Also, franchisors often sell off corporate units to franchisees.
- Contacting other franchisees in the area, and asking if they or any of their colleagues are thinking about retiring or doing something else.
- Contacting local business brokers.

Stay away from systems where a lot of franchises are for sale. That's a sign that franchisees are not making money.

If you find an available franchise that seems profitable, the first thing you want to do, says Liss, is find out why the person is selling. Is the unit doing so well, he or she wants to sell it at a profit? Is the franchisee retiring? Does he or she or a family member have health problems? Or does he or she know something you don't, like the landlord is raising rents, the city is changing the way the road goes by or is about to ban smoking in his or her restaurant? If the franchise is located in a shopping center, talk to the other tenants about upcoming changes.

If the franchise is not in a system you've already researched, you'll have to begin due diligence on the concept at the same time you and your accountant are poring over the franchisee's books. Liss says you'll want to see three years of income statements, tax returns, and sales analysis reports. Do the tax returns match the financial statements and bank deposits? You're looking for consistency.

You and the seller will have to agree on a price, says Liss, "and valuing any ongoing business is an art form." Franchises generally sell for between two and four times their net annual profits; but, as we've seen in previous chapters, some franchisees take profits while others use excess monies to pay business-related (and personal) expenses. To find out if the price the seller proposes is fair, call five other franchisees in similar locations and ask what they'd sell for. You can also contact a local business broker and ask what similar franchised and independent businesses have sold for recently.

> *"Valuing any ongoing business is an art form."*

Like any prospective franchisee, you'll have to be approved by the franchisor, which will want you to submit financial information and attend Discovery Day and training. About three-fourths of the time, says Liss, the franchisor will want you to sign a new franchise agreement, which means that what you're buying is not the same business the old operator is selling. If royalties and ad fund fees are higher under the new contract, the seller may give you a concession on the price.

Other inside tips for buying an existing franchise include:

- If seller-financing is available, take it, says Liss. "It's a kind of truth serum, because the seller wants the buyer to be successful, so he'll get paid. If you discover he lied to you, he knows you won't pay him."

- You'll probably be able to assume the seller's old lease, but ask the landlord for amendments, so that it can be extended to cover the term of your new franchise agreement.

- Use a franchise attorney and tell him or her to include clauses in your purchase contract that make the seller liable for problems that occurred when he or she owned the business, like disputes with customers, unpaid bills, and lawsuits.

- Taking over may not be easy. Chris Butler says, "We had to start making tough decisions immediately. And while we had employees, they were not the people we would have hired. Since we started in 2003, we've had a 100 percent turnover in our office staff."

Here's something else to keep in mind: Attorney Justin Klein says that when a system gets into a lot of trouble, you can sometimes buy a franchise at fire sale prices. During the mid-2000s, when many franchisees of Quiznos were having problems, some advertised that they'd sell units they spent $300,000 to build for only $25,000, for example. "If you don't have debt service, you might be able to make some money," Klein says. "But be careful. If an entire system is faltering, you could lose your investment, too."

Searching for a Site

According to research firm FRANdata, only about 4.7 percent of franchises change owners in any given year. Unless you happen to find one of them—or have opted to operate a home business—you'll have to find a site for your business. Besides your eagerness to get started, you may have extra pressure from your lender, who wants you to have a place for your franchise before he or she approves your loan.

Not that long ago, a new franchisee would choose between buying land and putting up his or her own building or renting space in an enclosed mall. Today, land prices are so high that most new franchisees can't afford the option of buying an acre and putting up a freestanding unit. Enclosed malls are losing favor, too, because rents are higher than in open strip centers, and the mall's required hours of operation may not suit your concept. Mall ice cream franchises, for example, have to open at 10:00 A.M., and usually don't sell their first cones until noon. "Shopping malls are still great for impulse item franchises, like Auntie Anne's Hand-Rolled Soft Pretzels, or Cinnabon," says iFranchise president Dave Hood, "because they require lots of people walking by."

A Franchise Resale Champion

Harvey Nevins, of Tucson, Arizona, bought his first Midas Automotive Center in 1980. Since then, he's bought and sold so many units, including some twice, he's lost count, but thinks the number is around 40.

Nevins says he was living in Tucson, where no Midas centers were available, when the franchisor alerted him to an existing franchise for sale in Chico, California. "I left my family in Arizona and I moved up there," Nevins says. "For the first three months, I lived in the back office. Every night, I'd lay out some cardboard to sleep on, then put it away in the morning."

"When everything was working fine, I sold my Tucson house and brought my family to California. Midas named me 'Rookie of the Year,'" he remembers. Nevins soon acquired a second Midas, 50 miles away in Marysville, California. He then sold those centers—"always at a profit," he says—and, with a partner, bought eight more in Las Vegas. When the partnership ended, Nevis used his proceeds to buy up existing Midas shops and open new ones in Arizona and Idaho.

In the meantime, the man who'd purchased his two California stores with seller financing asked him to take back the Marysville store in exchange for the rest of his debt. "I drove up there," Nevins says, "and you wouldn't believe what the store was like. So many lights were out, it looked like a cave, and the lifts were inoperable. How can you fix cars if the lifts don't work? I checked into a motel across the street, assembled a workforce, and spent every night for two weeks replacing lightbulbs and repairing things. As soon as everything was fixed, sales volume in the store doubled."

Nevins says you can do the same thing, skipping the cardboard bed part. "If you buy a franchise operating to its maximum, you'll have to pay a high price, and you may have a big debt to pay off," he says. "If you buy an underperforming unit at a bargain price, you have no start-up costs, no Grand Opening, and a customer base already coming in. All you have to do is take good care of them, and you'll soon have more customers than you can handle."

This means that you'll be looking for rental space in strip centers or, if your franchise is a service concept, in office parks and industrial areas. Finding a site to rent and signing a lease can take from 6 to 12 weeks, says commercial real estate broker Phil Baugh.

Finding a Site through Your Franchisor

Begin with your franchisor. Many franchise companies hire third-party firms that research who their customers are, then use Global Positioning Systems (GPS) and Census data to find out where they live. Urban Science, in Detroit, Michigan, for example, uses car registration information to help automotive franchisors determine where to locate new stores. The technology can even tell you which other stores your future customers shop at or which other services they use, and pinpoint the best places in your community to attract their attention.

And some franchisors, like Clix, a digital photography studio franchise based in Marietta, Georgia, refer all new franchisees to a single national commercial real estate firm. CEO David Asarnow says, "We prefer to deal with one broker who knows what we're looking for and our co-tenancy requirements. If a franchisee is searching outside that broker's geographic area, he can find the best broker in that market, who'll report back to him."

Going It Alone

If your franchisor doesn't offer such a service, you'll have to find a commercial real estate broker on your own. Like residential brokers, commercial real estate brokers expect you to work with them exclusively. They are paid by the landlord after leases are signed, at rates that vary from market to market.

You can find a broker by:

- Asking other franchisees in the area who they used. Or ask the owners of businesses that attract the same kind of customer you're seeking.

- Driving through your target shopping or industrial areas and writing down the phone numbers on "For Rent" signs. Most brokers represent both landlords and renters. Call or check out the companies on the Internet to see who else they represent.

- Asking members of the chamber of commerce, local merchant's association, or other group whom they recommend.

When you start contacting brokers, present yourself in a professional manner, says Baugh. "Tell her, 'I'm looking to open this business, and here's my business plan and my financial information,'" he says. "Some brokers are hesitant to work with individual franchisees unless they feel you have the ability to get the lease completed."

No matter how impressed he or she may be, the broker can't work with you until he or she understands what you're looking for. Ask someone from your franchisor's real estate office to call the broker and explain the concept, the criteria of the space you'll need, and how much you can afford to pay.

> *"Some brokers are hesitant to work with individual franchisees unless they feel you have the ability to get the lease completed."*

Setting a rent ceiling can be tricky. Most real estate experts, including your broker, perhaps, say you should choose a great location over a bargain rental fee. Talk to other franchisees about what they're paying and ask whether they could still make a profit if they paid more than your franchisor recommends. In almost all cases, your franchisor must approve your site before you sign a lease. If you're looking at a site that's too expensive, your franchisor may reject it, and you'll have to start the search process all over again.

It will take the broker one or two weeks to identify what's out there. Then he or she will take you to see the top few properties, Baugh says. If you like a location, play detective again. Sit in the parking lot at different times of the day, making notes on traffic that comes in and out. Who shops there? Go in and talk to the other tenants. What's business like? What do they think of their landlord? Does he or she take good care of the place?

Next Steps

When you've found a space that seems feasible, your broker will submit a letter of intent to the landlord, outlining the business conditions under which you'll consider renting it. Here's where the timeline gets stretched out, Baugh says. The landlord will negotiate on those business terms (Signage, parking, early termination rights, etc.) for one to three weeks. If you agree to those terms, it will take the landlord another week or two to prepare a lease.

That lease, even for a 1,200-square-foot space, will be over 100 pages long, says attorney Liss. And you'll have to pay a commercial real estate attorney to review it, "because everything's negotiable," he says.

If your franchise attorney isn't local, you can ask your broker or other franchisees to recommend a commercial real estate attorney. The lease negotiation process can take up to a month, Liss says, and will cost you $3,000 to $4,000 in legal fees. Not using an attorney, however, can be much more costly. Here are some important issues to focus on:

- Make sure you can rent the property for the length of your franchise agreement. If your lease is for five years and your agreement is for ten, include options to extend it for additional periods and set future rental rates now.

- If your franchisor recommends that you locate in a shopping center with a grocery store, a big-box retailer like Wal-Mart or, in the case of Clix, a Toys "R" Us or other children's store, ask for co-tenancy provisions that let you out of the lease should that important tenant move away.

- Don't agree to pay rent that's a percentage of your gross sales. Such rent may look like a bargain when you're starting, but can escalate quickly once you're doing well.

- Beware of how taxes, insurance, and common area maintenance (CAM)—the cost of keeping up the strip center or shopping mall, including trimming the shrubs, plowing the entranceways, paving the parking lot, maintaining the shared eating space in an enclosed mall, removing the rubbish, and so on—are assessed. You should pay a pro rata share, based on the leasable space at the center, not the leased space. If your share is calculated on leased space, you'll have to pay more, should some tenants move out.

- Expect to sign a personal guarantee, make a large security deposit, or produce a letter of credit so your landlord has some recourse, should you default.

- If you default on your franchise agreement, your franchisor has the option of taking over the location immediately, says Liss. Your franchisor must approve your lease, and almost all of them add cross-default clauses that give them the right to have you evicted if you stop paying your royalties, he warns.

Building Out Your Space

The general rule for all construction projects is "It takes twice as long and costs twice as much as you thought it would." For some franchisees, the odds are even higher. We met a gourmet ice cream franchisee who thought he'd save money by using the guy who put an addition on his house to build out his store. The franchisee had to spend an extra $30,000 to have the residential contractor's work torn out and replaced, and he missed opening up during the summer, when most ice cream sales occur.

> *"The general rule for all construction projects is 'It takes twice as long and costs twice as much as you thought it would.'"*

Just how smoothly your buildout goes depends on the quality of the contractor you hire, the support of your franchisor, and the vagaries of the permitting process in your own community. Christopher Nellis and Jay Charlesworth, who are in their mid-forties, had been friends since college, and had spent countless hours talking about going into business together. In the fall of 2005, they started exploring meal preparation franchises and, by April 2006, had signed a contract with Super Suppers, had found a site in downtown Northbrook, Illinois, within biking distance of Jay's house, and had even driven back from training class in Fort Worth, Texas, with a trailer full of accessories to give their store the franchise's signature Tuscany-styled décor.

They hired a commercial contractor, who worked from architectural plans e-mailed from franchise headquarters, and planned to open August 1. But getting their buildout approved by village inspectors added another month to the process. "All the inspectors have to sign off on everything," says Nellis, "so one will approve something and put it in the next inspector's inbox. If he happens to be on vacation, your project is delayed."

When they thought they were close to opening, an inspector checking their Americans with Disabilities Act (ADA) requirements noted that the food carts they planned to use were two inches too tall for customers in wheelchairs. "When we called Fort Worth," says Charlesworth, "none of their other 200 franchisees had ever encountered this problem. They said we had to figure it out on our own." Once they'd located accessible carts on the Internet, another inspector said they had to replace all the lightbulbs in their overhead recessed fixtures with shatterproof glass. "The devil's in the details," says Nellis.

Bryan Hildebrand, a new Dinner by Design franchisee in Lemont, Illinois, recommends building relationships with local inspectors while your franchise is being built. "I started asking questions before we submitted our plans," Hildebrand says. "They were appreciative that I wanted my plans to be as right as possible. Later, when the plumbing inspector wanted revisions, he got back to see our changes within one or two days every time. He's not obligated to respond for two weeks."

Letting Others Do the Dirty Work

Soon, all buildouts may pick up speed. The Total Resource Group (TRG) in Lincolnwood, Illinois, specializes in "Buildings in a Box." Company founder Bruce Olans says, "Rather than send franchisees out to hire architects and contractors and find equipment vendors, we take over the whole process. We get the permits and, when the time to build comes, we pull a truck up to the franchisee's front door with everything he needs to open—flooring, millwork, graphics, his exterior sign, equipment, and even his office and cleaning supplies. Our contractors do all the work, and, in the best case, the franchisee goes away until we're finished and hand him the keys."

Clix president Asarnow, who requires new franchisees to use TRG to put up their photography studios, says that the full-service buildout costs about 10 percent more than doing everything yourself. "Having someone else do the construction work allows a new franchisee to work on his business and marketing plans," Asarnow says. "Since our model includes events photography at local schools and sporting events, our new franchisees can be out earning money instead of supervising the construction process."

The Thirty-Four-Day Buildout

When Jim Railing and his daughter finished training at Cousins Subs in Wisconsin, in late October 2006, they told their franchisor they planned to open their first unit in Columbus, Indiana, before Christmas. "Cousins said it couldn't be done," Railing says. But during the restaurant chain's three-and-a-half-week training program, Railing had been on his cell phone, negotiating lease terms and talking to his architect and contractor. The contractor had their permits lined up in record time and started construction on November 15.

Cousins marketing department warned Railing how foolish he'd look if customers who read his Opening Day newspaper ads arrived at an unfinished store. "My daughter was quite nervous," Railing admits. "We had four or five subcontractors working in the store at any one time, and she had to interview prospective employees in the lobby of a hotel a block away. But all the restaurant equipment arrived on November 30 and we opened on December 19, right on schedule."

Ask the Professor

What should prospective franchisees watch out for when buying existing units?

Prospective franchisees need to determine the reason why the existing franchisee is selling the unit. It could be because of life changes—for example, retirement, divorce, a death in the family, or health reasons. Perhaps the franchisee simply wasn't cut out to be in the business, or it wasn't what she expected it would be. It may be a distressed unit, and the current franchisee doesn't have the available capital to renovate and upgrade the unit. Prospective franchisees need to ensure that the brand name is still intact and there are no negative connotations associated with it. You certainly don't want to inherit someone else's negative image in the marketplace.

Consider your options. In many mature franchise systems, the only way to get in is by purchasing an existing unit. Most franchisors have a listing of units for sale. You might even get a bargain if you buy an underperforming unit and have the capital to upgrade it and bring it to the current operating standards. You will already have a built-in customer and employee base.

How much support should a franchisor provide when looking for locations?

Remember: location, location, location. This is one of the big advantages of being part of a franchise system. The mature franchisor has experience in finding sites that work and sites that don't. Almost all franchisors will provide some input into your site selection process. It may be guidelines they have established, or sending support staff to help you look for the location. You'll find their level of involvement outlined in the franchise agreement.

Good franchisors will point you in the right direction, based on their experience. They may provide you with criteria for evaluating prospective sites that lists specifications for the site and meets their system's standards. In discussing prospective locations with franchisors, they should provide you with information on what your site will look like, why it will attract customers, customer traffic counts, and competitors in the area. Often, franchisors have demographic information on areas because they use data from research companies.

Some franchisors may provide considerable support in finding the site and accompanying you in your hunt for a location. Other franchisors will approve a general area for your location, and then it is up to you to find a site within those boundaries. Once you find a site, the franchisor will approve or disapprove the site you select.

Most franchise agreements will state that the franchisor is only approving or disapproving the site; it is not guaranteeing that it will work for you. The franchisor's approval indicates that the site is acceptable. The franchisor does not know what kind of operator you will be; nor does the franchisor force you to accept its suggestion. The franchisor distances itself from the final decision because of potential liability. It is your responsibility to find and accept a good location; it is not the franchisor's.

What are the dangers in waiting for a new shopping center to be built?

By the time you are driving through town looking for "For Sale" or "For Rent" signs, many of the prime spots in a new shopping center that is going to be built have probably already been secured. Major franchisors have real estate departments that specialize in understanding and negotiating tenant leases. Many other franchise organizations work with commercial real estate brokers.

You can work with an experienced real estate broker or attorney or investigate future development opportunities on your own. Check with city hall, real estate developers and brokers, and the local zoning and planning departments. Attend the exhibitions where shopping center developers disclose their construction plans. Visit the International Council of Shopping Centers at its Web site at www.icsc.org.

CHAPTER FIFTEEN

Getting Your Franchise Up and Running

It's crunch time. After those long weeks of waiting for your lease to be signed and contractor hired, now everything needs your attention at once. Equipment vendors are calling, the plumber is waiting for you to pick out a sink for the store's bathroom, the painter is complaining that he can't match the color your franchisor wants on the walls, and the franchise's marketing person is insisting that you turn in your opening day (the day you officially open for business, which some franchisors call your grand opening) budget and plan immediately. And, don't forget employees. If you don't hire some, it won't matter what color is on those walls—no one will see them.

Because every franchise is so different, we can't provide one hassle-free checklist to get you through outfitting and opening your franchise. Instead, we'll give you tips for handling some of the decisions you'll have to make. We'll show you details from the opening day schedules and budgets of a couple of different franchises. And we'll share marketing tips from professionals, franchisees, and franchisors, to keep your new customers coming back.

New or Used Equipment?

Buying all the equipment to run a restaurant, a fitness center, or almost any kind of franchise is expensive, and you may be tempted to save money by buying some of it used. This only works well, says Dan Levy of the iFranchise Group, if the equipment is something like the Hobart Mixers used in restaurants "that have the reputation of lasting 100 years." Sometimes equipment vendors can sell you reconditioned equipment that is under warranty. Otherwise, Levy says, you'll want your equipment to be new, with warranties in place. You don't want to experience malfunctions during your first few months in business.

If you plan to lease your equipment, most of those lending programs are only available for new equipment packages. Your operating manual specifies everything you'll have to purchase, and your franchisor may have arrangements with distributors that can deliver all of it at once, perhaps at a discount.

Setting Up Your Business

That delivery may include cash registers and computers, but, Levy says, you'll probably have to choose and set up an accounting program yourself. Talk to other fran-

> *"You don't want to experience malfunctions during your first few months in business."*

chisees about what they use and ask your accountant for recommendations. Your accountant can help you set up programs to calculate withholding taxes and Social Security payments for your employees and, if required, workers' compensation accounts. Talk to your insurance agent about coverage for your franchise. And if you turn part of your home into a franchise office, you'll need business coverage there, too.

If your franchise is a retail store or restaurant, you'll have to order supplies and inventory well in advance of your opening. If your store's shelves look sparse, or if you don't have the ingredients for menu items when you open, your first customers may never return. Again, your franchisor will provide a list of what to order, although a field consultant from headquarters may review the list and help you adapt it for regional preferences or tastes.

Some operations manuals are so explicit, they tell you just where to store or display every item that gets delivered. If you don't know what to do with something, call a franchisee whose building layout is similar to yours for advice.

If you need a special license or certification to operate your franchise, that subject will have been covered in training. But everyone, even home-based franchise owners, need business licenses. Levy suggests you contact your local town or city hall several weeks before you open and ask how to obtain one.

Beginning the Selling Process—Before You Have Something to Sell

During the weeks it takes to get your franchise built, you can get a jump-start on marketing your business and checking out the competition. "It's never too early to promote your new franchise," says Laurie Hobbs, director of marketing

"It's never too early to promote your new franchise."

communications for Dinner by Design. "We've had franchisees who joined their chambers of commerce six months in advance," she says, "and left our brochures and monthly menus on everyone's chairs before each meeting. It created a groundswell of interest." Other things you can do include:

- Buy ads in upcoming Yellow Pages. Service businesses depend on such listings. A new franchisee of Mr. Rooter, the Dwyer Group's plumbing concept, says he and his wife timed their opening with the delivery of new telephone books to residents of their Michigan town. But the books were sent out three weeks early that year, and by the time the couple returned from training, their voicemail was full of requests from new customers.

- Sign up for community events. The Super Suppers partners, Chris Nellis and Jay Charlesworth, and their families marched in their town's July 4th parade and passed out sample food at local events during the summer before their opening. At each event, they gathered names, phone numbers, and e-mail addresses for their database.

- Offer to provide free products or services as prizes for golf tournaments, fun runs, Little League tournaments, or other local sporting events.

- Purchase ads in program books of upcoming events. As you'll see in our section on advertising, your ads must follow a format provided by your franchisor. During training you were probably given a booklet of sample ads, brochures, and press releases. If your franchisor's marketing department doesn't offer the service, you may want to work with a local graphic designer now to lay out a simple format for the ads you place now and after you open.

- Approach local charities about cross-promotion opportunities during your Grand Opening. One Dinner by Design franchisee, for example, set aside an introductory night for volunteers of a local cancer research organization and donated part of her proceeds to the charity.

- Put together a local media list and gather rates for newspaper and radio advertising. Pay attention to advertising you see and hear now, to determine what stands out.

- Be on the lookout for local celebrities, politicians, community leaders, and other people you can invite to a VIP night. Check out other VIP events in your community to see who's there.

While you wait to open your doors, you should also attend the grand openings of other franchisees, to see what works. Even better, you can volunteer to help them.

Check Out the Competition

Linda Duke, president of Duke Marketing in San Rafael, California, suggests you spend part of your preopening time analyzing your competition. "If you don't know the weaknesses and promotional offers of your competitors, you will not be able to overcome your competitors' marketing strategy and attract their guests into your business," Duke says.

Find your competitors by looking up like businesses in the Yellow Pages, chamber of commerce or other local business directories, and online, by finding local units of competing franchise companies. Duke gives the following tips for analyzing their places in the market:

- Identify the basics—where they are, the hours they operate, and their price points.

- Examine their local and/or corporate Web sites to see how they're promoting their products or services. Are they targeting the same customers?

- If they have retail locations, stop in and build relationships with their front-line employees. By earning their confidence now, they may tell you information, like the results of sales events, that will be valuable later.

- Get on your competitors' mailing lists and join their special programs or clubs. "Naturally," Duke says, "you'll have to be discreet about whose name you put down. Perhaps you can use a relative with a different last name."

- Monitor the media to determine competitors' advertising programs and estimated expenditures. Figure out patterns. Do they advertise on certain days? What's their creative approach? When do they schedule special programs or sales?

- Count how many guests are walking in their doors at different times of the day and week. Do this again three months after you've opened, to see if you're taking away some of their market share.

Once you know what your competition offers, Duke says, you can schedule special sales events before theirs, for example. More important, once you know how your business differs from theirs, you can stress those points of differentiation in your promotional materials and advertising.

Hiring Employees to Help You Run Your Franchise

Unless you're opening a home-based business, you'll need people to help you run your new franchise. If you hired (and fired) workers in your previous jobs, you'll be way ahead of the curve here. Otherwise, you'll want to take your time finding and vetting the right employees. Your franchisor may offer guidelines, and even some personality tests, you can use to make the recruiting task easier. If not, you can check out the following suggestions offered by several franchisees.

Finding Your First Employees

While he was waiting for his Snip-its franchise to be built, Brian McMullin, of The Woodlands, Texas, had his hair cut in a different barbershop every two weeks. "If the stylist was good," he says, "I'd ask her if she wanted a new job." None of them did, but a couple referred him to friends who still work in his children's hair salon.

Although the labor market is tight, and it's more difficult to recruit people now, you have more options to find them, Levy says. It's much cheaper to post a job on Monster or other online job boards than it is to run a print ad in a daily metropolitan newspaper. If you're looking for young workers, they're more likely to see an online ad anyway. You can also run classified ads in local newspapers or stick "Help Wanted" signs in the window of your unopened business.

Christopher Nellis and Jay Charlesworth held a two-day job fair in their Super Suppers franchise during buildout. "We made a sign ourselves," says Nellis, "and hung it in the window. We were amazed at the quality of the women who walked in and applied—attorneys, teachers, a woman who'd had a catering company. They were all doing the stay-at-home mom thing and were looking for something else to do part-time."

If the people you're hiring require special training, like hair stylists, go to nearby vocational schools and make friends with the instructors. When they graduate, you can have "the pick of the litter," Levy says. Harry Johns, whose Cartridge World franchise sits between two Rutgers University dormitories, posted help-wanted signs on their bulletin boards.

If your franchise requires a lot of workers, you may want to follow San Antonio Church's Chicken franchisee Wayne Baker's strategy of mixing age groups. "Most of my employees are older people," Baker says, "but I like to hire a few teenagers, because they can bring in so much enthusiasm." Baker, by the way, nurtures his young workers and lets them fit their shift schedules around their studies. A young man who worked part-time while attending college "just graduated at the top of his class," Baker says.

Grady Love says he and his wife, Nancy, take on all help at their Honey-Baked Ham store in Rock Hill, South Carolina, on a conditional basis. "We spend a few weeks evaluating whether it will work for all of us," he says.

Unless all your applicants are attorneys with young children, you'll want to check their references. Past employers, however, are unlikely to verify anything on the telephone. Write to them on your new letterhead and ask when they employed an applicant. Because of the fear of litigation, companies no longer share information about former employees beyond these simple facts—when they worked there, what positions they held and, possibly, their salaries.

If your franchise deals with children, or if your employees will be working in customers' homes, you will want to pay a firm to do a thorough background check on them first, says Dave Hood of the iFranchise Group. Your franchisor may also provide a personality test to help you screen applicants. These tests can highlight candidates' strengths and weaknesses and may help you decide which applicants are best suited to your business.

"I like to hire a few teenagers, because they can bring in so much enthusiasm."

No matter whether you hire introverts or extroverts, one thing is almost certain: You'll hire too many of them. Levy says most new business owners overhire because they're afraid of being short-staffed. You'll probably lose some to attrition, or decide in a few weeks that some workers are more efficient than others and let some go.

Who Handles the Cash Register and Cleans the Bathroom?

If you're opening a small franchise and hiring a handful of people, it seems silly to spend your time writing out lengthy job descriptions. As Jay Charlesworth says of his new team, "They're all five-tool players. In baseball, that means they can handle any task—wash dishes, set up food stations, take reservations, and so on." But opening day is unlike any other day. As you'll see shortly, you'll be spending thousands of dollars to invite the community into your new business. This is not the time to be allocating tasks.

Your operations manual lists the number of employees you should have on duty for each shift or for each business day, and goes into detail about what they should do.

If you assign specific tasks to each new employee, it will be easier for your franchisor's opening team when it arrives to train them.

> *"They're all five-tool players. In baseball, that means they can handle any task."*

Here's a tip. Levy says new franchisees tend to hover. As soon as possible during your preopening trial run, leave your employees alone in your location. "If you keep bailing them out of every difficult situation, you'll all have a false sense of security," Levy says. It's better to let them learn to handle things on their own, before the real rush arrives.

Motivating Your New Workers

Fifty years ago, motivating employees was easier, because everyone came from the same population cohort and held similar values. Today, your workers may come from four distinct generations, with their own values, beliefs, and expectations. Linda Haneborg, senior vice president of marketing/communications for Express Personnel Services, recently outlined the four generation groups at the Annual Leadership Conference, hosted by the Women's Franchise Committee, at the 2007 International Franchise Association Convention.

According to Haneborg, your employees will fall into one—or all—of these groups: traditionalists, baby boomers, Generation Xers, and millennials.

Traditionalists

These are the 76 million people born between 1900 and 1945, who make up 10 percent of the workforce. They tend to be loyal, respectful, courteous, and fiscally conservative, and are motivated by flexible retirement options and a structured workplace environment. "Their worst discipline problem in school was chewing gum," Haneborg says.

"The traditionalist's worst discipline problem in school was chewing gum."

Here are some suggestions for recruiting and retaining Traditionalists:

- Stick to your schedule.
- Don't use slang or vulgar language.
- Dress appropriately.
- Respect their years of experience.

Baby Boomers

Boomers represent the largest contingent, the 80 million people born between 1946 and 1964, who make up 45 percent of our current workforce. Baby boomers, or the "me generation," are optimistic workaholics, with a strong work ethic and competitive edge. They grew up questioning authority and prefer to be asked, not told. They expect their bosses to be politically correct and to recognize their contributions.

Other tips for working with baby boomers include:

- Value their experiences.
- Provide new retirement options and flexible work schedules.
- Follow proper business etiquette.

Generation Xers

These are the baby boomers' children, and their exact opposites. The 46 million people born between 1965 and 1980 make up 30 percent of the workforce—

if they show up at all. They grew up in dual-income households, and many had TV sets as babysitters. They tend to be independent, suspicious of authority, and technologically savvy. In the workplace, they like to multitask, but hate to be micromanaged. They're driven more by work/life balance perks than money.

You can motivate Gen Xers by:

- Giving them fast feedback.
- Grooming them for management.
- Allowing them to multitask.

Millennials

The 76 million young people born between 1981 and 2000 are just entering the workforce. They make up 15 percent of employees now, but will become the bulk of your workers soon. Millennials are the antithesis of their Gen X older siblings and have characteristics that make their grandparents proud. They, too, tend to be hopeful, collaborative, and polite, in addition to having an innate talent for technology that keeps them on the Internet almost 24/7. Haneborg says. "They've never known a TV without a remote." Millennials like to be kept busy—perhaps because they're sleep-deprived—and will accept advice from mentors.

"They've never known a TV without a remote."

Other tips for hiring and keeping millennials happy include:

- Allow them to multitask.
- Appeal to old-fashioned values, like "making a difference."
- Don't move too slowly—they're used to a fast-paced world.

Unlike other small business owners who must hire employees and hope they work out, and work together, you belong to a system where dozens, or hundreds, of franchisees operate similar businesses. Before you extend job offers to anyone, talk to seasoned franchisees about which types, and ages, of employees do best in your business. Such advice, of course, is just a guideline. Your final hiring decisions will also be based on an applicant's industry experiences and other qualifications.

The mixture of ages and expectations makes motivating today's intergenerational workforce really difficult, as some franchisees have learned. Church's Chicken franchisee Wayne Baker (a traditionalist) says he uses cash bonuses to motivate his employees, who are baby boomers with a scattering of millennials. "If I'm making more money, my employees must be doing something right. Every month when my sales go over a certain level, I'll give my manager and employees a bonus," Baker says.

But cash bonuses may not work with some Generation Xers and other employees because:

- After a few months, employees expect to get bonuses, and become resentful when they don't.

- They don't link their behavior to the extra money.

- They don't care that much about money, and would prefer another incentive.

Baby boomer and MAACO franchisee Mike Murphy says, "When I first started, I told my workers (who are mostly Gen Xers), 'If you get all this done by 5:00 today, I'll give you a $25 bonus.' I never paid one out. But when I said, 'If you finish the week's work by Thursday, you can have Friday off without pay,' they were done by Thursday evening. They cared more about time off than about money."

The baby boomer franchisee of a Valvoline Instant Oil Change center reports that his employees, like most Gen Xers, respond best to instant rewards. Now he keeps $50 bills in his pocket, and hands one to any worker he sees providing extra customer service. And baby boomer John Ricky Garmon says the multigenerational cleaning crews of his Maids International franchise appreciate little things, like ice cream after a hard day. He's the one getting the bonus because, "my employees reproduce themselves, by bringing in their friends to work, too," Garmon says.

The Difficulty of Employee Discipline

Dealing with employees across generations is exacerbated when they're doing something wrong. JoAnne Shaw, CEO of the Coffee Beanery, Ltd. in Flushing,

Michigan, recommends that when you hire new employees, talk to them about how they like to communicate. Traditionalists and baby boomers, she says, like face-to-face conversations, while younger workers prefer e-mail, which they see as nonconfrontational. If a conflict arises, make employees aware of the problem via their chosen form of communication.

Other tips for dealing with difficult employees include this advice from *The Intentional Leader* by Kenneth Shaw, former chancellor of Syracuse University:

- Give praise and recognition when someone does a job well.
- Avoid blame and embarrassment when he or she doesn't.
- Focus on behavior, not the person.
- Have employees assess their own performances.
- Give timely, specific, and descriptive feedback.
- Provide modeling and training.

Multigenerational conflicts are not limited to employees. Shaw says, "When we started franchising, we had a lot of older franchisees who had taken buyouts from corporate jobs. Over the past couple of years we've accepted some younger (Generation Xer) franchisees who are into instant gratification. This generation has unrealistic expectations."

Opening Day Countdown

Your Opening Day (or Grand Opening), when you officially launch your business, is the most important day in your franchise career. The purpose of Opening Day is to create a customer base by inviting your community into your new location to sample your food, view your wares, or learn about your services. A successful Opening Day for any franchise with a retail location combines a strategic marketing campaign with a bit of street theater. Yes, you can have balloons, clowns, big blow-up gorillas, and even a band if it draws attention to your store.

During the training session I attended at Dinner by Design, Laurie Hobbs showed videos of successful franchisee openings. Dinner by Design's opening celebration is a two-day event, with a ribbon-cutting ceremony and product demonstrations for that VIP list of civic leaders on a Thursday or Friday, followed by a day of family-oriented activities on Saturday. In one video, we saw someone in a SpongeBob SquarePants costume jumping up and down and waving at traffic or posing for photos with little kids.

"I did that," said trainee Bryan Hildebrand, "when my friends opened their franchise in Frankfort (Illinois). They'd better reciprocate when I open mine."

Hobbs said that meal preparation is such a new field, franchisees (and their friends) have to pull out all stops to draw attention to their businesses. She said each franchisee is expected to spend a minimum of $7,500 on her Grand Opening, then passed out budgets from franchisees who spent even more. "Opening Day is like running a marathon," says Hobbs. "If you open strong, it's a lot easier to maintain the momentum than if you're running from behind."

> *"Opening Day is like running a marathon. If you open strong, it's a lot easier to maintain the momentum than if you're running from behind."*

Your Opening Day Game Plan

Your franchisor may not expect you to spend as much, but it will want you to submit an Opening Day budget and plan several weeks before you open. Here are some of the elements of a Grand Opening plan and their costs:

- *Trade area demographics.* Collect demographic data from your chamber of commerce, local realtors, and local newspapers and radio stations. Who lives in your community, in the neighborhoods your location is closest to? Study their ages, incomes, education levels, places of employment, number of children, whether they rent or own their homes, and so on, to target your product or service to their immediate needs. Cost: Free.

- *Local organizations.* What groups do your target customers belong to? Parent-teacher clubs? Rotary or other business-related groups? Trade associations? Join them or, if that's not possible, ask about renting their mailing lists. Many local chambers of commerce will give new members a one-time use of their mailing lists. Cost: Dues to whichever organizations you join.

- *Local visibility.* Provide giveaways, like T-shirts with your logo, during parades and community events, or distribute gift cards that give a discount when redeemed in your location. Cost: Varies—typically, $50 to several hundred dollars.

- *Preopening press releases and invitations to local media.* Call the local print media and ask how they want to receive press release information—by e-mail, fax, or snail-mail. Should it be double-spaced? Your franchisor should provide fill-in-the-blanks press releases you can retype and send out. Ask your franchise marketing department for templates or design help in creating Opening Day invitations to send to the press and your VIP list. Cost: A few hundred dollars, depending on size of mailing.

- *E-mail announcements.* Send to all those e-mail addresses you've been gathering. Cost: Free.

- *Postcards to residents of targeted neighborhoods.* Your franchisor can recommend a mailing service. Cost: Approximately $500.

- *Refreshments for a "soft" opening for your friends and family.* You and your new employees will demonstrate your services, show off your products, cook your menu items, and so forth in a nonthreatening atmosphere. Cost: If your franchise is not food-related, approximately $200 for wine and cheese or other treats.

- *Printed flyers and door hangers.* Distribute to targeted businesses and neighborhoods. Cost: a few hundred dollars, plus pizza for the kids who distribute them.

- *Advertising.* Hobbs says your choice of ad media depends on your location, your type of franchise, and your target market. A series of radio commercials on one or more local stations can cost $2,000 or more, but is only effective if you live in a suburb or rural area without many competing stations. Remote radio broadcasts from your location during your opening cost $1,000 to $2,000. Inclusion in direct mail coupon envelopes from Money Mailer or other services can cost a few hundred dollars, but upscale customers may not open them. Dinner by Design franchisees spend most of their media budgets on display ads and inserts in local newspapers. Inserts, Hobbs says, are often more effective because, "Our customers don't have time to read the paper." Cost: $4,000 to $6,000.

- *Balloons, banners, "Coming Soon" signs, pennants, and the like.* Many franchisors will sell you a kit of attention-getters. Cost: The one at Dinner by Design costs $350.

- *Costume rental for Opening Day mascot.* Cost: About $100—more if you don't have a friend like Bryan Hildebrand and have to pay someone to wear it.

Opening Day is so important to Sport Clips franchisees, says CEO Gordon Logan, that the franchise requires them to spend $15,000 to promote the launch of their "man-friendly" hair salons. "We're thinking of increasing that to $20,000," Logan says. "If a great Grand Opening means you can get to breakeven faster, wouldn't you rather spend the money on advertising now than on working capital later?"

Logan says franchisees spend most of that budget on direct mailings to targeted customers, radio, and, in some regions, TV advertising. "It's worth it to pay a talent fee for a radio disc jockey to broadcast from your store," he says.

Like many franchisors, Sport Clips sends out a member of the franchise marketing team a week before a franchisee's Opening Day, to help with the last-minute details. "It's important to contact all the businesses in town to let them know you're opening," Logan says. "We're at the high end of value salons, and compete with franchises like Fantastic Sam's and Supercuts, and have to get men inside our stores to appreciate what we offer. Men and teenage boys like our sports theme and flat-screen TVs, and once they realize we provide hot towels for their necks, and shoulder massages, they'll drive an extra mile or two to return."

Office-Based Openings

Contacting local businesses is even more important for new office-based franchises, like personnel services and accounting firms. The other tenants of your building would probably frown on an inflatable gorilla in the lobby, but they would like a tour of your office space—if it includes a buffet table with donuts and coffee in the morning or sandwiches and cold drinks at lunchtime. Opening Day

> *"The other tenants of your building would probably frown on an inflatable gorilla in the lobby, but they would like a tour of your office space."*

promotions for such franchises include advertising in local business journals, press releases, and direct mail announcements to local companies.

Launching Your Franchise from Your Living Room—and Other Spaces

You'll have more of a challenge launching your home-based franchise—unless you want to invite the press and a clown or two into the spare bedroom you just converted to an office. Most home-based franchisees announce their openings by sending press releases to local newspapers, paying for ads in newspapers, sending out general and targeted mailings, networking through the chamber of commerce and other organizations, and telling everyone they meet about their business. As you recall, Carleen Peaper drew attention to her new Cruise Planners franchise by offering to write a column on cruises for her local newspaper.

Paige Schulte says that when she and her friend, Jessica Inzaina, started their KidzArt franchise in Sacramento, every day was Opening Day. "We offer after-school art programs in school buildings, so we had to do grassroots marketing, and introduce ourselves to the principals and staffs of dozens of schools," Schulte says. The effort paid off, because the women now offer programs in 44 schools and serve more than 700 students a month. At the end of their first year in business, Schulte and Inzaina were named their system's Franchisees of the Year.

Opening Softly First

Since Opening Day is so important, most franchisors recommend that you begin with a dry run. Restaurant franchises have shakedown periods, called "soft" openings, which can last from a couple of days to several weeks before they officially open to the public. During this time, the franchisee and his or her employees prepare and serve menu items to their friends and relatives, who act like customers but don't pay for their food. To simulate the pressure of serving strangers, you can invite members of the organizations you belong to, or groups from your kids' school or your church or synagogue in for free meals.

Franchisees of hotels and retail food operations also hold soft openings to enable their employees to practice their skills without annoying paying guests. In fact, franchisees of any concept that serves customers directly can benefit from trying out their business first on friends and relatives. As you recall from the chapter on training, Luxury Bath Systems suggests that new installers line the bathtubs of their neighbors before offering their services to the general public. LearningRX franchisee Betsy McLaughlin practiced her franchise's techniques for helping children with learning difficulties on a neighbor's son.

If your franchisor provides no guidance in this area, you can design your own shakedown by offering to clean carpets, install blinds, repair dripping faucets, trim hair or lawns, or provide any other service for free to people who will give you an honest assessment of your services. As a bonus, you may turn these faux customers into real ones.

After Opening Day: Keeping Those Customers Coming Back

When you own a small business, you're marketing all the time. In franchising, your marketing program begins within your business, making every aspect of your customers' visit or service call so positive they'll use you again and tell their friends about you.

My first job after college was in the public relations department of the Drake Hotel in Chicago (now a Hilton property, but then privately owned). Often, as I walked through the front door, I'd hear a bellman greet an incoming guest by name: "Mr. Morris, it's so good to see you again. Is Mrs. Morris with you? I believe we have your favorite room, with a view of Lake Michigan, all ready." The personal greeting was repeated again at the reservation desk. I was amazed that the employees remembered so much about guests they hadn't seen in months.

Of course, they didn't remember. A VIP list circulated each morning with the names and descriptions of previous guests checking in that day. The Drake was famous for entertaining dignitaries—Queen Elizabeth stayed there once. But it was also famous for making each guest feel as special as a queen.

You can do the same with your franchise. Wayne Baker is in his Church's Chicken restaurant every day, greeting customers by name. You can easily create a computer database to help you remember customers' names and preferences. If you operate a hotel or restaurant that takes reservations, circulate your own VIP list each day to your employees. Service franchisees can alert workers about who is coming in that day to pick up a print order or repaired car. Order takers with caller ID can quickly access customer databases and personalize their greetings: "Mrs. Morris, it's so good to hear from you. Do you want us to clean all the carpets in your downstairs again?"

Here are some additional tips for winning repeat customers:

- Offer loyalty cards that give customers a discount after a certain number of purchases.

- Send birthday cards and/or provide discounts for the month of each customer's birthday.

- Act on customers' suggestions. At Dinner by Design, for example, franchisees started meal delivery services after customers requested them.

- Celebrate events, like Cinco de Mayo, that are important to segments of your customer base.

- Provide unexpected amenities, like free gourmet coffee to customers waiting to pick something up. One retail franchisee we visited fills her customer bathroom with fancy lotions and soaps.

- Hire friendly employees who look customers in the eye during conversations. You can hold "friendliest employee" contests or pass out instant bonuses to workers who provide excellent customer interactions.

- Agree to do something extra, even if it may not be cost-effective. Express Personnel franchisee Becky Kortjohn says, "A speaker's group once needed 80 people to work a one-day special event. I passed the request on to an office that was struggling, but the franchisee turned it down. 'Do you know how many people we'd have to call to get 80 workers?' she asked. Of course I knew, because that's the kind of service we provide our customers every day."

Your Franchise Ad Fund

You're contributing 1 to 5 percent of your revenues to an ad fund, so once you're open, your franchisor will take care of all advertising—right? The short answer is, probably not. Franchisees of strong national brands, like Subway and McDonald's, certainly benefit from national television commercials. But the majority of franchisors have fewer than 100 units and can't afford national, or even local, television ads. Even if they could afford them, such commercials would not be appropriate to promote the majority of franchise businesses.

"If you ask our franchisees what they want," says Jim Wassell, chief marketing officer for the ServiceMaster Clean of Memphis, "they'll say they want to be on TV or want our name on the side of a NASCAR vehicle. But neither one of those will hit our target market."

ServiceMaster Clean has more than 4,500 franchisees that provide cleaning and janitorial services to residences and commercial buildings and disaster Restoration, to homes and businesses. In 2007, ServiceMaster Clean had a $4.8 million ad fund budget, with franchisees contributing 0.5 to 1 percent of their revenues, and corporate contributing 5 percent of their revenues. Expenditures are: regional marketing, 30 percent; internal and external sales force, 30 percent; national trade shows, 15 percent; and Web initiatives, 14 percent.

"If you ask our franchisees what they want, they'll say they want to be on TV or want our name on the side of a NASCAR vehicle. But neither one of those will hit our target market."

As in over half of franchise systems, an elected group of franchisees, called the National Franchise Council at ServiceMaster Clean, meet with corporate executives to approve those expenditures. An outside accounting firm audits the fund annually, and reports on all expenditures are communicated to franchisees via the franchise's intranet site and in newsletters.

As you'll see in Chapter Sixteen on disputes, the administration of an ad fund can become a contentious issue between franchisees and their franchisor. Issues may include:

- Does the fund pay the salaries of corporate marketing employees?
- Who gets the 15 percent commissions paid for media placements?
- Who decides which regions or cities get an advertising blitz?
- Must every franchisee also contribute to a regional ad fund or participate in an advertising co-operative?

At Batteries Plus, says director of advertising and marketing support Cathleen Stewart, franchisees contribute 1 percent of their sales to a national marketing fund. "But it's a misconception that the national fund is used for national advertising," she says. "We have about 300 stores and feel we need 500 to 600 to benefit from a national ad campaign."

In the meantime, a 16-person in-house team designs ad formats that can be used by franchisees to run in their local newspapers, in the Yellow Pages, and as wraps for their vehicles, Stewart says. The team includes two people who specialize in helping new franchisees with their Grand Openings. The franchise ad fund is used to help support in-house services, for new market development, and to pay for services like the store locator on the franchise Web site and its 800-number. An elected six-person franchisee council must approve all ad fund distributions.

You may also be required to contribute another percentage of your sales to a local advertising co-op or regional ad fund. Franchisees in a geographic region meet frequently to plan marketing strategies and pool their resources to save money on media buys, including the costs of newspaper, radio, and cable television advertising. A by-product of participation, say many of the franchisees we've talked to, is the chance to share tips and war stories with fellow franchisees.

Stuart Johnson was an area developer for two fast-food concepts, operating six stores himself and supporting five subfranchisees who operated the others. Johnson, who sold his stores and now teaches classes on franchising, offers these tips about working with a regional ad co-op:

- The first time you attend an ad co-op meeting, notice which franchisees are the leaders. Are they successful? "These are the people you want to get to know, so you can pick their brains on how to succeed in your local market area," Johnson says.

"We could easily have disputes over whether to advertise on the local country or rock radio station."

- Does the co-op have a marketing plan? If not, Johnson says, ask your franchisor to help you develop one for your region. "Your franchisor is in a better position than you are to know who your target market is and what types of advertising—coupons, radio spots, newspaper inserts, and so forth—work best to reach them," he advises.

- Be aware that ad co-op members make decisions according to the votes of those present—and that votes are usually allocated according to the number of stores/territories each franchisee has. Since Johnson had five stores in one system, he was entitled to five votes, while the individual operators in his group each had one vote.

- Discussions can get heated. Johnson warns, "We could easily have disputes over whether to advertise on the local country or rock radio station."

Promoting Your Franchise on Your Own

Your franchisor may also require you to spend another percentage of your revenues on local marketing. Even if no such number is stipulated in your UFOC, you'll want to spend as much as you can afford to attract customers during your first year in business. Again, your franchisor's ad team can help you design a campaign. By planning ahead, you can receive discounts on display ads or 30-second announcements from your local radio station by ordering several such "buys" in advance. You'll want to time your ads according to the promotion schedules of your competitors and to coincide with any special promotions planned by your franchisor.

Marketing communications expert Linda Duke offers these tips to promote your franchise on an ongoing basis:

- Run newspaper display ads on a consistent basis in your community newspaper. Always request that your ad be placed on the right-hand page, preferably in the bottom right corner. Always inquire about the possibility of using trade in place of cash.

- Contact your local cable television station about the cost of advertising. It may be less expensive than you'd think. Talk to your customers about which cable programs they watch, and then advertise there.

- If your business is near a movie theater complex, consider buying one of the on-screen ads they run before the trailers.

Community Spirit

Part of local advertising involves weaving your business into the fabric of the local community. During a luncheon for franchisees attending a recent IFA convention, speaker Nancy Michaels, president of Grow Your Business Network,

Yeah, There's a Franchise for That...

Wherever there's a market gap, we can be sure a new franchise will jump into it. David Hearld, of Hinsdale, Illinois, has created Profit-Tell whose franchisees help small businesses with their marketing. Hearld says his franchisees can provide services "on the fly and on the cheap," including writing and sending out one-shot press releases, for $350 or creating and recording 30- or 60-second radio commercials for $400. Regular services include writing and recording promotional messages for overhead announcements in your store or for your telephone when you put customers on hold. Hearld says, "We know franchisees can't afford to run half-page ads in newspapers. We help them find marketing touchpoints where they can reach their customers and spread out their marketing dollars."

of Concord, Massachusetts, and attending franchisees offered these tips for generating local goodwill:

- Ask good customers for testimonials. Frame them and hang them on the walls.

- Celebrate the unexpected. Instead of sending her clients Christmas gifts, Michaels says she sends gifts during the Chinese New Year or the Fourth of July.

- Sponsor sports teams. A Sport Clips franchisee gives free haircuts to the coaches and assistant coaches of the team he sponsors and passes out discount coupons to the players.

- A Dunkin' Donuts franchisee passes out cards that say "Good for a free donut and coffee" to everyone he meets.

- A Dairy Queen franchisee decorates his restaurant according to the local high school's sports season. He hangs poster-sized action shots of players on the walls, and paints their names and numbers on his parking lot curb stops. "It costs nothing to do," he says, "and the players bring their friends in. We're building loyalty."

- Admit your mistakes. When a print shop franchisee made a mistake on an important order, he had the local Cookies by Design franchise create a giant cookie eraser, and delivered it with his apologies.

- Plan special events with noncompeting businesses. A Dinner by Design kitchen teamed up with a nearby wine shop for an evening of wine and food, for instance.

- Educate your customers by bringing in a speaker on a topic of interest, suggests Linda Duke. Of course, you'll pass out samples or demonstrate your services after the speech.

E-mail Marketing

A surprisingly inexpensive way to promote your business is e-mail newsletters.

Alternative Board franchisee Paul Detlefs says he uses an e-mail service to send an electronic newsletter to the members of the boards he facilitates, prospects, and business networks every month. He says, "I met a business owner at an informational meeting we'd sponsored and added his name to my e-mail list. Two years later, the man called and said he'd just read the newsletter and was ready to join one of our groups. Group members pay us $400 to

Franchise-Style Guerilla Marketing

MAACO franchisee Mike Murphy says he never wears shirts or drives cars that don't say MAACO. "The biggest gripe waiters have is that customers are always stealing their pens, so everywhere I eat, I give the waiter a handful of pens—that all say MAACO," Murphy says. "During political campaigns, I send workers out with campaign signs that say 'Vote for MAACO.'"

Murphy once cut an old VW bug in half, wedged the rear part against the wall of his store, and drew skidmarks across the lawn, to make it look like a car crash. "When I drove by later, the police and TV camera crews were there," Murphy says. "I kept driving and let them figure it out for themselves."

$1,000 a month to belong, according to the size of their companies, and this guy was in the middle of that range. The cost to recruit him: zero."

E-mail marketing is an inexpensive tool you can use to keep in touch with customers and recruit new ones. Kevin O'Brien, director of business partner programs for Constant Contact in Waltham, Massachusetts, says his company helps thousands of franchisees create and distribute e-mail newsletters at rates as low as $15 a month for 100 addresses. Abrakadoodle franchise CEO Mary Rogers says each of her system's 70-plus franchisees use Constant Contact to send quarterly newsletters to parents, teachers, and representatives of the facilities where they hold their children's art enrichment classes. "We keep parents informed of upcoming events, like our summer camp registrations, and sometimes have tie-ins with our business partners. Last summer we included a coupon for ice cream at MaggieMoo's and an art lesson for creating a collage sundae," Rogers says.

If you mail a print newsletter, you never know if it gets read or tossed. With e-mail, you can see exactly who opens it and when he or she does. Rogers says, "Our franchisees say they can send a newsletter out at 5:00 P.M. and by 7:00 P.M. mothers are on their Web sites, signing up their children for classes." You can even call up a status report to see which customers failed to open your newsletter and which ones forward it on to their friends.

Ask the Professor

What mistakes do new franchisees make when setting up their first franchise?

Franchisees make some common mistakes in setting up their first franchise. Many of the mistakes are predictable, and include:

- Going into a franchise that you can't afford. You need to set aside adequate working capital to operate and advertise the business until you get enough customers through the door to provide positive cash flow.

- Underestimating the amount of time you will spend in the business if you are an owner/operator. You will be working long hours with little or no time off to get the business operating smoothly.

- Thinking that you can sit behind the counter waiting for the customers to walk through the door and come to you, or sitting by the phone waiting for it to ring. You need to be proactive in marketing your product or service. In order to succeed in your first, and subsequent, franchises, you need to be a people person and have good interpersonal skills. You will be in direct contact with your customers, vendors, employees, and the franchisor. You need to be able to negotiate good terms with your vendors; greet your customers with warmth and friendliness, and motivate them to come back; and you need to communicate effectively with your employees, motivate them, and get them to buy into your vision for the business.

- Staffing is one of the most stressful aspects of setting up a first franchise for many franchisees. Many new franchisees don't know how to hire employees, what to pay them without breaking the bank, or how to fire undesirable employees. They may hire someone who is overqualified because he or she has such excellent credentials, but the person will quickly become bored and move on. Franchisees need help from the franchisor in determining how to best staff their stores during busy seasons. I made the mistake when I was a franchisee of hiring all but three of my employees from the university that was two blocks away. At spring break, all my university employees left for a week. Fortunately, the customer base

(continued)

didn't leave, and we were swamped. The high school students who worked in the store started calling their friends to come in and be trained. After that experience, I employed a mixture of high school and college students. Additionally, I hired local kids who came home for the summers and school holidays from their out-of-state universities to work in the store when my regulars were gone. Many of them were already trained because they worked in the same franchise in another state.

- Paying your initial employees too much is a problem that many new franchisees face. Test the market to see what it will bear. You may want to pay a little more than minimum wage.

- Trying to be everyone's best friend is another common mistake that new franchisees make. You need to be able to motivate, guide, inspire, and, perhaps, fire your employees. It is difficult if you're going to have to fire your best friend.

How long should you test your concept before your Grand Opening?

It depends whether you are a new concept in the area. You need to decide whether to conduct soft-opening advertising or grand-opening advertising.

A soft opening means opening your location without any unusual fanfare or special attention. You keep the advertising and promotional efforts to a minimum and follow the retail marketing programs generally recommended by the franchisor for that time of year. You may throw a party for your family and friends when you first open your doors, to give your employees a feeling for what it is like to serve customers. This allows you to work with your new staff and develop good team spirit while ensuring all the bugs are ironed out. The soft-opening period is considered as a trial run and is usually six to eight weeks before the Grand Opening.

Grand Openings are the official introduction of the franchise to the community. You should send special invitations to local politicians, dignitaries, media, and community groups. These events are designed to be exciting for everyone. Many franchisors will have you set aside $5,000 to $10,000 in an account for your Grand Opening. You may want to have local ranking dignitaries perform the ribbon-cutting ceremony.

PART FOUR

Franchising Today… and Tomorrow

In our final chapters, we'll look at franchising within a larger context. Unfortunately, franchisor/franchisee relationships are not always harmonious, so in Chapter Sixteen we include information about the main causes of contention—and how to avoid them. In Chapter Seventeen, we look at the advances women and minorities have made in franchising, and point out where improvements are needed. And, in our final chapter, we introduce you to franchisee millionaires and show how you, too, may one day make the Forbes list of wealthiest people. We also look at franchising's future and the roles you can play in your newly chosen industry.

CHAPTER SIXTEEN

Trouble in Paradise: Keeping the Peace with Your Franchisor

We hate to keep coming back to the marriage analogy, but it's really apt in a discussion of relationship problems. Franchisees begin their new relationships with the highest of hopes. They've spent months researching the industry and their chosen franchisor, been empowered by positive Discovery Day and training experiences, and been assisted through their own Grand Openings. Everything's wonderful—until it isn't.

Disputes between franchisees and their franchisors are common. Most are over minor issues—not enough visits from the regional support team, too many unannounced inspections—and most are settled quickly. Sometimes, though, disputes become so contentious they make headlines. We've recently seen newspaper articles about Subway franchisees suing company founder Fred DeLuca, or about Quiznos franchisees and their legal battles with their Denver franchisor.

So, What Can Go Wrong?

Thankfully, most franchisee/franchisor disputes don't make headlines. The majority of franchisors work hard to settle disagreements long before they reach class-action status. Lawsuits are bad for business. Prospective franchisees shy away from systems embroiled in litigation and too many lawsuits paint the industry with a tainted brush. Old-timers fear a return to the Minnie Pearl era, and the resources of young franchise companies are stretched thin now, without adding heavy legal expenses.

This does not mean your franchisor will back down over issues you feel are unfair. Your Franchise Agreement, after all, was written by the franchisor's attorneys and is tipped in its favor for a purpose. That long list of franchisee obligations in Item 11 isn't there to hassle you; it's there to maintain consistency.

Most franchise relationship problems, including high-profile lawsuits, revolve around a few basic issues. We'll look at each of them, and talk about what they can mean to your system.

Your Franchisor Is Purchased by Another Company

Private equity firms love the steady returns of franchising, and if your franchisor is sold to one, it could be good news. In recent years, private equity firms, alone or in partnerships, have purchased Dunkin' Brands, Burger King, Shoney's, Jamba Juice, Damon's Grill, Marie Callender's Restaurant & Bakery, Schlotzsky's, Sbarro, Church's Chicken, Lady of America, Del Taco, and Sylvan Learning Centers.

Financial firms tend to buy underperforming concepts that they can turn around, then sell at a profit three to five years later to another private equity firm or to the public, through an initial public offering (IPO). In late 2004, for example, investment bank Arcapita purchased Church's Chicken, a chain whose franchisees had suffered under years of stagnant growth and falling same-store sales. "The first thing we did," says Church's new CEO Harsha Agadi, "was go out to visit our franchisees."

In less than two years, the new owners moved Church's from negative growth to same-store sales increases, introduced new products, and opened 200 more stores. The franchisees we talked to are thrilled.

But franchisors are also purchased by strategic buyers, corporations, or other franchise companies that want to expand in the same industry. The Kahala Group in Scottsdale, for example, is building a stable of compatible fast-food brands, including Ranch 1, TacoTime, Samurai Sam's, and Blimpie's. If your fast-food franchisor were to be purchased by Kahala, you'd gain a seasoned management team and the opportunity to co-brand (two concepts within a single unit) with one of its other concepts.

But if your franchisor is purchased by a company with a competing brand, all you might gain is trouble. Until the Arcapita buyout, Church's Chicken had been owned by AFC, America's Favorite Chicken, which also owned Popeyes Fried Chicken. Church's franchisees felt that Popeyes operators were awarded the best sites and were given a better choice in menu items.

Mail Boxes, Etc. franchisees expected no such conflict in 2003, when shipping giant UPS bought their franchisor from its previous owner, a cash-strapped office products conglomerate. Three thousand franchisees followed their new owners' directives, redecorating their red, white, and blue stores in UPS brown. But about 400 franchisees fought the change. Most of the dissidents sold out, closed, or went independent, but 130 resisted and still operate from flag-colored outlets. Another 300 made the switch to brown, but claim that the new business model is less profitable. When they felt their franchisor was not responding to their complaints, both groups filed lawsuits and, as of press time, decisions were still pending.

Encroachment: When a New Franchise Steals Your Market Share

A Connecticut Quiznos franchisee told *Franchise Times* that his sales dropped from $15,000 a week to $8,000 after a second store opened in his town. He complained to his franchisor, but had no recourse, because Quiznos offers no protected territories in its UFOC.

Encroachment is a major issue in franchising. Once you develop a strong market for your product or service, your franchisor may see an opportunity to make even more money, by placing a second unit nearby. If you have no exclusive rights to your territory—and if you haven't paid the franchisor additional fees to add more units to your area—you have no way to stop competing franchises from being built.

But that doesn't stop franchisees from filing suits against their encroaching franchisors. Each year the American Bar Association's Forum on Franchising publishes its Annual Franchise and Distribution Law Developments book, a synopsis of franchise lawsuits filed in the previous year. Every edition contains a few encroachment lawsuits; and in every situation, if the franchise agreement provides no exclusive territories, the franchisor wins.

The courts see franchising as a business model based on a contract, and judges make their decisions on what is written in your franchise contract, not what you think is fair.

> *"Judges make their decisions on what is written in your franchise contract, not what you think is fair."*

Encroachment from Cyberspace

Many disputes now focus on Internet sales. What if your franchisor launches a Web site and starts to sell its products directly to your customers? Most franchisors and their franchisees reach compromises on Internet sales, by redirecting orders to local franchisees or by sharing revenues with their franchise communities, as we'll see in the Sylvan case study in this chapter.

When the franchisor refuses to share Internet proceeds, frustrated franchisees file lawsuits. Because Internet selling came after many franchise agreements were written, judges often have no language to interpret, and sometimes these franchisees prevail. In a 2006 case filed by franchisees of Pro Golf of America, their UFOC authorized the franchisor to sell directly over the Internet "as long as those sales did not occur in a franchisee's territory." The judge still ruled in favor of the franchisor, because, he said, there was no proof that customers were within franchisees' territories when they placed their orders.

Misrepresentation: When You're Promised One Thing and . . .

Disputes arise over what franchisees believed when buying their franchises and what actually occurs. Too often these disagreements are based on oral promises made during the selling process—"Don't worry that there's no protected territory. We'd never open a store within four miles of yours"—that run counter to what's in the franchise agreement. If your sales representative said something during courtship and you didn't get it in writing, you have little chance of winning a lawsuit.

In 2006, franchisees of Moe's Southwest Grill, for example, filed a lawsuit against their Atlanta, Georgia, franchisor, claiming, according to the ABA book, "that Moe's misrepresented the overall initial investment expenses and that it had perfected a system for operating its restaurants." Since none of these promises were tied to express terms in their franchise agreement, the court dismissed their claim.

When Your Business Model Changes

Sometimes a franchisor will change its business model in a way that affects franchisees' ability to make money.

For years, franchisees of General Nutrition Centers (GNC) of Pittsburgh, for example, were free to purchase products from outside vendors, says a longtime New Jersey franchisee. But when other franchisors that also sell vitamins and health products moved into the marketplace, the franchisor changed its policies, requiring franchisees to purchase products only through GNC warehouses. And to win customers from its competitors, the operators of corporate GNC stores often sold products on a "buy one, get one free promotion" at prices lower than they charged franchisees for the same items, the franchisees allege. A group of franchisees filed a class-action lawsuit, accusing their franchisor of "predatory pricing."

"You can't always count on the concept of fairness to help you in a dispute."

The action is still pending, says Gerald Marks, of Marks & Klein in Red Bank, New Jersey, who is representing the franchisees. "Underlying every contract is something called the 'implied covenant of good faith and fair dealing,'" says Marks. "You can't, during the term of a franchise, give something with your right hand and take it away with your left hand. The law recognizes fairness."

But you can't always count on the concept of fairness to help you in a dispute. When a McDonald's franchisee in Washington state sued his franchisor over his rights to acquire more restaurants, the judge ruled for McDonald's, saying that "there is no 'free floating' duty of good faith" that overrides specific contract terms.

When Your Franchisor's Business Model Doesn't Change

Franchisees also get upset when their franchisor fails to adapt its business model to current times—not adding healthy options to its menus, for example.

When Snap-on Tools, of Kenosha, Wisconsin, started franchising in 1991, most Americans drove cars that needed frequent repairs. Franchisees purchased service routes, of 200 to 225 service stations and mechanic shops, and purchased Snap-on tools to resell to these customers. But as cars became more efficient and broke down less frequently, business dropped off. Franchisees were still required to buy tools from their franchisor on a regular basis, but couldn't sell them, so several thousand of them joined a class-action lawsuit against the company.

In July 2006, Snap-on settled with more than 6,000 current and former franchisees, paying out $38 million and forgiving more than twice that amount in debts owed by former franchisees. The tool company also pledged to update its franchise model.

When Your Franchisor Controls the Supply Line

One of the reasons anyone joins a franchise is to benefit from the cost efficiencies a large system provides. Since franchisees use so many chicken breasts, or ceramic tiles, during a year, the franchisor negotiates lower prices. Often, suppliers pay a commission, or rebate, to the franchisor for placing all those orders. Or the franchisor may take over the supply chain itself, buying up and warehousing products, then delivering them to franchisees on an as-needed basis.

Many franchisee/franchisor disputes focus on supply rebates and pricing. In lawsuits, judges rely on the contract. If a franchise agreement explicitly states that a franchisor will collect rebates on supply orders and does not specify what the money will be used for, the franchisees tend to lose their lawsuits.

A decision in a major lawsuit focusing on what happens when a franchisor takes over an entire supply chain is still pending. Franchisees and former franchisees of Quiznos Subs filed a class-action lawsuit in November 2006, contending they were forced to buy food and supplies from Quiznos or their affiliates at inflated prices, forcing many of them out of business.

When Your Franchisor Controls Your Ad Monies

Another area ripe for disagreement is the ad fund that franchisees contribute a percentage of their sales to each month. Disputes arise when ad dollars seem to favor one region of the country, and its franchisees, over another, or when franchisors use funds at their own discretion, paying for a trade show booth to attract more franchisees, for instance. A few years ago, so many franchisees filed complaints with the FTC or lawsuits over this issue that many franchisors gave franchisee representatives a seat on committees that determine how ad monies are doled out.

At Subway, in Milford, Connecticut, the franchisor answered complaints by forming the Subway Franchisee Advertising Fund Trust, setting up a franchisee-run national advertising program. In 2006, the franchisor began drafting new franchise agreements that would take back control of ad fund contributions. The North American Association of Subway Franchisees, representing more than 14,500 restaurants, filed a lawsuit against their franchisor, claiming that company owners were unlawfully taking control of their advertising fund program. The case is pending.

Noncompetes: Why Can't I Operate Wanda's Window Washing Company?

Even former franchisees have disputes with their franchisors. Most franchise agreements contain noncompete clauses, forbidding a former franchisee from operating a similar business from the same location, or within the same territory, for a number of years after they've left the system. Courts generally rule in favor of franchisors when ex-franchisees do something blatant, like take down the franchisor's signs but continue to serve the same menu items or perform the same services.

But not always. The reasoning behind noncompetes is that an entire franchise system is weakened if a former franchisee uses trade secrets—proprietary information, secret recipes, confidential procedures, and so on—to compete against franchisees that are still in the system. In a recent Florida case, a judge ruled in favor of former franchisees of Pirtek USA, a Rockledge, Florida, company that provides hydraulic hoses and accessories for on-site replacement. Pirtek sued when the ex-franchisees continued offering customers the same services. The judge ruled that the franchise had no trade secrets to protect, and that since no other franchisee operated within 200 miles of the ex-franchisees no one was getting hurt.

Terminations: Getting Those Signs Down

Franchisors spend almost as much money getting rid of franchisees as they do attracting them in the first place. All franchise agreements spell out the reasons a franchisor can oust franchisees from its system—not paying royalties, not keeping their premises up to system standards, being convicted of a crime, not paying taxes, and others. Agreements also include a "cure" date, a time period during which the franchisee has to catch up on royalty payments or make necessary repairs to his or her unit.

If the franchisee still doesn't comply, the franchisor sends out a notice of termination, requiring the franchisee to take down its signs and remove all its trademarks from the location. If that doesn't work, the franchisor goes into court for an injunction (a court order requiring a person or corporation to stop doing something). Such court actions are so common that when the *New York*

Times printed a list of the top ten companies that have the most lawsuits over trademark issues, it included three franchisors—Cendant (the parent company of several hotel and real estate chains), Dunkin' Donuts, and Baskin-Robbins.

What If You, Too, Fall Behind in Your Royalties?

We've just seen cases in which franchisors went to court to get rid of franchisees. Is that the fate you're facing if you fall behind in your royalty payments or can't afford required renovations to your unit?

When Things Get Really Ugly

Here's a synopsis of some colorful termination disputes:

- A Kumon franchisee in California refused to stop operating his franchise, which tutors young children in math, after he'd been convicted of battery to a child.

- The operator of a Ramada Hotel in upstate New York stopped paying royalties, but refused to take down the sign because the termination notice had been sent to his brother George, who had been dead for three years. It seems that when the original franchisee passed on, his brother continued to run the hotel in George's name.

- A terminated GNC franchisee in Pennsylvania would not give up his stores, even though his franchisor held the leases. When GNC sent people to take them back, he refused to let them in the door.

- A&W Restaurants tried to stop a new Illinois franchisee from opening a restaurant (and offered to refund his investment) when they learned that a Dairy Queen was about to open next door. The franchisee opened anyway. When he lost all his money and had to close, he sued A&W for misrepresentation.

- Baskin-Robbins terminated a California franchisee who had been convicted of tax evasion, for putting tens of thousands of dollars people paid him for ice cream directly into his own pockets. The franchisee countersued, claiming that shutting him down would be a "breach of his contract."

Not necessarily, says an attorney whose clients are franchisors. "No franchisor wants to throw a good franchisee out on his ear," she says. "If you're behind in your payments, you'll have to pay something, but most of my clients will give you a longer time to cure a default than the period they list in their UFOCs."

> *"No franchisor wants to throw a good franchisee out on his ear."*

If the problem is noncompliance with franchise standards, your franchisor may ask you to draw up a compliance plan, detailing how and when you'll improve your unit. Most franchisors will give you extra time to order required equipment and make other changes to your premises, the attorney says.

Should you try to shut down your franchise, your contract gives the franchisor the right to demand back royalties, and may require you to pay future royalties for the duration of the franchise agreement. If you refuse, the franchisor can sue you.

Most franchisors would prefer to avoid such lawsuits. They're expensive, bad for business, and take too much attention away from daily operations. No franchisor will let you just walk away without paying anything, says the attorney, "but I've seen plenty of cases where the franchisor and the unhappy franchisee came to a mutual agreement." Of course, franchisors don't want other franchisees to know about such concessions, so a condition of your exit deal may be your legal promise not to tell anyone about it.

When a Dispute Can't Be Settled

If you're having a disagreement with your franchisor, call other franchisees to see if they're having the same problem. One franchisee says she believed she was the only one with support issues, until she called franchisees in adjoining states. Together, they discovered the field representative assigned to their region was billing their franchisor for monthly support calls she never made, and they reported the situation to their franchisor.

If your franchise system has an independent franchisee association, you can go there with your complaint. Independent franchisee associations have become a strong influence in franchising. Some are run by elected volunteers; others have offices and full-time executives, paid for by member dues. Class-action lawsuits,

Solving a Dispute without Litigation

In the early 2000s, Baltimore-based Sylvan Learning Centers' executives wanted to take advantage of online learning, but realized that recruiting students for Internet instruction would steal market share from their 550 franchisees, who all operated under pre-Internet contracts.

Sylvan president Peter Cohen says, "When we brought up the subject, franchisees were concerned that we'd take away business they'd spent their lifetimes building." Sylvan executives and a team of 12 franchisees from the system's franchisee association spent months negotiating a solution, in person at company headquarters and during daily conference calls. Franchisee Barry Miller, a member of the negotiation team says, "We finally reached a compromise. We wouldn't sue if Sylvan set up a separate company, called e-Sylvan, to operate its online learning function." The franchisee association received a seat on the e-Sylvan board and all franchisees received stock in the new company. Franchisees who help sign up online students get paid a royalty from their fees.

"I thought for sure we'd be in litigation over this," says Cohen. "But we put our differences aside and we're building a new business together."

Now, seven years later, the agreement has evolved even further. Every franchisee can offer online tutoring through his or her own center, and e-Sylvan has become a service provider for the system's franchisees.

including those filed against GNC, Snap-on, and Quiznos, are often organized by franchisee associations.

Independent franchisee associations serve noncontentious functions as well. In some systems, elected association representatives meet regularly with franchisor executives to discuss everything from new product rollouts to insurance coverage.

If you'd like to organize a franchisee association for your system, the American Association of Franchisees and Dealers in San Diego (www.aafd.org) or the American Franchisee Association in Chicago (www.franchisee.org) can help you get started.

Ask the Professor

How can franchise disputes be settled before reaching litigation stages?

In order to preserve the business and franchise relationship, many franchisors and franchisees are recognizing the benefits of mediation as a way of minimizing the legal costs and risks. Alternative dispute resolution (ADR) refers to any means of settling disputes outside of the courtroom. Mediation is a form of ADR, and it has become an important first step in the dispute resolution process. In mediation, the franchisor and franchisee attempt to settle a legal dispute through active participation of a neutral third party (mediator) who works to find points of agreement between them and strives to make these conflicting parties agree on a fair result. An important benefit of mediation is that it helps franchisors and franchisees preserve valued business relationships with minimal risk, and it provides them with a unique opportunity to discuss their disputes in a privileged setting without fear or concern that their discussions will yield a bad result since there is no loser in mediation. Franchisees are allowed the opportunity to vent their frustrations with the franchisor. Arbitration is another popular form of alternative dispute resolution; however, it is a much slower process than mediation. It lasts longer and it is more costly.

The International Franchise Association (IFA) is committed to helping the franchising community build strong systems centered on healthy franchise relationships. The IFA's Franchise Sales Compliance Program is a critical component of the association's Self-Regulation program. The Self-Regulation program was designed to improve compliance, education, and dispute resolution within the franchise sector. Components of the Self-Regulation program include the IFA Code of Ethics, enforcement mechanism, ombudsman, and a reward/recognition program.

Another key component of the Self-Regulation program is the National Franchise Mediation Program (NFMP). The NFMP, founded in 1993, is a mediation program designed specifically for the franchise industry. Governed by a steering committee consisting of both franchisors and franchisees and administered by the CPR Institute for Dispute Resolution, the program allows franchisors and franchisees to go through a process whereby disputes between them

(continued)

can be resolved without the high costs of litigation. Through the mediation process both the franchisor and the franchisee can maintain focus on their core business, reduce stress, and continue to enhance the franchisor-franchisee relationship—things that often suffer during the litigation process. The CPR Institute for Dispute Resolution estimates that its member companies save $25 million per year through mediation.

Who is hurt most by litigation—the franchisee or the franchisor?

It is important to remember that Franchise Agreements have been carefully drafted and reviewed by the franchisor's attorneys. Therefore, franchisees should assume that the document reflects the franchisor's best interests. Additionally, most franchise companies have attorneys and executives who have been trained on handling disputes and litigation matters that might arise.

Obviously, the goal in franchising is to run a successful business where you can make money and be satisfied with the business that you are operating. Try to avoid litigation from the start by doing your due diligence. Speak to existing and former franchisees. Find out if there have been disputes in the past, and what kind. Were the disputes initiated by disgruntled franchisees who were unhappy with the system? Did things not go as they planned? How were the disputes resolved? Usually, before a dispute goes to litigation, the franchisee and the franchisor will have a pretty good idea that things aren't working.

When it comes to litigation, franchisees are at a disadvantage. Remember that team of lawyers and executives that the franchisor has at its disposal. If litigation is pending, don't just ignore it and be silent. Take it seriously. Get an estimate of what it will cost you in terms of time and money. Consider alternative dispute resolution—that is, mediation.

In the past, I would have said that franchisees suffered the most from litigation. However, I know of several franchise systems now that have spent close to a million or more in defending lawsuits brought against them by franchisees. In the end, no one really wins.

CHAPTER SEVENTEEN

The Diverse Faces of Franchising

In April 1992, rioters, furious that four Los Angeles policemen had been acquitted of assaulting African-American motorist Rodney King—a beating that was caught on videotape and widely broadcast—did $1 billion worth of damage to LA businesses. Not a single McDonald's was harmed.

Ronald Harrison, chairman of the Diversity Institute of the International Franchise Association, was an executive with PepsiCo, then the parent of Pizza Hut, KFC, and Taco Bell, when the riots occurred. "Some of our stores were looted," Harrison says. "But nobody touched McDonald's, because people in the community felt that 'this is my McDonald's. I worked there, or my kids worked there.' McDonald's was a role model on how to build connectivity with a community."

Today, McDonald's is even more connected, because the franchisor's mission is to mirror its consumers, by ensuring that its demographics reflect those of its customer base. Patricia Harris, McDonald's vice president of global diversity, says that over 40 percent of the chain's U.S. franchisees are women and minorities, 25 percent of company officers are minorities, and 50 percent of all managers are women. The head of the franchisees' Leadership Council, like Harris, is African-American, and the president of McDonald's North America, Ralph Alvarez, is Hispanic.

If McDonald's is the role model, it's a great time for women and minorities to be looking at franchising, because almost all the other systems have a lot of catching up to do. Although minorities make up over 30 percent of the U.S. population, less than 10 percent of franchisees belong to minority groups—and that number is inflated by the success of Asian Indians, who own about 40 percent of the nation's budget and midpriced

> *"McDonald's was a role model on how to build connectivity with a community."*

hotels. Women own an estimated 30 percent of all franchises and the number of female franchisors, although growing, is still under 50.

Why Are Women and Minorities Underrepresented in Franchising?

Diversity experts cite several reasons for the disparity in franchisee ownership:

- Most franchises are owned by white males, says C. Everett Wallace, co-founder of the National Minority Franchise Initiative in Durham, North Carolina, an organization that helps minorities become franchisees. When these franchisors look for new franchisees, "they keep fishing in the same pond."

- Minorities who do not see people like themselves running franchises "feel they don't want me," says Harrison.

- Minorities, especially new immigrants, are opening new businesses at five times the rate of the majority population, says Harrison. "Most of them are unaware that joining a franchise provides you with a partner that can lend you its expertise," he says.

- Many minorities grow up in traditional families with a history of holding traditional jobs, says Undray Baker, an African-American Subway franchisee in Benning, California. "We're not risk-takers."

- Some minorities and their families may be asset-poor and lack access to capital.

- Franchisors have done a poor job of recruiting corporate employees and franchisees from the minority communities.

The people who have done the best job of recruiting minorities are minority franchisees themselves. When Aslam Khan, CEO of Falcon Holdings in Oak Brook, Illinois, arrived in this country from Pakistan, his first job was washing dishes in a fast-food restaurant. Today, he owns more than 100 Church's Chicken restaurants and runs a company whose employees are 95 percent minorities. He's helping his senior managers become franchisees, too, by loaning them money directly or co-signing their bank loans. "If we don't get more minority franchisees into our brands," he says, "we'll be in trouble."

California, our largest state, is also the most diverse. According to the U.S. Census Bureau, African-Americans, Asians, Native Americans, and Hispanics make up 64 percent of the state's 36 million people. Almost 40 percent of them speak a language other than English at home. Minorities have also become the majority in over half of our major cities.

Harrison says, "African-Americans, Hispanic-Americans, and Asian-Americans represent exploding purchasing power. They set the pace in consumer trends and they are a major segment of the new-business-owner population. To be successful in our changing demographic environment, franchisors must find ways to connect with these populations."

> *"African-Americans, Hispanic-Americans, and Asian-Americans represent exploding purchasing power."*

Providing a Leg Up

Today, many franchisors are trying to provide opportunities to minorities:

- Hotel chain Accor North America in Carrollton, Texas, for example, has an Ambassador Program for Hispanic-Americans, African-Americans, and women, groups that have historically not owned hotels. The program assigns each participant a mentor/manager who oversees the development and operation of the hotel property until the franchisee feels ready to handle things him- or herself. The program's first graduate, James Manning, who is African-American, opened a Motel 6 in Spring Lake, North Carolina, in 2006.

- Marriott International, headquartered in Washington, D.C., launched a Diversity Ownership Initiative in 2005, which educates potential minority owners about the industry and provides financial tools to help them get started.

- Choice Hotels International, in Silver Spring, Maryland, has a Minority Incentive Program that provides financial assistance to qualified applicants.

- Antonio Swad, founder of Pizza Patron in Dallas, a chain that caters to Hispanic consumers, is working with banks to establish special lending programs for minorities who want to become his franchisees.

From Migrant Worker to President of the Chamber of Commerce

Carmen Hummel's mother was from El Salvador and her father from Texas. In the summer of 1976, Hummel picked strawberries and cucumbers in Washington State. "When the season was over," she says, "I bought a $5 bus ticket and rode as far as it would take me, which was Centralia, Washington. I started looking for a job in the only clothes I had—dirty jeans and boots—and walked into the local unemployment office. The woman at the front desk said, 'We have an opening for a clerk in the CETA [a since-discontinued government program called the Comprehensive Employment and Training Act] office.'"

CETA's policy was to hire minorities, "and it was a blessing to me that Centralia had no blacks, no Hispanics, and no Asians. Just white people," Hummel says. "It was a Friday, the job started on Monday, and I had no clothes and no place to live. I was walking around when a woman in a long boat of a car pulled up and asked if I needed a ride. I told her my story. She said she had clothes that would fit me and drove me to the home of her friend, who let me stay there in exchange for cleaning. The house was three or four miles out of town, and on Monday I started walking to work in my 'new' dress, panty hose, and sandals. An older man picked me up and gave me a ride every day until I could afford to move into town. He got me talking, and I told him my dreams of someday owning my own house and car."

Throughout the 1980s, the owner of a local personnel office helped Hummel find other jobs, then finally hired her to work there. Years later, after affiliating with franchisor Express Personnel of Oklahoma City, the owner told Hummel she was retiring "and I was the only person she wanted to buy her business. The price was $90,000; I had to come up with $40,000 and she'd hold a contract on the balance. I went to lots of banks and they all acted as though it was a joke," Hummel says.

One of Hummel's early jobs had been in a local stockbroker's office, so she approached an investor she knew about a loan. "He said he'd do it, but told my husband and me to make a list of everything we owned as collateral. We did, then crossed off the tent, so our kids would have a place to live if I failed."

Hummel didn't fail, and paid her loans off within five years. She opened a second Express Personnel office in Yakima, and, in 1998, was elected president of the Centralia Chamber of Commerce. "They told me I could pick anyone I wanted to sit at my table during my first meeting as president, so I found that man who used to give me rides and introduced him as the person who never laughed at my dreams."

Hummel often sits at the reception desk of her franchises and talks to job seekers. "They don't know I'm the owner," she says. "The applicant can be Hispanic, black, Asian, or have only one arm or one leg. I ask them, 'What are your dreams?' Then I tell them my story, to show what a half-Latino fruit picker with a high school education can accomplish, given the right opportunity."

- ServiceMaster in Memphis offers a discounted franchisee fee to qualified minorities.

- Jerome Williams, master franchisee for northern New Jersey and northeast Pennsylvania for hair salon franchisor Fantastic Sams in Beverly, Massachusetts, provides technical assistance to minority candidates. Williams, who is African-American, says, "Minorities have a great fear of losing their money, and the UFOC is a massive, paralyzing document. I help them focus on key sections and tell them how to find attorneys and real estate brokers."

Color-Blind Applications

If you're a minority interested in a particular franchise, you'll have to do more than send in an online application. Federal laws prohibit franchisors from asking applicants their race.

African-American Philip Wilkins, of Lexington, Kentucky, says that in the early 1990s, his employer, a large health care company, was involved in restructurings. "I knew I'd eventually be displaced out of a job," he recalls. "I was reading an article in *Money* magazine about McDonald's franchises and thought, I can do that. I sent in an application, but because I lacked the $200,000 of unencumbered cash they wanted, I was rejected. They had no way of knowing I was

The Cement Ceiling

Valerie Daniels-Carter, of Milwaukee, decided she wanted to own a Burger King restaurant in 1982. "As you can imagine, it wasn't easy being an African-American female in a white male-dominated industry. Young people talk about the glass ceiling today. Well, I was up against a cement ceiling."

Daniels-Carter says it took her and her brother, an attorney who is her financial partner, two years to get through the process. They finally opened a Burger King on the city's north side in 1984. They opened a second Burger King in 1985, a third in 1987, and then expanded rapidly. Today, Daniels-Carter operates 130 Burger King and Pizza Hut franchises in five states and employs 3,500 people. She was the president of the Minority Franchise Association of Burger King for several years and now serves on Burger King's Diversity Action Council.

"If I hadn't had rigorous determination and stamina," Daniels-Carter says, "I would have given up and it would be the same old story."

"Young people talk about the glass ceiling today. Well, I was up against a cement ceiling."

an African-American. I wonder how many other minorities are immediately cut off like that, even by franchisors that provide special programs that could help them. Franchisors are losing that potential person forever."

Wilkins didn't give up. He called the McDonald's licensing manager and told him they made a mistake. "When he told me money was the problem, I wrote McDonald's a letter a month, letting them know where we were financially, and networked real hard with area McDonald's executives," Wilkins says. Three years later, he was accepted into the franchisor's training program, and worked at restaurants nights and weekends for another three years before being offered his first store. Today, Wilkins owns four McDonald's franchises and is president of the Ohio chapter of the Black McDonald's Operators Association.

Longtime franchise executive Cynthia Gartman, who has served as the chair of the IFA's Minorities in Franchising Committee and on its Diversity Institute board, makes the following suggestions for minorities interested in franchising:

> *"I wrote McDonald's a letter a month, letting them know where we were financially, and networked real hard with area McDonald's executives."*

- Get educated. Read as much as you can about the industry and learn about franchise programs that target minority applicants.

- Network. "Go out and get involved in your local community. Join the chamber of commerce," Gartman says. Attend regional franchising events like the Franchise Business Network that meets four times a year. (You can find information on the IFA's Web site, www.franchise.org.)

- Build a serious banking relationship. "You don't want to meet a banker for the first time when you have an SBA loan application in your hands," she says. "Meet local bankers at chamber of commerce mixers and social events. Banks are more likely to loan money to people they recognize."

- If your credit score isn't great, get it up.

- Learn about the SBA loan process.

- Learn about any program that can help you—government loans, SCORE (the Service Corps of Retired Executives, mentioned in Chapter Twelve), local business incubators, and others.

- Begin your franchise search by sorting through the hundreds of franchisors listed on the IFA's Web site that are participating in the IFA's MinorityFran program and are actively seeking minority franchisees. Also look for franchisors that advertise in minority publications, serve customers that speak your language, or whose Web sites seem to target minorities.

Wilkins's caveat: "Many franchisors offer initiatives to minority franchisees who will help them expand into inner-city neighborhoods. This is fine if your demographic background matches those locations. I grew up in a small town and would not feel comfortable operating in the inner city. And the government grants and tax credits they offer may not offset the security costs of operating there."

Easing into a Grind

After 30 years as a corporate executive, African-American Mary Forte wanted to start her own business. She found a franchise broker on the Internet, who introduced her to coffeehouse franchise It's a Grind, of Long Beach, California. "All the people I met there during Discovery Day and training were very accommodating," Forte says.

When she agreed to put her coffeehouse in a redevelopment area in downtown Oakland, California, the city arranged two loans to get her started. And because most of her employees come from surrounding neighborhoods, she's eligible for tax credits. Now her coffeehouse serves downtown office workers during the day and neighborhood residents in the evenings and on weekends. "I wish I'd done this earlier," Forte says.

Women and Franchising

The first time I attended a networking reception organized by the IFA's Women's Franchise Committee at the trade group's annual convention, the event was held in a small room in a far corner of the convention hall. It was sponsored by a male franchisor, who stood at the door and welcomed the sparse group of women as we arrived. At today's IFA conventions, the annual WFC networking reception is a crowded event and it's sponsored by a female franchisor. The Women's Committee also holds a day-long Leadership Conference that's always sold out.

Women are making so much headway in franchising that diversity leader Ron Harrison no longer considers them a minority. Things were very different in the 1980s, says Cynthia Gartman, who was senior director of support services for Accor North America before leaving in 2006 to start her own company, GP Sports Centers.

Gartman, of Eulass, Texas, started her franchise career right out of college, as an administrator for a real estate franchisor. "I walked into the regional office to talk to 40 real estate affiliates, and they were all male," she says. "It was quite a learning curve." Female executives were so rare that the few women who were brave enough to attend IFA events "drew blank stares," she says.

Today, women run many large franchise companies. Heidi Morrissey is CEO of Kitchen Tune-up, an Aberdeen, South Dakota, franchise started by her father; Melanie Bergeron runs Two Men and a Truck, a moving franchise in Lansing, Michigan, that was launched by her mother, Mary Ellen Sheets; and Dina Dwyer-Owens is the CEO of the Dwyer Group in Waco, Texas. In 2000, another executive, JoAnne Shaw, president of the Coffee Beanery in Flushing, Michigan, became the IFA's first female chairman.

"Franchising is attractive to women," says Udo Schlentrich, director of the William Rosenberg Center of International Franchising at the University of New

> *"I walked into the regional office to talk to 40 real estate affiliates, and they were all male."*

Programs That Assist Minority Franchisees

- The IFA, through its Minorities in Franchising Committee and Diversity Institute, offers programs and scholarships.

- The Urban Entrepreneur Partnership, co-founded by the National Urban League, the Kauffman Foundation (www.kauffman.org), and other groups, is opening offices in U.S. cities to help minorities start their own businesses.

- The SBA sponsors Small Business Development Centers (www.sba.gov/sbdc) that can help you find loans and prepare business plans.

- The Minority Business Development Agency (www.mbda.gov) is a federal agency that can link you to loans and programs targeting minorities.

- Local redevelopment areas and Enterprise Zones provide funding and tax credits if you open within their borders and employ local residents.

Hampshire, "because it allows them to be their own boss on terms that can fit well within their family and social structure."

Lori Barrett, of Queens, New York, left a career as a social worker when her first child was born. "I was in a quandary," Barrett says. "I wanted to work, but I didn't want to go back full-time. At the same time, I saw the lack of good programs for young children." Barrett launched Thinkertots in 1998, a parent-child education program for babies, toddlers, and preschoolers. She started franchising in 2006.

"This is a low-investment business that can be run out of a retail store-front," Barrett says. "I'm aiming it at women who want something to channel their creative energy into until 2:30 each afternoon, when they pick up their own children at the school bus stop."

Veterans and Franchising

For 20 years, Linda and Vaughn Harker got up early every morning, put on their Army uniforms and followed whatever military order they were issued. Today, the Harkers may get up a little later, but they still dress in uniforms and follow procedures laid out in the operations manual that came with the UPS Store franchise they opened in Titusville, Florida, in 2004.

The Harkers are among more than 700 veterans who have obtained franchises through VetFran (the Veterans Transition Franchise Initiative). The IFA-sponsored program has more than 250 franchisor members who provide discounts on franchise fees to honorably discharged members of the armed services who meet franchisors' net worth, experience, and other criteria. The UPS Store in San Diego, for example, offers veterans a 15 percent discount off their franchise fee. In 2006, the company reports, over 10 percent of new franchisees were veterans like the Harkers who took advantage of the program.

The late Don Dwyer, founder of the Dwyer Group in Waco, Texas, started VetFran in 1991, during the first Gulf War. The program languished until 2003, when his daughter, Dwyer CEO Dina Dwyer-Owens, revived it with the IFA's support. VetFran is promoted on the IFA's Web site and by the Department of Veterans Affairs and the SBA.

The program has an unexpected dividend, because veterans and franchises make a perfect match. "I like the franchise because everything's spelled out for

Two Men (and Two Women) and a Truck

In the early 1980s, Mary Ellen Sheets was a single parent with three kids and a computer job with the state of Michigan. One summer, her two teenage sons started a short-haul moving business. When they went back to school in the fall, Sheets continued their business, buying an old moving truck for $395 and hiring two men, named Joe and Elmer. "I paid them in cash," she says, "and if they didn't feel like coming to work, we did no jobs that day. We had no pads or ramps—I told the men such things are for wimps—and no license and no insurance. We moved people all over and I made $1,000 in my first year. I gave it all away, writing ten checks for $100 each to local charities. I'd never felt so empowered."

In 1987, Sheets bought a second truck and stored them both in her mother's barn. When appearing on a small business panel at Michigan State University, Sheets met a franchise attorney, who suggested she started selling franchises. "I quit my job," Sheets says, "and moved onto a houseboat, where I wrote our operations manual."

Sheets' first franchisee was her daughter, Melanie Bergeron, a pharmaceutical salesperson in Atlanta, who agreed to run a franchise on the side. When other franchisees arrived, Sheets says training class was "their sitting on my couch for a week while I read through the manuals."

Sheets remodeled an old gas station into franchise headquarters, and then moved to the attic of an old house in a neighborhood so bad that "ladies in the driveway were negotiating their affections." By 1994, Sheets had 39 franchisees, 35 employees, and a request to run for public office, so she asked Melanie to come home to run the business.

"We didn't know about the IFA," Bergeron says. "We'd read no books about franchising and had a lot of problems with our franchisees. Some had yellow trucks, some had white ones; some were paying royalties, and others were not." The women received a grant from the State of Michigan that paid the fee of a franchise consultant who helped them set compliance standards, raise royalties, and get rid of franchisees who didn't want to follow the new rules.

(continued)

(Two Men (and Two Women) and a Truck continued)

Today, Two Men and a Truck International has almost 200 franchises and 74 corporate employees, who work in a sleek new building. Training is conducted there, in a fully furnished training house that franchisees learn to pack and unpack. Sheets certainly knows about the IFA, because she recently received the trade association's highest award, that of Entrepreneur of the Year. Bergeron serves as CEO, but her two brothers now work for the company, too. And, just as Sheets did that first year, Two Men and a Truck donates a portion of its annual revenues to charity.

you, from A to Z, just the way I was taught in my military career," says Linda Harker. Vaughn says, "In the military, one of the rules is, 'If the procedure works, use it.'" This, of course, is the premise of franchising. As for the uniforms, Linda says, "We've gone from wearing Army puke green to UPS beige and black."

"I like the franchise because everything's spelled out for you, from A to Z, just the way I was taught in my military career."

In 2007, Michael Ilitch, founder of the Little Caesars Pizza franchise in Detroit, increased his VetFran ante, by offering discounts and credits that can reach $68,000 for disabled veterans. Ex-Marine Ilitch made the change after reading about a serviceman who lost his legs in a roadside bombing in Iraq. Today, that soldier and an Army buddy operate a Little Caesars in Paducah, Kentucky. More information about VetFran is available on the IFA Web site (www.franchise.org).

Ask the Professor

How has the position of women changed since you first became involved in franchising?

I've been involved in franchising since 1984 so I've seen considerable changes. One of the most significant and rewarding changes has been building bridges to women and minorities. It has been a long process; there is much work to be done, but headway is being made.

In 1999, the IFA's Women's Franchise Committee (WFC) hosted its first networking reception at the annual convention, and a few women found their way to the event. The WFC held its eighth annual Leadership Conference at the 2007 IFA Convention in Las Vegas—for a standing-room-only crowd. The WFC Franchise Network (WFN) provides opportunities for women to meet and learn from other women on the local level. WFN chapters meet regularly around the country. The Women's Franchise and Distribution Forum (WFDF) and the Women's Food-service Forum also offer educational and networking opportunities for women. These resource groups, and others like them, provide networking and mentoring opportunities for women, and role models for them to look up to—very few women were involved in leadership positions in franchising back in 1984.

Women are opening businesses at a rate twice as fast as men. Franchisors that are expanding their organizations should consider women as key ingredients in their growth strategies. The number of women franchisees has increased in recent years. When I first entered franchising, women had a hard time getting financing, and it was often necessary for a spouse to be a partner or to co-sign for the loan. Primary barriers for women entering franchising today are still much the same—lack of capital for initial investments and lack of collateral to guarantee loans. The up-front investment franchising requires prevents women from bootstrapping a launch, as many women entrepreneurs would do. This financing barrier is not exclusive to franchising, however. It is a barrier that confronts many women in business.

How has the role of minorities in franchising changed?

Franchisors are seeking to attract more minority franchisees today than in the past. Minorities account for over 30 percent of the U.S. population, and they own

(continued)

nearly 15 percent of the nation's businesses. New minority-owned businesses have grown at five to six times the rate of all U.S. firms and at nearly twice the rate of all American firms in annual sales, according to U.S. Census data.

The changing complexion of the domestic market is having a dramatic impact on many franchising companies' recruiting and retention efforts. Franchisors are increasingly viewing minority franchise recruitment as a business imperative and a key component of corporate diversity initiatives, as African-Americans, Asian-Americans, Hispanics, and Native Americans represent 90 percent of the projected population growth over the next 50 years. According to the 2000 Census, in two of our largest states, California and Texas, the minority population already outnumbers non-Hispanic whites.

Challenges, new opportunities, changing demographics, alternative financing strategies for women and minority franchises and candidates—these are all topics that are of importance as women and minorities shape and boost franchise expansion into new and underserved markets. At the IFA's forty-seventh annual convention held in 2007, the convention's Diversity Summit, developed by the Minorities in Franchising Committee and the Diversity Institute, detailed these issues and financing programs for women and minority franchisees.

It is refreshing to go to IFA events and other franchising events today and see more women and minorities in attendance and on the speaker's platform, and to see that initiatives and programs are being put into place to encourage business growth and opportunities in these sectors.

CHAPTER EIGHTEEN

The Roles You Can Play in Franchising's Future

One of my first assignments for *Franchise Times* was to write about franchisee millionaires. I called around to various systems and found men and women doing quite well operating a couple dozen fast-food restaurants, a chain of hair salons, and a handful of auto care franchises. Then I called Gary Tharaldson in Fargo, North Dakota.

Tharaldson had been a high school teacher and an insurance salesman until 1982, when he used $100,000 of his own money to make a down payment on a rundown 30-room Super 8 motel in the town of Valley City. The owner, he told me, carried a contract for the rest of the debt. He bought his second motel in tiny Devil's Lake on contract, too, then pledged the ongoing commissions from his previous insurance work as collateral for a bank loan to buy his third motel in Beulah, population 2,300.

After buying and refurbishing four motels, Tharaldson started building hotels himself and soon organized his own construction company. He began with Super 8s, and then moved on to Choice Hotels International's Comfort Inns and Sleep Inn brands and no-frills Marriott concepts. When I talked to him in 1996, Tharaldson owned 204 motel or hotel properties and, he said, his total net worth was about $300 million.

I was flabbergasted. Finding someone who had parlayed a $100,000 investment into a lodging empire worth $300 million was my introduction to the power of multiunit franchising. I realized that anyone willing to invest a little money and a lot of energy—as I recall, Tharaldson was pretty funny about cleaning up that old Super 8 himself—can build real wealth.

Since 1996, I've met scores of franchisee millionaires. Each summer the *Restaurant Finance Monitor* (a publication that targets the restaurant and finance industries) publishes its Top 200 list of restaurant franchisees whose annual sales are $28 million and above. The 2006 leader was NPC International in

Lenexa, Kansas, whose 785 Pizza Huts earned almost $600 million in 2005. (Merrill Lynch Global Private Equity purchased NPC later that year.) In second place was Harman Management Corporation in Los Altos, California, which was started by high school dropout Leon "Pete" Harman, in 1952, when he purchased the very first Kentucky Fried Chicken franchise offered by Colonel Harland Sanders. Today, Harman Management owns 327 KFCs and other Yum! Brands, and takes in $425 million annually.

Multiunit wealth isn't limited to hotels and restaurants. An industry publication devoted to area developers recently profiled Jim Traweek and John Marett, who operate 45 showrooms for ProSource Wholesale Floorcoverings in Earth City, Missouri. The partners, whose offices are in Florida, employ more than 300 people who sell hardwood, carpet, and ceramic floor coverings to

---

Report from the Trenches

Graduating into Lawn Care

Michael Carlo majored in math and economics, but the day after he graduated from the University of Connecticut, in 1990, he moved back to Florida to work in a new U.S. Lawns franchise owned by his sister and brother-in-law. "I came in with zero experience in both landscaping and business," Carlo says.

Carlo spent his first six months working in the field, "something I'll never do again," he says. But within a couple of years he liked the business so much, he borrowed $20,000 to buy it. He sold that franchise in 1995 "at a good profit," to open another one in Sarasota. In 1998, Carlo joined forces with longtime friend and fellow franchisee Todd Moerchen and today the men operate five U.S. Lawns franchises in Florida and a sixth in Lexington, Kentucky.

"We've hired managers to do all the field work," Carlo says, "while we oversee the finances, marketing, and policies. Although we consider homeowners our number-one customers, we also have accounts to maintain the landscaping for banks, office buildings, shopping malls, hotels, and hospitals." Their total annual revenues are over $6 million. "Ultimately," Carlo says, "we'll buy more territories."

contractors, decorators, and other professionals. In 2006, their revenues topped $170 million. Other muliunit mavens include a former Big Four accountant who owns 55 Liberty Tax Service centers, and the son of a dairy farmer who operates 26 Cost Cutters and Supercuts hair salons.

Vehicles for Multiple-Unit Franchising

Just a few years ago, single-unit operators owned the vast majority of franchises. Today, says FRANdata president Darrell Johnson, 82 percent of franchisees are single-unit operators, but they control only half of all U.S. franchised units. One-fourth of all units are owned by franchisees who operate two to five units, and one-fourth are owned by franchisees with five or more units.

Multiunit operators are hot commodities in franchising today. Franchisors target multiunit franchisees of compatible concepts to become area developers of their brands as well. And private equity groups that have run out of franchisors to purchase are buying up large multiunit operations outright—a private equity group is the largest IHOP (International House of Pancakes) franchisee, for example—or investing in multiunit operations, to help those franchisees expand even more. See Figure 18-1 for a summary of the percentage of multiunit franchisees by industry.

Selling a franchisee more than one unit has several advantages for franchisors, says Brett Lowell, a partner in the Reston, Virginia, office of international law firm DLA Piper US LLP, in a report he prepared for the IFA. They include:

- A chance to develop more rapidly
- Use of another person's financial and human resources
- Shared risk with another person
- Potential for rapid cash flow from sale of multiple-unit franchise rights

There are several routes you can take to owning a handful, or several hundred, units. The least risky is the path Tharaldson took in his early years, opening one unit at a time. Undray Baker, for example, purchased an existing Subway in Banning, California, in 2005, and six months later opened a second unit inside a Wal-Mart in nearby Beaumont. "My goal is to have ten stores," he says. "You can support a family off one or two Subways. I don't want to be the

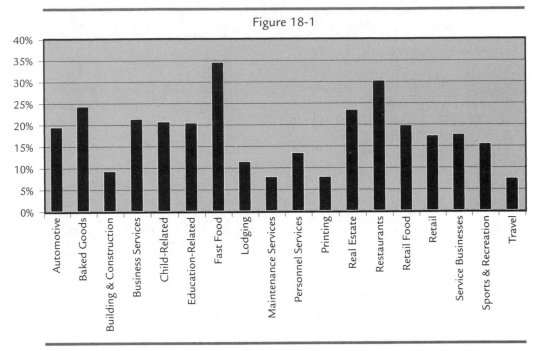

Figure 18-1

BY INDUSTRY, PERCENTAGE OF FRANCHISEES WHO OWN MORE THAN 1 UNIT

richest person, but with ten, I feel we can be comfortable." According to a spokesman at Subway, 47 percent of that system's 12,000 North American franchisees operate more than one unit.

As we've seen, many franchisors would prefer you take a faster road, by signing a multiunit deal at the starting line. According to Lowell's report, "Multiple-Unit Franchising: The Key to Rapid System Growth," franchisors offer multiple units using three different techniques, although some use a combination of the following:

1. *Area development.* The franchisor sells you the right to establish and operate more than one unit within a specified territory. You pay an up-front fee for the right, a portion of which may be applied toward the franchise fees of your future units. You are obligated to open a fixed number of units according to a specific schedule and, each time you open one, you sign a new franchise agreement. You may open all the units yourself or form partnerships with other individuals who operate them.

2. *Subfranchising.* Here, the franchisor sells you the right to become a franchisor yourself within a specified territory. Some franchisors insist that their subfranchisors operate at least one unit themselves; others prohibit that activity. A subfranchisor solicits prospects, signs contracts with the franchisees he or she has attracted, and provides support and standards enforcement. For these efforts, the subfranchisor receives a portion of each franchisee's fees and monthly royalties. Subfranchising is used when franchisors want to develop a territory far from their home offices; and it's the way many franchisors expand overseas. This technique is used less often within the states, Lowell says.

3. *Area representation.* Here a person who knows the system well, like a seasoned franchisee, may or may not pay for the right to solicit prospective franchisees within a certain territory, and may provide services to them once they've opened, in exchange for a share of the franchisee fee and royalties. Unlike subfranchising, each franchisee signs his or her contract directly with the franchisor.

All three techniques pose disadvantages for franchisors, which can lose control of their sales process and who can lose out if an area developer, subfranchisor, or area representative falls behind in his or her development schedule. And by granting the rights to develop a territory, the franchisor "freezes" expansion there by committing to a schedule that may not be rapid enough, should competitors arrive, Lowell says.

Walk before You Run

But the real disadvantages of signing a multiple-unit deal fall on the shoulders of the new franchisee. "Until you have experience with that first unit, you're not in a real good position to take on more units," says Johnson. "The challenges of opening a second unit don't increase arithmetically—it's not simply twice as hard. When you operate one unit, you're physically there all the time. When you open a second one, you have to rely on someone else to supervise it. And training that person requires a different skill set."

The challenges compound when you add in the financial burden of opening a second, and even third, unit before your first one starts to break even. It's not surprising that Johnson says, "Development agreements today are seldom

> *"The challenges of opening a second unit don't increase arithmetically—it's not simply twice as hard."*

realized under the time limits required." No matter how alluring it sounds to "own a territory" or "become the master of a multimillion dollar franchise business," walk before you run, Johnson advises.

When I asked Tharaldson for advice in 1996, he said, "Start small. It gives you a chance to learn everything about the business and leaves a lot of room for error. Once I could show bankers that I had three units operating at a good profit level, they started believing in me."

In 1998, Tharaldson was number 385 on *Forbes* magazine's list of the country's 400 richest people. Today, Tharaldson Property Management Inc. in Fargo manages 370 franchised hotels in 36 states, including Fairfield Inns and 4 other Marriott brands; Homewood Suites and Hampton Inns by Hilton; Comfort Inns by Choice; and Holiday Inn Express. Tharaldson Lodging owns 240 of them; the family sold 130 others to Whitehall Real Estate Funds in 2006, for $1.2 billion.

Charles Krumwiede, Tharaldson Lodging's vice president of operations, says the company always has 15 to 20 hotels "in the pipeline." "Gary's still buying land and developing hotels, and his goal is to open another hundred."

Krumwiede says, "Gary and I were both teachers and high school basketball coaches. One day when our teams were competing against each other, he said to me, 'This is a very difficult way to make a living.' We often laugh about that now."

A New Breed of Franchisee

Most of the early franchisee millionaires began like Pete Harman and Tharaldson did, as successful operators who slowly grew into businessmen or businesswomen. Many of the newest multiunit owners were businesspeople first.

C.H. James & Company, the oldest African-American-owned business in the United States, was founded in 1883 by the first Charles H. James, who sold vegetables from a mule-drawn cart. Successive generations moved the company beyond selling produce to distributing a full line of food products to grocery stores and restaurants. The current CEO, Charles H. James III was a banker who earned his MBA from the Wharton School at the University of Pennsylvania before joining the company in 1985. James III bought a company that supplied precut lettuce and onions to McDonald's and other fast-food operators, sold that, and had a fling with e-commerce (he sold his Internet company for $20 million before the dot-com bust).

In 2004, James III and the Goldman Sachs Urban Investment Group purchased a 37-unit Burger King multiunit operation in Deerfield, Illinois, from a franchisee who wanted to retire. "There's a lot more to franchising than people on the outside realize," says James III. "It's like running thirty-seven $1 million to $2 million businesses with 30 to 50 employees each."

After Adam Schmitz received his master's degree in economics, he planned to move to Wall Street and become an investment banker. Instead, he moved to Arizona and became a partner in his father-in-law's fast-food restaurants. Today, he and Gary Behmer operate 11 Jack in the Box restaurants in Arizona and plan to open more. "Franchising was a better fit for my career goals," Schmitz says.

> *"There's a lot more to franchising than people on the outside realize."*

Adding More Units

Even if you don't have advanced degrees and family wealth, you can still grow your franchise into a multiple-unit operation. Your first hurdle, of course, is financing. We've met franchisees who did so well with their first unit, they were able to finance the next ones themselves. Most, however, have to borrow more money from their original lenders or from nonbank lenders with which their franchisors have relationships. Luckily, franchising is a better known quantity than it was in the 1980s, when Tharaldson's bankers were wary until he had three motels running at a profit. You may not need three profitable units, but you will have to be making money with your first one, and have a history of increasing sales, before any institution will approve your loan for a second unit. GE Capital Solutions Franchise Finance, in Scottsdale, for example, has a lending program targeted to small franchisees who want to expand. Popular Small Business Capital, a division of Banco Popular North America in Panama City, Florida, provides expansion loans to franchisees who have been in business for at least one year.

Darrell Johnson says the other hurdle is operational. Each franchise system is a little different, but you can usually run three units yourself, he says, by driving from one to the next each day, checking in with your managers and making most of the decisions yourself. But if you want to get bigger, you must make the transformation from being an individual with multiple locations to being a sophisticated businessperson. "You have to build an infrastructure to support your new business of franchising," Johnson says.

Once you have that business in place, you can expand rapidly. You'll recall that it took Valerie Daniels-Carter five years to open her first three Burger King franchises; within another five years she owned dozens of fast-food restaurants. Mahendra Nath, of Bloomington, Minnesota, was a commercial real estate developer when he was attracted to two troubled Burger Kings in Minneapolis. "I'd built my company by acquiring underperforming assets and improving them. I bought the restaurants as a challenge, to see if I could fix up their curb appeal and make them profitable," he says.

When he succeeded, commercial real estate brokers and operators all over the country offered to sell him more troubled Burger Kings. Within a short time, Nath Companies owned about 100 of them in six states.

Operating More Than One Brand

Nath didn't stop with Whoppers. His family company purchased eight Denny's, built a hotel, and opened an independent fine dining restaurant. FRANdata reports that 13 percent of multiunit franchisees are involved in more than one franchise system, and 9 percent of multiunit franchisees, like Nath, have units in different industry sectors. Three generations of the Scott family in Erie, Pennsylvania, for example, operate three Applebee's, two Quaker Steak & Lubes, a Damon's Grill, and eight franchised hotels at exits along Pennsylvania's Route 95, plus an independent indoor water park, whose design they may eventually franchise themselves.

Franchise Agreements are quite strict about not allowing you to open a franchise of a competing brand—a McDonald's franchisee can't operate a Burger King, for example. But when aggressive franchisees have opened all the units of their brand a territory will support, franchisors allow them to take on another concept. Some franchisors, like The Franchise Company (TFC) in Toronto, have several brands available themselves. Once your Certa Pro Painters franchise is established, you can use the same office to operate one of TFC's other brands, like a Handyman Connection or a California Closets.

Combining Two Concepts

If you go into food franchising, you can start operating two concepts early, through co-branding, putting two or more food franchises into a single location. While the numbers are small—FRANdata reports that less than 1 percent of the nation's franchisees operate cross-branded outlets—more and more prospective restaurant franchisees are shopping for dual brands.

After Andy Lanz graduated from the University of Wisconsin with a degree in economics, his parents offered to help him get started in a business. He found a location, in a new strip mall in Verona, Wisconsin, and started talking to Figaro's Pizza in Salem, Oregon, about putting a franchise there. "The space was too big," Lanz says, "so I added a Cousins Subs franchise and a Chocolate Shoppe Ice Cream dipping station." The three concepts share a single, large walk-in cooler, a dishwashing sink, and a freezer, and require only one set of restrooms. Lanz says his sub shop is busiest at lunchtime, while dinner guests order more pizza, and customers drop in throughout the afternoon and evening for ice cream.

Dennis Lombardi, vice president of foodservice strategies for WD Partners, a restaurant design and development firm in Columbus, Ohio, says that co-branding offers two advantages: reduced cost and increased customer counts. If Lanz had built separate stores for each of his three concepts, he would have spent over $500,000; his tribranded restaurant cost only $330,000.

The co-branding champion is Yum! Brands of Louisville, Kentucky, with more than 3,000 locations sharing two or more of its concepts—KFC, Taco Bell, Pizza Hut, A&W, and Long John Silver's. Franchisees of Wienerschnitzel, a hot dog and burger concept in Newport Beach, California, had so much success when they added Tastee-Freez soft-serve ice cream to their restaurants that Wienerschnitzel's parent, the Galardi Group, purchased the Tastee-Freez company.

If you're thinking of co-branding two food concepts, it's safest to match brands that have been co-branded before. When a New York franchisee tried to combine a Cinnabon with a Quizno's, both franchisors were new to co-branding and threw up roadblocks, insisting that the employees of each concept wear different uniforms. (In most co-branded outlets, employees wear shirts or caps that bear both brands' logos.) Since his workers look and feel different, they're less likely to help each other out, the franchisee says.

Becoming a Franchisee Leader

Whether you have one unit or 200, you can become a leader within your system and the entire franchising community. Lee Staak, a Hardee's franchisee from Iowa City, with only four stores, for example, was elected president of the Independent Hardee's Franchisee Association in 2004 by its 1,400 members, some of whom own dozens of Hardee's. If your franchise has an independent franchisee association, you can volunteer to help with its committees and programs now and move up in the ranks later.

Franchisees were excluded from membership in the IFA when the trade group started 50 years ago, because many franchisors then were often at odds with their franchisees. In 1993, when the IFA board finally voted to admit franchisees as members, it's not surprising that only a few of them joined. One who did was Steve Siegel, an attorney and partner in 35 Dunkin' Donuts franchises in Massachusetts. Siegel founded the IFA's Franchisee Forum, a committee of elected franchisees that meets three times a year to discuss franchisee-related issues, and whose members are eligible for election to the IFA Board. In 2002, Siegel became the first franchisee chairman of the IFA; and in 2006, Lawrence "Doc" Cohen, a Great American Cookie franchisee in Tomball, Texas, became the second.

To boost franchisee membership, in 2001, the IFA board voted to allow its franchise system members to automatically enroll all their franchisees as members for free. Therefore, if your system is an IFA member, that means that you are one, too, and you should be receiving IFA materials by e-mail. Although the IFA now claims more than 30,000 franchisees as members, very few of them participate in IFA events. If you're interested in getting involved, you can find information on the IFA's annual convention, Franchise Business Network meetings held four times a year around the country, and the Franchisee Forum on the IFA's Web site (www.franchise.org).

The Future of Franchising

"Franchising today is the fastest-growing method of sharing the opportunities of small business ownership with those who want more control over their destinies," says IFA president Matthew Shay. "Franchising's adaptability to virtually any type of enterprise is one of the leading keys to its growth. Advances in technology, more efficient financial systems, instant communication, and effective marketing techniques have also given franchising significant boosts in just the past decade."

Shay predicts a smoothing out of franchisee and franchisor relations. He recounts, "William Rosenberg, the founder of Dunkin' Donuts and one of the founders of the IFA often said, 'You can't be a successful franchisor without having successful franchisees, and you can't be a successful franchisee without having a successful franchisor.'"

"Good franchisee-franchisor relations are more crucial to the future growth and development of franchising than any technological advance or business technique," Shay summarizes. "Those who are joined together in franchises that will be the leading brands 50 years from now understand that and practice it daily."

> *"You can't be a successful franchisor without having successful franchisees, and you can't be a successful franchisee without having a successful franchisor."*

Your Future in Franchising

Becoming a franchisee is a huge commitment. We hope that the advice contained in these pages will help you choose a franchise that is one of the leading brands 50 years from now. We also hope that sharing the stories of franchisees we've met in the past decade will help you decide whether or not to join them.

If you decide franchising is not for you, learning about this unique business model should give you a greater appreciation of the people who serve your food, cut your grass, and clean your clothes. The owner of each of the businesses you frequent every day may have been a top executive, a dot-com guru, or the person who held fish in her mouth during a dolphin act.

If you do decide to join a franchise system, we hope you'll stay in touch, so we can share your stories someday, too. As John Kohler says: "You're not buying a job. You're investing in an adventure." Good luck!

Ask the Professor

How has franchising changed since you first became involved?

Over the past 20-plus years, I have taught degree courses in franchising and entre-preneurship to undergraduate and graduate students, and conducted executive education programs for franchise executives in the United States and over a dozen foreign countries. Needless to say, since I became involved in franchising there have been significant changes.

There seems to be more thought put into training franchisees and executives in franchise systems today. The IFA's Institute for Certified Executives awards Certified Franchise Executive (CFE) credits to people who complete approved courses from a variety of course providers—including the International Institute for Franchise Education (IIFE). There are also programs offered through the Diversity Institute, the Women's Franchise Committee, Women's Franchise Networks, IFA's Franchise Business Network, and *Franchise Times* Franchise Finance and Development Conference and Restaurant Finance and Development Conference.

Franchising has evolved to keep up with technological advances and changing demographics. Franchisees today are more sophisticated than they were 20 years ago, and there are fewer mom-and-pop franchisees. A franchising trend that will continue into the foreseeable future is the growth in multiunit and multibrand ownership. There are an ever-increasing number of franchisees who own more than one unit, and even more than one brand.

Many U.S. companies have begun to look elsewhere for locations to sustain their company's growth, as the traditional domestic market is rapidly reaching the saturation point for mature franchise systems. In the last ten years, a number of franchisors have taken their concepts into foreign countries. Additionally, I've seen more and more global concepts entering the lucrative U.S. marketplace. I remember making a presentation in Paris in the spring of 1989. At that time, I could only name a handful of international concepts that were operating success-fully in the United States. Now there are companies that specialize in taking U.S. concepts to other countries and in bringing foreign concepts to the United States.

In the previous chapter, we discussed the increase in the number of opportu-nities for women and minorities in franchising. Even though women and minorities make up only a small percentage of franchisees today, the number has been increasing steadily since I've been involved in franchising. Many people believe that the underserved minority population represents the future of franchising.

PART FIVE

Franchise Company Directory

The 300 franchise companies found in this directory come from *Franchise Times* magazine's 2006 ranking of the largest U.S.-based franchise companies, as measured by systemwide sales for calendar year 2005. Unit counts represent actual businesses operating as of year-end 2005, and parent companies are those that were in place at that date.

Data related to investment estimates, royalty and advertising rates, and SBA Franchise Registry status were compiled by FRANdata and represent the most current data available at the time of publication. FRANdata provides unbiased research and analysis to a variety of franchise industry stakeholders utilizing their proprietary database of franchise companies, the brands they manage, and the franchisees who invest in those brands.

Please be aware that the franchises listed were chosen and ranked only according to their total sales. In no way should you consider the listings an endorsement by *Franchise Times* or the author. If you select a franchise from the following list, you must perform due diligence on the company and its officers and talk to current franchisees, just as you would any other franchise system.

Explanation of Terms

Date Began Franchising. The date the company began selling franchises. In some instances, where companies have changed ownership or have otherwise reorganized, this is the date when the current iteration of the company began selling franchises.

Systemwide Sales. This figure represents sales for calendar year 2005, generated by both franchise and company units around the world. It *does not* include various payments, such as franchise fees or royalties, made to franchisors from franchisees. For those companies that refused to disclose sales, the figure has been estimated. For real estate companies, the systemwide sales figure measures commissions generated by real estate transactions.

Total Units. This figure represents all units, company and franchised, in operations around the world.

Franchise Percent. This figure represents the percentage of franchised units to total units as of year-end 2005.

International Percent. This figure represents the percentage of international units to total units.

Minimum and Maximum Investment. These provide an estimated range of initial investment requirements necessary to get the franchise business up and running. The specific up-front investment a franchise requires varies, depending on the type of business operated and the associated inventory, building, equipment, and/or territory considerations. Restaurants, for instance, generally have a standard prototype for their building design, and the ranges given incorporate the differences in construction expenses a franchisee may incur in building a typical prototype. Additionally, the ranges account for such expenses as furniture, fixtures and equipment (FF&E), utility deposits, opening inventory, franchise fees, and other incidental expenses.

It is important to note that the initial investment figures *do not* include estimates for real estate acquisitions. That is, the investment estimates include the costs associated with constructing or remodeling a restaurant, hotel, and so on, but do not include the cost of actually buying the real estate it sits on. Since the large majority of franchise companies do not require the franchisee to own real estate, and in fact assume that the franchisee will rent or lease, the investment ranges will often include an estimate for the first month's rent or lease payment.

Investment ranges vary widely for a number of reasons other than construction costs, as well. Inventory requirements for businesses that rent cars, machinery, or other high-ticket items can lead to large initial investment ranges. For service and maintenance businesses, differences in the size and location of a franchise territory will impact the required initial investment.

Royalty. Franchisors collect royalties from franchisees, generally as a percentage of sales. In many instances, royalty fees are the product of complex calculations, depending on unit age, territory demographics, revenue levels, or other criteria. "Variable" indicates complex royalty criteria.

National Advertising. Not all franchisors have national advertising funds, and many have both national and local marketing programs. As with royalties, national advertising fees can be dependent on a number of variables, and franchisors reserve the right to change advertising fee requirements.

SBA Franchise Registry. The SBA Franchise Registry is a national online listing of franchise systems whose franchisees receive expedited loan processing when applying for financial assistance from the U.S. Small Business Administration (SBA). By centralizing the review process, the registry allows the SBA to make consistent eligibility decisions regarding franchise systems, to cut red tape in the system, and to speed access to SBA financial assistance. Administered by FRANdata, the registry is a successful partnership between the SBA, franchise lenders, franchisors, and franchisees.

The SBA Franchise Registry is updated constantly, so companies identified as "Not Listed" may have changed status since the publishing of the directory. Please visit www.franchiseregistry.com for additional information and for an updated listing of participating companies.

How the Directory Is Organized

To make it easier to find the information you're looking for, we've organized the directory in three ways:

1. *Directory by Category.* Here you'll find full profiles of the 300 entries, divided into the following eight groupings:

- Automotive Services and Rental (page 295)

- Lodging (page 300)

- Maintenance, Restoration, and Cleaning (page 311)

- Printing, Graphic Design, Signage, and Shipping (page 317)

- Real Estate and Travel Agencies (page 320)

- Restaurants and Prepared Food (page 323)

- Retail (page 350)

- Services (page 357)

2. *Directory by Minimum Investment.* If you're not exactly sure what kind of franchise you're looking for, but you know how much you'd like to invest, you can find options here. In this section, we've organized franchises by the following minimum investment ranges:

- $0–$100,000 (page 365)

- $100,001–$250,000 (page 367)

- $250,001–$1,000,000 (page 370)

- $1,000,000-plus (page 373)

As discussed, the minimum investment includes such expenses as the initial franchise fee, utility deposits, leasehold improvements, and the initial rent payment, but does not include the ongoing working capital needs of the business and assumes any real estate will be leased, not purchased. For each franchise in this part of the directory, we've listed the corresponding category. You can find the full profile for each of these franchises in the Directory by Category listing.

3. *Alphabetical Listing of Franchises.* If you already know which franchise you're interested in, you can go straight to that entry for more information.

Directory by Category

Automotive Services and Rental

AAMCO Transmissions
201 Gibraltar Road
Horsham, PA 19044
Telephone: (800) 462-2626
Web Site: www.aamcotransmissions.com
Description: An automotive services and
repairs chain
Parent Company: American Driveline
Systems, Inc.
Date Began Franchising: January 1, 1963
Sales ($Million): 454
Total Units: 743
Franchised: 100%
International: 4%
Minimum Investment: $197,650
Maximum Investment: $222,414
Royalty: 7.0%
National Advertising: $150/mo.
SBA Registry Status: Listed

Batteries Plus
925 Walnut Ridge Dr.
Hartland, WI 53029
Telephone: (262) 912-3000
Web Site: www.batteriesplus.com
Description: Specialty battery retailer and
wholesaler franchises
Parent Company: Batteries Plus LLC
Date Began Franchising: April 1, 1992
Sales ($Million): 149
Total Units: 250
Franchised: 94%
International: 0%
Minimum Investment: $176,485

Maximum Investment: $327,485
Royalty: 4.0%
National Advertising: 1%
SBA Registry Status: Listed

Big O Tires, Inc.
12650 E .Briarwood Ave., Ste. 2-D
Centennial, CO 80112
Telephone: (303) 728-5500
Web Site: www.bigotires.com
Description: A chain of automotive tire
and service shops
Parent Company: TBC Corporation
Date Began Franchising: December 30,
1982
Sales ($Million): 700
Total Units: 557
Franchised: 100%
International: 0%
Minimum Investment: $364,300
Maximum Investment: $607,800
Royalty: 2.0%
National Advertising: 0.2%
SBA Registry Status: Listed

CARSTAR
8400 W. 110th St., Ste. 200
Overland Park, KS 66210
Telephone: (913) 451-1294
Web Site: www.carstar.com
Description: Automotive collision repair
center consolidator
Parent Company: CARSTAR Franchise
Systems, Inc.
Date Began Franchising: August 1, 1989
Sales ($Million): 510
Total Units: 374
Franchised: 97%

International: 29%
Minimum Investment: $280,100
Maximum Investment: $788,500
Royalty: 1.0%
National Advertising: 1.3%
SBA Registry Status: Not Listed

Cottman Transmission
204 Gibraltar Road
Horsham, PA 19044
Telephone: (215) 643-5885
Web Site: www.cottman.com
Description: North American chain of
    transmission repair shops
Parent Company: American Driveline
    Systems, Inc.
Date Began Franchising: January 1, 1964
Sales ($Million): 156
Total Units: 354
Franchised: 100%
International: 1%
Minimum Investment: $161,000
Maximum Investment: $208,700
Royalty: 7.5%
National Advertising: $730/wk
SBA Registry Status: Listed

Dollar Rent A Car
5310 E. 31st Street, CIMS #7060
Tulsa, OK 74135
Telephone: (918) 669-3000
Web Site: www.dollar.com
Description: A global chain of car
    rental agencies
Parent Company: Dollar Thrifty
    Automotive Group, Inc.
Date Began Franchising: January 1, 1966
Sales ($Million): 1,023
Total Units: 574
Franchised: 67%
International: 57%
Minimum Investment: $113,575

Maximum Investment: $713,575
Royalty: Variable
National Advertising: 0%
SBA Registry Status: Not Listed

Express Oil Change
190 W. Valley Ave.
Birmingham, AL 35209
Telephone: (205) 945-1771
Web Site: www.expressoil.com
Description: A chain of automotive oil
    change and maintenance shops
Parent Company: Express Oil Change, LLC
Date Began Franchising: February 22, 1996
Sales ($Million): 104
Total Units: 158
Franchised: 68%
International: 0%
Minimum Investment: $114,500
Maximum Investment: $149,500
Royalty: 5.0%
National Advertising: 2.0%
SBA Registry Status: Not Listed

Glass Doctor
1020 N. University Parks Dr.
Waco, TX 76707
Telephone: (254) 759-5891
Web Site: www.glassdoctor.com
Description: A repair and replacement
    service for home, auto, and business
    glass panes
Parent Company: The Dwyer Group, Inc.
Date Began Franchising: January 1, 1984
Sales ($Million): 66
Total Units: 190
Franchised: 74%
International: 0%
Minimum Investment: $107,581
Maximum Investment: $259,581
Royalty: Variable
National Advertising: 2.0%
SBA Registry Status: Listed

Grease Monkey

7100 East Belleview, Ste. 305
Greenwood Village, CO 80111
Telephone: (303) 308-1660
Web Site: www.greasemonkeyintl.com
Description: A chain of automotive oil
  change and maintenance shops
Parent Company: Grease Monkey
  International
Date Began Franchising: September 28,
  1978
Sales ($Million): 99
Total Units: 231
Franchised: 99%
International: 20%
Minimum Investment: $158,000
Maximum Investment: $259,000
Royalty: 5.0%
National Advertising: 1.0%
SBA Registry Status: Listed

J.D. Byrider

12802 Hamilton Crossing Blvd.
Carmel, IN 46032
Telephone: (317) 249-3000
Web Site: www.jdbyrider.com
Description: Used car sales and financing
  franchises
Parent Company: JD Byrider Systems, Inc.
Date Began Franchising: May 1, 1989
Sales ($Million): 527
Total Units: 123
Franchised: 89%
International: 0%
Minimum Investment: $514,193
Maximum Investment: $3,287,500
Royalty: 3.0%
National Advertising: Variable
SBA Registry Status: Not Listed

Jiffy Lube International, Inc.

700 Milam Street
Houston, TX 77002
Telephone: (713) 546-4000
Web Site: www.jiffylube.com
Description: A chain of automotive quick
  lube shops
Parent Company: Pennzoil Quaker State
Date Began Franchising: January 1, 1979
Sales ($Million): 1,470
Total Units: 2,205
Franchised: 87%
International: 2%
Minimum Investment: $214,000
Maximum Investment: $273,000
Royalty: 5.0%
National Advertising: 5.0%
SBA Registry Status: Not Listed

LINE-X Spray-On Truck Bedliners

2400 S. Garnsey Street
Santa Ana, CA 92707
Telephone: (714) 850-1662
Web Site: www.line-xfranchise.com
Description: A chain of shops specializing
  in applying spray-on truck bedliners
Parent Company: Line-X Franchise
  Development Corp.
Date Began Franchising: April 1, 1999
Sales ($Million): 60
Total Units: 526
Franchised: 100%
International: 5%
Minimum Investment: $115,183
Maximum Investment: $202,450
Royalty: 0%
National Advertising: 1.5%
SBA Registry Status: Listed

MAACO Auto Painting & Body Works

381 Brooks Rd.
King of Prussia, PA 19406
Telephone: (610) 265-6606
Web Site: www.franchise.maaco.com
Description: Automotive body shop
    franchise
Parent Company: Maaco Enterprises, Inc.
Date Began Franchising: February 1, 1972
Sales ($Million): 408
Total Units: 476
Franchised: 100%
International: 8%
Minimum Investment: $417,460
Maximum Investment: $460,550
Royalty: 9.0%
National Advertising: $850
SBA Registry Status: Listed

Matco Tools

4403 Allen Road
Stow, OH 44224-1096
Telephone: (330) 929-4949
Web Site: www.matcotools.com
Description: Automotive equipment and
    tools manufacturer and distributor
Parent Company: Danaher Corporation
Date Began Franchising: January 1, 1979
Sales ($Million): 428
Total Units: 1,463
Franchised: 100%
International: 0%
Minimum Investment: $74,139
Maximum Investment: $169,554
Royalty: 0%
National Advertising: 0%
SBA Registry Status: Listed

Meineke Car Care Centers

128 S. Tryon Street, Ste. 900
Charlotte, NC 28202
Telephone: (704) 377-8855

Web Site: www.meinekefranchise.com
Description: An automotive services and
    repairs chain
Parent Company: Driven Brands, Inc.
Date Began Franchising: September 1, 1972
Sales ($Million): 409
Total Units: 888
Franchised: 100%
International: 6%
Minimum Investment: $205,103
Maximum Investment: $268,090
Royalty: Variable
National Advertising: 8.0%
SBA Registry Status: Listed

Midas

1300 Arlington Heights Rd.
Itasca, IL 60143
Telephone: (630) 438-3000
Web Site: www.midas.com
Description: Automotive service providing
    franchises
Parent Company: Midas International
    Corporation
Date Began Franchising: January 1, 1956
Sales ($Million): 1,500
Total Units: 2,610
Franchised: 97%
International: 39%
Minimum Investment: $243,150
Maximum Investment: $311,800
Royalty: 10.0%
National Advertising: Variable
SBA Registry Status: Listed

Payless Car Sales, Inc.

2350 North 34th St. North
St. Petersburg, FL 33713
Telephone: (727) 323-0943
Web Site: www.paylessfranchising.com
Description: A chain of preowned
    vehicle sellers

Parent Company: Avalon Global
    Group, Inc.
Date Began Franchising: January 1, 1993
Sales ($Million): 240
Total Units: 50
Franchised: 100%
International: 0%
Minimum Investment: $351,650
Maximum Investment: $3,079,500
Royalty: Variable
National Advertising: Variable
SBA Registry Status: Not Listed

Precision Tune Auto Care
748 Miller Drive SE
Leesburg, VA 20175
Telephone: (703) 669-2311
Web Site: www.precisiontune.com
Description: A chain of automotive
    repair shops
Parent Company: Precision Auto Care
Date Began Franchising: June 1, 1977
Sales ($Million): 168
Total Units: 414
Franchised: 100%
International: 24%
Minimum Investment: $123,000
Maximum Investment: $208,075
Royalty: 6.0%–7.5%
National Advertising: 1.5%
SBA Registry Status: Listed

SpeeDee Oil Change & Tune-Up
159 Hwy. 22E
Madisonville, LA 70447
Telephone: (985) 845-1919
Web Site: www.speedeeoil.com
Description: A chain of automotive quick
    lube and tune-up shops
Parent Company: G.C. & K.B.
    Investments, Inc.
Date Began Franchising: July 1, 1987
Sales ($Million): 89

Total Units: 185
Franchised: 100%
International: 35%
Minimum Investment: $202,500
Maximum Investment: $361,500
Royalty: 6.0%
National Advertising: 8.0%
SBA Registry Status: Listed

Thrifty Car Rental
P.O. Box 35250
Tulsa, OK 74153-0250
Telephone: (918) 665-3930
Web Site: www.thrifty.com
Description: A global chain of car
    rental agencies
Parent Company: Dollar Thrifty
    Automotive Group, Inc.
Date Began Franchising: December 10,
    1998
Sales ($Million): 957
Total Units: 975
Franchised: 81%
International: 62%
Minimum Investment: $836,700
Maximum Investment: $4,434,600
Royalty: Variable
National Advertising: 2.5%–4.5%
SBA Registry Status: Listed

Transmission USA/Mr. Transmission
4444 W. 147th Street
Midlothian, IL 60445
Telephone: (708) 389-5922
Web Site: www.moranindustries.com
Description: A chain of transmission
    service and repair shops
Parent Company: Moran Industries, Inc.
Date Began Franchising: January 1, 1970
Sales ($Million): 62
Total Units: 155
Franchised: 100%
International: 0%

Minimum Investment: $149,000
Maximum Investment: $149,000
Royalty: 7.0%
National Advertising: 1.0%
SBA Registry Status: Listed

Tuffy/Car-X
1414 Baronial Plaza Dr.
Toledo, OH 43615
Telephone: (419) 865-6900
Web Site: www.tuffy.com/www.carx.com
Description: A chain of automotive
    repair centers
Parent Company: Tuffy Associates Corp.
Date Began Franchising: April 1, 1986
Sales ($Million): 256
Total Units: 429
Franchised: 92%
International: 0%
Minimum Investment: $209,000
Maximum Investment: $317,000
Royalty: 5.0%
National Advertising: 5.0%
SBA Registry Status: Not Listed

Lodging

AmericInn
250 Lake Drive East
Chanhassen, MN 55317
Telephone: (952) 294-5000
Web Site: www.americinn.com
Description: A midscale hotel chain
    without dining services
Parent Company: AmericanInn
    International, LLC
Date Began Franchising: July 1, 1986
Sales ($Million): 194
Total Units: 202
Franchised: 100%
International: 0%
Minimum Investment: $2,726,150

Maximum Investment: $3,622,550
Royalty: 5.0%
National Advertising: 2.0%
SBA Registry Status: Listed

AmeriHost Franchise Systems
1 Sylvan Way
Parsippany, NJ 07054
Telephone: (973) 496-2800
Web Site: www.amerihostinn.com
Description: A midscale hotel chain
    without dining services
Parent Company: Wyndham Hotel Group
Date Began Franchising: September 30,
    2000
Sales ($Million): 96
Total Units: 110
Franchised: 100%
International: 0%
Minimum Investment: $3,714,500
Maximum Investment: $4,700,300
Royalty: 4.0%
National Advertising: 3.5%
SBA Registry Status: Listed

Baymont Inn & Suites
1 Sylvan Way
Parsippany, NJ 07054
Telephone: (973) 496-2800
Web Site: www.baymontinns.com
Description: A midscale hotel chain
    without dining services
Parent Company: Wyndham Hotel Group
Date Began Franchising: September 1,
    2004
Sales ($Million): 182
Total Units: 118
Franchised: 100%
International: 0%
Minimum Investment: $4,255,000
Maximum Investment: $5,280,000
Royalty: 4.0%
National Advertising: 2.5%
SBA Registry Status: Listed

Candlewood Suites

Three Ravinia Drive, Ste. 100
Atlanta, GA 30346
Telephone: (770) 604-2000
Web Site: www.candlewoodsuites.com
Description: A midscale, extended-stay,
  all-suites hotel chain
Parent Company: InterContinental
  Hotels Group
Date Began Franchising: June 1, 1995
Sales ($Million): 209
Total Units: 112
Franchised: 32%
International: 0%
Minimum Investment: $3,927,000
Maximum Investment: $5,358,000
Royalty: 5.0%
National Advertising: 2.5%
SBA Registry Status: Listed

Clarion Inn & Suites

10750 Columbia Pike
Silver Spring, MD 20901
Telephone: (301) 592-5032
Web Site:
  www.choicehotelsfranchise.com
Description: A midscale hotel chain with
  dining services
Parent Company: Choice Hotels
  International
Date Began Franchising: January 1, 1987
Sales ($Million): 529
Total Units: 263
Franchised: 100%
International: 42%
Minimum Investment: $7,413,883
Maximum Investment: $11,835,066
Royalty: 4.3%
National Advertising: 2.0%
SBA Registry Status: Listed

Comfort Inn & Suites

10750 Columbia Pike
Silver Spring, MD 20901
Telephone: (301) 592-5032
Web Site:
  www.choicehotelsfranchise.com
Description: A midscale hotel chain
  without dining services
Parent Company: Choice Hotels
  International
Date Began Franchising: January 1, 1981
Sales ($Million): 2,938
Total Units: 2,418
Franchised: 100%
International: 24%
Minimum Investment: $3,303,301
Maximum Investment: $4,858,075
Royalty: 5.7%
National Advertising: 2.1%
SBA Registry Status: Listed

Country Inns & Suites

P.O. Box 59159
Minneapolis, MN 55459
Telephone: (763) 212-1000
Web Site: www.countryinns.com
Description: A midscale hotel chain
  without dining services
Parent Company: Carlson Hotels
  Worldwide
Date Began Franchising: January 1, 1987
Sales ($Million): 551
Total Units: 380
Franchised: 97%
International: 7%
Minimum Investment: $3,182,471
Maximum Investment: $5,469,471
Royalty: 4.5%
National Advertising: 2.5%
SBA Registry Status: Not Listed

Courtyard

Marriott Drive, Dept 977.01
Washington, DC 20058
Telephone: (301) 380-7770
Web Site: www.marriot.com
Description: An upscale hotel chain serving North America
Parent Company: Marriott International, Inc.
Date Began Franchising: October 1, 1990
Sales ($Million): 2,566
Total Units: 670
Franchised: 58%
International: 10%
Minimum Investment: $6,050,600
Maximum Investment: $9,757,450
Royalty: 5.5%
National Advertising: 2.0%
SBA Registry Status: Not Listed

Crowne Plaza

Three Ravinia Drive, Ste. 100
Altanta, GA 30346
Telephone: (770) 604-2000
Web Site: www.crowneplaza.com
Description: A global upscale hotel and resort chain
Parent Company: InterContinental Hotels Group
Date Began Franchising: February 1990
Sales ($Million): 1,734
Total Units: 235
Franchised: 64%
International: 54%
Minimum Investment: $4,923,775
Maximum Investment: $26,467,459
Royalty: 5.0%
National Advertising: 2.5%
SBA Registry Status: Listed

Days Inns Worldwide

1 Sylvan Way
Parsippany, NJ 07054
Telephone: (973) 496-2800
Web Site: www.daysinn.com
Description: An economy hotel chain
Parent Company: Wyndham Hotel Group
Date Began Franchising: February 1, 1992
Sales ($Million): 1,567
Total Units: 1,844
Franchised: 100%
International: 8%
Minimum Investment: $3,711,800
Maximum Investment: $5,702,900
Royalty: 5.0%
National Advertising: 5.0%
SBA Registry Status: Listed

Doubletree

9336 Civic Center Drive
Beverly Hills, CA 90210
Telephone: (310) 278-4321
Web Site: www.doubletreefranchise.com
Description: An upscale hotel and resort chain
Parent Company: Hilton Hotels Corporation
Date Began Franchising: February 1, 1989
Sales ($Million): 1,224
Total Units: 169
Franchised: 72%
International: 2%
Minimum Investment: $24,583,750
Maximum Investment: $35,953,250
Royalty: 4.0%
National Advertising: 4.0%
SBA Registry Status: Not Listed

Econo Lodge

10750 Columbia Pike
Silver Spring, MD 20901
Telephone: (301) 592-5032

Web Site:
www.choicehotelsfranchise.com
Description: An economy hotel chain
Parent Company: Choice Hotels
International
Date Began Franchising: January 1, 1990
Sales ($Million): 444
Total Units: 848
Franchised: 100%
International: 5%
Minimum Investment: $1,987,819
Maximum Investment: $3,071,904
Royalty: 4.5%
National Advertising: 3.5%
SBA Registry Status: Listed

Embassy Suites Hotels
9336 Civic Center Drive
Beverly Hills, CA 90210
Telephone: (301) 278-4321
Web Site: www.embassyfranchise.com
Description: An upscale all-suites
hotel chain
Parent Company: Hilton Hotels
Corporation
Date Began Franchising: January 1, 1984
Sales ($Million): 1,547
Total Units: 185
Franchised: 55%
International: 3%
Minimum Investment: $17,043,000
Maximum Investment: $22,836,000
Royalty: 4.0%
National Advertising: Variable
SBA Registry Status: Not Listed

Fairfield Inn
Marriott Dr., Dept. 977.01
Washington, DC 20058
Telephone: (301) 380-7770
Web Site: www.marriot.com
Description: A midscale hotel chain
without dining services

Parent Company: Marriott
International, Inc.
Date Began Franchising: October 1, 1989
Sales ($Million): 894
Total Units: 524
Franchised: 100%
International: 1%
Minimum Investment: $4,560,100
Maximum Investment: $7,073,175
Royalty: 4.5%
National Advertising: 2.5%
SBA Registry Status: Not Listed

Four Points by Sheraton
1111 Westchester Ave.
White Plains, NY 10604
Telephone: (914) 640-4498
Web Site:
www.development.starwood.com
Description: An upscale hotel chain
Parent Company: Starwood Hotels and
Resorts Worldwide, Inc.
Date Began Franchising: January 1, 1995
Sales ($Million): 565
Total Units: 124
Franchised: 85%
International: 27%
Minimum Investment: $13,720,000
Maximum Investment: $23,945,000
Royalty: 6.0%
National Advertising: 1.0%
SBA Registry Status: Not Listed

Hampton Inn and
Hampton Inn & Suites
9336 Civic Center Drive
Beverly Hills, CA 90210
Telephone: (310) 278-4321
Web Site: www.hamptonfranchise.com
Description: A midscale hotel chain
dining services
Parent Company: Hilton Hotels
Corporation

Date Began Franchising: January 1, 1983
Sales ($Million): 3,056
Total Units: 1,369
Franchised: 97%
International: 2%
Minimum Investment: $4,348,000
Maximum Investment: $6,981,000
Royalty: 4.0%
National Advertising: 4.0%
SBA Registry Status: Not Listed

Hawthorn Suites

13 Corporate Sq., Ste. 250
Atlanta, GA 30329
Telephone: (404) 321-4045
Web Site: www.hawthorn.com
Description: An upscale all-suites
   hotel chain
Parent Company: US Franchise Systems,
   Inc.
Date Began Franchising: March 20, 1996
Sales ($Million): 189
Total Units: 98
Franchised: 100%
International: 2%
Minimum Investment: $5,725,000
Maximum Investment: $7,360,000
Royalty: 5.0%
National Advertising: 2.5%
SBA Registry Status: Listed

Hilton

9336 Civic Center Drive
Beverly Hills, CA 90210
Telephone: (310) 278-4321
Web Site: www.hiltonfranchise.com
Description: An upscale hotel and
   resort chain
Parent Company: Hilton Hotels
   Corporation
Date Began Franchising: September 1, 1965
Sales ($Million): 3,654
Total Units: 260

Franchised: 67%
International: 7%
Minimum Investment: $33,760,500
Maximum Investment: $57,443,500
Royalty: 5.0%
National Advertising: 4.0%
SBA Registry Status: Not Listed

Hilton Garden Inn

9336 Civic Center Drive
Beverly Hills, CA 90210
Telephone: (310) 278-4321
Web Site:
   www.hiltongardeninnfranchise.com
Description: An upscale hotel chain with
   dining services
Parent Company: Hilton Hotels
   Corporation
Date Began Franchising: July 23, 1962
Sales ($Million): 1,033
Total Units: 279
Franchised: 97%
International: 6%
Minimum Investment: $8,743,000
Maximum Investment: $14,321,000
Royalty: 5.0%
National Advertising: 4.3%
SBA Registry Status: Not Listed

Holiday Inn Express

Three Ravinia Drive, Ste. 100
Atlanta, GA 30346-2149
Telephone: (770) 604-2000
Web Site: www.hiexpress.com
Description: A midscale hotel chain
   without dining services
Parent Company: InterContinental
   Hotels Group
Date Began Franchising: January 1, 1990
Sales ($Million): 2,672
Total Units: 1,590
Franchised: 98%
International: 15%

Minimum Investment: $5,401,020
Maximum Investment: $8,887,030
Royalty: 5.0%
National Advertising: 2.5%
SBA Registry Status: Listed

Holiday Inn Hotels & Resorts

Three Ravinia Drive, Ste. 100
Atlanta, GA 30346-2149
Telephone: (770) 604-2000
Web Site: www.holidayinn.com
Description: A midscale hotel and resort
    chain with dining services
Parent Company: InterContinental
    Hotels Group
Date Began Franchising: January 1, 1990
Sales ($Million): 5,474
Total Units: 1,435
Franchised: 84%
International: 38%
Minimum Investment: $5,401,020
Maximum Investment: $8,887,030
Royalty: 5.0%
National Advertising: 2.5%
SBA Registry Status: Listed

Homewood Suites by Hilton

9336 Civic Center Drive
Beverly Hills, CA 90210
Telephone: (310) 278-4321
Web Site:
    www.homewoodsuitesfranchise.com
Description: An upscale all-suites brand
    of residential-style hotels
Parent Company: Hilton Hotels
    Corporation
Date Began Franchising: January 1, 1988
Sales ($Million): 537
Total Units: 178
Franchised: 76%
International: 2%
Minimum Investment: $9,144,500

Maximum Investment: $14,487,000
Royalty: 4.0%
National Advertising: 4.0%
SBA Registry Status: Not Listed

Howard Johnson International

1 Sylvan Way
Parsippany, NJ 07054
Telephone: (973) 496-2800
Web Site: www.howardjohnson.com
Description: A global midscale hotel
    chain with dining services
Parent Company: Wyndham Hotel Group
Date Began Franchising: January 1, 1935
Sales ($Million): 455
Total Units: 458
Franchised: 100%
International: 21%
Minimum Investment: $793,000
Maximum Investment: $1,055,000
Royalty: 2.0%
National Advertising: 0.3%
SBA Registry Status: Listed

Knights Franchise Systems

1 Sylvan Way
Parsippany, NJ 07054
Telephone: (973) 496-2800
Web Site: www.knightsinn.com
Description: An economy hotel chain
Parent Company: Wyndham Hotel Group
Date Began Franchising: September 1, 1991
Sales ($Million): 94
Total Units: 216
Franchised: 100%
International: 5%
Minimum Investment: $3,504,300
Maximum Investment: $4,424,900
Royalty: Variable
National Advertising: 5.0%
SBA Registry Status: Listed

La Quinta Franchise LLC

909 Hidden Ridge, Ste. 600
Irving, TX 75038
Telephone: (214) 492-6753
Web Site: www.laquintafranchise.com
Description: A midscale hotel chain
  without dining services
Parent Company: LQ Management LLC
Date Began Franchising: January 1, 2003
Sales ($Million): 895
Total Units: 528
Franchised: 30%
International: 0%
Minimum Investment: $4,478,300
Maximum Investment: $6,098,400
Royalty: 4.0%
National Advertising: 2.5%
SBA Registry Status: Listed

Luxury Collection

1111 Westchester Ave.
White Plains, NY 10604
Telephone: (914) 640-4498
Web Site:
  www.development.starwood.com
Description: A global luxury hotel and
  resort chain
Parent Company: Starwood Hotels &
  Resorts Worldwide Inc.
Date Began Franchising: January 1, 1998
Sales ($Million): 642
Total Units: 45
Franchised: 33%
International: 82%
Minimum Investment: $47,700,000
Maximum Investment: $93,160,000
Royalty: Variable
National Advertising: 1.0%
SBA Registry Status: Not Listed

Marriott Hotels, Resorts & Suites

Marriott Dr., Dept. 977.01
Washington, DC 20058
Telephone: (301) 380-7770
Web Site: www.marriott.com
Description: An upscale hotel and
  resort chain
Parent Company: Marriott International
Date Began Franchising: January 1, 1968
Sales ($Million): 6,760
Total Units: 498
Franchised: 39%
International: 34%
Minimum Investment: $42,414,100
Maximum Investment: $66,707,200
Royalty: Variable
National Advertising: 1.0%
SBA Registry Status: Not Listed

Microtel Inns & Suites

13 Corporate Sq., Ste. 250
Atlanta, GA 30329
Telephone: (404) 321-4045
Web Site: www.microtelinn.com
Description: An economy hotel chain
Parent Company: US Franchise
  Systems, Inc.
Date Began Franchising: October 1, 1995
Sales ($Million): 202
Total Units: 260
Franchised: 100%
International: 4%
Minimum Investment: $3,870,800
Maximum Investment: $5,452,500
Royalty: Variable
National Advertising: Variable
SBA Registry Status: Listed

Motel 6

4001 International Parkway
Carrollton, TX 75007
Telephone: (972) 360-9000

Web Site: www.motel6.com
Description: An economy hotel chain
Parent Company: Accor North America
Date Began Franchising: December 1, 1993
Sales ($Million): 886
Total Units: 865
Franchised: 22%
International: 1%
Minimum Investment: $2,211,500
Maximum Investment: $2,684,650
Royalty: 4.0%
National Advertising: 3.5%
SBA Registry Status: Listed

Quality Inn & Suites
10750 Columbia Pike
Silver Spring, MD 20901
Telephone: (301) 592-5032
Web Site: www.choicehotelsfranchise.com
Description: A midscale hotel chain with
   dining services
Parent Company: Choice Hotels
   International
Date Began Franchising: January 1, 1968
Sales ($Million): 1,297
Total Units: 1,056
Franchised: 100%
International: 38%
Minimum Investment: $3,984,540
Maximum Investment: $6,285,275
Royalty: 4.7%
National Advertising: 2.1%
SBA Registry Status: Listed

Radisson Hotels & Suites
P.O. Box 59159
Minneapolis, MN 55459
Telephone: (763) 212-1000
Web Site: www.radisson.com
Description: A global upscale hotel and
   resort chain
Parent Company: Carlson Hotels
   Worldwide

Date Began Franchising: January 1, 1983
Sales ($Million): 2,497
Total Units: 415
Franchised: 94%
International: 56%
Minimum Investment: $2,222,785
Maximum Investment: $2,757,830
Royalty: 5.0%
National Advertising: 2.0%
SBA Registry Status: Not Listed

Ramada Worldwide
1 Sylvan Way
Parsippany, NJ 07054
Telephone: (973) 496-2800
Web Site: www.ramada.com
Description: A midscale hotel chain with
   dining services
Parent Company: Wyndham Hotel Group
Date Began Franchising: December 1,
   1989
Sales ($Million): 1,396
Total Units: 916
Franchised: 100%
International: 27%
Minimum Investment: $4,487,300
Maximum Investment: $6,003,900
Royalty: 4.0%
National Advertising: 4.5%
SBA Registry Status: Listed

Red Roof Inn
4001 International Parkway
Carrollton, TX 75007
Telephone: (972) 360-9000
Web Site: www.redroof.com
Description: An economy hotel chain
Parent Company: Accor North America
Date Began Franchising: January 1, 1972
Sales ($Million): 371
Total Units: 338
Franchised: 29%
International: 0%

Minimum Investment: $2,636,100
Maximum Investment: $2,985,450
Royalty: 4.5%
National Advertising: 4.0%
SBA Registry Status: Listed

Renaissance
Marriott Dr., Dept. 977.01
Washington, DC 20058
Telephone: (301) 380-7770
Web Site: www.marriot.com
Description: An upscale hotel and
    resort chain
Parent Company: Marriott
    International, Inc.
Date Began Franchising: January 1, 1957
Sales ($Million): 1,499
Total Units: 124
Franchised: 38%
International: 52%
Minimum Investment: $34,781,500
Maximum Investment: $54,636,300
Royalty: 5.0%
National Advertising: 1.5%
SBA Registry Status: Not Listed

Residence Inn
Marriott Dr., Dept. 977.01
Washington, DC 20058
Telephone: (301) 380-7770
Web Site: www.marriot.com
Description: An upscale hotel and
    resort chain
Parent Company: Marriott
    International, Inc.
Date Began Franchising: July 1, 1987
Sales ($Million): 1,750
Total Units: 489
Franchised: 73%
International: 3%
Minimum Investment: $7,340,800

Maximum Investment: $11,360,350
Royalty: 5.0%
National Advertising: 2.5%
SBA Registry Status: Not Listed

Rodeway Inn
10750 Columbia Pike
Silver Spring, MD 20901
Telephone: (301) 592-5032
Web Site:
    www.choicehotelsfranchise.com
Description: An economy hotel chain
Parent Company: Choice Hotels
    International
Date Began Franchising: January 1, 1990
Sales ($Million): 84
Total Units: 185
Franchised: 100%
International: 3%
Minimum Investment: $2,128,435
Maximum Investment: $3,291,904
Royalty: 3.5%
National Advertising: 1.3%
SBA Registry Status: Listed

Sheraton Hotels & Resorts
1111 Westchester Ave.
White Plains, NY 10604
Telephone: (914) 640-4498
Web Site:
    www.development.starwood.com
Description: An upscale hotel and
    resort chain
Parent Company: Starwood Hotels and
    Resorts Worldwide, Inc.
Date Began Franchising: June 1, 1962
Sales ($Million): 4,854
Total Units: 391
Franchised: 43%
International: 51%
Minimum Investment: $25,730,000

Maximum Investment: $61,175,000
Royalty: 6.0%
National Advertising: 1.0%
SBA Registry Status: Not Listed

Sleep Inn
10750 Columbia Pike
Silver Spring, MD 20901
Telephone: (301) 592-5000
Web Site:
www.choicehotelsfranchise.com
Description: A midscale hotel chain
without dining services
Parent Company: Choice Hotels
International
Date Began Franchising: January 1, 1987
Sales ($Million): 351
Total Units: 335
Franchised: 100%
International: 5%
Minimum Investment: $35,201
Maximum Investment: $53,049
Royalty: 4.7%
National Advertising: 2.1%
SBA Registry Status: Listed

SpringHill Suites
Marriott Dr., Dept. 977.01
Washington, DC 20058
Telephone: (301) 380-7770
Web Site: www.marriot.com
Description: An upscale all-suites
hotel chain
Parent Company: Marriott
International, Inc.
Date Began Franchising: September 1,
1998
Sales ($Million): 381
Total Units: 136
Franchised: 83%
International: 1%
Minimum Investment: $5,553,125

Maximum Investment: $9,784,975
Royalty: 5.0%
National Advertising: 2.5%
SBA Registry Status: Not Listed

Staybridge Suites
Three Ravinia Drive, Ste. 100
Atlanta, GA 30346
Telephone: (770) 604-2000
Web Site: www.staybridge.com
Description: An upscale all-suites
hotel chain
Parent Company: InterContinental
Hotels Group
Date Began Franchising: November 1, 1997
Sales ($Million): 246
Total Units: 87
Franchised: 55%
International: 5%
Minimum Investment: $5,890,800
Maximum Investment: $8,031,000
Royalty: 5.0%
National Advertising: 2.5%
SBA Registry Status: Listed

Super 8 Motels
1 Sylvan Way
Parsippany, NJ 07054
Telephone: (973) 496-2800
Web Site: www.super8.com
Description: An economy hotel chain
Parent Company: Wyndham Hotel Group
Date Began Franchising: January 1, 1972
Sales ($Million): 1,279
Total Units: 2,040
Franchised: 100%
International: 6%
Minimum Investment: $2,273,450
Maximum Investment: $2,832,450
Royalty: 5.0%
National Advertising: 5.0%
SBA Registry Status: Listed

TownePlace Suites
Marriott Dr., Dept. 977.01
Washington, DC 20058
Telephone: (301) 380-7770
Web Site: www.marriot.com
Description: A midscale hotel chain
without dining services
Parent Company: Marriott
International, Inc.
Date Began Franchising: April 1, 1996
Sales ($Million): 370
Total Units: 122
Franchised: 72%
International: 0%
Minimum Investment: $5,916,450
Maximum Investment: $8,624,550
Royalty: 5.0%
National Advertising: 1.5%
SBA Registry Status: Not Listed

Travelodge Hotels
1 Sylvan Way
Parsippany, NJ 07054
Telephone: (973) 496-2800
Web Site: www.travelodge.com
Description: An economy hotel chain
Parent Company: Wyndham Hotel Group
Date Began Franchising: January 1, 1966
Sales ($Million): 388
Total Units: 513
Franchised: 100%
International: 23%
Minimum Investment: $3,556,800
Maximum Investment: $5,692,900
Royalty: 4.5%
National Advertising: 4.0%
SBA Registry Status: Listed

Westin Hotels and Resorts
1111 Westchester Ave.
White Plains, NY 10604
Telephone: (914) 640-4498

Web Site:
www.development.starwood.com
Description: A global upscale hotel and
resort chain
Parent Company: Starwood Hotels and
Resorts Worldwide, Inc.
Date Began Franchising: January 1, 1992
Sales ($Million): 2,462
Total Units: 123
Franchised: 31%
International: 34%
Minimum Investment: $31,530,000
Maximum Investment: $72,660,000
Royalty: 7.0%
National Advertising: 2.0%
SBA Registry Status: Not Listed

Wingate Inns International
1 Sylvan Way
Parsippany, NJ 07054
Telephone: (973) 496-2800
Web Site: www.wingateinns.com
Description: A global midscale hotel
chain without dining services
Parent Company: Wyndham Hotel Group
Date Began Franchising: May 1, 1995
Sales ($Million): 245
Total Units: 146
Franchised: 100%
International: 1%
Minimum Investment: $5,931,550
Maximum Investment: $6,485,250
Royalty: 4.5%
National Advertising: 4.0%
SBA Registry Status: Listed

Wyndham Hotels & Resorts
1 Sylvan Way
Parsippany, NJ 07054
Telephone: (973) 496-2800
Web Site: www.wyndham.com
Description: An upscale hotel and
resort chain

Parent Company: Wyndham Hotel Group
Date Began Franchising: January 1, 1996
Sales ($Million): 659
Total Units: 98
Franchised: 77%
International: 16%
Minimum Investment: $96,828
Maximum Investment: $97,528
Royalty: 5.0%
National Advertising: 1.5%
SBA Registry Status: Not Listed

Maintenance, Restoration, and Cleaning

ABC Seamless
3001 Fiechtner Dr.
Fargo, ND 58103
Telephone: (701) 293-5952
Web Site: www.abcseamless.com
Description: A provider of seamless gutter, siding, and window installation
Parent Company: ABC, Inc.
Date Began Franchising: September 1, 1979
Sales ($Million): 62
Total Units: 124
Franchised: 97%
International: 0%
Minimum Investment: $100,480
Maximum Investment: $219,500
Royalty: Variable
National Advertising: 0.5%
SBA Registry Status: Listed

Basement Finishing System
One Owens Corning Pkwy.
Toledo, OH 43659
Telephone: (800) GET-PINK
Web Site: www.owenscorning.com
Description: Chain of complete basement remodeling and finishing franchises
Parent Company: Owens Corning

Date Began Franchising: 2000
Sales ($Million): 149
Total Units: 28
Franchised: 100%
International: 0%
Minimum Investment: $24,100
Maximum Investment: $43,100
Royalty: 5.0%
National Advertising: Variable
SBA Registry Status: Not Listed

Benjamin Franklin Plumbing
50 Central Avenue, Ste. 920
Sarasota, FL 34236
Telephone: (941) 552-5111
Web Site: www.benfranklinplumbing.com
Description: Franchises offering residential plumbing services
Parent Company: Clockwork Home Services, Inc.
Date Began Franchising: January 9, 2001
Sales ($Million): 80
Total Units: 166
Franchised: 100%
International: 0%
Minimum Investment: $165,290
Maximum Investment: $386,790
Royalty: Variable
National Advertising: 4.0%
SBA Registry Status: Not Listed

CertaPro Painters
PO Box 836
Oaks, PA 19456
Telephone: (610) 650-9999
Web Site: www.gocerta.com
Description: Franchises offering residential and commercial painting and decorative sevices
Parent Company: The Franchise Company
Date Began Franchising: September 1, 1992
Sales ($Million): 119
Total Units: 301

Franchised: 100%
International: 9%
Minimum Investment: $85,000
Maximum Investment: $106,000
Royalty: 5.0%
National Advertising: 10.0%
SBA Registry Status: Listed

Certified Restoration Drycleaning Network

2060 Coolidge Highway
Berkeley, MI 48072
Telephone: (248) 246-7878
Web Site:
    www.restorationdrycleaning.com
Description: An international organization
    of textile restoration specialists
Parent Company: Certified Restoration
    Drycleaning Network, LLC
Date Began Franchising: July 2001
Sales ($Million): 56
Total Units: 141
Franchised: 99%
International: 19%
Minimum Investment: $37,350
Maximum Investment: $222,000
Royalty: Variable
National Advertising: 1.0%
SBA Registry Status: Not Listed

ChemStation

3400 Encrete Lane
Dayton, OH 45439
Telephone: (937) 294-8265
Web Site: www.chemstation.com
Description: Franchises offering delivery
    of custom-formulated cleaning and
    processing chemicals
Parent Company: ChemStation
    International
Date Began Franchising: January 1, 1985
Sales ($Million): 60
Total Units: 54

Franchised: 91%
International: 2%
Minimum Investment: $193,500
Maximum Investment: $283,500
Royalty: 4.0%
National Advertising: 2.0%
SBA Registry Status: Not Listed

CleanNet USA Inc.

9861 Broken Land Pkwy, Ste. 208
Columbia, MD 21046
Telephone: (410) 720-6444
Web Site: www.cleannetusa.com
Description: A chain of commercial
    office-cleaning franchises
Parent Company: CleanNet USA, Inc.
Date Began Franchising: March 1, 1988
Sales ($Million): 105
Total Units: 2,969
Franchised: 100%
International: 0%
Minimum Investment: $3,942
Maximum Investment: $35,507
Royalty: 3.0%
National Advertising: 1.0%
SBA Registry Status: Not Listed

Coverall Cleaning Concepts

5201 Congress Ave., Ste. 275
Boca Raton, FL 33487
Telephone: (561) 922-2500
Web Site: www.coverall.com
Description: A franchise system offering
    commercial cleaning services
Parent Company: Coverall North
    America, Inc.
Date Began Franchising: July 1, 1985
Sales ($Million): 302
Total Units: 8,872
Franchised: 100%
International: 6%
Minimum Investment: $6,291
Maximum Investment: $35,920

Royalty: 5.0%
National Advertising: 0%
SBA Registry Status: Not Listed

Disaster Kleenup International
611 Busse Road, Ste. 205
Bensenville, IL 60106
Telephone: (630) 350-3000
Web Site: www.disasterkleenup.com
Description: A network of property
damage restoration contractors
Parent Company: DKI Services
Corporation
Date Began Franchising: July 10, 1995
Sales ($Million): 1,095
Total Units: 161
Franchised: 100%
International: 33%
Minimum Investment: $15,235
Maximum Investment: $40,235
Royalty: Variable
National Advertising: Variable
SBA Registry Status: Not Listed

Dryclean USA
290 NE 68th Street
Miami, FL 33138
Telephone: (305) 754-9966
Web Site: www.drycleanusa.com
Description: A chain of dry-cleaning
franchises
Parent Company: Dryclean USA, Inc.
Date Began Franchising: June 9, 1999
Sales ($Million): 104
Total Units: 484
Franchised: 100%
International: 63%
Minimum Investment: $78,300
Maximum Investment: $189,750
Royalty: Variable
National Advertising: $527/mo.
SBA Registry Status: Not Listed

Handyman Connection
10250 Alliance Road, Ste. 100
Cincinnati, OH 45242
Telephone: (513) 771-3003
Web Site: www.handymanconnection.com
Description: A chain of home repair and
light remodeling providers
Parent Company: Mamar, Inc.
Date Began Franchising: January 1, 1993
Sales ($Million): 72
Total Units: 162
Franchised: 99%
International: 15%
Minimum Investment: $71,110
Maximum Investment: $192,745
Royalty: 5.0%
National Advertising: 2.0%
SBA Registry Status: Listed

INTERIORS by Decorating Den
8659 Commerce Dr.
Easton, MD 21601
Telephone: (410) 822-9001
Web Site: www.decoratingden.com
Description: A full-service home interior
decorating chain
Parent Company: Decorating Den
Systems Inc.
Date Began Franchising: January 1, 1974
Sales ($Million): 56
Total Units: 473
Franchised: 100%
International: 6%
Minimum Investment: $24,038
Maximum Investment: $36,747
Royalty: Variable
National Advertising: 4.0%
SBA Registry Status: Not Listed

Jani-King International
16885 Dallas Pkwy.
Addison, TX 75001
Telephone: (972) 991-0900

Web Site: www.janiking.com
Description: A global chain of commercial cleaning franchises
Parent Company: Jani-King International, Inc.
Date Began Franchising: January 1, 1969
Sales ($Million): 525
Total Units: 11,407
Franchised: 100%
International: 19%
Minimum Investment: $112,100
Maximum Investment: $155,500
Royalty: 5.0%
National Advertising: 1.0%
SBA Registry Status: Not Listed

Lawn Doctor

142 State Rte. 34
Holmdel, NJ 07733
Telephone: (732) 946-0029
Web Site: www.lawndoctor.com
Description: A chain offering lawn, tree, and pest services
Parent Company: Lawn Doctor Inc.
Date Began Franchising: January 1, 1967
Sales ($Million): 79
Total Units: 490
Franchised: 100%
International: 0%
Minimum Investment: $97,900
Maximum Investment: $108,300
Royalty: 10.0%
National Advertising: 5.0%
SBA Registry Status: Listed

Maid to Perfection

1101 Opal Court, Floor 2
Hagerstown, MD 21740
Telephone: (301) 790-7900
Web Site: www.maidtoperfectioncorp.com
Description: Residential and commercial contract cleaning franchises
Parent Company: Maid to Perfection Corp.

Date Began Franchising: October 1, 1990
Sales ($Million): 89
Total Units: 303
Franchised: 100%
International: 8%
Minimum Investment: $48,590
Maximum Investment: $55,990
Royalty: Variable
National Advertising: 4.5%
SBA Registry Status: Not Listed

The Maids Home Services

4820 Dodge Street
Omaha, NE 68132
Telephone: (402) 558-5555
Web Site: www.maids.com
Description: A franchise system providing residential cleaning services
Parent Company: The Maids International
Date Began Franchising: November 1, 1979
Sales ($Million): 86
Total Units: 937
Franchised: 97%
International: 2%
Minimum Investment: $148,600
Maximum Investment: $173,200
Royalty: Variable
National Advertising: 2.0%
SBA Registry Status: Not Listed

Molly Maid

3948 Ranchero Drive
Ann Arbor, MI 48108
Telephone: (888) 700-6177
Web Site: www.mollymaid.com
Description: A chain of residential cleaning services franchises
Parent Company: Service Brands International
Date Began Franchising: January 1, 1979
Sales ($Million): 116
Total Units: 715
Franchised: 100%

International: 48%
Minimum Investment: $61,125
Maximum Investment: $106,400
Royalty: Variable
National Advertising: 2.0%
SBA Registry Status: Listed

Mr. Rooter
1010 N. University Parks Drive
Waco, TX 76707
Telephone: (254) 759-5891
Web Site: www.mrrooter.com
Description: A chain providing plumbing
  and drain-cleaning services
Parent Company: The Dwyer Group, Inc.
Date Began Franchising: July 30, 1993
Sales ($Million): 250
Total Units: 317
Franchised: 100%
International: 34%
Minimum Investment: $50,950
Maximum Investment: $142,000
Royalty: Variable
National Advertising: 2.0%
SBA Registry Status: Listed

One Hour Heating &
Air Conditioning
50 Central Avenue, Ste. 920
Sarasota, FL 34236
Telephone: (941) 552-5100
Web Site: www.onehourheatandair.com
Description: A franchise system providing
  residential HVAC services
Parent Company: Clockwork Home
  Services, Inc.
Date Began Franchising: April 1, 2003
Sales ($Million): 171
Total Units: 155
Franchised: 93%
International: 3%
Minimum Investment: $261,660

Maximum Investment: $435,920
Royalty: $1,500.00
National Advertising: 4.0%
SBA Registry Status: Not Listed

One Hour Martinizing Dry Cleaning
422 Wards Corner Rd.
Loveland, OH 45140
Telephone: (513) 351-6211
Web Site: www.martinizing.com
Description: A chain of dry-cleaning
  franchises
Parent Company: Martin Franchises Inc.
Date Began Franchising: May 1, 1978
Sales ($Million): 140
Total Units: 614
Franchised: 100%
International: 39%
Minimum Investment: $275,500
Maximum Investment: $476,000
Royalty: 4.0%
National Advertising: 3.5%
SBA Registry Status: Listed

Paul Davis Restoration
One Independent Drive, Ste. 2300
Jacksonville, FL 32202
Telephone: (904) 737-2779
Web Site: www.pdrestoration.com
Description: A building repair and
  remodeling franchise
Parent Company: First Service
Date Began Franchising: January 1, 1970
Sales ($Million): 365
Total Units: 226
Franchised: 100%
International: 0%
Minimum Investment: $104,464
Maximum Investment: $164,774
Royalty: 3.5%
National Advertising: $125/mo.
SBA Registry Status: Listed

Pillar to Post

13902 N. Dale Mabry Hwy., Ste. 300
Tampa, FL 33618
Telephone: (813) 962-4461
Web Site: www.pillartopost.com
Description: A chain of home inspection
   franchises
Parent Company: The Franchise Company
Date Began Franchising: September 15,
   1999
Sales ($Million): 125
Total Units: 519
Franchised: 100%
International: 16%
Minimum Investment: $36,600
Maximum Investment: $57,000
Royalty: 7.0%
National Advertising: 4.0%
SBA Registry Status: Not Listed

Rainbow International Restoration and Cleaning

1010 N. University Parks Dr.
Waco, TX 76707
Telephone: (254) 759-5891
Web Site: www.rainbowintl.com
Description: Franchises offering disaster
   restoration and cleaning services
Parent Company: The Dwyer Group
Date Began Franchising: January 1, 1981
Sales ($Million): 94
Total Units: 315
Franchised: 100%
International: 46%
Minimum Investment: $68,600
Maximum Investment: $121,400
Royalty: 4.0%–7.0%
National Advertising: 2.0%
SBA Registry Status: Listed

Roto-Rooter Corporation

300 Ashworth Road
West Des Moines, IA 50265
Telephone: (515) 223-1343
Web Site: www.rotorooter.com
Description: A chain of plumbing and
   drain-cleaning service providers
Parent Company: Chemed Corporation
Date Began Franchising: January 1, 1936
Sales ($Million): 547
Total Units: 596
Franchised: 83%
International: 5%
Minimum Investment: $45,000
Maximum Investment: $70,000
Royalty: Variable
National Advertising: 0%
SBA Registry Status: Not Listed

ServiceMaster Clean

3839 Forest Hill Irene Rd.
Memphis, TN 38120
Telephone: (901) 597-7500
Web Site: www.ownafranchise.com
Description: Residential and commercial
   cleaning franchises
Parent Company: ServiceMaster
Date Began Franchising: January 1, 1948
Sales ($Million): 1,459
Total Units: 4,133
Franchised: 100%
International: 23%
Minimum Investment: $31,333
Maximum Investment: $102,316
Royalty: 10.0%
National Advertising: 1.0%
SBA Registry Status: Listed

Stanley Steemer Carpet Cleaner

5500 Stanley Steemer Pkwy.
Dublin, OH 43016
Telephone: (614) 764-2007

Web Site: www.stanleysteemer.com
Description: A home-cleaning franchise
Parent Company: Stanley Steemer
  International, Inc.
Date Began Franchising: January 1, 1972
Sales ($Million): 371
Total Units: 286
Franchised: 81%
International: 0%
Minimum Investment: $80,990
Maximum Investment: $213,775
Royalty: 7.0%
National Advertising: 2.0%
SBA Registry Status: Not Listed

TruGreen ChemLawn

860 Ridge Lake Blvd.
Memphis, TN 38120
Telephone: (901) 681-1820
Web Site: www.trugreen.com
Description: Lawn fertilization and pest
  control franchises
Parent Company: ServiceMaster Co.
Date Began Franchising: January 1, 1977
Sales ($Million): 1,071
Total Units: 317
Franchised: 29%
International: 18%
Minimum Investment: $107,900
Maximum Investment: $143,300
Royalty: Variable
National Advertising: 0%
SBA Registry Status: Not Listed

Printing, Graphic Design, Signage, and Shipping

Allegra Network

21680 Haggerty Rd.
Northville, MI 48167
Telephone: (248) 596-8600
Web Site: www.allegranetwork.com

Description: A printing and graphics
  franchise
Parent Company: Allegra Network LLC
Date Began Franchising: December 1, 1996
Sales ($Million): 345
Total Units: 623
Franchised: 100%
International: 8%
Minimum Investment: $41,200
Maximum Investment: $62,850
Royalty: 6.0%
National Advertising: 1.0%
SBA Registry Status: Listed

AlphaGraphics

268 S. State Street, Ste. 300
Salt Lake City, UT 84111
Telephone: (801) 595-7270
Web Site: www.alphagraphics.com
Description: Franchises offering design,
  copy, and print services
Parent Company: AlphaGraphics, Inc.
Date Began Franchising: January 1, 1992
Sales ($Million): 285
Total Units: 262
Franchised: 100%
International: 13%
Minimum Investment: $365,000
Maximum Investment: $550,900
Royalty: Variable
National Advertising: 2.0%
SBA Registry Status: Listed

FASTSIGNS International, Inc.

2542 Highlander Way
Carrollton, TX 75006-2333
Telephone: (214) 346-5616
Web Site: www.fastsigns.com
Description: Franchises offering signs,
  banners, displays, and digital signage
Parent Company: Roark Capital
Date Began Franchising: April 30, 1986
Sales ($Million): 240

Total Units: 504
Franchised: 100%
International: 17%
Minimum Investment: $187,491
Maximum Investment: $282,955
Royalty: 6.0%
National Advertising: 2.0%
SBA Registry Status: Listed

Kwik Kopy Printing
12175 Telge Road
Cypress, TX 77429
Telephone: (281) 256-4100
Web Site: www.kwikkopy.com
Description: A franchise system of retail
    print and copy centers
Parent Company: International Center for
    Entrepreneurial Development
Date Began Franchising: January 1, 1988
Sales ($Million): 298
Total Units: 598
Franchised: 100%
International: 58%
Minimum Investment: $237,170
Maximum Investment: $270,995
Royalty: 7.0%
National Advertising: Variable
SBA Registry Status: Listed

Minuteman Press
61 Executive Drive
Farmingdale, NY 11735
Telephone: (631) 249-1370
Web Site: www.minutemanpress.com
Description: A printing services franchise
Parent Company: Minuteman Press
    International
Date Began Franchising: March 1, 1975
Sales ($Million): 400
Total Units: 946
Franchised: 100%
International: 21%
Minimum Investment: $122,171

Maximum Investment: $242,793
Royalty: 6.0%
National Advertising: 0%
SBA Registry Status: Listed

Pak Mail
7173 S. Havana, Suite 600
Englewood, CO 80122
Telephone: (303) 957-1000
Web Site: www.pakmail.com
Description: A chain of packaging and
    shipping stores
Parent Company: Pak Mail Centers of
    America, Inc.
Date Began Franchising: January 27, 1984
Sales ($Million): 177
Total Units: 508
Franchised: 98%
International: 22%
Minimum Investment: $117,180
Maximum Investment: $150,895
Royalty: Variable
National Advertising: 2.0%
SBA Registry Status: Listed

PIP Printing & Document Services
26722 Plaza Dr.
Mission Viejo, CA 92691
Telephone: (949) 348-5400
Web Site: www.pip.com
Description: Franchises offering printing,
    copying, and document services
Parent Company: Franchise Services, Inc.
Date Began Franchising: January 1, 1968
Sales ($Million): 132
Total Units: 203
Franchised: 100%
International: 3%
Minimum Investment: $261,413
Maximum Investment: $286,413
Royalty: Variable
National Advertising: 2.0%
SBA Registry Status: Listed

PostNet

181 Wazee Street, Bldg. A, Ste. 100
Denver, CO 80202
Telephone: (303) 771-7100
Web Site: www.postnet.com
Description: A global copy and print
    shop chain offering postal and
    business services
Parent Company: PostNet International
    Franchise Corporation
Date Began Franchising: October 27, 1992
Sales ($Million): 232
Total Units: 860
Franchised: 100%
International: 42%
Minimum Investment: $175,875
Maximum Investment: $197,600
Royalty: 5.0%
National Advertising: 2.0%
SBA Registry Status: Listed

Proforma

8800 E. Pleasant Valley Rd.
Cleveland, OH 44131
Telephone: (216) 520-8400
Web Site: www.proforma.com
Description: A printing and promotional
    products distributor
Parent Company: Proforma
Date Began Franchising: January 1, 1985
Sales ($Million): 293
Total Units: 610
Franchised: 100%
International: 7%
Minimum Investment: $7,230
Maximum Investment: $70,195
Royalty: 6.0%–8.0%
National Advertising: 0.5%–1.0%
SBA Registry Status: Not Listed

Sign-A-Rama

2121 Vista Parkway
West Palm Beach, FL 33411
Telephone: (561) 640-5570
Web Site: www.signarama.com
Description: Customized sign production
    franchise
Parent Company: Sign-A-Rama, Inc.
Date Began Franchising: April 1, 1987
Sales ($Million): 451
Total Units: 755
Franchised: 100%
International: 31%
Minimum Investment: $50,260
Maximum Investment: $105,690
Royalty: 6.0%
National Advertising: $150/mo.
SBA Registry Status: Listed

Signs Now

6976 Professional Parkway East
Sarasota, FL 34240
Telephone: (941) 373-1958
Web Site: www.signsnow.com
Description: A provider of signs and
    digital graphic solutions
Parent Company: Allegra Network LLC
Date Began Franchising: July 1, 1986
Sales ($Million): 78
Total Units: 215
Franchised: 100%
International: 7%
Minimum Investment: $135,750
Maximum Investment: $397,000
Royalty: 5.0%
National Advertising: 2.0%
SBA Registry Status: Listed

Sir Speedy, Inc.

26722 Plaza Drive
Mission Viejo, CA 92691
Telephone: (949) 348-5000
Web Site: www.sirspeedy.com

Description: A printing and business
  services chain
Parent Company: Franchise Services, Inc.
Date Began Franchising: July 9, 1968
Sales ($Million): 400
Total Units: 492
Franchised: 100%
International: 22%
Minimum Investment: $342,000
Maximum Investment: $477,000
Royalty: 6.0%
National Advertising: 2.0%
SBA Registry Status: Listed

The UPS Store/Mail Boxes Etc.
6060 Cornerstone Court West
San Diego, CA 92121
Telephone: (877) 623-7258
Web Site: www.theupsstore.com
Description: Retail shipping, postal, and
  business service centers
Parent Company: United Parcel Service
Date Began Franchising: June 11, 1980
Sales ($Million): 1,759
Total Units: 5,673
Franchised: 100%
International: 22%
Minimum Investment: $149,754
Maximum Investment: $187,471
Royalty: 5.0%
National Advertising: 2.5%
SBA Registry Status: Listed

Unishippers Association
746 E. Winchester, Ste. 200
Salt Lake City, UT 84107
Telephone: (801) 487-0600
Web Site: www.unishippers.com
Description: Franchise locations providing
  express and freight shipping services
Parent Company: Unishippers Association
Date Began Franchising: July 2, 1990
Sales ($Million): 253

Total Units: 275
Franchised: 100%
International: 0%
Minimum Investment: $31,125
Maximum Investment: $8,758,050
Royalty: Variable
National Advertising: Variable
SBA Registry Status: Not Listed

Real Estate and Travel Agencies

Carlson Wagonlit Travel
701 Carlson Parkway, MS 8207
Minneapolis, MN 55305
Telephone: (866) 225-9026
Web Site: www.carlsontravel.com
Description: Travel management and
  consulting services agencies
Parent Company: Carlson Companies, Inc.
Date Began Franchising: June 24, 1984
Sales ($Million): 25,600
Total Units: 2,872
Franchised: 38%
International: 69%
Minimum Investment: $2,490
Maximum Investment: $10,440
Royalty: Variable
National Advertising: $250/mo.
SBA Registry Status: Listed

Century 21 Real Estate, LLC
1 Campus Drive
Parsippany, NJ 07054
Telephone: (973) 496-0094
Web Site: www.century21.com
Description: Real estate brokerages for
  residential and commercial properties
Parent Company: Realogy Corporation
Date Began Franchising: December 1, 1995
Sales ($Million): 5,129
Total Units: 7,877

Franchised: 100%
International: 44%
Minimum Investment: $11,713
Maximum Investment: $522,511
Royalty: 6.0%
National Advertising: 2.0%
SBA Registry Status: Not Listed

Coldwell Banker Real Estate Corporation

1 Campus Drive
Parsippany, NJ 07054
Telephone: (973) 428-9700
Web Site: www.coldwellbanker.com
Description: Real estate brokerages for residential, luxury, resort, and commercial properties
Parent Company: Realogy Corporation
Date Began Franchising: December 31, 1998
Sales ($Million): 9,055
Total Units: 3,835
Franchised: 75%
International: 14%
Minimum Investment: $29,650
Maximum Investment: $101,400
Royalty: Variable
National Advertising: 2.0%
SBA Registry Status: Not Listed

Cruise Holidays International, Inc.

701 Carlson Parkway, MS 8207
Minneapolis, MN 55305
Telephone: (763) 212-8234
Web Site: www.cruiseholidays.com
Description: A chain of franchises offering cruise travel services
Parent Company: Carlson Companies, Inc.
Date Began Franchising: July 1, 1984
Sales ($Million): 171
Total Units: 125
Franchised: 100%
International: 24%

Minimum Investment: $67,669
Maximum Investment: $126,219
Royalty: 1.0%
National Advertising: $400/mo.
SBA Registry Status: Listed

CruiseOne

1415 NW 62nd Street, Ste. 205
Ft. Lauderdale, FL 33309
Telephone: (954) 958-3701
Web Site: www.cruiseonefranchise.com
Description: Home-based cruise travel franchises
Parent Company: National Leisure Group
Date Began Franchising: June 16, 1992
Sales ($Million): 135
Total Units: 475
Franchised: 100%
International: 0%
Minimum Investment: $6,970
Maximum Investment: $26,315
Royalty: 3.0%
National Advertising: 0%
SBA Registry Status: Listed

Cruise Planners / American Express

3300 University Drive, Ste. 602
Coral Springs, FL 33065
Telephone: (954) 227-2545
Web Site: www.beacruiseagent.com
Description: Cruise travel agencies for business and leisure travelers
Parent Company: CPFranchising, LLC
Date Began Franchising: 1999
Sales ($Million): 100
Total Units: 639
Franchised: 100%
International: 0%
Minimum Investment: $3,245
Maximum Investment: $19,940
Royalty: 3.0%
National Advertising: 0%
SBA Registry Status: Not Listed

ERA Franchise Systems Inc.
1 Campus Drive
Parsippany, NJ 07054
Telephone: (973) 428-9700
Web Site: www.era.com
Description: A global chain of residential
real estate brokerages
Parent Company: Realogy Corporation
Date Began Franchising: January 31, 1996
Sales ($Million): 1,270
Total Units: 2,898
Franchised: 99%
International: 59%
Minimum Investment: $42,700
Maximum Investment: $205,900
Royalty: 6.0%
National Advertising: 2.0%
SBA Registry Status: Not Listed

GMAC Real Estate
2021 Spring Rd., Ste. 300
Oak Brook, IL 60523
Telephone: (630) 214-1600
Web Site: www.gmacrealestate.com
Description: Real estate brokerages offering
residential and relocation services
Parent Company: GMAC Home Services
Date Began Franchising: March 1, 2000
Sales ($Million): 1,292
Total Units: 1,220
Franchised: 92%
International: 3%
Minimum Investment: $19,368
Maximum Investment: $193,212
Royalty: 5.0%
National Advertising: 2.0%
SBA Registry Status: Not Listed

Keller Williams Realty
807 Las Cimas Pkwy., Ste. 200
Austin, TX 78746
Telephone: (512) 327-3070
Web Site: www.kw.com

Description: Real estate brokerages
across North America
Parent Company: Keller Williams Realty
Date Began Franchising: November 22,
1995
Sales ($Million): 2,145
Total Units: 533
Franchised: 100%
International: 2%
Minimum Investment: $123,650
Maximum Investment: $459,750
Royalty: 6.0%
National Advertising: 0.5%
SBA Registry Status: Not Listed

Results Travel
701 Carlson Parkway, MS 8207
Minneapolis, MN 55305
Telephone: (281) 955-1569
Web Site: www.resultstravel.com
Description: A low-cost travel agency chain
Parent Company: Carlson Companies, Inc.
Date Began Franchising: June 1, 1984
Sales ($Million): 2,300
Total Units: 915
Franchised: 100%
International: 0%
Minimum Investment: $25
Maximum Investment: $8,925
Royalty: $300/yr.
National Advertising: 0%
SBA Registry Status: Listed

UNIGLOBE Travel International
18662 MacArthur Blvd., Ste. 100
Irvine, CA 92612
Telephone: (604) 718-2600
Web Site: www.uniglobetravel.com
Description: A chain of full-service
travel agencies
Parent Company: Charlwood Pacific Group
Date Began Franchising: January 1, 1995
Sales ($Million): 2,028

Total Units: 700
Franchised: 100%
International: 0%
Minimum Investment: $1,895
Maximum Investment: $7,295
Royalty: 1.0%
National Advertising: 0%
SBA Registry Status: Listed

Restaurants and Prepared Foods

A&W All-American Food Restaurants
P.O. Box 34550
Louisville, KY 40232
Telephone: (859) 543-6000
Web Site: www.awrestaurants.com
Description: A quick-service drive-in hamburger chain
Parent Company: Yum! Brands Inc.
Date Began Franchising: April 28, 1950
Sales ($Million): 300
Total Units: 668
Franchised: 98%
International: 35%
Minimum Investment: $212,400
Maximum Investment: $407,000
Royalty: 5.0%
National Advertising: 4.0%
SBA Registry Status: Not Listed

Applebee's Neighborhood Grill & Bar
4551 W. 107 Street
Overland Park, KS 66207
Telephone: (913) 967-4000
Web Site: www.applebees.com
Description: A full-service casual dining restaurant chain
Parent Company: Applebee's International Inc.
Date Began Franchising: March 16, 1988
Sales ($Million): 4,306

Total Units: 1,804
Franchised: 73%
International: 4%
Minimum Investment: $2,724,500
Maximum Investment: $5,379,000
Royalty: 4.0%
National Advertising: 2.8%
SBA Registry Status: Not Listed

Arby's
1155 Perimeter Center West
Atlanta, GA 33334
Telephone: (678) 514-4100
Web Site: www.arbys.com
Description: A quick-service chain specializing in roast beef sandwiches
Parent Company: Triarc Companies, Inc.
Date Began Franchising: January 1, 1965
Sales ($Million): 3,067
Total Units: 3,506
Franchised: 70%
International: 4%
Minimum Investment: $750,700
Maximum Investment: $2,434,400
Royalty: 4.0%
National Advertising: 1.2%
SBA Registry Status: Not Listed

Atlanta Bread Co.
1955 Lake Park Dr., Ste. 400
Smyrna, GA 30080
Telephone: (770) 432-0933
Web Site: www.atlantabread.com
Description: A fast casual bakery café
Parent Company: Atlanta Bread Company International, Inc.
Date Began Franchising: December 28, 1995
Sales ($Million): 181
Total Units: 156
Franchised: 99%
International: 0%
Minimum Investment: $629,700

Maximum Investment: $806,300
Royalty: 5.0%
National Advertising: 3.0%
SBA Registry Status: Not Listed

Auntie Anne's

160A Route 41
Gap, PA 17527
Telephone: (717) 442-4766
Web Site: www.auntieannes.com
Description: A quick-service chain offering
    hand-rolled soft pretzels
Parent Company: Auntie Anne's, Inc.
Date Began Franchising: January 1, 1991
Sales ($Million): 270
Total Units: 1,058
Franchised: 99%
International: 16%
Minimum Investment: $192,550
Maximum Investment: $382,500
Royalty: 6.0%
National Advertising: 1.0%
SBA Registry Status: Listed

Back Yard Burgers

1657 N. Shelby Oaks Dr., Ste. 105
Memphis, TN 38134
Telephone: (901) 367-0888
Web Site: www.backyardburgers.com
Description: A quick-service
    hamburger chain
Parent Company: Back Yard Burgers, Inc.
Date Began Franchising: March 23, 1987
Sales ($Million): 139
Total Units: 171
Franchised: 74%
International: 0%
Minimum Investment: $352,000
Maximum Investment: $1,943,000
Royalty: 4.0%
National Advertising: 1.0%
SBA Registry Status: Not Listed

Baja Fresh Mexican Grill

100 Moody Court, Ste. 200
Thousand Oaks, CA 91360
Telephone: (805) 495-4704
Web Site: www.bajafresh.com
Description: A quick-service Mexican
    fare chain
Parent Company: Wendy's
    International Inc.
Date Began Franchising: May 15, 1991
Sales ($Million): 349
Total Units: 299
Franchised: 53%
International: 0%
Minimum Investment: $656,110
Maximum Investment: $1,095,090
Royalty: 5.0%
National Advertising: 1.0%
SBA Registry Status: Not Listed

Baskin-Robbins

130 Royall St.
Canton, MA 02021
Telephone: (781) 737-3000
Web Site: www.dunkinbrands.com
Description: A global chain of ice cream
    specialty stores
Parent Company: Dunkin' Brands, Inc.
Date Began Franchising: January 1, 1960
Sales ($Million): 1,148
Total Units: 5,636
Franchised: 100%
International: 51%
Minimum Investment: $135,800
Maximum Investment: $521,400
Royalty: 5%
National Advertising: 5.0%
SBA Registry Status: Listed

Beef O' Brady's

5510 W. LaSalle Street
Tampa, FL 33670
Telephone: (813) 226-2333

Web Site: www.beefobradys.com
Description: A full-service family sports pub chain
Parent Company: Family Sports Concepts, Inc.
Date Began Franchising: January 1, 1998
Sales ($Million): 148
Total Units: 183
Franchised: 98%
International: 0%
Minimum Investment: $246,800
Maximum Investment: $405,500
Royalty: 4.0%
National Advertising: 1.5%
SBA Registry Status: Listed

Bellacino's Pizza and Grinders

10096 Shaver Road
Portage, MI 49024
Telephone: (877) 379-0700
Web Site: www.bellacinos.com
Description: A chain of restaurants serving oven-baked pizza and grinders
Parent Company: Bellacino's Inc.
Date Began Franchising: June 15, 1998
Sales ($Million): 58
Total Units: 89
Franchised: 100%
International: 0%
Minimum Investment: $275,000
Maximum Investment: $345,000
Royalty: 3.0%
National Advertising: 1.0%
SBA Registry Status: Not Listed

Bennigan's Grill & Tavern

6500 International Parkway, Ste. 1000
Plano, TX 75093
Telephone: (972) 588-5000
Web Site: www.bennigans.com
Description: A full-service casual dining restaurant chain

Parent Company: Metromedia Restaurant Group
Date Began Franchising: January 1, 1995
Sales ($Million): 610
Total Units: 309
Franchised: 47%
International: 16%
Minimum Investment: $1,497,784
Maximum Investment: $2,681,866
Royalty: 4.0%
National Advertising: 2%
SBA Registry Status: Listed

Big Boy

One Big Boy Drive
Warren, MI 48091
Telephone: (586) 759-6000
Web Site: www.bigboy.com
Description: A full-service family restaurant chain
Parent Company: Big Boy Restaurants International, Inc.
Date Began Franchising: January 1, 1952
Sales ($Million): 624
Total Units: 362
Franchised: 93%
International: 26%
Minimum Investment: $1,761,050
Maximum Investment: $3,009,250
Royalty: 4.0%
National Advertising: 2%
SBA Registry Status: Not Listed

Blimpie Subs & Salads

7730 E. Greenfield Road, Ste. 104
Scottsdale, AZ 85260
Telephone: (480) 443-0200
Web Site: www.kahalacorp.com
Description: A quick-service sandwich chain
Parent Company: Kahala Corp.
Date Began Franchising: 1970
Sales ($Million): 327
Total Units: 1,649

Franchised: 99%
International: 1%
Minimum Investment: $137,970
Maximum Investment: $391,600
Royalty: 6%
National Advertising: 4%
SBA Registry Status: Listed

Bojangles' Restaurants, Inc.

9432 Southern Pine Blvd.
Charlotte, NC 28273
Telephone: (704) 527-2675
Web Site: www.bojangles.com
Description: A quick-service chicken
    restaurant chain
Parent Company: Bojangles'
    Restaurants, Inc.
Date Began Franchising: January 1, 1990
Sales ($Million): 449
Total Units: 337
Franchised: 67%
International: 1%
Minimum Investment: $270,100
Maximum Investment: $478,000
Royalty: 4.0%
National Advertising: 1.0%
SBA Registry Status: Not Listed

Boston's the Gourmet Pizza / Boston Pizza

1505 LBJ Freeway, Ste. 450
Dallas, TX 75234
Telephone: (972) 484-9022
Web Site: www.bostonsgourmet.com
Description: A full-service casual dining
    restaurant chain
Parent Company: Boston Pizza
    Restaurants LP/Boston Pizza
    International
Date Began Franchising: October 1, 1995
Sales ($Million): 577
Total Units: 259

Franchised: 98%
International: 86%
Minimum Investment: $1,625,000
Maximum Investment: $2,295,000
Royalty: 5.0%
National Advertising: 3.0%
SBA Registry Status: Listed

Bruegger's Bagels

159 Bank Street
Burlington, VT 05401
Telephone: (802) 660-4020
Web Site: www.brueggers.com
Description: A fast casual bagel and
    sandwich café
Parent Company: Bruegger's
    Franchise Corp.
Date Began Franchising: March 1, 1993
Sales ($Million): 155
Total Units: 240
Franchised: 39%
International: 0%
Minimum Investment: $217,250
Maximum Investment: $481,500
Royalty: 5.0%
National Advertising: 1.0%
SBA Registry Status: Listed

Buffalo Wild Wings Grill & Bar

1600 Utica Ave. South, Ste. 700
Minneapolis, MN 55446
Telephone: (952) 593-9943
Web Site: www.buffalowildwings.com
Description: A full-service casual dining
    restaurant chain
Parent Company: Buffalo Wild Wings, Inc.
Date Began Franchising: April 15, 1991
Sales ($Million): 656
Total Units: 370
Franchised: 67%
International: 0%
Minimum Investment: $1,340,200

Maximum Investment: $2,418,700
Royalty: 5.0%
National Advertising: 2.5%
SBA Registry Status: Listed

Burger King
5505 Blue Lagoon Dr.
Miami, FL 33126
Telephone: (305) 378-7690
Web Site: www.burgerking.com
Description: A quick-service
    hamburger chain
Parent Company: Burger King Holdings Inc.
Date Began Franchising: January 1, 1954
Sales ($Million): 12,004
Total Units: 11,104
Franchised: 89%
International: 30%
Minimum Investment: $1,399,000
Maximum Investment: $2,875,000
Royalty: 4.5%
National Advertising: 4.0%
SBA Registry Status: Listed

Captain D's Seafood
1717 Elm Hill Pike, Ste. A-1
Nashville, TN 37210
Telephone: (949) 462-7320
Web Site: www.captainds.com
Description: A quick-service seafood chain
Parent Company: Sagittarius Acquisitions
    II, Inc.
Date Began Franchising: January 1, 1971
Sales ($Million): 519
Total Units: 589
Franchised: 46%
International: 0%
Minimum Investment: $684,000
Maximum Investment: $843,000
Royalty: 4.0%
National Advertising: 1.25%
SBA Registry Status: Listed

Carl's Jr.
6307 Carpinteria Ave., Ste. A
Carpinteria, CA 93013
Telephone: (866) 253-7655
Web Site: www.ckefranchise.com
Description: A quick-service
    hamburger chain
Parent Company: CKE Restaurants, Inc.
Date Began Franchising: January 1, 1984
Sales ($Million): 1,275
Total Units: 1,050
Franchised: 59%
International: 7%
Minimum Investment: $913,000
Maximum Investment: $1,354,000
Royalty: 4%
National Advertising: 5.3%
SBA Registry Status: Listed

Carvel Ice Cream
200 Glenridge Point Parkway, Ste. 200
Atlanta, GA 30342
Telephone: (404) 255-3250
Web Site: www.carvel.com
Description: A quick-service ice cream
    treat chain
Parent Company: FOCUS Brands
Date Began Franchising: January 1, 1947
Sales ($Million): 146
Total Units: 561
Franchised: 96%
International: 5%
Minimum Investment: $247,474
Maximum Investment: $388,724
Royalty: 6.0%
National Advertising: 1.50%
SBA Registry Status: Listed

Checkers/Rally's
4300 West Cypress Street, Ste. 600
Tampa, FL 33607
Telephone: (813) 283-7000

Web Site: www.checkers.com

Description: A quick-service drive-in hamburger chain

Parent Company: Checkers Drive-In Restaurants, Inc.

Date Began Franchising: September 1, 1991

Sales ($Million): 625

Total Units: 804

Franchised: 75%

International: 1%

Minimum Investment: $487,100

Maximum Investment: $644,100

Royalty: 4.0%

National Advertising: 5.0%

SBA Registry Status: Listed

Chester's

3500 Colonnade Parkway, Ste. 325

Birmingham, AL 35243

Telephone: (800) 288-1555

Web Site: www.chestersinternational.com

Description: A quick-service chicken restaurant chain

Parent Company: Giles Enterprises

Date Began Franchising: March 1, 2004

Sales ($Million): 484

Total Units: 1,784

Franchised: 100%

International: 23%

Minimum Investment: $181,441

Maximum Investment: $395,000

Royalty: 4.0%

National Advertising: 2.0%

SBA Registry Status: Listed

Chick-fil-A

5200 Buffington Rd.

Atlanta, GA 30349

Telephone: (404) 765-8000

Web Site: www.chickfila.com

Description: A quick-service chicken restaurant chain

Parent Company: Chick-fil-A, Inc.

Date Began Franchising: May 4, 1992

Sales ($Million): 1,975

Total Units: 1,237

Franchised: 100%

International: 0%

Minimum Investment: $225,890

Maximum Investment: $775,851

Royalty: Contact franchisor for information

National Advertising: Variable

SBA Registry Status: Not Listed

Chili's Grill & Bar

6820 LBJ Frwy.

Dallas, TX 75240

Telephone: (972) 980-9917

Web Site: www.brinker.com

Description: A full-service, casual dining restaurant chain

Parent Company: Brinker International, Inc.

Date Began Franchising: January 1, 1984

Sales ($Million): 3,335

Total Units: 1,130

Franchised: 23%

International: 9%

Minimum Investment: $2,090,000

Maximum Investment: $3,488,000

Royalty: 4.0%

National Advertising: 2.7%

SBA Registry Status: Not Listed

Church's Chicken

980 Hammond Dr. NE,
    Building 2, Ste. 1100

Atlanta, GA 30328

Telephone: (770) 350-3800

Web Site: www.churchs.com

Description: A quick-service chicken restaurant chain

Parent Company: Arcapita, Inc.

Date Began Franchising: 1964

Sales ($Million): 988

Total Units: 1,562
Franchised: 82%
International: 23%
Minimum Investment: $459,800
Maximum Investment: $798,600
Royalty: 5.0%
National Advertising: 5.0%
SBA Registry Status: Listed

CiCi's Pizza

1080 W. Bethel Rd.
Coppell, TX 75019
Telephone: (972) 745-4204
Web Site: www.cicispizza.com
Description: Franchisor of pizza buffet
  restaurants and smaller pizza
  take-out units
Parent Company: CiCi's Enterprises, LP
Date Began Franchising: May 1, 1988
Sales ($Million): 490
Total Units: 579
Franchised: 97%
International: 0%
Minimum Investment: $404,400
Maximum Investment: $646,400
Royalty: 4.0%
National Advertising: 3.0%
SBA Registry Status: Listed

Cinnabon, Inc.

200 Glenridge Point Parkway, Ste. 200
Atlanta, GA 30342
Telephone: (404) 255-3250
Web Site: www.cinnabon.com
Description: A quick-service chain offering
  baked goods
Parent Company: FOCUS Brands
Date Began Franchising: January 1, 1986
Sales ($Million): 216
Total Units: 617
Franchised: 100%
International: 35%

Minimum Investment: $255,200
Maximum Investment: $343,000
Royalty: 5.0%
National Advertising: 3.0%
SBA Registry Status: Listed

Cold Stone Creamery

9311 East Via De Ventura
Scottsdale, AZ 85258
Telephone: (480) 362-4800
Web Site: www.coldstonecreamery.com
Description: Franchise serving customizable
  ice cream creations
Parent Company: Cold Stone
  Creamery, Inc.
Date Began Franchising: April 1, 1994
Sales ($Million): 408
Total Units: 1,224
Franchised: 97%
International: 0%
Minimum Investment: $294,250
Maximum Investment: $438,850
Royalty: 6.0%
National Advertising: 3.0%
SBA Registry Status: Listed

Country Kitchen

801 Deming Way,
Madison, WI 53717
Telephone: (608) 833-9633
Web Site:
  www.countrykitchenrestaurants.com
Description: A full-service family dining
  restaurant chain
Parent Company: Country Kitchen
  International
Date Began Franchising: January 1, 1965
Sales ($Million): 142
Total Units: 145
Franchised: 80%
International: 0%
Minimum Investment: $661,600

Maximum Investment: $1,581,700
Royalty: 4.0%
National Advertising: 1.0%
SBA Registry Status: Not Listed

Cousins Subs
N83 W. 13400 Leon Rd.
Menomonee Falls, WI 53051
Telephone: (262) 253-7700
Web Site: www.cousinssubs.com
Description: A chain of quick-service
  sandwich shops
Parent Company: Cousins Subs, Inc.
Date Began Franchising: January 1, 1979
Sales ($Million): 70
Total Units: 157
Franchised: 87%
International: 0%
Minimum Investment: $159,300
Maximum Investment: $291,600
Royalty: Variable
National Advertising: 2.0%
SBA Registry Status: Listed

Culver's ButterBurgers &
Frozen Custard
540 Water St.
Prairie du Sac, WI 53578
Telephone: (608) 643-7980
Web Site: www.culvers.com
Description: A quick-service
  hamburger chain
Parent Company: Culver Franchising
  System, Inc.
Date Began Franchising: January 1, 1987
Sales ($Million): 481
Total Units: 312
Franchised: 98%
International: 0%
Minimum Investment: $185,000
Maximum Investment: $2,923,000

Royalty: 4.0%
National Advertising: 2.0%
SBA Registry Status: Listed

Dairy Queen
7505 Metro Boulevard, P.O. Box 39286
Edina, MN 55439
Telephone: (952) 830-0200
Web Site: www.dairyqueen.com
Description: A quick-service ice cream
  and hamburger chain
Parent Company: IDQ Companies
Date Began Franchising: January 1, 1958
Sales ($Million): 2,688
Total Units: 5,190
Franchised: 99%
International: 7%
Minimum Investment: $461,150
Maximum Investment: $920,100
Royalty: 4.0%
National Advertising: 5.0%
SBA Registry Status: Listed

Damon's Grill
4645 Executive Dr.
Columbus, OH 43220
Telephone: (614) 442-7900
Web Site: www.damons.com
Description: A full-service casual dining
  restaurant chain
Parent Company: Damon's
  International, Inc.
Date Began Franchising: January 1, 1982
Sales ($Million): 225
Total Units: 99
Franchised: 80%
International: 6%
Minimum Investment: $1,166,500
Maximum Investment: $1,759,000
Royalty: 4.0%
National Advertising: 2.0%
SBA Registry Status: Not Listed

D'Angelo Grilled Sandwiches

600 Providence Hwy.
Dedham, MA 02026
Telephone: (781) 461-1200
Web Site: www.dangelos.com
Description: A fast casual sandwich chain
Parent Company: Papa Gino's Corp.
Date Began Franchising: 1988
Sales ($Million): 120
Total Units: 200
Franchised: 25%
International: 0%
Minimum Investment: $205,944
Maximum Investment: $348,280
Royalty: 6.0%
National Advertising: 3.0%
SBA Registry Status: Listed

Del Taco LLC

25521 Commercentre Dr.
Lake Forest, CA 92630
Telephone: (949) 462-7319
Web Site: www.deltaco.com
Description: A quick-service Mexican
    fare chain
Parent Company: Sagittarius Brands
Date Began Franchising: March 28, 1988
Sales ($Million): 523
Total Units: 462
Franchised: 42%
International: 0%
Minimum Investment: $272,000
Maximum Investment: $626,000
Royalty: 5.0%
National Advertising: 4.0%
SBA Registry Status: Not Listed

Denny's

203 E. Main Street
Spartanburg, SC 29319-9912
Telephone: (864) 597-8000
Web Site: www.dennys.com
Description: A full service family
    restaurant chain
Parent Company: Denny's Corporation
Date Began Franchising: January 1, 1963
Sales ($Million): 2,362
Total Units: 1,578
Franchised: 66%
International: 5%
Minimum Investment: $1,090,230
Maximum Investment: $1,759,450
Royalty: 4.0%
National Advertising: 3.0%
SBA Registry Status: Not Listed

Domino's Pizza

30 Frank Lloyd Wright Dr.
Ann Arbor, MI 48106
Telephone: (734) 930-3030
Web Site: www.dominos.com
Description: A quick-service pizza
    delivery chain
Parent Company: Domino's Pizza, Inc.
Date Began Franchising: January 1, 1967
Sales ($Million): 5,000
Total Units: 8,080
Franchised: 93%
International: 37%
Minimum Investment: $118,350
Maximum Investment: $450,100
Royalty: 5.5%
National Advertising: 4.0%
SBA Registry Status: Listed

Dunkin' Donuts

130 Royall St.
Canton, MA 02021
Telephone: (781) 737-3000
Web Site: www.dunkindonuts.com
Description: Restaurants offering
    quick-service coffee, doughnuts and
    baked goods
Parent Company: Dunkin' Brands, Inc.
Date Began Franchising: January 1, 1955

Sales ($Million): 4,143
Total Units: 7,021
Franchised: 100%
International: 27%
Minimum Investment: $548,100
Maximum Investment: $1,313,400
Royalty: 5.0%
National Advertising: 5.0%
SBA Registry Status: Listed

El Pollo Loco
3333 Michelson Drive, Ste. 550
Irvine, CA 92612
Telephone: (949) 399-2000
Web Site: www.elpolloloco.com
Description: A fast casual Mexican
    restaurant chain
Parent Company: Trimaran Capital
    Partners
Date Began Franchising: October 2, 1989
Sales ($Million): 478
Total Units: 341
Franchised: 57%
International: 0%
Minimum Investment: $425,000
Maximum Investment: $630,000
Royalty: 4.0%
National Advertising: 4.0%
SBA Registry Status: Not Listed

Elmer's Breakfast–Lunch–Dinner
11802 SE Stark Street
Portland, OR 97292
Telephone: (503) 252-1485
Web Site: www.elmers-restaurants.com
Description: A full-service family dining
    restaurant chain
Parent Company: Elmer's Restaurants, Inc.
Date Began Franchising: January 1, 1982
Sales ($Million): 58
Total Units: 43
Franchised: 77%

International: 0%
Minimum Investment: $1,569,000
Maximum Investment: $1,948,000
Royalty: 4.0%
National Advertising: 2.0%
SBA Registry Status: Not Listed

Famous Dave's
12701 Whitewater Drive, Ste. 200
Minnetonka, MN 55343
Telephone: (952) 294-1300
Web Site: www.famousdaves.com
Description: A full-service casual dining
    restaurant chain
Parent Company: Famous Dave's of
    America, Inc.
Date Began Franchising: January 1, 1998
Sales ($Million): 310
Total Units: 136
Franchised: 70%
International: 0%
Minimum Investment: $907,000
Maximum Investment: $1,504,500
Royalty: 5.0%
National Advertising: 1.0%
SBA Registry Status: Not Listed

Firehouse Subs
3410 Kori Road
Jacksonville, FL 32257
Telephone: (904) 886-8300
Web Site: www.firehousesubs.com
Description: A quick-service sandwich chain
Parent Company: Firehouse Restaurant
    Group, Inc.
Date Began Franchising: February 20, 1995
Sales ($Million): 123
Total Units: 233
Franchised: 85%
International: 0%
Minimum Investment: $161,200
Maximum Investment: $305,475

Royalty: 6.0%
National Advertising: 2.0%
SBA Registry Status: Not Listed

Fox's Pizza Den
3243 Old Franktown Rd.
Pittsburgh, PA 15239
Telephone: (724) 733-7888
Web Site: www.foxpizza.com
Description: A pizza and sandwich delivery
    and take-out chain
Parent Company: Fox's Pizza Den, Inc.
Date Began Franchising: January 1, 1997
Sales ($Million): 150
Total Units: 284
Franchised: 100%
International: 0%
Minimum Investment: $93,550
Maximum Investment: $115,550
Royalty: $300/mo.
National Advertising: 0%
SBA Registry Status: Listed

Friendly's Restaurants Franchise, Inc.
1855 Boston Road
Wilbraham, MA 01095
Telephone: (413) 731-4211
Web Site: www.friendlys.com
Description: A full-service family
    restaurant chain
Parent Company: Friendly's Ice Cream
    Corporation
Date Began Franchising: May 1, 1996
Sales ($Million): 531
Total Units: 521
Franchised: 40%
International: 0%
Minimum Investment: $498,500
Maximum Investment: $1,954,250
Royalty: 4.0%
National Advertising: 3.0%
SBA Registry Status: Listed

Fuddruckers
5700 Mopac Expressway South, Ste. C300
Austin, TX 78749
Telephone: (512) 275-0400
Web Site: www.fuddruckers.com
Description: A full-service family
    restaurant chain
Parent Company: Magic Restaurants, LLC
    & King Cannon, Inc.
Date Began Franchising: January 1, 1999
Sales ($Million): 328
Total Units: 234
Franchised: 53%
International: 0%
Minimum Investment: $740,000
Maximum Investment: $1,550,000
Royalty: 5.0%
National Advertising: 4.0%
SBA Registry Status: Not Listed

Golden Corral Family Restaurants
5151 Glenwood Ave.
Raleigh, NC 27612
Telephone: (919) 881-5135
Web Site:
    www.goldencorralfranchise.com
Description: A full-service family
    restaurant chain
Parent Company: Golden Corral Corp.
Date Began Franchising: April 1, 1986
Sales ($Million): 1,380
Total Units: 476
Franchised: 74%
International: 0%
Minimum Investment: $2,382,650
Maximum Investment: $4,282,000
Royalty: 4.0%
National Advertising: Variable
SBA Registry Status: Not Listed

Great Harvest Bread Co.

28 S. Montana St.
Dillon, MT 59725
Telephone: (406) 683-6842
Web Site: www.greatharvest.com
Description: A franchise system of
    whole-grain bakeries
Parent Company: Great Harvest
    Franchising Inc.
Date Began Franchising: May 1, 1980
Sales ($Million): 82
Total Units: 175
Franchised: 99%
International: 0%
Minimum Investment: $97,834
Maximum Investment: $566,538
Royalty: Variable
National Advertising: 0%
SBA Registry Status: Listed

Great Steak & Potato Co.

7730 E. Greenway Rd., Ste. 104
Scottsdale, AZ 85260
Telephone: (480) 443-0200
Web Site: www.kahalacorp.com
Description: A quick-service sandwich chain
Parent Company: Kahala Corp.
Date Began Franchising: Contact franchiser
Sales ($Million): 107
Total Units: 241
Franchised: 100%
International: 6%
Minimum Investment: $153,000
Maximum Investment: $280,000
Royalty: 6.0%
National Advertising: 4.0%
SBA Registry Status: Listed

Hardee's

One U.S. Bank Plaza, 505 N. 7th St.,
    Ste. 2000
St. Louis, MO 63101
Telephone: (866) 253-7655
Web Site: www.hardees.com
Description: A quick-service
    hamburger chain
Parent Company: CKE Restaurants, Inc.
Date Began Franchising: January 1, 1961
Sales ($Million): 1,760
Total Units: 2,001
Franchised: 67%
International: 8%
Minimum Investment: $820,800
Maximum Investment: $1,177,500
Royalty: 4.0%
National Advertising: 5.0%
SBA Registry Status: Listed

Hooters Restaurants

1815 the Exchange
Atlanta, GA 30339
Telephone: (770) 951-2040
Web Site: www.hooters.com
Description: A full-service casual dining
    restaurant chain
Parent Company: Hooters of America
Date Began Franchising: January 1, 1986
Sales ($Million): 828
Total Units: 402
Franchised: 71%
International: 9%
Minimum Investment: $591,500
Maximum Investment: $1,787,000
Royalty: 6.0%
National Advertising: 2.0%
SBA Registry Status: Not Listed

Hot Stuff Foods, LLC

2930 West Maple St.
Sioux Falls, SD 57107
Telephone: (605) 336-6961
Web Site: www.hotstufffoods.com
Description: Quick-service food offerings
    in convenience store locations
Parent Company: Hot Stuff Foods, LLC

Date Began Franchising: January 1, 1994
Sales ($Million): 315
Total Units: 1,207
Franchised: 100%
International: 2%
Minimum Investment: $49,995
Maximum Investment: $412,495
Royalty: 0%
National Advertising: $250/qtr
SBA Registry Status: Not Listed

Houlihan's

8700 State Line Rd., Ste. 100
Leawood, KS 66206
Telephone: (913) 901-2571
Web Site: www.houlihans.com
Description: A full-service casual dining
restaurant chain
Parent Company: Houlihan's
Restaurants, Inc.
Date Began Franchising: January 1, 1984
Sales ($Million): 255
Total Units: 91
Franchised: 67%
International: 2%
Minimum Investment: $1,662,500
Maximum Investment: $5,045,000
Royalty: 4.0%
National Advertising: Variable
SBA Registry Status: Listed

Huddle House, Inc.

5901-B Peachtree-Dunwoody Road,
Ste. 450
Atlanta, GA 30328
Telephone: (404) 377-5700
Web Site: www.huddlehouse.com
Description: A full-service diner chain
open 24 hours
Parent Company: HH Holdings
Date Began Franchising: January 1, 1964
Sales ($Million): 211
Total Units: 405

Franchised: 95%
International: 0%
Minimum Investment: $484,000
Maximum Investment: $1,026,000
Royalty: 4.0%
National Advertising: 1.0%
SBA Registry Status: Listed

Hungry Howie's Pizza

30300 Stephenson Hwy., Ste. 200
Madison Heights, MI 48071
Telephone: (248) 414-3300
Web Site: www.hungryhowies.com
Description: A quick-service pizza delivery
and carry-out chain
Parent Company: Hungry Howie's
Pizza, Inc.
Date Began Franchising: January 1, 1982
Sales ($Million): 254
Total Units: 524
Franchised: 100%
International: 0%
Minimum Investment: $84,100
Maximum Investment: $270,500
Royalty: 5.0%
National Advertising: 1.0%
SBA Registry Status: Not Listed

International House of Pancakes (IHOP)

450 N. Brand Blvd., 7th Floor
Glendale, CA 91203
Telephone: (818) 240-6055
Web Site: www.ihop.com
Description: A full-service family
restaurant chain
Parent Company: IHOP Corp.
Date Began Franchising: January 1, 1960
Sales ($Million): 1,991
Total Units: 1,242
Franchised: 100%
International: 1%
Minimum Investment: $836,000

Maximum Investment: $3,626,750
Royalty: 4.5%
National Advertising: 1.0%
SBA Registry Status: Listed

Jack in the Box Restaurant
9330 Balboa Ave.
San Diego, CA 92123
Telephone: (619) 571-2121
Web Site: www.jackinthebox.com
Description: A quick-service
    hamburger chain
Parent Company: Jack in the Box, Inc.
Date Began Franchising: January 1, 1982
Sales ($Million): 2,640
Total Units: 2,052
Franchised: 26%
International: 0%
Minimum Investment: $1,116,091
Maximum Investment: $2,181,760
Royalty: 5.0%
National Advertising: 5.0%
SBA Registry Status: Not Listed

Jason's Deli
2400 Broadway
Beaumont, TX 77702-1904
Telephone: (409) 838-1976
Web Site: www.jasonsdeli.com
Description: A fast casual sandwich chain
Parent Company: Deli Management, Inc.
Date Began Franchising: October 3, 1983
Sales ($Million): 329
Total Units: 152
Franchised: 41%
International: 0%
Minimum Investment: $680,000
Maximum Investment: $905,000
Royalty: 4.0%
National Advertising: 2.0%
SBA Registry Status: Not Listed

Jimmy John's Gourmet Sandwiches
2212 Fox Drive
Champaign, IL 61820
Telephone: (217) 356-9900
Web Site: www.jimmyjohns.com
Description: A quick-service sandwich chain
Parent Company: Jimmy John's Gourmet
    Sandwiches
Date Began Franchising: April 29, 1993
Sales ($Million): 215
Total Units: 366
Franchised: 95%
International: 0%
Minimum Investment: $211,400
Maximum Investment: $363,500
Royalty: 6.0%
National Advertising: 4.5%
SBA Registry Status: Not Listed

Johnny Carino's Italian
7500 Rialto Blvd., Ste. 250
Austin, TX 78735
Telephone: (512) 263-0800
Web Site: www.carinos.com
Description: A full-service casual dining
    restaurant chain
Parent Company: Fired Up, Inc.
Date Began Franchising: March 1, 1996
Sales ($Million): 375
Total Units: 167
Franchised: 55%
International: 4%
Minimum Investment: $1,228,000
Maximum Investment: $2,480,000
Royalty: 4.0%
National Advertising: 4.0%
SBA Registry Status: Not Listed

Johnny Rockets
25550 Commercentre Drive, Ste. 200
Lake Forest, CA 92630
Telephone: (949) 643-6134
Web Site: www.johnnyrockets.com

Description: A full-service diner chain
Parent Company: Johnny Rockets
    Group, Inc.
Date Began Franchising: January 9, 1987
Sales ($Million): 199
Total Units: 198
Franchised: 75%
International: 13%
Minimum Investment: $636,000
Maximum Investment: $920,000
Royalty: Variable
National Advertising: 1.5%
SBA Registry Status: Listed

KFC

1441 Gardiner Lane
Louisville, KY 40213
Telephone: (502) 874-8300
Web Site: www.kfc.com
Description: A quick-service chicken
    restaurant chain
Parent Company: Yum! Brands, Inc.
Date Began Franchising: January 1, 1952
Sales ($Million): 13,200
Total Units: 13,893
Franchised: 77%
International: 61%
Minimum Investment: $1,142,300
Maximum Investment: $1,732,300
Royalty: 4.0%
National Advertising: 2.0%
SBA Registry Status: Not Listed

Krispy Kreme

370 Knollwood St., Ste. 500
Winston Salem, NC 27103
Telephone: (336) 725-2981
Web Site: www.krispykreme.com
Description: A quick-service donut chain
Parent Company: Krispy Kreme
    Doughnuts, Inc.
Date Began Franchising: January 1, 1996
Sales ($Million): 1,062

Total Units: 402
Franchised: 67%
International: 17%
Minimum Investment: $1,225,000
Maximum Investment: $1,700,000
Royalty: 4.5%
National Advertising: 1.0%
SBA Registry Status: Not Listed

Krystal Company

One Union Square
Chattanooga, TN 37402
Telephone: (423) 757-5601
Web Site: www.krystal.com
Description: A quick-service
    hamburger chain
Parent Company: Port Royal Holdings, Inc.
Date Began Franchising: Contact
    franchisor for information
Sales ($Million): 420
Total Units: 423
Franchised: 42%
International: 0%
Minimum Investment: $560,500
Maximum Investment: $1,065,000
Royalty: 4.5%
National Advertising: 4.0%
SBA Registry Status: Listed

La Salsa Fresh Mexican Grill

6307 Carpinteria Ave., Ste. A
Carpinteria, CA 93013
Telephone: (805) 745-7500
Web Site: www.lasalsa.com
Description: A fast casual Mexican
    restaurant chain
Parent Company: CKE Restaurants, Inc.
Date Began Franchising: January 26, 1988
Sales ($Million): 82
Total Units: 101
Franchised: 39%
International: 0%
Minimum Investment: $431,000

Maximum Investment: $612,000
Royalty: 5.0%
National Advertising: 1.0%
SBA Registry Status: Listed

Long John Silver's

P.O. Box 34550
Louisville, KY 40232
Telephone: (859) 543-6000
Web Site: www.ljsilvers.com
Description: A quick-service seafood chain
Parent Company: Yum! Brands, Inc.
Date Began Franchising: September 1, 1969
Sales ($Million): 800
Total Units: 1,184
Franchised: 53%
International: 3%
Minimum Investment: $851,000
Maximum Investment: $1,220,000
Royalty: 5.0%
National Advertising: 5.0%
SBA Registry Status: Not Listed

Manchu Wok

P.O. Box 625
Deerfield Beach, FL 33443
Telephone: (954) 427-2163
Web Site: www.manchuwok.com
Description: A fast casual Chinese food
     restaurant chain
Parent Company: Manchu Wok
Date Began Franchising: 1985
Sales ($Million): 140
Total Units: 207
Franchised: 75%
International: 40%
Minimum Investment: $287,450
Maximum Investment: $469,000
Royalty: 7.0%
National Advertising: 1.0%
SBA Registry Status: Not Listed

Marble Slab Creamery

3100 S. Gessner, Ste. 305
Houston, TX 77063
Telephone: (713) 780-3601
Web Site: www.marbleslab.com
Description: A chain of ice cream shops
Parent Company: Marble Slab
     Creamery, Inc.
Date Began Franchising: January 1, 1984
Sales ($Million): 62
Total Units: 559
Franchised: 100%
International: 4%
Minimum Investment: $375,675
Maximum Investment: $225,275
Royalty: 6.0%
National Advertising: 2.0%
SBA Registry Status: Not Listed

Marco's Pizza

5252 Monroe St., 2nd Fl.
Toledo, OH 43623
Telephone: (419) 885-7000
Web Site: www.marcos.com
Description: A chain of take-out and
     delivery pizza and sub shops
Parent Company: Marco's Franshising, LLC
Date Began Franchising: January 1, 2004
Sales ($Million): 70
Total Units:148
Franchised: 100%
International: 0%
Minimum Investment: $184,300
Maximum Investment: $338,750
Royalty: 5.0%
National Advertising: 1.0%
SBA Registry Status: Listed

Max & Erma's

4849 Evanswood Dr.
Columbus, OH 43229
Telephone: (614) 431-5800

Web Site: www.maxandermas.com

Description: A full-service casual dining restaurant chain

Parent Company: Max & Erma's Restaurants, Inc.

Date Began Franchising: January 1, 1998

Sales ($Million): 232

Total Units: 91

Franchised: 23%

International: 0%

Minimum Investment: $622,500

Maximum Investment: $3,028,500

Royalty: 4.0%

National Advertising: 1.0%

SBA Registry Status: Not Listed

Mazzio's Italian Eatery

4441 S. 72nd East Ave.

Tulsa, OK 74145

Telephone: (918) 663-8880

Web Site: www.mazzios.com

Description: A fast casual Italian eatery chain

Parent Company: Mazzio's Corporation

Date Began Franchising: January 1, 1966

Sales ($Million): 148

Total Units: 175

Franchised: 66%

International: 0%

Minimum Investment: $759,000

Maximum Investment: $1,572,000

Royalty: 4.0%

National Advertising: 1.0%

SBA Registry Status: Not Listed

McAlister's Deli

731 S. Pear Orchard Rd., Ste. 51

Ridgeland, MS 39157

Telephone: (601) 952-1100

Web Site: www.mcalistersdeli.com

Description: A fast casual sandwich chain

Parent Company: McAlister's Corporation

Date Began Franchising: April 2, 1999

Sales ($Million): 207

Total Units: 181

Franchised: 87%

International: 0%

Minimum Investment: $879,500

Maximum Investment: $1,479,000

Royalty: 5.0%

National Advertising: 2.0%

SBA Registry Status: Listed

McDonald's

711 Jorie Blvd., Dept. 50

Oak Brook, IL 60523

Telephone: (630) 623-6196

Web Site: www.mcdonalds.com

Description: A quick-service hamburger chain

Parent Company: McDonald's Corporation

Date Began Franchising: January 1, 1955

Sales ($Million): 52,950

Total Units: 30,771

Franchised: 73%

International: 55%

Minimum Investment: $655,750

Maximum Investment: $1,255,000

Royalty: 4.0%

National Advertising: 4.0%

SBA Registry Status: Not Listed

The Melting Pot

8810 Twin Lakes Blvd.

Tampa, FL 33614

Telephone: (813) 881-0055

Web Site: www.meltingpot.com

Description: A full-service casual dining restaurant chain featuring fondue

Parent Company: The Melting Pot Restaurants, Inc.

Date Began Franchising: September 1, 1984

Sales ($Million): 175

Total Units: 100

Franchised: 96%
International: 0%
Minimum Investment: $671,395
Maximum Investment: $1,397,395
Royalty: 4.5%
National Advertising: 1.5%
SBA Registry Status: Listed

Moe's Southwest Grill
2915 Peach Tree Rd.
Atlanta, GA 30305
Telephone: (404) 844-8335
Web Site: www.moes.com
Description: A fast casual Mexican
   restaurant chain
Parent Company: Raving Brands, Inc.
Date Began Franchising: January 1, 2001
Sales ($Million): 185
Total Units: 266
Franchised: 100%
International: 0%
Minimum Investment: $252,000
Maximum Investment: $634,000
Royalty: 5.0%
National Advertising: 2.0%
SBA Registry Status: Listed

Old Chicago
248 Centennial Pkwy.
Louisville, CO 80027
Telephone: (303) 664-4200
Web Site: www.oldchicago.com
Description: A full-service casual dining
   restaurant chain
Parent Company: Rock Bottom
   Restaurants, Inc.
Date Began Franchising: February 1, 2000
Sales ($Million): 173
Total Units: 82
Franchised: 28%
International: 0%
Minimum Investment: $1,169,000
Maximum Investment: $2,076,000

Royalty: 4.0%
National Advertising: 1.0%
SBA Registry Status: Not Listed

Panera Bread
6710 Clayton Rd.
Richmond Heights, MO 63117
Telephone: (314) 633-7100
Web Site: www.panerabread.com
Description: A chain of fast casual
   bakery cafes
Parent Company: Panera, LLC
Date Began Franchising: December 1, 1993
Sales ($Million): 1,597
Total Units: 877
Franchised: 65%
International: 0%
Minimum Investment: $1,003,000
Maximum Investment: $2,235,175
Royalty: 5.0%
National Advertising: 2.6%
SBA Registry Status: Not Listed

Papa John's Pizza
P.O. Box 99900
Louisville, KY 40269
Telephone: (502) 261-7272
Web Site: www.papajohns.com
Description: A quick-service pizza
   delivery chain
Parent Company: Papa John's
   International, Inc.
Date Began Franchising: March 1, 1984
Sales ($Million): 1,922
Total Units: 2,926
Franchised: 83%
International: 11%
Minimum Investment: $171,283
Maximum Investment: $487,623
Royalty: 4.0%
National Advertising: 4.0%
SBA Registry Status: Listed

Papa Murphy's Take 'N' Bake Pizza

8000 NE Parkway Drive, Ste. 350
Vancouver, WA 98662
Telephone: (360) 449-4036
Web Site: www.papamurphys.com
Description: Take-and-bake pizza franchise
Parent Company: Papa Murphy's
   International, Inc.
Date Began Franchising: May 9, 1995
Sales ($Million): 411
Total Units: 944
Franchised: 95%
International: 0%
Minimum Investment: $183,600
Maximum Investment: $275,000
Royalty: 5.0%
National Advertising: 2.0%
SBA Registry Status: Listed

Penn Station East Coast Subs

8276 Teechmont Ave.
Cincinnati, OH 45255
Telephone: (317) 554-6360
Web Site: www.penn-station.com
Description: A fast casual sandwich chain
Parent Company: Penn Station
   Incorporated
Date Began Franchising: August 1, 1987
Sales ($Million): 86
Total Units: 195
Franchised: 90%
International: 0%
Minimum Investment: $229,640
Maximum Investment: $434,709
Royalty: Variable
National Advertising: 0.5%
SBA Registry Status: Not Listed

Perkins Restaurant & Bakery

6075 Poplar Avenue, Ste. 800
Memphis, TN 38119-4709
Telephone: (901) 766-6400

Web Site: www.perkinsrestaurants.com
Description: A full-service family
   restaurant chain
Parent Company: Perkins & Marie
   Callender's Inc.
Date Began Franchising: December 22,
   1999
Sales ($Million): 868
Total Units: 482
Franchised: 69%
International: 3%
Minimum Investment: $1,797,357
Maximum Investment: $2,940,588
Royalty: 4.0%
National Advertising: 3.0%
SBA Registry Status: Not Listed

Peter Piper Pizza

14635 N. Kierland Blvd., Ste. 160
Scottsdale, AZ 85254
Telephone: (480) 609-6400
Web Site: www.peterpiperfranchise.com
Description: A full-service family pizza
   restaurant chain
Parent Company: Peter Piper Inc.
Date Began Franchising: January 1, 1977
Sales ($Million): 171
Total Units: 138
Franchised: 72%
International: 22%
Minimum Investment: $1,253,000
Maximum Investment: $1,253,000
Royalty: 5.0%
National Advertising: 4.5%
SBA Registry Status: Not Listed

Pizza Hut

14841 Dallas Parkway
Dallas, TX 75254
Telephone: (972) 338-7700
Web Site: www.pizzahut.com
Description: A quick-service pizza dine-in
   and delivery chain

Parent Company: Yum! Brands, Inc.
Date Began Franchising: January 1, 1959
Sales ($Million): 9,100
Total Units: 12,548
Franchised: 80%
International: 40%
Minimum Investment: $338,000
Maximum Investment: $1,382,000
Royalty: 6.5%
National Advertising: 3.0%
SBA Registry Status: Not Listed

Pizza Inn
3551 Plano Pkwy.
The Colony, TX 75056
Telephone: (469) 384-5000
Web Site: www.pizzainn.com
Description: A full-service family pizza
    restaurant chain
Parent Company: Pizza Inn, Inc.
Date Began Franchising: January 1, 1963
Sales ($Million): 160
Total Units: 389
Franchised: 99%
International: 19%
Minimum Investment: $571,250
Maximum Investment: $697,250
Royalty: 4.0%
National Advertising: 1.0%
SBA Registry Status: Not Listed

Popeyes Chicken & Biscuits
5555 Glenridge Connector NE, Ste. 300
Atlanta, GA 30342
Telephone: (404) 459-4450
Web Site: www.popeyes.com
Description: A quick-service chicken
    restaurant chain
Parent Company: AFC Enterprises, Inc.
Date Began Franchising: November 5, 1992
Sales ($Million): 1,600
Total Units: 1,828
Franchised: 98%

International: 19%
Minimum Investment: $287,300
Maximum Investment: $380,100
Royalty: 5.0%
National Advertising: 3.0%
SBA Registry Status: Listed

Qdoba Mexican Grill
4865 Ward Rd., Ste. 500
Wheat Ridge, CO 80033
Telephone: (303) 629-5000
Web Site: www.qdoba.com
Description: A fast casual Mexican
    restaurant chain
Parent Company: Jack in the Box, Inc.
Date Began Franchising: September 1, 1995
Sales ($Million): 235
Total Units: 273
Franchised: 78%
International: 0%
Minimum Investment: $395,000
Maximum Investment: $605,000
Royalty: 5.0%
National Advertising: 2.0%
SBA Registry Status: Not Listed

Quiznos
1475 Lawrence St., Ste. 400
Denver, CO 80202
Telephone: (720) 359-3300
Web Site: www.quiznos.com
Description: A quick-service sandwich chain
Parent Company: The Quiznos Corporation
Date Began Franchising: January 1, 1991
Sales ($Million): 1,570
Total Units: 3,769
Franchised: 100%
International: 13%
Minimum Investment: $202,440
Maximum Investment: $302,500
Royalty: 7.0%
National Advertising: 1.0%
SBA Registry Status: Listed

Red Robin

6312 S. Fiddlers Green Circle, Ste. 200 N.
Greenwood Village, CO 80111
Telephone: (303) 846-6000
Web Site: www.redrobin.com
Description: A full-service casual dining
restaurant chain
Parent Company: Red Robin Gourmet
Burgers
Date Began Franchising: January 1, 1979
Sales ($Million): 840
Total Units: 299
Franchised: 45%
International: 6%
Minimum Investment: $2,145,900
Maximum Investment: $3,245,900
Royalty: 4.0%
National Advertising: 4.0%
SBA Registry Status: Not Listed

Rita's Ices, Cones, Shakes, and Other Cool Stuff

1525 Ford Rd.
Bensalem, PA 19020
Telephone: (215) 633-9899
Web Site: www.ritasice.com
Description: An italian ice, gelati, and
frozen custard shop chain
Parent Company: Rita's Water Ice
Franchise Company, LLC
Date Began Franchising: May 1, 1989
Sales ($Million): 74
Total Units: 391
Franchised: 100%
International: 0%
Minimum Investment: $161,900
Maximum Investment: $337,500
Royalty: 6.5%
National Advertising: 2.5%
SBA Registry Status: Listed

Round Table Pizza

1320 Willow Pass Rd., Ste. 600
Concord, CA 94520
Telephone: (925) 969-3900
Web Site: www.roundtablepizza.com
Description: A quick-service pizza dine-in
and delivery chain
Parent Company: Round Table Pizza, Inc.
Date Began Franchising: January 1, 1962
Sales ($Million): 409
Total Units: 506
Franchised: 75%
International: 1%
Minimum Investment: $521,000
Maximum Investment: $633,000
Royalty: 4.0%
National Advertising: 4.0%
SBA Registry Status: Not Listed

Roy Rogers

321 Ballenger Center Drive, Ste. 201
Frederick, MD 21703
Telephone: (301) 695-8563
Web Site: www.royrogersrestaurants.com
Description: A quick-service
hamburger chain
Parent Company: Roy Rogers Franchise
Company, LLC
Date Began Franchising: January 1, 1968
Sales ($Million): 85
Total Units: 54
Franchised: 72%
International: 0%
Minimum Investment: $1,130,250
Maximum Investment: $1,344,250
Royalty: 5.0%
National Advertising: 2.0%
SBA Registry Status: Not Listed

Ruby Tuesday

150 W. Church Ave.
Maryville, TN 37801

Telephone: (865) 379-5700
Web Site: www.rubytuesday.com
Description: A full-service casual dining
restaurant chain
Parent Company: Ruby Tuesday, Inc.
Date Began Franchising: January 1, 1997
Sales ($Million): 1,749
Total Units: 880
Franchised: 29%
International: 5%
Minimum Investment: $1,208,300
Maximum Investment: $3,920,000
Royalty: 4.0%
National Advertising: 0.5% –3%
SBA Registry Status: Not Listed

Ruth's Chris Steak House
500 International Parkway
Heathrow, FL 32746
Telephone: (407) 333-7440
Web Site: www.ruthschris.com
Description: A full-service upscale
steak house
Parent Company: Ruth's Chris Steak
House, Inc.
Date Began Franchising: January 1, 1985
Sales ($Million): 415
Total Units: 95
Franchised: 52%
International: 11%
Minimum Investment: $2,050,000
Maximum Investment: $3,568,000
Royalty: 5.0%
National Advertising: 1.0%
SBA Registry Status: Not Listed

Sbarro
401 Broadhollow Road
Melville, NY 11747
Telephone: (631) 715-4146
Web Site: www.sbarro.com
Description: A quick-service Italian chain
Parent Company: Sbarro, Inc.

Date Began Franchising: November 1, 1977
Sales ($Million): 601
Total Units: 952
Franchised: 48%
International: 19%
Minimum Investment: $244,000
Maximum Investment: $331,500
Royalty: 7.0%
National Advertising: 0%
SBA Registry Status: Not Listed

Schlotzsky's
301 Congress Ave., Ste. 1100
Austin, TX 78701
Telephone: (800) 846-2867
Web Site: www.cooldeli.com
Description: A fast casual sandwich chain
Parent Company: Schlotzsky's, Ltd.
Date Began Franchising: February 23, 1987
Sales ($Million): 231
Total Units: 384
Franchised: 96%
International: 4%
Minimum Investment: $509,300
Maximum Investment: $719,500
Royalty: 6.0%
National Advertising: 4.0%
SBA Registry Status: Listed

Shoney's Restaurants
1717 Elm Hill Pike, Ste. B-1
Nashville, TN 37210
Telephone: (615) 391-5395
Web Site: www.shoneys.com
Description: A full-service family dining
restaurant chain
Parent Company: Shoney's LLC
Date Began Franchising: January 1, 1971
Sales ($Million): 470
Total Units: 290
Franchised: 78%
International: 0%
Minimum Investment: $568,000

Maximum Investment: $2,799,000
Royalty: 2.5% –3.5%
National Advertising: 0.5% –1.0%
SBA Registry Status: Not Listed

Sirloin Stockade

2908 N. Plum
Hutchinson, KS 67502
Telephone: (620) 669-9372
Web Site: www.stockadecompanies.com
Description: Steakhouse and buffet
    restaurants in the United States
    and Mexico
Parent Company: Stockade Companies
Date Began Franchising: March 23, 1984
Sales ($Million): 83
Total Units: 48
Franchised: 98%
International: 31%
Minimum Investment: $1,259,000
Maximum Investment: $2,784,000
Royalty: 3.0%
National Advertising: 1.0%
SBA Registry Status: Not Listed

Sizzler Restaurants

6101 W. Centinela Ave., Ste. 300
Culver City, CA 90230
Telephone: (310) 846-8750
Web Site: www.sizzler.com
Description: A full-service casual dining
    restaurant chain
Parent Company: Sizzler USA, Inc.
Date Began Franchising: May 6, 1997
Sales ($Million): 500
Total Units: 302
Franchised: 77%
International: 24%
Minimum Investment: $933,000
Maximum Investment: $1,787,000
Royalty: 4.0%
National Advertising: 2.0%
SBA Registry Status: Not Listed

Smoothie King

121 Park Place
Covington, LA 70433
Telephone: (985) 635-6973
Web Site: www.smoothieking.com
Description: A chain offering smoothies
    and supplement-enhanced beverages
Parent Company: Smoothie King Systems
Date Began Franchising: May 1, 1988
Sales ($Million): 96
Total Units: 444
Franchised: 97%
International: 3%
Minimum Investment: $121,000
Maximum Investment: $251,000
Royalty: 6.0%
National Advertising: 1.0%
SBA Registry Status: Listed

Sonic Drive-In

300 Johnny Bench Dr.
Oklahoma City, OK 73104
Telephone: (405) 225-5000
Web Site: www.sonicdrivein.com
Description: A quick-service drive-in ham-
    burger chain
Parent Company: Sonic Corp.
Date Began Franchising: December 3, 1974
Sales ($Million): 3,000
Total Units: 3,039
Franchised: 81%
International: 0%
Minimum Investment: $821,500
Maximum Investment: $2,172,500
Royalty: 5.0%
National Advertising: 0.75%
SBA Registry Status: Not Listed

Subway Restaurants

325 Bic Drive
Milford, CT 06460
Telephone: (203) 877-4281
Web Site: www.subway.com

Description: A quick-service sandwich chain
Parent Company: Doctor's Associates Inc.
Date Began Franchising: January 1, 1974
Sales ($Million): 9,050
Total Units: 24,810
Franchised: 100%
International: 21%
Minimum Investment: $92,050
Maximum Investment: $222,800
Royalty: 8.0%
National Advertising: 4.5%
SBA Registry Status: Listed

T.G.I. Friday's

4201 Marsh Lane
Carrollton, TX 75007
Telephone: (972) 662-5400
Web Site: www.fridays.com
Description: A full-service casual dining
    restaurant chain
Parent Company: Carlson Restaurants
    Worldwide, Inc.
Date Began Franchising: November 13,
    1969
Sales ($Million): 2,580
Total Units: 805
Franchised: 64%
International: 32%
Minimum Investment: $2,120,000
Maximum Investment: $3,640,000
Royalty: 4.0%
National Advertising: 4.0%
SBA Registry Status: Not Listed

Taco Bell

17901 Von Karman Ave.
Irvine, CA 92614
Telephone: (949) 863-4500
Web Site: www.tacobell.com
Description: A quick-service Mexican
    fare chain
Parent Company: Yum! Brands, Inc.
Date Began Franchising: January 1, 1964

Sales ($Million): 6,400
Total Units: 5,868
Franchised: 79%
International: 4%
Minimum Investment: $242,800
Maximum Investment: $536,000
Royalty: 5.5%
National Advertising: 3.0%
SBA Registry Status: Not Listed

Taco John's

808 W. 20th Street
Cheyenne, WY 82001
Telephone: (307) 635-0101
Web Site: www.tacojohns.com
Description: A quick-service Mexican
    fare chain
Parent Company: Taco John's
    International, Inc.
Date Began Franchising: March 1, 1995
Sales ($Million): 250
Total Units: 418
Franchised: 98%
International: 0%
Minimum Investment: $637,500
Maximum Investment: $968,500
Royalty: 4.0%
National Advertising: 3.5%
SBA Registry Status: Listed

Taco Time

7730 E. Greenway Rd., Ste. 104
Scottsdale, AZ 85260
Telephone: (480) 443-0200
Web Site: www.tacotime.com
Description: A quick-service Mexican
    fare chain
Parent Company: Kahala Corp.
Date Began Franchising: January 1, 1971
Sales ($Million): 135
Total Units: 357
Franchised: 99%
International: 31%

Minimum Investment: $137,000
Maximum Investment: $598,000
Royalty: 5.0%
National Advertising: 4.0%
SBA Registry Status: Listed

TCBY

2855 E. Cottonwood Parkway, Ste. 400
Salt Lake City, UT 84121
Telephone: (801) 736-5600
Web Site: www.tcby.com
Description: A chain offering frozen
    yogurt treats and smoothies
Parent Company: TCBY Systems
Date Began Franchising: June 1, 1982
Sales ($Million): 297
Total Units: 1,249
Franchised: 100%
International: 24%
Minimum Investment: $159,800
Maximum Investment: $398,000
Royalty: 5.0%
National Advertising: 3% –5%
SBA Registry Status: Listed

Tim Horton's

4150 Tuller Rd., Ste. 236
Dublin, OH 43017-0256
Telephone: (614) 791-4200
Web Site: www.timhortons.com
Description: A Canadian-based quick-
    service coffee and baked goods chain
Parent Company: Tim Horton's Inc.
Date Began Franchising: July 1, 1984
Sales ($Million): 3,129
Total Units: 2,885
Franchised: 97%
International: 90%
Minimum Investment: $373,200
Maximum Investment: $616,900
Royalty: 4.5%
National Advertising: 4.0%
SBA Registry Status: Not Listed

Togo's Eatery

130 Royall St.
Canton, MA 02021
Telephone: (781) 737-3000
Web Site: www.togos.com
Description: A quick-service sandwich chain
Parent Company: Dunkin' Brands, Inc.
Date Began Franchising: January 1, 1977
Sales ($Million): 166
Total Units: 356
Franchised: 100%
International: 0%
Minimum Investment: $194,225
Maximum Investment: $559,800
Royalty: 5.0%–5.9%
National Advertising 5.0%
SBA Registry Status: Listed

Tony Roma's

9304 Forest Lane, Ste. 200
Dallas, TX 75243
Telephone: (214) 343-7800
Web Site: www.tonyromas.com
Description: A full-service casual dining
    restaurant chain
Parent Company: Romacorp, Inc.
Date Began Franchising: March 29, 1994
Sales ($Million): 402
Total Units: 216
Franchised: 90%
International: 55%
Minimum Investment: $1,420,800
Maximum Investment: $2,215,800
Royalty: 4.0%
National Advertising: 0.5%
SBA Registry Status: Not Listed

Tumbleweed Southwest Grill

2301 River Rd., Ste. 200
Louisville, KY 40206
Telephone: (502) 893-0323
Web Site:
    www.tumbleweedrestaurants.com

Description: A full-service casual dining
  restaurant chain
Parent Company: Tumbleweed, Inc.
Date Began Franchising: May 22, 1981
Sales ($Million): 125
Total Units: 59
Franchised: 56%
International: 17%
Minimum Investment: $1,006,000
Maximum Investment: $1,653,000
Royalty: Variable
National Advertising: 1.0%–3.0%
SBA Registry Status: Not Listed

Uno Chicago Grill

100 Charles Park Rd.
West Roxbury, MA 02132
Telephone: (617) 218-5205
Web Site: www.unos.com
Description: A full-service casual dining
  restaurant chain
Parent Company: Uno Restaurant Corp.
Date Began Franchising: January 1, 1996
Sales ($Million): 454
Total Units: 213
Franchised: 43%
International: 1%
Minimum Investment: $1,103,500
Maximum Investment: $2,708,000
Royalty: 5.0%
National Advertising: 1.0%
SBA Registry Status: Not Listed

Villa Pizza

25 Washington Street
Morristown, NJ 07960
Telephone: (973) 539-5849
Web Site: www.villaenterprises.com
Description: A quick-service Italian chain
Parent Company: Villa Enterprises
  Management
Date Began Franchising: February 1, 1997

Sales ($Million): 120
Total Units: 222
Franchised: 41%
International: 10%
Minimum Investment: $161,950
Maximum Investment: $402,000
Royalty: 6.0%
National Advertising: 1.0%
SBA Registry Status: Listed

Village Inn Restaurants

400 West 48th Avenue
Denver, CO 80216
Telephone: (303) 672-2229
Web Site: www.vicorpinc.com
Description: A full-service family dining
  restaurant chain
Parent Company: VICORP Restaurants, Inc.
Date Began Franchising: January 1, 1961
Sales ($Million): 342
Total Units: 237
Franchised: 42%
International: 0%
Minimum Investment: $599,000
Maximum Investment: $2,723,000
Royalty: 4.0%
National Advertising: 2.0%
SBA Registry Status: Not Listed

Wendy's

One Dave Thomas Blvd.
Dublin, OH 43017-0256
Telephone: (614) 764-8434
Web Site: www.wendys-invest.com
Description: A quick-service
  hamburger chain
Parent Company: Wendy's
  International, Inc.
Date Began Franchising: January 1, 1971
Sales ($Million): 8,684
Total Units: 6,746
Franchised: 78%
International: 11%

Minimum Investment: $1,308,500
Maximum Investment: $2,350,000
Royalty: 4.0%
National Advertising: 2.0%
SBA Registry Status: Not Listed

Western Sizzlin

1338 Plantation Road
Roanoke, VA 24012
Telephone: (540) 345-3195
Web Site: www.westernsizzlin.com
Description: A full-service family dining
    restaurant chain
Parent Company: Western Sizzlin Corp.
Date Began Franchising: March 30, 1993
Sales ($Million): 234
Total Units: 130
Franchised: 96%
International: 0%
Minimum Investment: $811,000
Maximum Investment: $2,280,000
Royalty: 2.0%
National Advertising: 0.5%
SBA Registry Status: Not Listed

Whataburger

One Whataburger Way
Corpus Christi, TX 78411
Telephone: (361) 878-0352
Web Site: www.whataburger.com
Description: A quick-service
    hamburger chain
Parent Company: Whataburger, Inc.
Date Began Franchising: Not available
Sales ($Million): 885
Total Units: 674
Franchised: 38%
International: 0%
Minimum Investment: Contact franchisor
    for information
Maximum Investment: Contact franchisor
    for information

Royalty: Contact franchisor for information
National Advertising: Contact franchisor
    for information
SBA Registry Status: Not Listed

Wingstop

1101 E. Aprapaho Road, Ste. 150
Richardson, TX 75081
Telephone: (972) 686-6500
Web Site: www.wingstop.com
Description: Dine-in and carryout chicken
    wing restaurant chain
Parent Company: Wingstop
    Restaurants, Inc.
Date Began Franchising: May 1, 1997
Sales ($Million): 118
Total Units: 276
Franchised: 97%
International: 0%
Minimum Investment: $257,500
Maximum Investment: $400,900
Royalty: 5.0%
National Advertising: 2.0%
SBA Registry Status: Listed

Zaxby's

1040 Founder's Blvd.
Athens, GA 30606
Telephone: (706) 433-2225
Web Site: www.zaxbys.com
Description: A quick-service chicken
    restaurant chain
Parent Company: Zaxby's Franchising Inc.
Date Began Franchising: September 8, 1994
Sales ($Million): 339
Total Units: 301
Franchised: 80%
International: 0%
Minimum Investment: $230,500
Maximum Investment: $488,800
Royalty: 6.0%
National Advertising: 4.0%
SBA Registry Status: Listed

Retail

7-Eleven
2711 North Haskell Avenue
Dallas, TX 75204-2906
Telephone: (800) 255-0711
Web Site: www.7-11.com
Description: A global chain of
    convenience stores
Parent Company: 7-Eleven, Inc.
Date Began Franchising: January 1, 1964
Sales ($Million): 37,999
Total Units: 29,465
Franchised: 92%
International: 80%
Minimum Investment: $191,230
Maximum Investment: $574,102
Royalty: 50.0% (turnkey offering)
National Advertising: Variable
SBA Registry Status: Not Listed

Ace Hardware
2200 Kensington Court
Oak Brook, IL 60523
Telephone: (630) 990-6900
Web Site: www.myace.com
Description: Retail hardware and home
    improvement cooperative stores
Parent Company: Ace Hardware Corp.
Date Began Franchising: January 1, 1928
Sales ($Million): 13,000
Total Units: 4,868
Franchised: 100%
International: 5%
Minimum Investment: $236,000
Maximum Investment: $1,051,245
Royalty: 2.0%
National Advertising: Variable
SBA Registry Status: Listed

ampm
4 Centerpoint Dr.
La Palma, CA 90623
Telephone: (818) 894-2676
Web Site: www.ampmfranchising.com
Description: A fuel and food convenience
    store chain
Parent Company: BP Amoco, plc
Date Began Franchising: January 1, 1979
Sales ($Million): 3,000
Total Units: 2,898
Franchised: 92%
International: 69%
Minimum Investment: $333,930
Maximum Investment: $2,745,024
Royalty: 11.0%
National Advertising: 3.5%
SBA Registry Status: Not Listed

The Athlete's Foot
1412 Oakbrook Drive, Ste. 100
Norcross, GA 30093
Telephone: (770) 514-4523
Web Site: www.theathletesfoot.com
Description: A sporting goods retailer
Parent Company: The Athlete's Foot
Date Began Franchising: March 17, 1972
Sales ($Million): 340
Total Units: 593
Franchised: 100%
International: 62%
Minimum Investment: $220,800
Maximum Investment: $683,100
Royalty: 5.0%
National Advertising: 1%
SBA Registry Status: Listed

Blockbuster
1201 Elm Street, Ste. 2100
Dallas, TX 75270
Telephone: (214) 854-3000
Web Site: www.blockbuster.com

Description: Retail video rental with
online and in-store renting options
Parent Company: Blockbuster, Inc.
Date Began Franchising: January 1, 1986
Sales ($Million): 5,864
Total Units: 8,821
Franchised: 21%
International: 38%
Minimum Investment: $219,500
Maximum Investment: $714,500
Royalty: Variable
National Advertising: 2.0%
SBA Registry Status: Listed

Candy Bouquet

423 E. 3rd St.
Little Rock, AR 72201
Telephone: (501) 375-9990
Web Site: www.candybouquet.com
Description: A chain of stores offering
floral-like designer gifts and gourmet
confections
Parent Company: Candy Bouquet
International, Inc.
Date Began Franchising: January 1, 1994
Sales ($Million): 72
Total Units: 821
Franchised: 100%
International: 12%
Minimum Investment: $14,550
Maximum Investment: $50,330
Royalty: 0%
National Advertising: 0%
SBA Registry Status: Listed

Cartridge World

6460 Hollis St.
Emmeryville, CA 94608
Telephone: (510) 594-9900
Web Site: www.cartridgeworldusa.com
Description: Global franchise system
providing printer cartridge refilling
and recycling

Parent Company: Cartridge World
Date Began Franchising: January 1, 2006
Sales ($Million): 300
Total Units: 1,252
Franchised: 100%
International: 71%
Minimum Investment: $135,000
Maximum Investment: $568,200
Royalty: 2.40%
National Advertising: 2.0%
SBA Registry Status: Not Listed

Circle K Convenience Stores

1130 West Warner Road
Tempe, AZ 85284
Telephone: (602) 728-8000
Web Site: www.circlek.com
Description: A fuel and food convenience
store chain
Parent Company: Alimentation
Couche-Tard Inc.
Date Began Franchising: January 1, 1995
Sales ($Million): 8,121
Total Units: 6,124
Franchised: 65%
International: 56%
Minimum Investment: $531,000
Maximum Investment: $1,163,000
Royalty: 4.0%
National Advertising: 2.0%
SBA Registry Status: Listed

EmbroidMe

2121 Vista Parkway
West Palm Beach, FL 33411
Telephone: (561) 640-7367
Web Site: www.embroidme.com
Description: A full-service embroidery,
screen printing, and promotional
products chain
Parent Company: EmbroidMe, Inc.
Date Began Franchising: September 1, 2000
Sales ($Million): 80

Total Units: 306
Franchised: 100%
International: 8%
Minimum Investment: $44,560
Maximum Investment: $104,490
Royalty: 5.0%
National Advertising: 1.0%
SBA Registry Status: Listed

Foot Solutions

2359 Windy Hill Rd., Ste. 220
Marietta, GA 30067
Telephone: (770) 955-0099
Web Site: www.footsolutions.com
Description: A chain selling specialty
custom shoes
Parent Company: Foot Solutions, Inc.
Date Began Franchising: September 1, 2000
Sales ($Million): 58
Total Units: 222
Franchised: 100%
International: 10%
Minimum Investment: $174,700
Maximum Investment: $242,300
Royalty: 5.0%
National Advertising: 2.0%
SBA Registry Status: Listed

General Nutrition Centers

300 Sixth Avenue
Pittsburg, PA 15222
Telephone: (412) 338-2503
Web Site: www.gncfranchising.com
Description: Retail health supplement
and vitamin chain
Parent Company: GNC Franchising, LLC
Date Began Franchising:
November 2, 1987
Sales ($Million): 1,300
Total Units: 4,799
Franchised: 42%
International: 21%

Minimum Investment: $129,573
Maximum Investment: $228,003
Royalty: 6.0%
National Advertising: 3.0%
SBA Registry Status: Listed

Glamour Shots

1300 Metropolitan Ave.
Oklahoma City, OK 73108
Telephone: (405) 951-7323
Web Site: www.glamourshots.com
Description: Mall-based studios offering
professional portraits
Parent Company: Glamour Shots
Licensing, Inc.
Date Began Franchising: December 29,
1989
Sales ($Million): 59
Total Units: 93
Franchised: 98%
International: 8%
Minimum Investment: $78,866
Maximum Investment: $113,866
Royalty: 7.0%
National Advertising: 2.0%
SBA Registry Status: Not Listed

Golf USA, Inc.

3705 W. Memorial Rd., Ste. 801
Oklahoma City, OK 73134
Telephone: (405) 751-0015
Web Site: www.golfusa.com
Description: A chain of retail golf
equipment, accessories, and
apparel stores
Parent Company: Golf USA, Inc.
Date Began Franchising: June 1, 1989
Sales ($Million): 100
Total Units: 116
Franchised: 92%
International: 31%
Minimum Investment: $320,800
Maximum Investment: $488,000

Royalty: 2.0%
National Advertising: 1.0%
SBA Registry Status: Listed

HobbyTown USA

6301 S. 58th St.
Lincoln, NE 68516
Telephone: (402) 434-5064
Web Site: www.hobbytown.com
Description: A chain of retail hobby and
toy stores
Parent Company: Hobby Town
Unlimited, Inc.
Date Began Franchising: September 1,
1985
Sales ($Million): 131
Total Units: 183
Franchised: 99%
International: 0%
Minimum Investment: $134,825
Maximum Investment: $237,999
Royalty: Variable
National Advertising: 2.0%
SBA Registry Status: Listed

Hollywood Tans

11 Enterprise Court
Sewell, NJ 08080
Telephone: (856) 716-2150
Web Site: www.hollywoodtans.com
Description: A chain of tanning salons
Parent Company: Hollywood Tanning
Systems, Inc.
Date Began Franchising: September 1, 1998
Sales ($Million): 96
Total Units: 260
Franchised: 98%
International: 2%
Minimum Investment: $310,500
Maximum Investment: $390,500
Royalty: 7.0%
National Advertising: 1.0%
SBA Registry Status: Listed

Merle Norman Cosmetic Studio

9130 Bellanca Avenue
Los Angeles, CA 90045
Telephone: (310) 641-3000
Web Site: www.merlenorman.com
Description: Retail stores selling Merle
Norman cosmetic products
Parent Company: Merle Norman
Cosmetics, Inc.
Date Began Franchising: January 1, 1934
Sales ($Million): 97
Total Units: 1,911
Franchised: 100%
International: 5%
Minimum Investment: $44,854
Maximum Investment: $155,862
Royalty: 0%
National Advertising: Variable
SBA Registry Status: Listed

Norwalk–The Furniture Idea

100 Furniture Parkway
Norwalk, OH 44857
Telephone: (800) 837-2565
Web Site: www.norwalkfurnitureidea.com
Description: Retail stores selling custom-
ordered upholstered furniture
Parent Company: Norwalk Furniture
Corporation
Date Began Franchising: September 1, 1992
Sales ($Million): 110
Total Units: 66
Franchised: 83%
International: 5%
Minimum Investment: $495,000
Maximum Investment: $495,000
Royalty: 0%
National Advertising: $1,000
SBA Registry Status: Listed

Once Upon a Child

4200 Dahlberg Drive, Ste. 100
Minneapolis, MN 55422
Telephone: (763) 520-8490
Web Site: www.ouac.com
Description: Retail franchises selling new and used children's clothing, toys, and accessories
Parent Company: Winmark Corporation
Date Began Franchising: January 1, 1993
Sales ($Million): 105
Total Units: 208
Franchised: 100%
International: 9%
Minimum Investment: $127,575
Maximum Investment: $219,927
Royalty: 5.0%
National Advertising: $500/yr.
SBA Registry Status: Listed

Party America

980 Atlantic Avenue, Ste. 103
Alameda, CA 94501
Telephone: (510) 747-1800
Web Site: www.partyamerica.com
Description: A chain of party supply retailers
Parent Company: PA Acquisition
Date Began Franchising: October 1, 1987
Sales ($Million): 271
Total Units: 270
Franchised: 24%
International: 0%
Minimum Investment: $348,000
Maximum Investment: $532,000
Royalty: 4.0%
National Advertising: 4.0%
SBA Registry Status: Listed

Pet Supplies "Plus"

22670 Haggerty Rd., Ste. 100
Farmington Hills, MI 48335
Telephone: (248) 374-1900
Web Site: www.petsuppliesplus.com
Description: A pet supplies franchise
Parent Company: Pet Supplies "Plus" USA, Inc.
Date Began Franchising: December 1, 1991
Sales ($Million): 432
Total Units: 217
Franchised: 100%
International: 0%
Minimum Investment: $423,300
Maximum Investment: $714,000
Royalty: $2,000
National Advertising: $2,500
SBA Registry Status: Not Listed

Petland

250 Riverside Street
Chillicothe, OH 45601
Telephone: (740) 775-2464
Web Site: www.petlandinc.com
Description: A chain of retail pet product stores
Parent Company: Petland, Inc.
Date Began Franchising: January 1, 1972
Sales ($Million): 245
Total Units: 206
Franchised: 97%
International: 27%
Minimum Investment: $334,000
Maximum Investment: $801,300
Royalty: 4.5%
National Advertising: 2.0%
SBA Registry Status: Listed

Plato's Closet

4200 Dahlberg Drive, Ste. 100
Minneapolis, MN 55422
Telephone: (763) 520-8581
Web Site: www.platoscloset.com
Description: A buyer and seller of gently used clothing for children, teens, and twenty-somethings
Parent Company: Winmark Corporation

Date Began Franchising: March 1, 1999
Sales ($Million): 81
Total Units: 159
Franchised: 100%
International: 0%
Minimum Investment: $144,825
Maximum Investment: $285,427
Royalty: 4.0%
National Advertising: $1,000
SBA Registry Status: Listed

Play It Again Sports

4200 Dahlberg Drive, Ste. 100
Minneapolis, MN 55422
Telephone: (763) 520-8480
Web Site: www.playitagainsports.com
Description: A retail chain of used
    sporting equipment
Parent Company: Winmark Corporation
Date Began Franchising: August 1, 1988
Sales ($Million): 251
Total Units: 410
Franchised: 100%
International: 10%
Minimum Investment: $185,772
Maximum Investment: $353,873
Royalty: 5.0%
National Advertising: $500
SBA Registry Status: Listed

Pro Golf Discount/
Pro Golf of America

32735 Enterprise Ct., Ste. 600
Farmington Hills, MI 48331
Telephone: (248) 994-0553
Web Site: www.progolfamerica.com
Description: A chain of retail golf
    equipment, accessories, and
    apparel stores
Parent Company: Pro Golf
    International, Inc.
Date Began Franchising: September 22,
    1975

Sales ($Million): 208
Total Units: 138
Franchised: 100%
International: 7%
Minimum Investment: $250,000
Maximum Investment: $2,500,000
Royalty: 2.5%
National Advertising: 1.0%
SBA Registry Status: Listed

RadioShack

300 RadioShack Circle
Fort Worth, TX 76102
Telephone: (817) 415-3499
Web Site: www.radioshack.com
Description: A consumer electronics
    specialty retailer of wireless communi-
    cations, electronic parts, batteries,
    accessories, and more
Parent Company: RadioShack Corp.
Date Began Franchising: January 1, 1972
Sales ($Million): 5,082
Total Units: 6,782
Franchised: 27%
International: 3%
Minimum Investment: $69,900
Maximum Investment: $69,900
Royalty: 0%
National Advertising: 0%
SBA Registry Status: Not Listed

Relax the Back Corporation

6 Centerpointe Drive, Ste. 350
La Palma, CA 90623
Telephone: (714) 736-7952
Web Site:
    www.relaxthebackfranchise.com
Description: A chain of stores offering
    furniture and massage products for
    back pain
Parent Company: Dominion Ventures
Date Began Franchising: October 1, 1989
Sales ($Million): 92

Total Units: 106
Franchised: 100%
International: 2%
Minimum Investment: $192,200
Maximum Investment: $320,500
Royalty: 4.0%
National Advertising: 2.0%
SBA Registry Status: Listed

Rocky Mountain Chocolate Factory
265 Turner Drive
Durango, CO 81303
Telephone: (970) 259-0554
Web Site: www.sweetfranchise.com
Description: A chain of retail gourmet
    chocolate confections
Parent Company: Rocky Mountain
    Chocolate Factory, Inc.
Date Began Franchising: November 1, 1982
Sales ($Million): 111
Total Units: 307
Franchised: 98%
International: 11%
Minimum Investment: $230,400
Maximum Investment: $435,515
Royalty: 5.0%
National Advertising: 1.0%
SBA Registry Status: Listed

Snap-on Tools
2801 80th Street
Kenosha, WI 53143
Telephone: (262) 656-6516
Web Site: www.snapon.com
Description: Home-based mobile tool
    sales franchises
Parent Company: Snap-on Incorporated
Date Began Franchising: January 1, 1991
Sales ($Million): 742
Total Units: 4,420
Franchised: 99%
International: 27%
Minimum Investment: $149,634

Maximum Investment: $262,862
Royalty: $62.50/mo.
National Advertising: 0%
SBA Registry Status: Not Listed

USA BABY
793 Springer Dr.
Lombard, IL 60148
Telephone: (630) 652-0600
Web Site: www.usababy.com
Description: A chain of retail stores offering
    merchandise for mothers and babies
Parent Company: USA BABY, Inc.
Date Began Franchising: January 1, 1987
Sales ($Million): 88
Total Units: 61
Franchised: 100%
International: 3%
Minimum Investment: $343,900
Maximum Investment: $649,700
Royalty: 1.5%–3.0%
National Advertising: 0.5%
SBA Registry Status: Not Listed

White Hen Pantry, Inc.
3003 Butterfield Rd., Ste. 300
Lombard, IL 60148
Telephone: (630) 366-3100
Web Site: www.whitehen.com
Description: Convenience stores that
    will soon be converted to the
    7-Eleven brand
Parent Company: 7-Eleven, Inc.
Date Began Franchising: January 1, 1985
Sales ($Million): 284
Total Units: 271
Franchised: 96%
International: 0%
Minimum Investment: $53,264
Maximum Investment: $204,257
Royalty: Variable
National Advertising: 1.0%
SBA Registry Status: Not Listed

Wild Birds Unlimited
11711 N. College Avenue, Ste. 146
Carmel, IN 46032
Telephone: (317) 571-7100
Web Site: www.wbu.com
Description: A chain of retail bird feeding
 and nature stores
Parent Company: Wild Birds Unlimited, Inc.
Date Began Franchising: June 8, 1983
Sales ($Million): 100
Total Units: 315
Franchised: 100%
International: 4%
Minimum Investment: $98,916
Maximum Investment: $154,733
Royalty: 4.0%
National Advertising: 0.5%
SBA Registry Status: Not Listed

Services

@WORK Personnel Services
3215 John Sevier Highway
Knoxville, TN 37920
Telephone: (865) 609-6911
Web Site: www.atworkfranchise.com
Description: Franchises providing
 staffing and payroll services to
 businesses
Parent Company: @WORK Franchise Inc.
Date Began Franchising: April 20, 1992
Sales ($Million): 97
Total Units: 47
Franchised: 100%
International: 0%
Minimum Investment: $65,000
Maximum Investment: $110,500
Royalty: Variable
National Advertising: 0%
SBA Registry Status: Not Listed

Aaron Rents
309 E. Paces Ferry Road NE
Atlanta, GA 30305
Telephone: (404) 231-0011
Web Site: www.aaronsfranchise.com
Description: A chain of stores leasing
 consumer durable goods
Parent Company: Aaron's Rents, Inc.
Date Began Franchising: May 1, 1992
Sales ($Million): 1,524
Total Units: 1,204
Franchised: 33%
International: 0%
Minimum Investment: $253,670
Maximum Investment: $558,980
Royalty: 6.0%
National Advertising: 0.5%
SBA Registry Status: Not Listed

Comfort Keepers
6640 Poe Ave., Ste. 200
Dayton, OH 45414
Telephone: (937) 264-1933
Web Site: www.comfortkeepers.com
Description: A global franchise system pro-
 viding in-home independent living care
Parent Company: CK Franchising, Inc.
Date Began Franchising: March 1, 1999
Sales ($Million): 167
Total Units: 492
Franchised: 100%
International: 1%
Minimum Investment: $44,525
Maximum Investment: $66,700
Royalty: Variable
National Advertising: Variable
SBA Registry Status: Listed

Cost Cutters
7201 Metro Blvd.
Edina, MN 55439
Telephone: (952) 947-7777

Web Site: www.regiscorp.com
Description: A chain of family hair salons
Parent Company: Regis Corporation
Date Began Franchising: January 1, 1982
Sales ($Million): 222
Total Units: 775
Franchised: 66%
International: 0%
Minimum Investment: $82,333
Maximum Investment: $175,100
Royalty: Variable
National Advertising: 4.0%
SBA Registry Status: Not Listed

Curves and Curves for Women
100 Ritchie Rd.
Waco, TX 76712
Telephone: (254) 399-9285
Web Site: www.curvesinternational.com
Description: A global chain of women's
    fitness centers
Parent Company: Curves International, Inc.
Date Began Franchising: October 1, 1995
Sales ($Million): 1,297
Total Units: 9,904
Franchised: 100%
International: 19%
Minimum Investment: $38,425
Maximum Investment: $53,450
Royalty: 5.0%
National Advertising: 3.0%
SBA Registry Status: Listed

Express Personnel Services
8516 NW Expressway
Oklahoma City, OK 73162
Telephone: (405) 840-5000
Web Site: www.expresspersonnel.com
Description: Business-to-business staffing
    and human resources services
Parent Company: Express Services, Inc.
Date Began Franchising: January 31, 1985

Sales ($Million): 1,549
Total Units: 512
Franchised: 98%
International: 6%
Minimum Investment: $114,350
Maximum Investment: $161,800
Royalty: 8.0%
National Advertising: 0.6%
SBA Registry Status: Not Listed

Fantastic Sams
50 Dunham Rd., Floor 3
Beverly, MA 01915
Telephone: (978) 232-5600
Web Site: www.FantasticSams.com
Description: A hair salon franchise
Parent Company: Fantastic Sams
    Franchise Corporation
Date Began Franchising: January 1, 1995
Sales ($Million): 360
Total Units: 1,385
Franchised: 100%
International: 2%
Minimum Investment: $71,165
Maximum Investment: $156,805
Royalty: $88.59/wk.
National Advertising: $191.39/wk.
SBA Registry Status: Listed

First Choice Haircutters
7201 Metro Blvd.
Edina, MN 55439
Telephone: (952) 947-7777
Web Site: www.firstchoice.com
Description: North American chain of
    hair salons
Parent Company: Regis Corporation
Date Began Franchising: January 1, 1985
Sales ($Million): 94
Total Units: 437
Franchised: 47%
International: 0%

Minimum Investment: $92,500
Maximum Investment: $121,150
Royalty: Variable
National Advertising: 3.0%
SBA Registry Status: Not Listed

The Goddard School
1016 W. Ninth Ave.
King of Prussia, PA 19406
Telephone: (610) 265-8510
Web Site: www.goddardschool.com
Description: Early childhood development and education centers
Parent Company: Goddard Systems, Inc.
Date Began Franchising: August 1, 1988
Sales ($Million): 191
Total Units: 207
Franchised: 100%
International: 0%
Minimum Investment: $447,010
Maximum Investment: $531,100
Royalty: 7.0%
National Advertising: 4.0%
SBA Registry Status: Listed

Gold's Gym Franchising
358 Hampton Dr.
Venice, CA 90291
Telephone: (214) 296-5035
Web Site: www.goldsgym.com
Description: A global chain of coed gyms
Parent Company: Gold's Gym International
Date Began Franchising: September 3, 1987
Sales ($Million): 1,168
Total Units: 778
Franchised: 94%
International: 13%
Minimum Investment: $442,000
Maximum Investment: $1,725,000
Royalty: 3.0%
National Advertising: 2.0%
SBA Registry Status: Listed

Great Clips
7700 France Ave. S, Ste. 425
Minneapolis, MN 55435
Telephone: (952) 893-9088
Web Site: www.greatclips.com
Description: A chain of no-appointment hair salons
Parent Company: Great Clips, Inc.
Date Began Franchising: January 1, 1983
Sales ($Million): 598
Total Units: 2,466
Franchised: 100%
International: 2%
Minimum Investment: $98,750
Maximum Investment: $184,350
Royalty: 6.0%
National Advertising: 5.0%
SBA Registry Status: Listed

H&R Block
One H&R Block Way
Kansas City, MO 64105
Telephone: (816) 854-4540
Web Site: www.hrblock.com
Description: A tax preparation and financial services chain
Parent Company: H&R Block, Inc.
Date Began Franchising: March 31, 1993
Sales ($Million): 4,873
Total Units: 13,548
Franchised: 36%
International: 10%
Minimum Investment: $27,528
Maximum Investment: $40,156
Royalty: Variable
National Advertising: 0%
SBA Registry Status: Not Listed

Home Instead Senior Care
13330 California St., Ste. 200
Omaha, NE 68154
Telephone: (402) 498-4466

Web Site: www.homeinstead.com

Description: A franchise system of caregivers/companions for senior citizens

Parent Company: Home Instead, Inc.

Date Began Franchising: January 1, 1995

Sales ($Million): 361

Total Units: 624

Franchised: 100%

International: 20%

Minimum Investment: $34,050

Maximum Investment: $46,050

Royalty: 5.0%

National Advertising: 0%

SBA Registry Status: Listed

Huntington Learning Centers

496 Kinderkamack Road

Oradell, NJ 07649

Telephone: (800) 653-8400

Web Site: www.huntingtonfranchise.com

Description: Franchises providing supplemental education and exam preparation

Parent Company: Huntington Learning Centers, Inc.

Date Began Franchising: February 25, 1985

Sales ($Million): 126

Total Units: 310

Franchised: 89%

International: 0%

Minimum Investment: $158,270

Maximum Investment: $273,400

Royalty: 8.0%

National Advertising: 2.0%

SBA Registry Status: Listed

Interim HealthCare

1601 Sawgrass Corporate Pkwy.

Sunrise, FL 33323

Telephone: (954) 858-6000

Web Site: www.interimhealthcare.com

Description: Franchises offering licensed medical and nonmedical home care and staffing

Parent Company: Interim HealthCare, Inc.

Date Began Franchising: January 1, 1968

Sales ($Million): 600

Total Units: 314

Franchised: 92%

International: 0%

Minimum Investment: $123,150

Maximum Investment: $404,750

Royalty: Variable

National Advertising: 1.0%

SBA Registry Status: Not Listed

Jackson Hewitt Tax Service

3 Sylvan Way

Parsippany, NJ 07054

Telephone: (973) 630-1040

Web Site: www.jacksonhewitt.com

Description: A chain of tax preparation franchises

Parent Company: Jackson Hewitt Tax Service Inc.

Date Began Franchising: January 1, 1986

Sales ($Million): 650

Total Units: 6,022

Franchised: 89%

International: 0%

Minimum Investment: $47,430

Maximum Investment: $75,205

Royalty: 15.0%

National Advertising: 6.0%

SBA Registry Status: Not Listed

Jenny Craig

5770 Fleet Street

Carlsbad, CA 92008

Telephone: (760) 696-4000

Web Site: www.jennycraig.com

Description: Weight loss centers franchise

Parent Company: Jenny Craig

Date Began Franchising: 1988
Sales ($Million): 400
Total Units: 650
Franchised: 34%
International: 23%
Minimum Investment: $122,600
Maximum Investment: $301,500
Royalty: Variable
National Advertising: Variable
SBA Registry Status: Listed

Labor Finders

11426 North Jog Road
Palm Beach Gardens, FL 33418
Telephone: (561) 627-6507
Web Site: www.laborfinders.com
Description: A temporary staffing franchise
Parent Company: Labor Finders
    International, Inc.
Date Began Franchising: June 1, 1992
Sales ($Million): 331
Total Units: 232
Franchised: 93%
International: 0%
Minimum Investment: $96,150
Maximum Investment: $157,320
Royalty: 2.5%
National Advertising: 0%
SBA Registry Status: Not Listed

Liberty Tax Service

1716 Corporate Landing Pkwy., Ste. 1040
Virginia Beach, VA 23454
Telephone: (757) 493-8855
Web Site: www.libertytax.com
Description: A chain of tax preparation
    franchises
Parent Company: JTH Tax, Inc.
Date Began Franchising: October 1, 1997
Sales ($Million): 182
Total Units: 2,044
Franchised: 98%

International: 13%
Minimum Investment: $33,350
Maximum Investment: $59,900
Royalty: Variable
National Advertising: 5.0%
SBA Registry Status: Listed

The Little Gym

7001 North Scottsdale Road, Ste. 1050
Scottsdale, AZ 85253
Telephone: (480) 948-2878
Web Site: www.thelittlegym.com
Description: Children's motor skill devel-
    opment centers
Parent Company: The Little Gym
    International
Date Began Franchising: June 1, 1990
Sales ($Million): 88
Total Units: 231
Franchised: 100%
International: 19%
Minimum Investment: $155,700
Maximum Investment: $238,000
Royalty: 8.0%
National Advertising: 1.0%
SBA Registry Status: Listed

Medicine Shoppe & Medicap Pharmacy

1100 N. Lindbergh Blvd.
St. Louis, MO 63132
Telephone: (314) 993-6000
Web Site: www.medicineshoppe.com
Description: Retail pharmacy and health-
    related products chain
Parent Company: Cardinal Health, Inc.
Date Began Franchising: January 1, 1970
Sales ($Million): 2,760
Total Units: 1,339
Franchised: 98%
International: 27%
Minimum Investment: $197,910

Maximum Investment: $253,418
Royalty: Variable
National Advertising: $200
SBA Registry Status: Listed

Miracle-Ear
5000 Cheshire Lane N.
Plymouth, MN 55446
Telephone: (763) 268-4000
Web Site: www.miracle-ear.com
Description: Retail locations providing
   hearing aids and hearing services
Parent Company: Amplifon S.p.A.
Date Began Franchising: January 1, 1984
Sales ($Million): 225
Total Units: 1,150
Franchised: 96%
International: 0%
Minimum Investment: $101,500
Maximum Investment: $305,500
Royalty: Variable
National Advertising: Variable
SBA Registry Status: Listed

Money Mailer
14721 Corporate Dr.
Garden Grove, CA 92843
Telephone: (888) 446-4648
Web Site: www.moneymailer.net
Description: A franchise system providing
   direct mail advertising
Parent Company: Money Mailer Holding
   Corporation
Date Began Franchising: July 8, 1985
Sales ($Million): 167
Total Units: 322
Franchised: 94%
International: 0%
Minimum Investment: $37,550
Maximum Investment: $71,250

Royalty: Variable
National Advertising: Variable
SBA Registry Status: Listed

Primrose School Franchising Company
3660 Cedarcrest Road
Acworth, GA 30101
Telephone: (770) 529-4100
Web Site: www.primroseschools.com
Description: Chain of preschool and child
   day care providers
Parent Company: American Capital
   Strategies Ltd.
Date Began Franchising: January 1, 1989
Sales ($Million): 135
Total Units: 161
Franchised: 99%
International: 0%
Minimum Investment: $1,989,400
Maximum Investment: $2,472,400
Royalty: 7.0%
National Advertising: 2.0%
SBA Registry Status: Listed

Spherion
925 North Point Parkway
Alpharetta, GA 30005
Telephone: (678) 867-3702
Web Site: www.spherion.com
Description: A full-time and temporary
   staffing services chain
Parent Company: Spherion
Date Began Franchising: July 7, 2000
Sales ($Million): 1,972
Total Units: 505
Franchised: 41%
International: 0%
Minimum Investment: $121,800
Maximum Investment: $391,700
Royalty: 6.0%
National Advertising: 0.25%
SBA Registry Status: Not Listed

SuperCuts

7201 Metro Blvd.
Edina, MN 55439
Telephone: (952) 947-7777
Web Site: www.regiscorp.com
Description: A chain of affordable salons
geared toward men
Parent Company: Regis Corporation
Date Began Franchising: January 1, 1988
Sales ($Million): 565
Total Units: 2,014
Franchised: 49%
International: 7%
Minimum Investment: $106,860
Maximum Investment: $169,080
Royalty: 6.0%
National Advertising: 5.0%
SBA Registry Status: Not Listed

Sylvan Learning Centers

1001 Fleet St.
Baltimore, MD 21202
Telephone: (410) 843-8000
Web Site: www.educate.com
Description: Tutoring franchises offering
personalized instruction for children
of all ages
Parent Company: Educate, Inc.
Date Began Franchising: January 1, 1993
Sales ($Million): 579
Total Units: 1,154
Franchised: 78%
International: 0%
Minimum Investment: $203,948
Maximum Investment: $297,400
Royalty: 8.0%
National Advertising: 1.5%–5%
SBA Registry Status: Listed

Two Men and a Truck

3400 Belle Chase Way
Lansing, MI 48911
Telephone: (800) 345-1070
Web Site: www.twomenandatruck.com
Description: Franchises providing home
and business moving services
Parent Company: Two Men and a Truck
International, Inc.
Date Began Franchising: February 1, 1989
Sales ($Million): 182
Total Units: 151
Franchised: 97%
International: 3%
Minimum Investment: $89,300
Maximum Investment: $246,500
Royalty: 6.0%
National Advertising: 1.0%
SBA Registry Status: Listed

Valpak Direct Marketing

8605 Largo Lakes Dr.
Largo, FL 33773
Telephone: (727) 399-3000
Web Site: www.valpak.com
Description: Franchise that advertises
local businesses through direct mail
and Internet coupons
Parent Company: Cox Target Media, Inc.
Date Began Franchising: January 1, 1971
Sales ($Million): 420
Total Units: 196
Franchised: 95%
International: 7%
Minimum Investment: $51,700
Maximum Investment: $84,300
Royalty: 0%
National Advertising: Variable
SBA Registry Status: Listed

Volvo Rents

One Volvo Drive
Asheville, NC 28803
Telephone: (828) 650-2000
Web Site: www.volvorents.com
Description: Franchises offering
    construction and industrial
    equipment rental
Parent Company: Volvo Construction
    Equipment North America, Inc.
Date Began Franchising: January 1, 1986
Sales ($Million): 144
Total Units: 127
Franchised: 97%
International: 49%
Minimum Investment: $2,017,250
Maximum Investment: $5,225,250
Royalty: 4.0%
National Advertising: 1.0%
SBA Registry Status: Not Listed

World Gym

3223 Washington Blvd.
Marina Del Ray, CA 90292
Telephone: (310) 827-7705
Web Site: www.worldgym.com
Description: A global chain of full-service
    fitness centers
Parent Company: World Gym
    International, Inc.
Date Began Franchising: January 1, 1982
Sales ($Million): 263
Total Units: 358
Franchised: 100%
International: 20%
Minimum Investment: $350,000
Maximum Investment: $1,200,000
Royalty: $7,200/yr.
National Advertising: 0%
SBA Registry Status: Not Listed

Directory by Minimum Investment

$0–$100,000

FRANCHISE	MINIMUM INVESTMENT	CATEGORY
Results Travel	$ 25	Real Estate and Travel Agencies
UNIGLOBE Travel International	$ 1,895	Real Estate and Travel Agencies
Carlson Wagonlit Travel	$ 2,490	Real Estate and Travel Agencies
Cruise Planners/American Express	$ 3,245	Real Estate and Travel Agencies
CleanNet USA Inc.	$ 3,942	Maintenance, Restoration, and Cleaning Services
Coverall Cleaning Concepts	$ 6,291	Maintenance, Restoration, and Cleaning Services
CruiseOne	$ 6,970	Real Estate and Travel Agencies
Proforma	$ 7,230	Printing, Graphic Design, Signage, and Shipping
Century 21 Real Estate, LLC	$ 11,713	Real Estate and Travel Agencies
Candy Bouquet	$ 14,550	Retail
Disaster Kleenup International	$ 15,235	Maintenance, Restoration, and Cleaning Services
GMAC Real Estate	$ 19,368	Real Estate and Travel Agencies
INTERIORS by Decorating Den	$ 24,038	Maintenance, Restoration, and Cleaning Services
Basement Finishing System	$ 24,100	Maintenance, Restoration, and Cleaning Services
H&R Block	$ 27,528	Services
Coldwell Banker Real Estate Corp.	$ 29,650	Real Estate and Travel Agencies
Unishippers Association	$ 31,125	Printing, Graphic Design, Signage, and Shipping
ServiceMaster Clean	$ 31,333	Maintenance, Restoration, and Cleaning Services
Liberty Tax Service	$ 33,350	Services
Home Instead Senior Care	$ 34,050	Services
Sleep Inn	$ 35,201	Lodging

FRANCHISE	MINIMUM INVESTMENT	CATEGORY
Pillar to Post	$ 36,600	Maintenance, Restoration, and Cleaning Services
Certified Restoration, Drycleaning Network, LLC	$ 37,350	Maintenance, Restoration, and Cleaning Services
Money Mailer	$ 37,550	Services
Curves and Curves for Women	$ 38,425	Services
Allegra Network	$ 41,200	Printing, Graphic Design, Signage, and Shipping
ERA Franchise Systems Inc.	$ 42,700	Real Estate and Travel Agencies
Comfort Keepers	$ 44,525	Services
EmbroidMe	$ 44,560	Retail
Merle Norman Cosmetic Studio	$ 44,854	Retail
Roto-Rooter Corporation	$ 45,000	Maintenance, Restoration, and Cleaning Services
Jackson Hewitt Tax Service	$ 47,430	Services
Maid to Perfection	$ 48,590	Maintenance, Restoration, and Cleaning Services
Hot Stuff Foods	$ 49,995	Restaurants and Prepared Foods
Sign-A-Rama	$ 50,260	Printing, Graphic Design, Signage, and Shipping
Mr. Rooter	$ 50,950	Maintenance, Restoration, and Cleaning Services
Valpak Direct Marketing	$ 51,700	Services
White Hen Pantry, Inc.	$ 53,264	Retail
Molly Maid	$ 61,125	Maintenance, Restoration, and Cleaning Services
@WORK Personnel Services	$ 65,000	Services
Cruise Holidays International, Inc.	$ 67,669	Real Estate and Travel Agencies
Rainbow International Restoration & Cleaning	$ 68,600	Maintenance, Restoration, and Cleaning Services
RadioShack	$ 69,900	Retail
Handyman Connection	$ 71,110	Maintenance, Restoration, and Cleaning Services
Fantastic Sams	$ 71,165	Services
Matco Tools	$ 74,139	Automotive Services and Rental

FRANCHISE	MINIMUM INVESTMENT	CATEGORY
Dryclean USA	$ 78,300	Maintenance, Restoration, and Cleaning Services
Glamour Shots	$ 78,866	Retail
Stanley Steemer Carpet Cleaner	$ 80,990	Maintenance, Restoration, and Cleaning Services
Cost Cutters	$ 82,333	Services
Hungry Howie's Pizza	$ 84,100	Restaurants and Prepared Foods
CertaPro Painters	$ 85,000	Maintenance, Restoration, and Cleaning Services
Two Men and a Truck	$ 89,300	Services
Subway Restaurants	$ 92,050	Restaurants and Prepared Foods
First Choice Haircutters	$ 92,500	Services
Fox's Pizza Den	$ 93,550	Restaurants and Prepared Foods
Labor Finders	$ 96,150	Services
Wyndham Hotels & Resorts	$ 96,828	Lodging
Great Harvest Bread Co.	$ 97,834	Restaurants and Prepared Foods
Lawn Doctor	$ 97,900	Restoration and Cleaning Services
Great Clips	$ 98,750	Services
Wild Birds Unlimited	$ 98,916	Retail

$100,001–$250,000

FRANCHISE	MINIMUM INVESTMENT	CATEGORY
ABC Seamless	$ 100,480	Maintenance, Restoration, and Cleaning Services
Miracle-Ear	$ 101,500	Services
Paul Davis Restoration	$ 104,464	Maintenance, Restoration, and Cleaning Services
SuperCuts	$ 106,860	Services
Glass Doctor	$ 107,581	Automotive Services and Rental
TruGreen ChemLawn	$ 107,900	Maintenance, Restoration, and Cleaning Services
Jani-King International	$ 112,100	Maintenance, Restoration, and Cleaning Services

FRANCHISE	MINIMUM INVESTMENT	CATEGORY
Dollar Rent A Car	$ 113,575	Automotive Services and Rental
Express Personnel Services	$ 114,350	Services
Express Oil Change	$ 114,500	Automotive Services and Rental
LINE-X Spray-On Truck Bedliners	$ 115,183	Automotive Services and Rental
Pak Mail	$ 117,180	Printing, Graphic Design, Signage, and Shipping
Domino's Pizza	$ 118,350	Restaurants and Prepared Foods
Smoothie King	$ 121,000	Restaurants and Prepared Foods
Spherion	$ 121,800	Services
Minuteman Press	$ 122,171	Graphic Design, Signage, and Shipping
Jenny Craig	$ 122,600	Services
Precision Tune Auto Care	$ 123,000	Automotive Services and Rental
Interim HealthCare	$ 123,150	Services
Keller Williams Realty	$ 123,650	Real Estate and Travel Agencies
Once Upon a Child	$ 127,575	Retail
General Nutrition Centers	$ 129,573	Retail
HobbyTown USA	$ 134,825	Retail
Cartridge World	$ 135,000	Retail
Signs Now	$ 135,750	Printing, Graphic Design, Signage, and Shipping
Baskin-Robbins	$ 135,800	Restaurants and Prepared Foods
Taco Time	$ 137,000	Restaurants and Prepared Foods
Blimpie Subs & Salads	$ 137,970	Restaurants and Prepared Foods
Plato's Closet	$ 144,825	Retail
The Maids Home Services	$ 148,600	Maintenance, Restoration, and Cleaning Services
Transmission USA/ Mr. Transmission	$ 149,000	Automotive Services and Rental
Snap-on Tools	$ 149,634	Retail
The UPS Store/Mail Boxes Etc.	$ 149,754	Printing, Graphic Design, Signage, and Shipping
Great Steak & Potato Co.	$ 153,000	Restaurants and Prepared Foods
The Little Gym	$ 155,700	Services

FRANCHISE	MINIMUM INVESTMENT	CATEGORY
Grease Monkey	$ 158,000	Automotive Services and Rental
Huntington Learning Centers	$ 158,270	Services
Cousins Subs	$ 159,300	Restaurants and Prepared Foods
TCBY	$ 159,800	Restaurants and Prepared Foods
Cottman Transmission Centers	$ 161,000	Automotive Services and Rental
Firehouse Subs	$ 161,200	Restaurants and Prepared Foods
Rita's Ices, Cones, Shakes and Other Cool Stuff	$ 161,900	Restaurants and Prepared Foods
Villa Pizza	$ 161,950	Restaurants and Prepared Foods
Benjamin Franklin Plumbing	$ 165,290	Restoration and Cleaning Services
Papa John's Pizza	$ 171,283	Restaurants and Prepared Foods
Foot Solutions	$ 174,700	Retail
PostNet	$ 175,875	Printing, Graphic Design, Signage, and Shipping
Batteries Plus	$ 176,485	Automotive Services and Rental
Chester's	$ 181,441	Restaurants and Prepared Foods
Papa Murphy's Take 'N' Bake Pizza	$ 183,600	Restaurants and Prepared Foods
Marco's Pizza	$ 184,300	Restaurants and Prepared Foods
Culver's ButterBurgers & Frozen Custard	$ 185,000	Restaurants and Prepared Foods
Play It Again Sports	$ 185,772	Retail
FASTSIGNS International, Inc.	$ 187,491	Printing, Graphic Design, Signage, and Shipping
7-Eleven	$ 191,230	Retail
Relax the Back Corporation	$ 192,200	Retail
Auntie Anne's	$ 192,550	Restaurants and Prepared Foods
ChemStation	$ 193,500	Maintenance, Restoration, and Cleaning Services
Togo's Eatery	$ 194,225	Restaurants and Prepared Foods
AAMCO Transmissions	$ 197,650	Automotive Services and Rental
Medicine Shoppe & Medicap Pharmacy	$ 197,910	Services

FRANCHISE	MINIMUM INVESTMENT	CATEGORY
Quiznos Sub	$ 202,440	Restaurants and Prepared Foods
SpeeDee Oil Change & Tune-Up	$ 202,500	Automotive Services and Rental
Sylvan Learning Centers	$ 203,948	Services
Meineke Car Care Centers	$ 205,103	Automotive Services and Rental
D'Angelo Grilled Sandwiches	$ 205,944	Restaurants and Prepared Foods
Tuffy/Car-X	$ 209,000	Automotive Services and Rental
Jimmy John's Gourmet Sandwiches	$ 211,400	Restaurants and Prepared Foods
A&W All-American Food Restaurants	$ 212,400	Restaurants and Prepared Foods
Jiffy Lube International, Inc.	$ 214,000	Automotive Services and Rental
Bruegger's Bagels	$ 217,250	Restaurants and Prepared Foods
Blockbuster	$ 219,500	Retail
The Athlete's Foot	$ 220,800	Retail
Chick-fil-A	$ 225,890	Restaurants and Prepared Foods
Penn Station East Coast Subs	$ 229,640	Restaurants and Prepared Foods
Rocky Mountain Chocolate Factory	$ 230,400	Retail
Zaxby's	$ 230,500	Restaurants and Prepared Foods
Ace Hardware	$ 236,000	Retail
Kwik Kopy Printing	$ 237,170	Printing, Graphic Design, Signage, and Shipping
Taco Bell	$ 242,800	Restaurants and Prepared Foods
Midas Auto Service Experts	$ 243,150	Automotive Services and Rental
Sbarro	$ 244,000	Restaurants and Prepared Foods
Beef O' Brady's	$ 246,800	Restaurants and Prepared Foods
Carvel Ice Cream	$ 247,474	Restaurants and Prepared Foods
Pro Golf Discount/Pro Golf of America	$ 250,000	Retail

$250,001–$1,000,000

Moe's Southwest Grill	$ 252,000	Restaurants and Prepared Foods
Aaron Rents	$ 253,670	Services

FRANCHISE	MINIMUM INVESTMENT	CATEGORY
Cinnabon, Inc.	$ 255,200	Restaurants and Prepared Foods
PIP Printing & Document Services	$ 261,413	Printing, Graphic Design, Signage, and Shipping
One Hour Heating & Air Conditioning	$ 261,660	Maintenance, Restoration, and Cleaning Services
Bojangles' Restaurants, Inc.	$ 270,100	Restaurants and Prepared Foods
Del Taco LLC	$ 272,000	Restaurants and Prepared Foods
Bellacino's Pizza and Grinders	$ 275,000	Restaurants and Prepared Foods
One Hour Martinizing Dry Cleaning	$ 275,500	Maintenance, Restoration, and Cleaning Services
CARSTAR	$ 280,100	Automotive Services and Rental
Popeyes Chicken & Biscuits	$ 287,300	Restaurants and Prepared Foods
Manchu Wok	$ 287,450	Restaurants and Prepared Foods
Cold Stone Creamery	$ 294,250	Restaurants and Prepared Foods
Wingstop	$ 297,800	Restaurants and Prepared Foods
Hollywood Tans	$ 310,500	Retail
Golf USA, Inc.	$ 320,800	Retail
ampm	$ 333,930	Retail
Petland	$ 334,000	Retail
Pizza Hut	$ 338,000	Restaurants and Prepared Foods
Sir Speedy, Inc.	$ 342,000	Printing, Graphic Design, Signage, and Shipping
USA BABY	$ 343,900	Retail
Party America	$ 348,000	Retail
World Gym	$ 350,000	Services
Payless Car Sales, Inc.	$ 351,650	Automotive Services and Rental
Back Yard Burgers	$ 352,000	Restaurants and Prepared Foods
Big O Tires, Inc.	$ 364,300	Automotive Services and Rental
AlphaGraphics	$ 365,000	Printing, Graphic Design, Signage, and Shipping
Tim Horton's	$ 373,200	Restaurants and Prepared Foods
Marble Slab Creamery	$ 375,675	Restaurants and Prepared Foods
Qdoba Mexican Grill	$ 395,000	Restaurants and Prepared Foods
CiCi's Pizza	$ 404,400	Restaurants and Prepared Foods

FRANCHISE	MINIMUM INVESTMENT	CATEGORY
MAACO Auto Painting & Bodyworks	$ 417,460	Automotive Services and Rental
Pet Supplies "Plus"	$ 423,300	Retail
El Pollo Loco	$ 425,000	Restaurants and Prepared Foods
La Salsa Fresh Mexican Grill	$ 431,000	Restaurants and Prepared Foods
Gold's Gym Franchising	$ 442,000	Services
The Goddard School	$ 447,010	Services
Church's Chicken	$ 459,800	Restaurants and Prepared Foods
Dairy Queen	$ 461,150	Restaurants and Prepared Foods
Huddle House, Inc.	$ 484,000	Restaurants and Prepared Foods
Checkers/Rally's	$ 487,100	Restaurants and Prepared Foods
Norwalk-The Furniture Idea	$ 495,000	Retail
Friendly's Restaurants Franchise, Inc.	$ 498,500	Restaurants and Prepared Foods
Schlotzsky's	$ 509,300	Restaurants and Prepared Foods
J.D. Byrider	$ 514,193	Automotive Services and Rental
Round Table Pizza	$ 521,000	Restaurants and Prepared Foods
Circle K Convenience Stores	$ 531,000	Retail
Dunkin' Donuts	$ 548,100	Restaurants and Prepared Foods
Krystal Company	$ 560,500	Restaurants and Prepared Foods
Shoney's Restaurants	$ 568,000	Restaurants and Prepared Foods
Pizza Inn	$ 571,250	Restaurants and Prepared Foods
Hooters Restaurants	$ 591,500	Restaurants and Prepared Foods
Village Inn Restaurants	$ 599,000	Restaurants and Prepared Foods
Max & Erma's	$ 622,500	Restaurants and Prepared Foods
Atlanta Bread Co.	$ 629,700	Restaurants and Prepared Foods
Johnny Rockets	$ 636,000	Restaurants and Prepared Foods
Taco John's	$ 637,500	Restaurants and Prepared Foods
McDonald's	$ 655,750	Restaurants and Prepared Foods
Baja Fresh Mexican Grill	$ 656,110	Restaurants and Prepared Foods
Country Kitchen	$ 661,600	Restaurants and Prepared Foods
The Melting Pot	$ 671,395	Restaurants and Prepared Foods
Jason's Deli	$ 680,000	Restaurants and Prepared Foods

FRANCHISE	MINIMUM INVESTMENT	CATEGORY
Captain D's Seafood	$ 684,000	Restaurants and Prepared Foods
Fuddruckers	$ 740,000	Restaurants and Prepared Foods
Arby's	$ 750,700	Restaurants and Prepared Foods
Mazzio's Italian Eatery	$ 759,000	Restaurants and Prepared Foods
Howard Johnson International	$ 793,000	Lodging
Western Sizzlin	$ 811,000	Restaurants and Prepared Foods
Hardee's	$ 820,800	Restaurants and Prepared Foods
Sonic Drive-In	$ 821,500	Restaurants and Prepared Foods
International House of Pancakes (IHOP)	$ 836,000	Restaurants and Prepared Foods
Thrifty Car Rental	$ 836,700	Automotive Services and Rental
Long John Silver's	$ 851,000	Restaurants and Prepared Foods
McAlister's Deli	$ 879,500	Restaurants and Prepared Foods
Famous Dave's	$ 907,000	Restaurants and Prepared Foods
Carl's Jr.	$ 913,000	Restaurants and Prepared Foods
Sizzler Restaurants	$ 933,000	Restaurants and Prepared Foods

$1,000,000-Plus

Panera Bread	$ 1,003,000	Restaurants and Prepared Foods
Tumbleweed Southwest Grill	$ 1,006,000	Restaurants and Prepared Foods
Denny's	$ 1,090,230	Restaurants and Prepared Foods
Uno Chicago Grill	$ 1,103,500	Restaurants and Prepared Foods
Jack in the Box Restaurant	$ 1,116,091	Restaurants and Prepared Foods
Roy Rogers	$ 1,130,250	Restaurants and Prepared Foods
KFC	$ 1,142,300	Restaurants and Prepared Foods
Damon's Grill	$ 1,166,500	Restaurants and Prepared Foods
Old Chicago	$ 1,169,000	Restaurants and Prepared Foods
Ruby Tuesday	$ 1,208,300	Restaurants and Prepared Foods
Krispy Kreme	$ 1,225,000	Restaurants and Prepared Foods
Johnny Carino's Italian	$ 1,228,000	Restaurants and Prepared Foods
Peter Piper Pizza	$ 1,253,000	Restaurants and Prepared Foods

FRANCHISE	MINIMUM INVESTMENT	CATEGORY
Sirloin Stockade	$ 1,259,000	Restaurants and Prepared Foods
Wendy's	$ 1,308,500	Restaurants and Prepared Foods
Buffalo Wild Wings Grill & Bar	$ 1,340,200	Restaurants and Prepared Foods
Burger King	$ 1,399,000	Restaurants and Prepared Foods
Tony Roma's	$ 1,420,800	Restaurants and Prepared Foods
Bennigan's Grill and Tavern	$ 1,497,784	Restaurants and Prepared Foods
Elmer's Breakfast – Lunch – Dinner	$ 1,569,000	Restaurants and Prepared Foods
Boston's The Gourmet Pizza/ Boston Pizza	$ 1,625,000	Restaurants and Prepared Foods
Houlihan's	$ 1,662,500	Restaurants and Prepared Foods
Big Boy	$ 1,761,050	Restaurants and Prepared Foods
Perkins Restaurant & Bakery	$ 1,797,357	Restaurants and Prepared Foods
Econo Lodge	$ 1,987,819	Lodging
Primrose School Franchising Co.	$ 1,989,400	Services
Volvo Rents	$ 2,017,250	Services
Ruth's Chris Steak House	$ 2,050,000	Restaurants and Prepared Foods
Chili's Grill & Bar	$ 2,090,000	Restaurants and Prepared Foods
T.G.I. Friday's	$ 2,120,000	Restaurants and Prepared Foods
Rodeway Inn	$ 2,128,435	Lodging
Red Robin	$ 2,145,900	Restaurants and Prepared Foods
Motel 6	$ 2,211,500	Lodging
Radisson Hotels	$ 2,222,785	Lodging
Super 8 Motels	$ 2,273,450	Lodging
Golden Corral Family Restaurants	$ 2,382,650	Restaurants and Prepared Foods
Red Roof Inn	$ 2,636,100	Lodging
Applebee's Neighborhood Grill & Bar	$ 2,724,500	Restaurants and Prepared Foods
AmericInn	$ 2,726,150	Lodging
Country Inn & Suites	$ 3,182,471	Lodging
Comfort Inn & Suites	$ 3,303,301	Lodging
Knights Franchise Systems	$ 3,504,300	Lodging
Travelodge Hotels	$ 3,556,800	Lodging
Days Inns Worldwide	$ 3,711,800	Lodging

FRANCHISE	MINIMUM INVESTMENT	CATEGORY
AmeriHost Franchise Systems	$ 3,714,500	Lodging
Microtel Inns & Suites	$ 3,870,800	Lodging
Candlewood Suites	$ 3,927,000	Lodging
Quality Inn & Suites	$ 3,984,540	Lodging
Baymont Inn & Suites	$ 4,255,000	Lodging
Hampton Inn & Hampton Inn & Suites	$ 4,348,000	Lodging
La Quinta Franchise LLC	$ 4,478,300	Lodging
Ramada Worldwide	$ 4,487,300	Lodging
Fairfield Inn	$ 4,560,100	Lodging
Crowne Plaza	$ 4,923,775	Lodging
Holiday Inn Hotels & Resorts	$ 5,401,020	Lodging
Holiday Inn Express	$ 5,401,020	Lodging
Springhill Suites	$ 5,553,125	Lodging
Hawthorn Suites	$ 5,725,000	Lodging
Staybridge Suites	$ 5,890,800	Lodging
TownePlace Suites	$ 5,916,450	Lodging
Wingate Inns International	$ 5,931,550	Lodging
Courtyard	$ 6,050,600	Lodging
Residence Inn	$ 7,340,800	Lodging
Clarion Inn and Clarion Suites	$ 7,413,883	Lodging
Hilton Garden Inn	$ 8,743,000	Lodging
Homewood Suites by Hilton	$ 9,144,500	Lodging
Four Points by Sheraton	$13,720,000	Lodging
Embassy Suites Hotels	$17,043,000	Lodging
Doubletree	$24,583,750	Lodging
Sheraton Hotels and Resorts	$25,730,000	Lodging
Westin Hotels and Resorts	$31,530,000	Lodging
Hilton	$33,760,500	Lodging
Renaissance	$34,781,500	Lodging
Marriott Hotels, Resorts & Suites	$42,414,100	Lodging
Luxury Collection	$47,700,000	Lodging

Alphabetical Listing of Franchises

Resources

Franchise Associations

American Association of Franchisees
and Dealers
San Diego, California
(800) 733-9858
www.aafd.org

American Franchisee Association
Chicago, Illinois
(312) 431-0545
www.franchisee.org

International Franchise Association
Washington, DC
(202) 628-8000
www.franchise.org

Franchise Research

FRANdata
Arlington, Virginia
(703) 740-4707
www.frandata.com

FranchiseHelp, Inc.
Elmsford, New York
(800) 401-1446
www.franchisehelp.com

Franchise Times
Minneapolis, Minnesota
(800) 528-3296
www.franchisetimes.com

GE Capital Solutions Franchise Finance
Scottsdale, Arizona
(866) 438-4333
www.getfranchisefinance.com

Restaurant Finance Monitor
Minneapolis, Minnesota
(800) 528-3296
www.restfinance.com

Smith Travel Research
Hendersonville, Tennessee
(615) 824-8664
www.smithtravelresearch.com

Other Resources

Better Business Bureau
Council of Better Business Bureaus
Arlington, Virginia
www.bbb.org for local chapter

SCORE, Service Corps of
Retired Executives
Washington, DC
(800) 634-0245
www.score.org

Small Business Administration
Washington, DC
(800) 827-5722
www.sba.gov
SBA Franchise Registry
www.franchiseregistry.com

Personality Assessment Companies

Accord Management Systems
Westlake Village, California
(800) 466-0105
www.accordsyst.com

Caliper
Princeton, New Jersey
(800) 422-5477
www.caliperonline.com

Dynamic Performance Systems, Inc.
Etobicoke, Ontario, Canada
(800) 719-9993
www.franchise-profiles.com/ssbo

Index

Note: Franchise companies that appear ***throughout the book*** are listed here. Franchise company names that are mentioned **only** in the Franchise Company Directory are listed in the Alphabetical Listing of Franchises (see pages 376 to 380).